DIPLOMATIC DISCOURSE: INTERNATIONAL CONFLICT AT THE UNITED NATIONS— ADDRESSES AND ANALYSIS

The Ablex
Communication, Culture, & Information Series
Eileen Mahoney, Series Editor

Communication, Organization and Performance
by Tom Dixon, Queensland University of Technology, 1996

Diplomatic Discourse: International Conflict at the United Nations—Addresses and Analysis
by Ray T. Donahue, Nagoya Gakuin University, and Michael H. Prosser, Rochester Institute of Technology, 1997

Unglued Empire: The Soviet Experience with Communications Technologies
by Gladys D. Ganley, Foreword by Marshall I. Goldman, 1996

Writing in a Milieu of Utility: The Move to Technical Communication in American Engineering Programs 1850–1950
by Teresa C. Kynell, Northern Michigan University, 1996

News Media and Foreign Relations: A Multifaceted Perspective
edited by Abbas Malek, Howard University, 1997

World Broadcasting: A Comparative View
edited by Alan Wells, Temple University, 1997

Mass Media & Society
edited by Alan Wells, Temple University, and Ernest A. Hakanen, Drexel University, 1997

Forthcoming:

The Information Revolution: Current & Future Consequences
edited by Alan Porter and William H. Read, Georgia Institute of Technology

Telecommunications Law, Regulation, and Policy
edited by William H. Read and Walter Sapronov, Georgia Institute of Technology

DIPLOMATIC DISCOURSE: INTERNATIONAL CONFLICT AT THE UNITED NATIONS— ADDRESSES AND ANALYSIS

RAY T. DONAHUE
NAGOYA GAKUIN UNIVERSITY
AND
MICHAEL H. PROSSER
ROCHESTER INSTITUTE OF TECHNOLOGY

ABLEX PUBLISHING CORPORATION
GREENWICH, CONNECTICUT
LONDON, ENGLAND

Printed in the United States of America

Library of Congress Cataloging-in-Publication Data

Donahue, Ray T.
Diplomatic discourse : international conflict at the United Nations : addresses and analysis / Ray T. Donahue & Michael H. Prosser.
p. cm. — (Communication, culture & information studies)
Includes bibliographical references (p.) and index.
ISBN 1-56750-290-3 (cloth). — ISBN 1-56750-291-1 (paper)
1. Diplomacy—Language. 2. International relations—Language. 3. International relations and culture. 4. United Nations—Language. 5. Speeches, addresses, etc. 6. Discourse analysis. 7. Rhetorical criticism. I. Prosser, Michael H., 1936– . II. Title. III. Series: Ablex communication, culture and information studies.
JZ1434.D66 1997
241.23′014—dc20 96–30457
CIP

Ablex Publishing Corporation
55 Old Post Road #2
P.O. Box 5297
Greenwich, CT 06830

Published in the U.K. and Europe by:
JAI Press Ltd.
38 Tavistock Street
Covent Garden
London WC2E 7PB
England

P

In order to keep this title in print and available to the academic community, this edition was produced using digital reprint technology in a relatively short print run. This would not have been attainable using traditional methods. Although the cover has been changed from its original appearance, the text remains the same and all materials and methods used still conform to the highest book-making standards.

For
Noriko Donahue, Eugene Donahue, Ken Donahue, Rene Donahue,
and in memory of Stella T. Donahue and Martin L. Donahue

Joan Ann Kirkeby-Prosser, Christine Ann Prosser, Elizabeth Marie Prosser,
Mary Catherine Rose Prosser, Lilia Epiphany Evans (In Memoriam, 1996)
Ashlie Michelle Adams, Heather Elizabeth Adams,
Emma Renstrom Hanley, Anne-Laure Dislaire,
Helene Dislaire, and Tanishia Nicole Mbuyisa

CONTENTS

PREFACE

Diplomatic Discourse considers the speech communication by world leaders at the United Nations. UN speeches, deserving of study in their own right, are a useful vehicle for developing culture and communication skills. UN speeches provide a lively way of doing so because they involve conflict about our most important world issues. Such conflicts challenge our worldviews, stimulating the growth of cultural awareness, while developing expertise for discourse analysis and rhetorical analysis. *Diplomatic Discourse,* interdisciplinary in focus, can be used effectively for upper-level courses in communication studies, discourse analysis, rhetoric and speech, international studies, and other courses dealing with language, culture, and communication.

Now that the UN has celebrated its 50th anniversary, more than a thousand speech addresses by world leaders have accumulated at this forum. This represents a rich, fertile field for communication studies, and *Diplomatic Discourse,* its first field guide. This guide uses illustrative messages from Nobel Peace Laureates and revolutionaries, kings and presidents. Demonstrated analyses are made throughout, as well as work with the elite media as consultative sources. Application exercises and discussion questions also are provided, as well as actual UN addresses for additional practice.

The authors have more than 50 years combined experience in intercultural communication and relations: Donahue, an applied linguist and professional cross-cultural counselor; and Prosser, a classical rhetorician and a founder of the academic field of intercultural communication. Both have separately and cooperatively contributed to *Diplomatic Discourse* and share full responsibility for all aspects of the book. Donahue has made major contributions to the Introduction, Chapters 1 through 5, and 12; Prosser, to Chapters 6 through 11, and 13.

Diplomatic Discourse had its genesis in the work of Prosser (1970), who has continued to work in collecting and documenting UN addresses made at the level of heads of state or government. His courses on UN diplomatic communication may have been originally the first in the field. Additionally, he has been a leader in advancing model UN student workshops held at national and international levels. It seems like fate that Prosser invited Donahue to his UN course at the University of Virginia, a course that made lasting impressions. They have been committed ever since to produce a work that would make UN diplomatic discourse accessible to more students and specialists in communication studies. They have further committed themselves by works-in-progress tentatively titled *Cultural Rhetorics/Cultural Logics*, a planned addition to the present Ablex series *Communication, Culture, and Information Studies*, as well as Prosser's forthcoming *United Nations Addresses: Toward the Millennium.* Related forthcoming volumes in the same Ablex series edited by Prosser (with K. S. Sitaram) merit mention also: *Multiculturalism, Cultural Diversity, and Global Communication* and *Intercultural, International, and Global Media.*

Special thanks are given to Nagoya Gakuin University and Rochester Institute of Technology for their institutional encouragement; and to Heather Fleck, who assisted in retrieving various mass media articles used. We offer special thanks to Anne Trowbridge, Book Production Manager of Ablex Publishing Co.

We are equally grateful to Cecilia M. Suzuki, editor, *Kokiku Magazine,* for permission to reproduce the May Yokomoto articles in Chapter 4, as well to Hisashi Kajiwara for his permission regarding his speech in Chapter 2.

Finally, our greatest debt is acknowledged to the United Nations, its cooperating agencies, and above all to the world leaders whose words grace these pages.

—Ray T. Donahue
Nagoya, Japan
Michael H. Prosser
Rochester, New York

INTRODUCTION

Diplomatic Discourse is the first of its kind. It breaks new ground in the field of international communication—the study of diplomatic speechmaking at the United Nations. As far as we know, there are no college textbooks that address this kind of study, especially in combining discourse analysis and rhetorical analysis. In general, diplomatic communication has remained an untapped field in communication studies (Gudykunst, 1990). It is our hope that *Diplomatic Discourse* will spur work in this new and exciting field.

This text develops a basis for applying discourse analysis and rhetorical analysis to speech communication at the United Nations. UN speech addresses involve important world issues and, through related conflicts, help exercise analytical skills applicable at either level, international or intercultural. International communication essentially involves group-to-group communication across cultures; and intercultural, person-to-person. Regardless of the level, critical communication requires analysis. Sample analyses are taken from the genre of diplomatic addresses given at the UN during its first 50 years, with guidance for independent analysis.

TERMS

Diplomatic

Diplomatic has at least two different meanings: "1. pertaining to, or engaged in diplomacy; 2. skilled in dealing with sensitive matters or people: tactful" (*Random House Webster's College Dictionary* [RHWCD], 1991). *Diplomatic Discourse* concerns the first meaning, that of diplomacy. When diplomatic does take on the second meaning of tactfulness, we trust that the context will help make the intended meaning clear.

Rhetoric, Discourse, Text

Rhetoric, as a classical study, was concerned with speaking persuasively. In the United States, it has also come to refer to writing, especially of composition in the schools. It may even refer to a handbook of composition, where rhetoric is "the study of effective expression" (Steinmann, 1982), a broadening of the classical definition. Both the classical and modern traditions apply to UN speech addresses because they are produced in both modes of speaking and writing—first as a speech and thereafter as a written document. The speech, however, may actually originate from a written script. Thus, rhetoric requires a broad view both in definition and scope.

Discourse, similarly, was first associated with spoken language but has come to refer to the written as well. *Text* refers to the physical (i.e., written) record of a discourse. In UN terminology, a formal speech at the UN is known as an "address"; other UN speeches are called "statements." The written transcription of an address or statement, in general terms, is called either a "text" or "speechtext."

Discourse Analysis/Rhetorical Analysis

As noted, a key feature of this book is the combining of discourse analysis and rhetorical analysis. (*Discoursal* might be parallel in form to *rhetorical,* but *discourse analysis* is the conventional term.) Discourse analysis, broadly, concerns how meaning evolves coherently in either oral or written language. It links linguistic elements with interpretation. Rhetorical (contemporary) analysis is largely a critical study of persuasion but of other types of communication also. Methods of argumentation have received central focus in rhetorical analysis.

Discourse analysis and rhetorical analysis overlap in many respects, and the terms, in fact, are sometimes used synonymously. However, if one had to state their essential difference, it might be this regarding their *emphasis*: Discourse analysis tends to be text-oriented and descriptive; traditional rhetorical analysis, author-oriented and prescriptive; and contemporary rhetorical analysis, audience-oriented and critical. All three types encompass much more in practice, for each attempts ideally to have an *interactional* view of the author, audience, text, and context. At least, an interactional view is what the present authors strive for. Finally, in some cases, a distinction in terms may be impractical.

PLAN OF THE BOOK

The book consists of three major parts: 1) discourse analysis; 2) rhetorical analysis; and 3) applications. Applications are found both at the end of chapters and as a collection in the final chapters. Part 1 develops an understanding of discourse analysis; Part 2, of rhetorical analysis. Discourse analysis is viewed as a tool of description; rhetorical analysis, a tool of criticism. Ideally, both can work hand-in-hand in aiming toward comprehensive analysis of a communication.

Descriptive tools are developed out of a knowledge of discourse organizational elements; critical tools, out of a knowledge of elements of logical argument and debate. Part 1 does so by an inventory of discourse frames, formats, and patterning devices; Part 2, by a survey of the historical development of rhetorical criticism from its classical roots to its contemporary thinkers. UN addresses are used in illustration, as well as others from outside the UN whenever appropriate. Although UN diplomatic communication is primarily our focus, it need not be. The analytical tools developed through *Diplomatic Discourse* have wide applicability to communication studies in general. And its international content offers to broaden our views toward other peoples and cultures, in an era when such sensitivities are ever at a premium.

SELECTION OF UN ADDRESSES

The authors have included UN addresses from its early period to its most recent. The bulk, however, comes from Prosser's (1970) collection. His collection contains all the known addresses by heads of state or government for the UN's first 25 years. Extracts from these addresses in *Diplomatic Discourse* were made almost entirely from convenience. Because the period of 1960–1965 accounts for more than 65 percent of the pages in Prosser's (1970) collection, this period happens to have become much represented. This period also has arguably some of the most colorful figures in the history of the UN, which became a factor, also. This period is balanced by the addresses provided unabridged or nearly so. These addresses come largely from the UN's most recent years and were chosen as for the speaker, his or her culture, the related conflict, and its period. Additional UN addresses can be found in Prosser (1970), Prosser (in press), and in UN depository collections at selected libraries.

LANGUAGE VERSION OF ADDRESSES

Diplomatic communication will frequently be through the medium of English, for "English has become the de facto common language of diplomacy, having overtaken French in recent decades" (Fisher, 1989:410). Even if a speech address is delivered in a different language, the speaker's delegation will often provide an official English version. Some delegations distribute only that version but not one in their own native language. English versions of the UN addresses, then, became a practical choice, if not the only choice, for the present contents.

This choice received further impetus by a recognition that English has fast become the world's lingua franca. For these reasons, we naturally consider a perspective for English-speaking cultures. However, we also make the point that, in our increasingly intercultural lives, a certain accommodation to international "Englishes" is required. However, this is not the same as saying that we are to relinquish our own cultural values. Within our own culture, western conventions of discourse are important and necessary for us to communicate effectively. When outside, they are still important, if only to help us determine or predict cross-cultural misunderstanding. If involved internationally, we wish to follow the expected norms of discourse and be flexible enough to do so. For UN addresses, at least those in English, the rhetorical standards appear similar to western convention. In cases when not, the tools developed through this text will still help to bridge such gaps in international communication.

Spelling Convention. The UN follows British spelling conventions in its records for the speech addresses even for US presidents. This suggests that the UN may convert speechtexts received from delegations. If so, any editing appears limited to spelling. Each national delegation, in any event, must approve the final form of any of its official messages distributed by the UN. However, American convention was followed for the speechtexts herein because it is consistent with the surrounding text. We trust that readers can comfortably make their own "switch," if ever the case need be.

Gender-Neutral Language

Because *Diplomatic Discourse* necessarily includes references to historical writings, even ancient ones, as well as to the many modern, the use of gender-neutral language cannot be uniformly applied. To do so would violate, perhaps, a higher order principle of preserving the orginal form(s) of historical writings. As a result, we follow a case-by-case basis on the issue. Editing for this purpose occurs in some cases but not in others. However, we have made the issue into an interesting exercise for analysis of a UN speech address in Chapter 2. By thus raising the issue, we hope that readers will be prepared for those left unedited in this regard.

AN INHERENT LIMITATION

The need to include actual diplomatic addresses, especially unabridged, immediately restricts space for other content. Although the authors believe an effective balance has been struck, it ought to be understood that *Diplomatic Discourse* is introductory in intent. If readers come away with new confidence in approaching discourse and an appreciation of international communication, the authors will feel justified in their attempt.

WORLD ISSUES

World issues offer an advantage in using UN addresses. This gives meaning to our purpose of developing skills in discourse analysis and rhetorical analysis. Although *Diplomatic Discourse* is not intended as a "discussion manual" for such issues, they will naturally spring up in the course of analysis. Space limits their separate treatment, for that is not the main purpose, of course. However, the Subject Index does include a number of relevant issues for those so interested. Indexing in some instances is suggestive and merely points to areas for potential use.

CRITICISM OF THE UNITED NATIONS

One issue that does merit separate attention, albeit briefly, is the viability of the United Nations. For a realistic assessment, we turn to Brian Saxton, UN correspondent for the BBC:

> The United Nations today labors under much criticism. It is criticized for appearing to be ineffective in times of emergencies; criticized for not having settled all the world's problems; and criticized for not having lived up to Harry Truman's hope that it would establish a worldwide rule of reason. The reason for this, of course, is simple enough. When the Charter was first drawn up, it appeared to promise the best of all possible worlds. And [people] took it literally. [They] didn't appreciate that much of the realization of that promise would be left to [them]. [One must] first understand and accept the principle that it is not a world government. It is, in fact, merely a body which reflects the political strategy of its membership at any one time. It is also a fact of life that the United Nations remains the most effective international forum for debate—a shelter where nations can seek protection from political storms and a safety catch to check political passions. Over the years, it has done much to improve the way the world behaves and the way it seeks to improve itself. (Saxton, 1972)

For example, ABC News (1995b) takes one day in that year to contrast the much talked about failure of the UN with its often overlooked success:

> It was last July 11 [during the Bosnian War] that UN troops lost [a city declared a safe haven] to Bosnian Serbs. Without firing a shot, the UN went into a full retreat with truckloads of women and children in tow. It was a day of disgrace for the United Nations and what it stands for—peace. Placenames like Bosnia or Somalia, these have become labels for spectacular United Nations failures. But less often talked about are all of those places where the UN gets it right. And that's all over the world everyday.
>
> July 11, for example, the same day that [its Bosnian safe haven] fell, 2,653 people at the border of Afghanistan crossed back into their home

country. They were among more than 3 million Afghans who have returned home, thanks to the UN almost 16 years after the Soviet invasion of Afghanistan. The UN helped these people start their lives again in their old homes. Afghan soldiers cleared the villages of mines while UN instructors gave classes on how to avoid getting hurt and also [taught] new [occupational] skills. . . . Among the UN staffers in Afghanistan on July 11 was Daniel Bellamy. "We are a kind of guarantee for the returnees. We are a guarantee for their right."

July 11 in China was another routine day at a UN-sponsored clinic administering polio vaccine to children. The goal is to stamp out polio there [within the next decade]. Worldwide the UN assists in health care for people in more than 160 countries. In the Gaza Strip the UN was laying down sewer lines on July 11 in the Palestinian refugee camps that it has supported since 1948. It was also picking up garbage—77 tons. And at the UN summer camp, the grownups were putting on a play. Fifteen thousand kids attend these camps every summer.

And finally, Mozambique. July was the tail end of a UN operation that brought home 1.6 million refugees of a long civil war. Andre Francisco ran with his pregnant wife in 1986 when they heard that soldiers were killing teachers. Without the UN he says, 'We wouldn't be alive. We would be dead because the government couldn't feed us.' This week back in the village, Andre's neighbors are settling in, feeling at home again. The UN has dug a new well in the village and is still providing food for some people but far fewer than last year because families, like Andre's, are getting back on their feet again working the land.

[That was a bad day in Bosnia], the kind of mission where the UN seems to get into trouble, but it is not the whole story of the difference the UN can make in so many places everyday.

Saxton's (1972) conclusion still applies decades later:

> In this temperamental world of ours we need an assembly like the United Nations to control the political pressures. [Probably] it will always suffer criticism, but its value as a stabilizing force and its influence is beyond question. For as long as [humankind] is willing to continue to dream of peace and is willing to try to achieve it, then the United Nations [will be in great demand].

That demand can only rise with today's spiraling world conflicts. The breakup of the former Soviet Union, the eruption of worldwide ethnic clashes, and the disunity among world political leaders all make this so. A critical view of such issues will be a requisite for the perceptive global citizen. The analytical skills needed find a basis in the following chapters.

PART I

DISCOURSE ANALYSIS

1

DISCOURSE ANALYSIS: A CONCEPTUAL FOUNDATION

Discourse is the language, spoken or written, produced for social, informational, and/or rhetorical purposes, such as conversations, speeches, novels, and technical reports. "Unlike 'language,' the term *discourse* itself is both a noun and a verb. So it is easier to retain the sense of discourse as an *act*, where the noun 'language' often seems to refer to a *thing*" (O'Sullivan, Hartley, Saunders, Montgomery, & Fiske, 1994, p. 93). The act of how language is purposefully used is the province of discourse analysis. Discourse analysis helps reveal to observers (researchers) how meaning evolves within a discourse event. Modern discourse analysis, anteceded in classical rhetoric (van Dijk, 1985), is a branch of linguistics (Clyne, 1994), which has had concurrent development in sociology, anthropology, philosophy, ethnology, psychology, and media and communication studies (Bhatia, 1993; McCarthy, 1991; Potter & Wetherell, 1987).

What explains all this fervent activity with discourse analysis? As voiced by Potter and Wetherell (1987, p. 9), "our talk and writing . . . are mediums for action"—action that gives shape to our lives. Explaining this shaping has become the task of discourse analysis (based on Crystal, 1987): Linguists work to show the linguistic patterning of discourse; psychologists, its comprehension and memory; ethnologists, its formation of social conversation; anthropologists, its embodiment of cultural myths and stories. Other researchers, in the same or different fields, study the social and political features of a society by how fairly or effectively legal, medical, and educational services are delivered through discourse. Because people's lives are mediated so much through language, discourse analytic skills will increasingly become integral to effective personal and professional functioning. Boardroom to bedroom, success ultimately depends on our skills related to the perception, comprehension, and interpretation of communicative messages. For this, discourse analysis promises a firm grounding.

Discourse analysis will vary in definition and methods according to the field or subfield, such that "it is perfectly possible to have two books on discourse analysis with no overlap in content at all (cf. Macdonell, 1986; Stubbs, 1983)" (Potter & Wetherell, 1987, p. 6). Consequently, universal procedures do not exist (Hatch, 1992), even within the same field (e.g., Bhatia, 1993; Schiffrin, 1994).

An Overview

To prepare for the discourse analysis of United Nations diplomatic discourse, this chapter provides essential grounding for appreciating the properties of language and discourse. The two concepts of contextualism and critical communication inform the discussion. Contextualism forms a rationale; whereas critical communication forms the means. Between these concepts rest some essential assumptions and principles for doing discourse analysis. Various examples are used in illustration, some demonstrating discourse analytic techniques.

These early chapters form related components that aim to provide a basis for discourse analysis. Some earlier points become clearer through later exposition. One such point concerns the concept of structure. Although reference is sometimes made to this concept, its fuller explanation is delayed until Chapter 4. Finally, examples ought to be tried and worked through before reading any further of the book.

CONTEXTUALISM

Contextualism is a paradigm newly emerging in the social sciences (Georgoudi & Rosnow, 1985; Jaeger & Rosnow, 1988; Morris 1988; Rosnow & Georgoudi, 1986; Scharfstein, 1989). Broadly, contextualism considers context essential for understanding human behavior and culture. Despite the importance of context, "neither historians nor social scientists have dealt intensively with the idea of context" (Scharfstein, 1989, p. 4). This point is especially true for mainstream psychology and linguistics. Work on context appears to have been left for the subfields, such as social psychology and sociolinguistics.

Context: The Matter of Definition

Defining context is complex and may turn out to be impossible (Goodwin & Duranti, 1992). In absence of a technical definition, a general one may suffice for this present volume: "the set of circumstances or facts that surround a particular event, situation, etc." (*Random House Webster's College Dictionary* [RHWCD], 1991, p. 294). *Context, situation,* and *context of situation* are sometimes used synonymously, a practice followed herein also.

Lavandera (1988) provided a useful summary of the relevant work on context in sociolinguistics. She distinguished between two types of context: *social* and *interpersonal.* The social context includes such factors as gender, age, race, and socioeconomic status; the interpersonal includes intention, beliefs, knowledge, and so on. Here, interpersonal may be termed *psychological* or *personal.* Both types are called simply *context* or *social context.*

Many people recognize the value of context, for personalities in the media seem to complain often of having been "taken out of context." Regarding research, the neglect of context, however, is a relative matter, not an absolute. Two factors may explain the research neglect of context found by Scharfstein: reductionism and individualism.

Reductionism

Reductionism places an emphasis on the irreducible unit of a phenomenon for study. Reductionism is a natural outgrowth of positivism that has dominated the social sciences since at least the 1930s (Morris, 1988). For biological organisms, reductionist approaches may be most appropriate. Moreover, analysis itself involves, by definition, dividing the phenomenon into its parts. The concern, however, is that an emphasis on parts may become extreme to the neglect of the associated phenomenon and its context.

This concern is well expressed by Weiss (1971):

> Modern scientists tend to foster "a militantly doctrinaire reductionism, which axiomatically prescribe[s] that all the relevant macroinformation about nature must, and eventually will, be derived completely from adding up and piecing together the microinformation about the smallest sample units. Never mind that physics had to give up that claim gradually as Bolzmann's thermodynamics, Planck's quantum theory, and Heisenberg's uncertainty principle came on the scene." (Weiss, 1971, p. 19; from Anttila, 1977, p. 1, as quoted by Alford, 1978, p. 493)

Various levels of experience may operate in different ways. Extrapolating from the lowest level to the highest, say from the amoebae to the human, would be, of course, quite tenuous. However, structural linguistics has sometimes made large leaps in (mis)applying phonological (sound) systems to the higher orders of language—sentences and discourse (Horowitz, 1987). Discourse simply does not follow a rigid set of rules, like the sentence:

> It would be a daring person indeed who risked declaring which combinations of [discourse] elements could not occur together in a text and which had to. When Kafka left a story apparently unfinished, and Hemingway began one by presenting as given information that was new, and Fowles ended one twice, they were exploiting the flexibility of [discourse]. One does not feel *The Burrow, For Whom the Bell Tolls,* and *French Lieutenant's Woman* to be deviant so much as different. [Discourse] analysts can describe what is common, the culturally popular patterns of organization, but they are not convincing when they seek to make predictive statements about what can and cannot occur. (Hoey, 1991, p. 204)

Individualism

Individualism, the emphasis on the person over that of the social group, appears relevant. American culture is often said to be individualistic. An example that some intercultural specialists use is the popularity of psychology as a major on American college campuses. As compared to sociology, the gap in specialties in favor of psychology is quite large as any perusal of the Graduate Record Examination (GRE) listing of program codes will show. (The GRE bulletin [Educational Testing Service, 1992] for that year lists 17 categories under the heading of psychology, but for sociology there are only two. This heavy specialization is neither necessarily favorable nor natural [Magnusson, 1988]).

A parallel gap is also found at the newsstand in a genre of literature known as "pop psychology." One recent example is *Psychology Today*, yet no similar publication is found for sociology. Another example is the mass market for books devoted to self-knowledge, enhancement, and satisfaction. Interestingly, culture and a contextual view of behavior appear related. Some cultures, like the American, appear less sensitive to contextual or situational explanations of behavior as compared to high-context cultures (Gudykunst & Kim, 1992). Whether a causal relation exists between individualism and reductionism is unclear, but for whatever reason, American mainstream psychology, behavioral and cognitive, has tended to ignore social context in theories of thinking and learning (Bredo, 1992). These two "isms" may, therefore, have their greatest expression in the United States.

Ignoring social context is not limited to mainstream psychology however. Even communication, a study many would readily consider context dependent, had until recently a predominantly mechanistic or reductionist view (Georgoudi & Rosnow, 1985). Similarly, "linguistics has also been dominated by an individualist ideology; Halliday (1978) observes that the angle of reasoning has been typically from the 'language outward' rather than from the social order 'into language' " (Horowitz, 1987, p. 121).

> For too long a time, linguistics has confined itself to the study of isolated sentences, either such sentences carefully selected from a corpus or, more often than not, artfully contrived so as to betray no need for further con-

> text. Thus boards in the linguistic classroom have been filled with such sentences as "John kissed Mary" or "Stephen knew that Mary knew something was wrong" to the avoidance of such sentences as "Consequently, he kissed her" or "Obviously he knew that Mary knew that something was wrong." (Longacre, 1983, p. xv)

We do not suggest that the study of isolated and devised sentences is worthless. On the contrary, that approach may be most effective for the study of sentence structure. The concern arises if the contrived sentence were then used to model the psycholinguistic dynamics of authentic discourse. Consequently, a functionalist approach has developed with the view that "language and [discourse] grow out of human needs to construct, negotiate, and interpret meaning for an audience and the personal intentions of a speaker or writer" (Horowitz, 1987, p. 122).

In brief, a concern for context by functionalist linguistics has emerged to treat as primary, the factors of audience and purpose for creating discourse. Functionalism views discourse from an opposite direction from that of structuralism: from the social situation of author and audience rather than from structural units of the sentence. This characterization is made in principle, for neither side would totally exclude context or structure. To consider context, Boxes 1.1 and 1.2 offer activities to do so.

Box 1.1: Exercise on Context: UN Speech Openings

Read the following openings from UN speeches delivered directly after or near the time of the death of Dag Hammarskjöld, a great humanitarian and UN Secretary General. Speaker identities have been withheld for the purposes of this exercise.

A.

We meet in an hour of grief and challenge: Dag Hammarskjöld is dead. But the United Nations lives. His tragedy is deep in our hearts, but the tasks for which he died are at the top of our agenda. A noble servant of peace is gone. But the quest for peace lies before us.

The problem is not the death of one man—the problem is the life of this Organization. It will either grow to meet the challenges of our age, or it will be gone with the wind, without influence, without force, without respect. Were we to let it die—to enfeeble its vigor—to cripple its powers—we would condemn our future.

For in the development of this Organization rests the only true alternative to war; and war appeals no longer as a rational alternative. . . . [Human]kind must put an end to war, or war will put an end to [human]kind.

So let us here resolve that Dag Hammarskjöld did not live—or die—in vain. Let us call a truce to terror.

(continued)

B.

The people of __X__ , on whose behalf I am addressing this Assembly, wish to support all those who have spoken here in favor of the maintenance of peace and friendship among all the peoples of the world. There is no more urgent and vital undertaking for the [people] of today—those of all regions of the world, of all beliefs and of all social classes—than that of preserving peace. . . .

I should like to pay a tribute of respect and admiration to the memory of Mr. Dag Hammarskjöld, the late Secretary General of the United Nations. Mr. Hammarskjöld was not only the administrative head of this Organization; he also fulfilled highly responsible functions in international life. By the vigor of his action and the exceptional qualities he displayed in the fulfillment of his task, Mr. Hammarskjöld became in this Organization an official whom it was difficult to replace, and his death in the line of duty constitutes a loss the magnitude of which will be fully realized as time goes by and all that his activities meant for peace becomes clear.

C.

I wish first to say how deeply moved I am at the thought that our Secretary General, Mr. Dag Hammarskjöld, is no more. On behalf of __X__ and its people, I desire to pay a formal tribute to the illustrious man who has fallen in the service of justice and peace. He was the friend of the small countries that are fighting for survival in a world where the law of the stronger is asserting itself ever more forcefully. He was an invaluable conciliator, a mediator of consummate tact, always available to help in the settlement of international disputes. . . . His memory will remain with us for all time.

As last year, and in my capacity as [head of the government] of __X__ , I have ventured to take part in the General Debate of the United Nations General Assembly at this sixteenth session; I am, however, fully aware of the delicate and difficult nature of the role which __X__ , as a non-aligned country, has to play.

1. Which opening do you personally like most?
2. Which, do you suppose, was the first speech at the UN after Dag Hammarskjöld's death? Which was the later one of the three?
3. How do the speeches reflect differences in psychological distance between the speaker and audience; and between him and Dag Hammarskjöld?
4. Which speech would have been more likely by a speaker at the center of world affairs?
5. How did the different uses of language by the speakers reflect your answers to the above questions?
6. Match the speeches with whom you think made them: Dr. Arturo Frondizi (Argentina); Prince Norodom Sihanouk (Cambodia); Pres. John F. Kennedy (USA). Spend just a few moments on this question; afterward see below.[1]

---

[1] As A appears most likely someone at the center of world affairs, we would correctly guess it as Kennedy's. C is Sihanouk's, perhaps understood by his reference to his country's non-aligned status. B, then, is Frondizi's. Sihanouk's [9-22-61] was the first of the three made; Kennedy's [9-25-61] and then Frondizi's [9-27-61]. Kennedy's reference to Hammarskjöld appears to have the least psychological distance among the three; Frondizi, the most. The same order appears concerning psychological distance with the audience (e.g., *we* vs. *this organization* or the *United Nations*).

Box 1.2: Japanese Silence and its Context

Structure is a central concept in linguistics, but as Chapter 4 will show, the concept can sometimes be overemphasized to the neglect of important sociocultural factors. To provide contextual awareness and an inkling for the evolving discussion on structure, this exercise concerns the topic of silence and how it is treated by an eminent linguist. However, what he says about the Japanese seems to require some explanation. That is, he leaves out some important contextual information. Read the passage and respond to the questions below:

> "Silence can . . . communicate a meaning in its own right. . . . Cross-cultural differences are common over when to talk and when to remain silent, or what a particular instance of silence means. In response to the question 'Will you marry me?', silence in English would be interpreted as uncertainty; in Japanese it would be acceptance. In Igbo, it would be considered a denial . . . " (Crystal 1987:172).

1. By the information given, which culture, Japanese or Igbo, appears more understandable to someone in an English-speaking culture?
2. What image about the Japanese comes to mind from this instance?

Images of Japanese silence and inscrutability are so prevalent that Crystal's description may seem unremarkable. His description is a bit misleading however. The problem is that it seems to have been shorn of its context. In Japan the romantic ideal is for a female to be so choked up with emotion that she becomes speechless. So, she expresses her acceptance by a headnod and tears. Without such nonverbal signs, the Japanese would be just as distraught as an American would. The Japanese have long been seen as inscrutable and at various times, this image is found reinvented in popular American and western media (Donahue, 1994). Here is an innocent but apt example how such imaging can be perpetuated, even in academic fare. It also suggests how context is easily ignored.

WORDS: EMPTY CONTAINERS?

In studies of communication, "meaning is the object of study, not a given [property] that exists prior to analysis. Hence meaning should not be assumed to reside *in* anything, be it [discourse], utterance . . . or behavior, even though such acts and objects may be understood as meaningful. Meaning is the product or result of communication" (O'Sullivan et al., 1994, p. 174). Technically, therefore, words do not "carry" meaning, despite how frequently this metaphor is heard. Incidently, *metaphor,* herein, has a conceptual sense rather than a literary one, for cognition is fundamentally metaphorical (Hobbs, 1979; Lakoff & Johnson, 1980), as is the "whole nature of [English]" (Holman, 1978, p. 315).

Bateson (1979) stated that, "without context, words and actions have no meaning at all" (p.15). Words can have multiple functions (Jakobson,

1960; Schiffrin, 1994) and are potentially unrestricted in meaning. A simple example is the greeting *How are you?*, often mistaken by foreigners as an inquiry into one's health. However, even some native speakers may sometimes respond with their "health report," which suggests that certain contextual factors trigger different responses.

Consider the various meanings of *"I love you."* J. A. M. Meerloo reported over 20 different meanings from love to hate to indifference (Adler & Towne, 1978), though that probably is just the tip of the iceberg. Some truth may lie in the impression held abroad (e.g., Japan) that because Americans appear so frequently to say "I love you," that the expression has become meaningless. The point of this section is that it was meaningless to begin with. Only through contextual features is meaning imbued. It has been suggested that the Gulf War could have been averted if it were not for the American Secretary of State's genteel manner in projecting little anger in giving Iraq a final ultimatum (e.g., Triandis, 1994). His words may have been too "empty."

All of this is so to the analyst, but what it means in daily life may be a different matter. Daily living would come to a standstill if we had to ponder the meaning of each word. Instead, people assume that their meanings are shared. Imperfect as this assumption may be, it does get us through our day. When it does not, the value of the empty container metaphor becomes evident. By this metaphor, people may be led to identify what word meanings they do not share. For the analyst, the metaphor enables him or her to objectify analysis and to include factors of communication that they may otherwise exclude.

SCRIPTED LANGUAGE

The locus of meaning for discourse—whether in the mind or in the text—will continue to be debated. Interestingly, this debate appears framed from a reductionist or individualist stance: It seems to preclude the wider context of social interaction. Instead of the "inside," as with internal elements of the mind or text, meaning may happen to reside "out there" in the social world. That is, language obtains meaning through social interaction—it is "scripted."

Language changes considerably depending on circumstances, such as that produced in an elevator or a church (Casse, 1980). Consider how language behavior may be preordained for church as suggested by this example:

> Sacred Heart, a church of virtual cathedral size, dominates the . . . neighborhood [in the] mostly Puerto Rican part of [this New England town]. . . . Sounds of Latin music, mostly salsa and meringue, came in from the streets

> outside during the quiet English Mass. Separate services were held at different hours in English and in Spanish. At the English Mass, [as Father Joyce] had observed, people stopped talking when they entered the church, they didn't bring in babies, and they spread out among the pews. Many took seats far from the altar. At the Spanish Mass, people came in talking, continuing the conversations that they'd begun outside. The Hispanic parishioners clustered together in the forward pews. The church always sat hushed after Communion at the English Mass, but voices murmured, babies cried, throughout the Spanish. "People clap their hands, and they're not afraid to sing," said Father Joyce. "There's a real noise level at the Spanish Mass that would drive most people crazy at the English Mass." He added, "*Vive la différence.* But it's hard to find ways to bring the two communities together." (Kidder, 1989. pp.231–232)

For a further example, imagine that a young man of the inner city is standing on a street corner when a policeman approaches him.[2] The cop asks, "What time is it?" The young man, pointing to his watch, replies, "This is mine."

How is this exchange explained? Explanation is helped by knowing the context of the inner city and the apparent propensity of "the man" (the police) to sometimes misidentify or stereotype young Black males. Yet, this exchange needs a reinterpretation, for the cop did not intend to harass the young man. Instead, the cop, who also attended night school, was merely trying to complete a homework assignment in sociology by asking strangers about the time. Considering this, one can see how the situation can exert profound influence on language and related behavior.

Verbal language, of course, is but one channel by which we communicate. Other channels—voice, face, posture—operate as well. The cop in the previous example may very well have communicated harassment nonverbally. If so, such behavior may have been elicited by the situation (whether rightly or wrongly). Language, then, is often dictated by a related sociocultural situation. This truism is often evident to those who live abroad.

When abroad, one's native language, figuratively, gets left behind, even if spoken in the new destination. CNN News (1994) appeared mistaken in broadcasting its *factoid* that said: *Door* in Japanese is *door*; *table* is *table*. The correct Japanese, if transliterated, is *doa* and *teeburu*. To the uninitiated, these loan words in Japanese are incomprehensible as English. Even if the native speakers of English understand, they can hardly feel at home with these foreign words. However, the matter is far more complex than unfamiliar sounds.

---

[2] This example was first heard from Prof. Ray P. McDermott in a graduate course in applied linguistics, Columbia University, 1984.

It is not necessarily the case that *door* in Japanese is *door* and *table* is *table.* Japanese is not limited to these loan words but also has corresponding words of native origin. Because traditional Japanese homes and furniture are considerably different in design and use from western, the concepts of *door* and *table* could be just as different. For example, sliding doors (*hikido*; *to*) are more prevalent than the hinged type in Japanese dwellings. *To* "door" can also refer to the hinged door of western design but usually not the reverse.

Technically, therefore, the CNN factoid is unclear about which concepts are involved. Although this may seem petty, it may not be to the expatriate in Japan who yearns for a dwelling of American design and proportion. Japanese sliding doors are of various types, some of which are made of fragile paper requiring careful use. This traditional Japanese aesthetic requires a certain lifestyle, actually, a discipline. Someone who had been raised differently may forever feel a bit amiss. Conversely, a Japanese may feel similarly amiss in the United States, despite having experienced "western" things in Japan.

Other misinformation could have been the result of the CNN factoid as well. Because the factoid ignored the Japanese words of native origin, the television audience could erroneously conclude that none exist. What may one, therefore, conclude about a people having no words for the most basic objects of everyday life? Furthermore, they "must" borrow the words from an alien language?! This progression can hardly be exaggerated, for a leading American Japanologist, interviewed by Kolker and Alvarez (1991), surprisingly said that the Japanese borrowed their "whole language" from China. That is untrue of course. However, such claims are not uncommon considering the history of western caricatures of Japan (Donahue, 1994).

Lastly, the implication exists that "they speak English," or even that "we speak the same language." However, some people may not realize that, once abroad, they will have to accommodate to a foreign English, if using English internationally. Sometimes, it may turn out that a *door* is not really a *door*, and a *table* is not a *table.*

In Japan, a common misunderstanding occurs when a visiting foreigner, say, an American, is told by his or her Japanese guide to meet at the "front" of a certain hotel (Sakamoto & Naotsuka, 1982). However, they miss meeting because "front" *(furonto)* to a Japanese means "front desk," but to the foreigner it means "outside in front."[3] This is not at all

[3] We are aware that *front desk* is sometimes shortened to *front* in English. However, that occurs after familiarity is established between the interlocutors about the front desk. In Japan, establishing this familiarity is not required for *furonto.* Thus, native speakers of English are caught unawares because its use is unexpected. Its use occurs even when one is not staying at a hotel: For example, making a hotel a place of meeting someone.

a reflection on the Japanese, but the point that communities have their own shared meanings. One's language only has communicative value to the extent that it is subordinated to the ways of the community. In fact, we will very likely never coin a word into the language.[4] The Japanese have borrowed words from English but have imbued them with their own meanings.

The rest of Sakamoto and Naotsuka's (1982) story is that the foreigner, convinced that he or she was duped, berates the Japanese guide. Despite the simple solution of testing that belief, people continue to fume. They are more distressed by an imagined wrong than the actual inconvenience itself. This story puts into relief how much language is dependent on the situation. Contrarily, we often think that language is "ours"; that it conforms to our wishes. Yet, it is not really ours but our community's. For if we do not use it, we lose it (e.g., Major, 1992; Pan & Gleason, 1986). With the breakup of the former Soviet Union, a previous American defector came "home." Gone for over 20 years, he needed an interpreter during his stay back in the United States. Milder effects from living abroad are more common. For example, after a couple of years abroad, some Americans may begin to sound "British" (different) to their folks back home. That impression may come from their acquired habits of enunciating words or using more formal expressions. Language is inextricably linked with a community. Language depends on context not only for its meaning, but also its very life.

EXPECTANCY: A KEY TO DISCOURSE

Meaning involves an inferential process, a process facilitated by expectancy (Faigley, Cherry, Jolliffe, & Skinner, 1985; Tannen 1993). A good example is the orienting function that titles often have for a discourse. Their absence allows one less way to prepare the reader or hearer. The importance of titles is cogently illustrated in an example taken from Dooling and Lachman (1971):

> With locked gems financing him, our hero bravely defied all scornful laughter that tried to prevent his scheme. "Your eyes deceive," he had said. "An egg, not a table, correctly typifies this unexplored planet." Now three sturdy sisters sought proof. Forging along, sometimes through calm vastness, yet more often over turbulent peaks and valleys, days became weeks as many doubters spread fearful rumors about the edge. At last, from nowhere, welcome winged creatures appeared signifying momentous success. (quoted in Sanford & Garrod, 1981, p. 9)

[4] This insight comes from Ray P. McDermott, 1984.

This text immediately becomes coherent once its thematic title, "Christopher Columbus's Discovery of America," is known.

Even before titles, readers or hearers usually have some expectation already about topic, style, content, view, and so on. Certainly, poetry elicits different expectations than what prose does. Within both, various genres exist with certain distinguishing features. For instance, front-page newspaper articles tend to preview its information with a "summary lead" at the start of the article (Fredrickson & Wedel, 1984). The summary lead, therefore, helps the reader to better digest the rest of the information by prior knowledge of the whos, the whats, and so forth. Clearly, the summary lead is more effectively placed at the start of the article than at the end (the bottom). By having this expectation, newspaper readers can locate summary leads and selectively read articles according to their interest and available time.

INTERACTIVE PROCESSING

The fact that reader/hearer expectations are used in the comprehension of discourse suggests the active role that the reader/hearer does play. In contrast, the writer and reader, under structuralism, take a back seat to that of language structure (Selden, 1985). This point, as seen earlier, can be reversed in favor of context. The truth, however, may lie somewhere between these competing views. Pragmatically, discourse comprehension is viewed as an interactive process by which a reader/hearer, given a particular purpose, activates textual, situational, and cognitive resources to derive meaning.

Such resources refer, for example, to a receiver's topic background knowledge; textual elements semantic, grammatical, and organizational in nature; situational cues related to role and relationship of the discourse participants; spatio–temporal factors, and so on. Comprehension probably varies according to the "mix" of these resources accessed. Most assuredly, comprehension will depend on the purpose of the receiver (e.g., Hoey, 1991; Hörmann, 1986). Different purposes result in different levels of understanding:

> Whoever reads a text for misprints understands it, if probably only at a relatively shallow level. Whoever repeats [after someone] the same text [in word for word utterances] also understands it. Whoever listens to a text to decide whether it is consistent understands it "more deeply"; and, finally, whoever listens to it so that he [or she] can paraphrase it in his [or her] own words afterwards understands it still better, on an even deeper level. (Hörmann, 1986, p. 269)

This interactive view explains, at least in part, a common observation about speeches: People who have heard the same speech can come to very different opinions about it. For diplomatic discourse especially, truths are not self-evident. World events are interpreted differently. Thus, a speech may be seen as onerous by one UN delegation, yet a delight by another. This is further reason to develop our capacity for critical communication.

Another point is that this view presupposes a "naturally occurring text." That is, one that occurs within a particular discourse community (see chapt. 3) and intended to be comprehensible (Beaugrande & Dressler, 1981). This stipulation excludes the nonsensical text made for experimental purposes—actually, a "nontext" (term, Beaugrande & Dressler, 1981). Hypothetically, a diplomat could produce a nontext as a political strategy, say, as a filibuster. However, the "general debate" atmosphere of the UN does not represent a legislative contest that invites a filibuster; rather the opposite. Heads of state, in particular, wish to be coherent for the sake of influencing policies of other governments, not to mention their personal image and that of their country. Although this does not preclude ineffectiveness, it does preclude nonsense.

Box 1.3: A Poster for World Economic Comparisons

In a poster titled "Economic Growth and Competition in the Global Economy,"[5] produced to accompany an American college textbook on economics, the following national names were taken from its international comparisons:

Argentina	Germany	Saudi Arabia
Australia	Indonesia	South Africa
Brazil	Japan, Inc.	South Korea
Canada	Mexico	United States
Chile	Poland	
China	Russia	

Consider this naming of Japan and these questions:

1. How might language be a factor in communication involving this poster?
2. How appropriate is this naming for use in a cross-cultural study? Why?
3. How would this naming, if made for a United Nations meeting, become a social factor in communication?
4. What prevents this kind of behavior in the United Nations?

[5] For *Economics* (Lipsey, Courant, Purves, Steiner, 1992). According to their publisher, as of July 1995, the poster was already out-of-print, which thwarted our attempt at confirmation.

This poster (see Box 1.3) was displayed under glass outside the economics department at a state university in Michigan. Close inspection appeared to show that the "inc." was not graffiti. Even if it were, it still merits our attention. That an economics department would display it suggests their complicity. The fact also that it occurred in Detroit's home state has bearing. People there have been adversely affected, no doubt, by competition from Japanese carmakers. This friction led to some Japanese to cancel their study abroad programs in Michigan for fear for their safety.

Despite trade friction, to display this poster by that academic department suggests poor judgment. This example shows that such thinking can be found even among the most highly educated—even our most elite—as anywhere else. International understanding goes only as far as the mutual respect held. This principle informs most discourse practices at the UN for good reason.

Consider the matter of respect more directly by comparing how speakers from North and South Korea were differentially treated at the UN (see Box 1.4).

Box 1.4: Different UN Receptions Received by North and South Korea (1988)*

Introduction by UN Chair

For South Korea	**For North Korea**
In accordance with the decision taken by the General Assembly at its 3rd plenary meeting held on Friday, 23 September 1988, I shall call on the President of the Republic of Korea, His Excellency Mr. Roh Tae Woo, who expressed the wish to participate in the considerationof this item.	In accordance with the decision taken by the General Assembly at its 3rd plenary meeting, held on Friday, 23 September 1988, I shall call on the First Deputy Minister for Foreign Affairs and Chairman of the delegation of the Democratic People's Republic of Korea, Mr. Kang Sok Ju, who has expressed the wish to participate in the consideration of this item. [end]
On behalf of the General Assembly, I have the honor to welcome to the United Nations the President of the Republic of Korea, His Excellency Mr. Roh Tae Woo, and to invite him to make his statement. [end]	

Conclusion by UN Chair

On behalf of the General Assembly, I wish to thank the President of the Republic of Korea for his statement. [end]	The Assembly has thus concluded its consideration of agenda item 146. [end]

*United Nations, General Assembly record A/43/PV.33 and A/43/PV. 34, October 18, 1988.

Was such differential treatment simply due to the speakers' relative diplomatic positions? Certainly, their relative positions had a large bearing: Diplomats reacted unfavorably toward North Korea because it was not represented by its top leader (Lewis, 1988, p. A6). So, despite the "great emphasis [placed] on the principle of the sovereignty and equality of nations large and small" at the UN (Bailey, 1964, p. 112), a social hierarchy between diplomats exists nonetheless. Still, was it too much for the presiding president (Caputo of Argentina) of the General Assembly to also thank the North Korean for his speech? Even speech communication at the UN does not begin with a clean slate. Given different ritualistic treatment, one must consider the possible effects on the audience (the General Assembly).

Do audiences become more predisposed to one speaker than another because of differential treatment received? This consideration is beyond the present scope, but research in social psychology and sociolinguistics shows that even the slightest social differences can predispose negative evaluations of others (e.g., Bourhis, 1979; Edwards & Giles, 1984; Giles 1979; Giles & Powesland, 1975; Sebastian & Ryan, 1985). We may think that, at a momentous occasion of bringing two combatants together, they could also be equally welcomed. This factor could be significant for North Korea, which may likely view the UN as too influenced by the United States. After all, the United States had been its enemy in war on the side of the South. Any slights received could then be misperceived as American inspired, encouraging North Korea to disparage the UN.

MOTIVATED DISCOURSE

Mention must also be made of Sigmund Freud. His name probably comes as a surprise in this context. However, much is owed him because of his principle, "behavior is caused," a basis on which studies of human affairs rest.[6] This principle assumes that a reason exists behind every human behavior. It thus allows the analyst to treat language as purposeful. Without this principle, discourse analysis would be severely impaired.

Because discourse, whether spoken or written, operates under constraints, the producer must make certain choices. Choice implies purpose. For example, referring to the nation of Japan as *Japan Incorporated* is plainly intentional and may suggest a certain ideology. Identifying the reason and ideology is a matter of interpretation. Because of Freud's principle, interpretation has the potential to become meaningful. Despite

[6] According to Professor Bacon in his graduate course on clinical psychology, Indiana University, 1975.

Freud's standing in therapeutic psychology today, his "behavior is caused" principle will long be remembered.

Another important contribution is the unconscious mind, although not entirely Freud's. No one is ever in complete control of his or her behavior. A diplomat makes a slip of the tongue. Insignificant? Perhaps, but, if investigated, could lead to insights about discourse segments elsewhere in his or her speech. Because most studies of UN speeches will be through print, such performance slips will not be encountered. Nevertheless, for contextual analysis, an example of a slip of the tongue is provided in Box 1.5 and elsewhere in this chapter. This speech phenomenon, in the context of diplomacy, is an area yet to be researched. In our small way, we hope that more attention is brought to it.

Box 1.5: A UN Slip of the Tongue

The year is 1960, the same year that the American U2 spy plane was shot down over the Soviet Union catching US President Dwight D. Eisenhower in a lie. It is also the same year that the Congo erupted into civil war with the super powers on opposite sides. President Eisenhower addressed the UN with these words but made a slight slip of the tongue while doing so. This slip, italicized here, does not appear in the official UN draft of the speech but is heard on its audio tape. Read the passage and think what meaning this slip could have had for Communist Bloc and Third World nations.

> This is, indeed, a moment for honest appraisal and historic decision. We can strive to master [problems in the world] for narrow national advantage or we can begin at once to undertake a period of constructive action which will subordinate selfish interest to the general well-being of the international community. . . . In response to the call of the Republic of the Congo, the United Nations, under its outstanding Secretary General, has recently mounted a large-scale effort to provide that new Republic with help. That effort has been flagrantly attacked by a few nations which wish to prolong strife in the Congo for their own purposes. The criticism directed by these nations against the Secretary General . . . is nothing less than a direct attack upon the [*United States its-*] the United Nations itself. In my opinion the Secretary General has earned the support and the gratitude of every peace-loving nation. (Eisenhower, 1960, pp. 186–187)

Although Americans may be well accustomed to having the UN headquartered on their soil, its location is probably still a sore spot to some in the world. For them, the American location is a conflict of interest. For example, Khrushchev (1960a) of the Soviet Union, in wake of tensions with the United States, proposed that the UN headquarters be moved to another country. Whether Eisenhower's slip contributed or not is unknown, but Khrushchev, soon thereafter, charged that the then UN Secretary General was biased in American favor: "Mr. Hammarskjöld [the Secretary General] has always been prejudiced in his attitude toward the socialist countries; he has always upheld the interests of the United States of America and the other monopoly-capitalist countries" (Khrushchev, 1960b, p. 541). Thus various implications follow, despite whatever we believe otherwise.

A basic principle of communication is that "We communicate whether we want to or not" (Prosser, 1989, p. 2). In the context of the Cold War, Eisenhower's slip could become a mother lode of interpretative riches. Each statement could be reinterpreted into newer or deeper meanings. For example, Eisenhower's words could suddenly be seen as irony (or subversion), for he spoke of the need for "honest appraisal" and the ignoring of "self-interest," not to mention his promoting of the Secretary General. Such tongue slips, then, could spark interpretations that might be otherwise missed. They are not necessarily correct, however. Interpretations must be based on reasonable evidence. Additionally, they need to be considered in light of other alternative views. Identifying alternative views is one of the most important skills to cultivate.

Appreciation of an opposing view is not synonymous with its acceptance. We can understand a viewpoint but still not accept it. The American U2 plane violated Soviet airspace and sovereignty. The Soviets were understandably upset. However, this must be tempered by the fact of the Cold War: the threat of nuclear war, active Soviet espionage, and the relatively closed nature of Soviet society. Although the Eisenhower government can be faulted for its timing and related behavior, it probably had little other choice. Still, the Soviet perspective requires exploration at least for its impact on Eisenhower's address.

In sum, motivation, expectancy, and interactive processing lead to an inescapable conclusion: Discourse is organized. Revealing that organization is a basic purpose of discourse analysis. To further prepare for that purpose, it would be instructive to consider critical communication concerning language and culture awareness. These twin awarenesses are relevant not only for the terminological issue with *discourse structure*, but also for contrastive discourse analysis and contrastive rhetoric, topics met in later chapters.

CRITICAL COMMUNICATION

The study of UN diplomatic discourse requires critical communication. Critical communication involves seeking alternative views. One way is by forming a dialectic between received opinion (or one's own) and related counterviews about a particular issue or idea related to communication. Ideally, one approaches the matter openly and fairly. Such dialectics lead to some resolution, usually with increased understanding of the problem or issue.

That may lead to reestablishing, modifying, or abandoning our original position. In any case, we can advance our thinking by the added insights.

At least, we would like to think so. For human problems require continual study and review: "There is no way to *conclusively verify* a [hypothesis or] model, because all possible evidence can never be assembled (cf. Popper, 1972); at most, the model can be *falsified* if it contradicts a significant body of evidence (cf. Lakatos, 1970)" (Beaugrande, 1984, p. 5). Consequently, critical communication is in order.

Ideally, we hope to employ critical awarenesses about language and culture throughout our analyses of discourses for study. To work toward such awarenesses, the next two sections provide a brief introduction and a related example.

Language Awareness

An age-old idea, now and then resurrected, believes that language determines thought. For instance, a Christian Scientist is known to have rejected vitamins when called "medicine" but accepted when called "food" (Dodd, 1991). The view that language can have such an influence underpins the movement to eradicate sexist language and thereby sexism itself. A change in behavior (language) is seen as a change in attitude (thought). Whether this relation holds true is still debatable. It is a chicken-and-egg thing—which came first? However, even if sexist attitudes went unchanged, a reduction in sexist language might be beneficial nonetheless.

Whether language really determines thought is open for debate. At present, linguistic determinism is generally accepted only in its qualified (weak) version (Berry, Poortinga, Segall, & Dasen, 1992; Clark & Clark, 1977; Crystal, 1987; Hill, 1988; Trudgill, 1983): "Language may not determine the way we think, but it does influence the way we perceive and remember, and it affects the ease with which we perform mental tasks" (Crystal, 1987, p. 15). The operative word here is *determine,* for the word appears too strong. However, if replaced by *influence,* as with "language or perception influencing thought," linguistic determinism, in modified form, appears a reasonable explanation in some cases.

How does this relate to discourse analysis? One good example is the metaphor of sentence structure for discourse. That could belie an attitude, which could affect our analysis in innumerable ways. One way may be to reduce contextual factors in analysis, an illustrated case of which is shown in Chapter 4. For now, discussion switches to cultural worldview and linguistic determinism through a convenient example of the American ethos of equality. This ethos is especially convenient because UN speeches necessarily involve conflict in views about forms of government or ways of living. If one were never to have reflected on the viability of one's own government or culture, then one may be that much less prepared for making effective discourse analyses.

Culture Awareness

We are all products of culture and possess an associated worldview. Worldview is "a distinctive set of attitudes, beliefs, and values" held by members of a particular culture (O'Sullivan et al., 1994, p. 333). A worldview forms a part of our perception through which we understand our world. By becoming aware of how culture influences our perception, we can begin to work at the control of cultural and personal biases. Sharpening our perception can increase our understanding of foreign views and thereby our discourse analysis of international communication. An early step is perceiving the links between our own culture and behavior.

An Illustrated Case

Toward developing culture awareness, the case of Tocqueville's classic study (1832) of the United States may prove helpful. In relation to American equality, his name is often evoked in the same breadth as that for the Founding Fathers. Political leaders like to underscore American uniqueness by citing Tocqueville's classic study; for from it "a consistent theme emerges that America is different from other countries because it was founded on a revolutionary idea that all men are created equal" (PBS, 1995).

Despite that famous phrase, the term *equality* neither appears in the original Constitution nor in the Bill of Rights (Bell, 1978). It only emerged in the former document by amendment—the 14th and 15th—nearly 4 decades after Tocqueville's departure. This fact surprises even some historians. Moreover, the United States today "has become the most economically stratified" society within the industrialized world (Bradsher, 1995, p. 1), yet as many as 95% of Americans see themselves as "middle class" (Francese, 1995; Sirevåg, 1991).

In explaining this cultural contradiction, cultural worldview may provide an answer. Americans believe that their nation, since its founding, has consisted of equality. This belief pertains more to prescriptive equality rather than descriptive, a fact often ignored by our national sentiment. How Tocqueville is translated may be illustrative of this (Donahue, 1995). According to Tocqueville, what most impressed him about the United States was *l'égalité des conditions*. Interestingly, American and British translations differ how *conditions* is rendered: The British keep the same form, but the Americans make it a mass/noncountable noun (condition). The mass form broadens the scope, as it does in the following pair: *communications* and *communication.*

Box 1.6: Difference in Translations

	French *conditions*
British (conditions)	**American** (condition)
Reeve 1835	Bowen—Bradley 1945; 1963
Lawrence—Mayer 1966; 1988	

Note: The French was taken from Tocqueville (1981) and is assumed identical to the original edition. For the "two-person" texts, the translator precedes that of the editor. Nationalities of the individuals have been surmised by this author from the sources available to him. Reeve's was the first translation into English and became the basis of Bowen's later translation in 1862 and subsequently retranslated by Bradley (Bradley, 1945).

Moreover, Tocqueville, in French, refers to *société* (society) when speaking of equality, yet American translators substitute that for *people,* again unlike the British versions. In short, Tocqueville seems originally to have been more restrictive and less concrete about individual social equality than what seems implied by American versions. For American readers, these differences may overstate American equality as compared to that for British readers.

A further use of discourse analysis reveals a possible case of linguistic determinism by which Tocqueville's idea of equality was much narrower than his American translations allow. In Tocqueville's day, "Classic liberalism defined equality as equality before the law" (Bell, 1978, p. 260). Individuals were to be treated equally under the law despite status or privilege. This restriction to political right is in marked contrast to modern liberalism, which conceives of equality as also encompassing social right regarding opportunity and sometimes even outcome (Bell, 1978). The definition of equality in classic liberalism can be best seen reflected in the fact that *equality* is a cognate of *legality* in French, Tocqueville's native language:

English	*French*
equality	*égalité*
legality	*légalité*

Even more striking is the following contrast between English and French when a grammatical article modifies *equality*:

English	*French*
the equality	*l'égalité*

Note the closeness of form in French between *légalité* (legality) and *l'égalité* (the equality), the term Tocqueville actually used. Because the orthography and phonology of these words are nearly identical in French, they are probably much harder to distinguish than in English. In fact, Tocqueville was found to have interchanged the terms of *equality, democracy,* and *free institutions* (Schleifer, 1980), terms related to political structure. Thus, he seemed more concerned with the political than the social. In view of his treatment of minorities at the time, his view on American equality appears solely related to mainstream White society (Donahue, 1995).

Another implication results, for equality is at the core of race relations. Blacks and Whites differ in their perception of equality of opportunity (Rice, 1995) and in their folk definitions of racism (Lichtenberg, 1992). For these reasons, it is unlikely that the two races will ever agree. How can they if they define the problem so essentially different? Blacks see racism as institutionalized—"it's out there"; whereas Whites see racism as an abnormality afflicting extremists (Lichtenberg, 1992). In effect, both definitions relieve one of personal racism by viewing racism as external to oneself. Although no racial group is immune from racism, the onus for change must be focused on White America—the majority—for that is the group most privileged by numbers, power, and historical legacy. In this regard, concern by Blacks over institutionalized racism is quite real and legitimate. However, personal racism and prejudice must become a concern for all.

The issues of equality and racism have particular relevance for our purposes, lest one assume that the United States or its people have inherent moral superiority. Mead (1995), an observer of American–Chinese relations, cautions us to recognize the ills of our own society before criticizing others. He points out that American missionaries to China in the 1830s seemed to have little compunction about criticizing social conditions there despite slavery and other ills in their own. One would be foolish to mistake American success in the world for its morality rather than its economic or military might. The American ethos has had a role to play, but the "American way" has its limitations. A modicum of nationalism is healthy but in excess, a peril. Its opposite—cynicism—is not a better stance either. As in most things, moderation appears best. Let us aspire toward our social ideals but be modest enough to recognize our personal and national shortcomings.

These examples, suggestive as they may be, intend to point out that a critical awareness about language and culture is integral to effective discourse analysis. As for discourse, the metaphor of *sentence structure* may or may not lead to extreme structuralist views, an issue reserved for later development. As for culture, language could influence one's worldview to assume cultural superiority. Until the proper opportunity, it suffices for now to have raised these cautions. If mindful of the implications, one may be on safer grounds.

CONCLUSION

In brief, discourse analysis focuses on the language of use. Because language mediates so much of human activities, discourse analysis has extensive applications across the social sciences. A necessary basis for its application is an understanding of the related context. Until recently, context had been rather ignored in favor of the constituent parts of a phenomenon. Fields such as sociolinguistics and social psychology have increasingly reminded us of its importance. However, its complexity makes it difficult to define context in scientific terms. A general definition suffices for present purposes.

Another important concept is critical communication, the practice of applying critical resources to a communicative message. Identifying alternative explanations or interpretations is an important outcome. This outcome is likely facilitated by the awareness of language and culture as factors affecting behavior. Illustration of this was made by comparing American and British translations of Tocqueville's sense of equality and related implications for racial relations today. Critical reflection on our society and culture appears to be a prerequisite for the study of diplomatic discourse.

Context and critical communication merit all the more attention considering that words and language are but "signposts" by which human receivers interpret meaning. Interpretation results from a constructed process by which receivers apply various resources including knowledge of the topic, purpose, relations between participants to the communication, and other situational matter. This construction of meaning occurs through interaction between person and text and associated factors. Construction is further facilitated by expectancy of such features as a certain title or type of discourse. With some situations, a discourse seems scripted in that certain routines or behaviors are expected and valued. Consider the "script" that is followed at weddings, funerals, restaurants, classrooms, and so on. Discourse, whether routine or spontaneous, is motivated, for it intends to serve a purpose, even if it is only at a nonconscious level.

APPLICATION

Performance Slips, or in Honor of Murphy's Law

As anyone who has studied actual speech knows, slips of the tongue are quite common. However, written transcripts often ignore them and other unintended vocalizations. As a result, people imagine speech to be far more fluent and "correct" than it actually is. This applies even for speeches that are read. To appreciate this fact about human performance, the following extracts from an actual UN speech ought to help. We know of no studies devoted to this phenomenon regarding diplomacy, but hope that, in a small way, this effort will draw attention to this area. We are not suggesting that such phenomena could have affected history. Or could they have?

Box 1.7

Read the following actual extracts from a speech made at the UN by Eisenhower (1960) on September 22, 1960. Each has a slip of the tongue as indicated and Eisenhower's self-correction:

(A) Second, the United Nations should be prepared to help the African countries maintain their security without wasteful and dangerous competition in armaments.

United Nations experts are being asked to train the Congo's security forces. If the Secretary General should find it useful to undertake increased activity in order to meet requests of this nature elsewhere, my country would be glad to join other Member States in making essential contributions to such United Nations activity.

More importantly, I **believe** that the Afr-. . . I hope that the African States will use existing, or establish new regional machinery in order to avert an arms race in this area. In so doing, they would help to spare their continent the ravages which the excesses of chauvinism have elsewhere inflicted in the past. If, through concerted effort, these nations can choke off competition in armaments, they can give the whole world a welcome lesson in international relations.

(B) The communist nations' walk-out at Geneva, when they learned that we were about to submit these proposals [for armaments control], brought negotiations to an abrupt halt. Their unexplained action does not, however, reduce the urgent need for arms control. My country believes that negotiations can—and should—soon be **removed** resumed.

Our aim is to reach agreement on all the various measures that will bring general and complete disarmament. Any honest appraisal, however, must recognize that this is an immense task. It will take time.

(C) The United States wants the Soviet Union and all the nations of the world to know enough about United States defense preparations to be assured that United States forces **extend** exist only for deterrence and defense—not for surprise attack. I hope the Soviet Union will similarly wish to assure the United States and other nations of the non-aggressive character of its security preparations.

(D) In urging progress towards a world community, I cite the American concept of the destiny of a progressive society. Here in this land, in what was once a wilderness, we have generated a society and a civilization drawn from many sources. Yet out of this mixture of many peoples and faiths we have developed unity in freedom.

This concept of unity in freedom, drawn from the diversity of many racial strains and cultures, we would like to see made a reality for all [human]kind. This concept should apply within every nation as it does among nations. . . . I should like to see a universal plebiscite in which every individual in the world would be given the opportunity freely and secretly to answer this question: "Do you want this right?" Opposed to the idea of two hostile, embittered worlds in **perfect** perpetual conflict, we envisage a single world community, as yet unrealized but advancing steadily towards fulfillment through our plans, our efforts and our collective ideas. (Eisenhower, 1960)

1. Comment on the possible interpretations by using the concepts or principles in Chapter 1. Provide related evidence from the extracts and your knowledge of the historical time.
2. These performance slips are not random—they still make sense. Does that fact give support to Freud's "behavior is caused" principle? Why or why not?
3. Try to think of several reasons, apart from pure chance, for accounting for slips of the tongue.
4. How and why may this speech phenomenon affect the role of written speechtexts distributed by the UN?
5. As compared to a television newscaster who may say "excuse me" for a slip in speech, Eisenhower says nothing other than his intended word(s). Explain this possible difference.[7]
6. Why are alternative views necessary to consider in discourse analysis?
7. What concept or principle in this chapter do you consider the most fundamental to discourse analysis? Why?

---

[7] An example of a TV newscaster follows: [paraphrased] . . . racial oppression has been charged to exist in Hollywood. This issue raised by Reggie Jackson, excuse me, Jesse Jackson, was the subject of the Nightline discussion (ABC News, 1996). (For those unfamiliar, Reggie Jackson is a retired Black baseball player; Jesse Jackson, a Black political leader.)

2

THE FRAMING AND FORMATTING OF DISCOURSE

This chapter aims to provide a systematic approach to the organizational elements of discourse. The approach developed is useful for the analysis of planned speech and writing in general and has benefitted from "functionalist" thought in linguistics, general and applied, as in Beaugrande (1984), Halliday (1994), Hoey (1983; 1991), Jordan (1984), McCarthy & Carter (1994), and Nunan (1993). A functional approach gives priority to the intentions or functions in a discourse rather than to mere form (structure) (Crystal, 1980). We attempt to link form and function without unduly reifying discourse forms into a highly rigid structure.

LINGUISTIC LEVELS

Traditionally, linguistics has viewed language as a "vertical space" of levels or strata (Halliday, 1994, p. 15). Based on Crystal (1987) and Halliday (1994), one way to visualize these linguistic levels is as follows:

meaning (semantics)	→	vocabulary/discourse
grammar (syntax)	→	clause/sentence
pronunciation (phonology)	→	sounds/syllables

Early in modern linguistics, linguistic analysis was ideally thought to first proceed from the phonological level (Crystal, 1987). This procedural order was pragmatic, especially in the United States, for linguists were pressed to study and preserve Native American languages before their disappearance. "Apocryphal stories abound of informants [i.e., native speakers] in field studies who have died before the investigating linguist got around to studying the meaning of the speech patterns that had been so painstakingly transcribed!" (Crystal, 1987, p. 83).

The development of such stories can symbolize how linguistics has been anchored at the sentence level and below. Again, this focus is in relative terms, as was similarly said before. However, it is still telling that the subfield text linguistics has come into being. In some views, text linguistics is concerned with the linguistic patterning of written texts; discourse analysis, with the spoken. This distinction between text and discourse is no longer generally held however (Crystal, 1987).

DISCOURSE LEVELS

Deciding the units and levels of discourse is a basic step in discourse analysis. Using an analogy from promotional advertising, imagine that a campaign for a new soap is planned to distribute free samples to each home in a specified city. How can this be done effectively using door to door distribution by workers from nearby supply trucks? Hardly can you send the workers off without a prior plan of distribution. How can the city be best divided into *units* and *levels*? Such divisions would help dividing the work among workers to ensure efficient completion of the campaign.

Planning may start by an overall view of the city by using a city map. The survey may be done by dividing the city into areas, access points, and routes. Thus, the view begins from the macro or global level, including areas from city wards and sections to communities and neighborhoods. At the opposite end is the micro or local level including the units of residential buildings or street blocks. The macro- and the microlevels are connected by major streets and thoroughfares. Because the campaign operates from trucks loaded with the soap samples, streets will probably be seen forming useful *networks* of city areas for planning efficient distribution. This is how a city may be perceived in units and levels.

Like the city survey, discourse analysis also benefits from a division into levels, although discourse is never as tightly connected as that. Typically, linguists define discourse as language beyond a single sentence, which forms a whole. Typically also, discourse is viewed in terms of two levels—the macro and micro. For example, the macrolevel may include an outline of headings or a major theme; the micro, those elements that tie or connect two sentences. The essential point is that overarching content or devices provide order for the discourse.

At least two more levels of discourse organization may be beneficial, not only because a vastness exists between sentence pairings and a major theme or outline, but also because an apparent paradox exists. If discourse means that which is "beyond the sentence," then there appears no role for the single sentence. However, even single, noncontiguous sentences contribute to discourse, if only as part of a collection. For that, the analyst must go into the microlevel examining the discourse sentence by sentence. Therefore, the common definition of discourse as that beyond the sentence is a bit of a misnomer, for it is through the sentence (or utterance) that discourse comes into being. For these reasons, we propose a discourse scheme consisting of four levels, which correspond to two strata—textual and sentential.

This view considers discourse, either spoken or written, as encompassing one or more texts. Viewing discourse as superordinate to text avoids the recent problem of discourse and text becoming identical in meaning. Originally, discourse and text were distinguished by language mode—spoken or written. However, as this distinction has lately become blurred, two terms appear excessive.

Another problem, however, relates to context: A priority is often given to verbal communication over the nonverbal. Indeed, the latter is defined in terms of the former. Yet, various specialists have estimated that the nonverbal can account for as much as 70% of the meaning of a communication. If discourse is conceived solely in terms of verbal language, then this may accentuate the tendency to devalue context. Viewing discourse as encompassing text encourages a broad view of communication. This appears necessary also because analysis must allow for references or associations to outside events or other texts or discourses. In other words, a discourse could conceivably consist of multiple texts, secondary texts contributing to comprehension of the main text (or discourse event). The quoting of other world leaders by a UN speaker, for example, may expand his or her context by integrating outside discourses or texts. Reference to other significant events or circumstances could have a similar effect.

A related example is silence. In some cultures, such as the Yanomamö of the Amazon or the Apaches and other Native American groups, sustained silences between intimates occur as ritualized behavior after a long absence (e.g., due to a trip), for example. To a lesser extent and perhaps less purposive, Fins and Lapps "remain silent for long periods across conversational turns" (McCarthy & Carter, 1994, p. 150). These silences may be full of meaning and may frame subsequent verbalizations. Ignoring such silences probably would result in a misunderstanding.

Although UN speechtexts may not present the analyst with nonverbal behavior, they still could manifest multiple texts as suggested earlier, and for that reason, the broad notion of discourse appears useful. Also, a restriction to only one variety of discourse (i.e., UN speeches), would appear to serve little purpose. The more varied our experience with discourse, the more skilled our analysis can become. For that reason, an attempt is made herein to provide a flexible approach and varied examples, wherever possible.

This idea of multiple texts may be how to distinguish conceptually context from situation. Context is a "set of circumstances," whereas situation has a base meaning of "locality" or "position" (RHWCD, 1991). Context appears more comprehensive in meaning. Suffice it to point out this technicality, although the two terms are still treated synonymously herein.

According to the scheme in Box 2.1, discourse consists of two strata, textual and sentential. The textual stratum includes three levels: macrolevel, midlevel, and microlevel. The sentential stratum includes the clause level and related elements.

Discourse analysis can proceed through any one of these levels. However, the optimal approach would seem to begin after one has a fair understanding of the text. For that, the macrolevel seems prominent early in comprehension. For example, knowledge of the title of a news article, speech, or essay can provide an orientation to the discourse or text as a whole. On the other hand, some texts may have few such linguistic signals of orientation. Also, the kind of discourse could be novel, providing few "leads" for the reader or listener. For example, foreign students, if inexperienced with satire, may misread Swift's "A Modest Proposal" to believe that the British actually ate Irish babies. Without the macro (the higher) order—satire—such works cannot be truly understood. Here the principle of interactive processing applies by which comprehension is heavily dependent on a reader's background knowledge.

Box 2.1: Discourse Levels

Textual Stratum

1. **macrolevel:** elements that tie together large segments of text from paragraph blocks or text sections to the whole text
2. **midlevel:** elements that tie one paragraph to another segment of text, paragraph, or that which forms paragraph blocks or sections of text
3. **microlevel:** elements that tie adjoining sentences up to that of the paragraph

Sentential Stratum

4. **clause level:** elements that form a single sentence

DISCOURSE INVENTORY

This discourse inventory suggests some important elements of text organization for either formally spoken or written discourse. The elements inventoried are briefly mentioned in anticipation of demonstrated analysis made later in the chapter. Not every element is realized with a particular text, nor must they. Their use will vary according to the factors of discourse, chief among them being author, audience, and purpose.

Terms for these elements, even within the same field, can differ. Thus, we tried to use terms for the widest applicability in view of an interdisciplinary audience. Some terms come directly from applied or theoretical linguistics, while others were renamed for our purposes. Others still are our own contribution. Beyond the language to talk about discourse, this inventory can also help coordinate discourse analyses to be done cooperatively in groups or teams.

Context of Situation

Context of situation, first originated by the anthropologist Malinowski and later expounded by the linguist Halliday, refers to the discourse as a whole. This term is used herein to distinguish context for the discourse from, say, context for a word or a sentence. Context of situation is not part of the inventory, by name, but its understanding is implicitly required. For example, consider Fidel Castro's assurance to the audience that he would be sparing in his remarks:

> Although we have been given the reputation of speaking at great length, the Assembly need not worry. We shall do our best to be brief, saying only what we regard it as our duty to say here. I also intend to speak slowly, in order to co-operate with the interpreters. (Castro, 1960, p. 326) (Cuba) (Note: Country affiliation in parentheses may accompany references to UN speakers.)

Yet, his address turned out to be over 4 hours in length, the longest ever for a head of state or government at the UN (ABC News, 1995a). He obviously came with a heavy agenda.

The analyst, by knowing that Castro and his delegation claimed that they had experienced discrimination by certain New York establishments and were under heavy police surveillance, may better understand his action. By this knowledge, certain words take on added significance, *duty* and *cooperate* for instance. Depending on the validity of Castro's complaints, he might indeed have a duty to address his concerns. *Duty* implies seriousness, which in turn may suggest to his audience that an extended speech is to come. With *cooperate,* the two words may function to shift responsibility away from the speaker for his wordiness. In this regard, note how he treats the *reputation* for wordiness: Something thrust not on him but his collective *(we have been given).* Also, the expressions *duty, cooperate, do our best* seem to reflect positively on the speaker's character. Finally, he seems to assert his rights for the podium, as if to say, "I have a right and I'll use it"; or as a rallying call ("let's stand up for our rights") for those of the same political bloc as his. Such double meanings or connotations become apparent in such situations of open conflict. Box 2.2 includes a related exercise.

Box 2.2: Exercise

Read the following last lines of UN speeches made within several days of each other in 1960. Choose which one you think is Castro's from the same speech above; the other two include Khrushchev's (USSR) and Tito's (Yugoslavia):

A. "The peoples of all States . . . expect the United Nations . . . to adopt decisions according with the aspirations of the peoples."

B. "I am convinced that . . . the so-called non-committed countries can make [important contributions to] the betterment of international relations as well as to the great role that the United Nations . . . should play. . . ."

C. "Some people wanted to know what the line of [our government] was. Well then, there you have our line."

The correct answer of which ending statement was Castro's is C. Khrushchev's was A. Castro's ending seems to fit with what had been earlier said about his opening lines, particularly his shifting the responsibility away from himself, the speaker.

Framing

> At a very general level, the notion of a "frame" provides an attractive metaphor for thinking about discourse understanding as, at least partially, "a process of fitting what one is told into the framework established by what one already knows." (Charniak, 1979) (as quoted by Brown & Yule, 1983, p. 239)

This general sense is intended herein by "framing." The speaker/writer engages in framing by orienting the audience about the content and its arrangement in a discourse. Frames are of two types: outer and inner.

Outer frame

The outer frame (term, Swales, 1990) consists herein of topic indicators, participant alignments, and content summation and final closure. Of these, participant alignments may need clarification.

Participant alignments order the social roles and expectations between a speaker or writer and the audience. For example, these discourse participants may behave differently according to the standing of the speaker/writer. Certain "powerful luminaries" in academic fields can run "rough shod over many of the accepted [discourse] conventions in their given field" (Swales, 1990, p. 128). Rank, reputation, and institutional affiliations held by a speaker or writer contribute to a person's standing. In international affairs, leaders of the superpowers generally gain more respect than those representing countries of least rank.

The *salutation* is an acknowledgment of a speaker's host or hosts and can mark either the opening or closing of a speech. *Footing* should not be confused with the standing of a speaker. Although the latter contributes to footing, they are different. Standing denotes the speaker's reputation; footing, the process engaged to align oneself with the audience about one's role and relationship (Goffman, 1981).

Footing manifests itself in the "textual self," or personification of authority (achievement) (Goffman, 1981). The textual self "can appear in full form in a printed version" without dependence on oral delivery and is conveyed by expertise and relevant personal experiences, the latter diplomats make great use of, according to Goffman (1981, p. 174). For example, Emperor Haile Selassie I of Ethiopia was the one person who addressed both the League of Nations and the United Nations (Prosser, 1970). It is no surprise that that is how he began: "Twenty-seven years ago, as Emperor of Ethiopia, I mounted the rostrum in Geneva to address the League of Nations an appeal [for war relief for my country]. . . . I spoke then both to and for the conscience of the world" (Selassie I, 1963, p. 959).

Exercise: Read Selassie's statement again and notice his word choices. For his first sentence, think of several alternative ways that he could have informed the audience of this fact. How different are they? Lastly, how do both sentences of his contribute to his footing with the audience?

Selassie, who spoke originally in English, cast himself as an experienced diplomat by stating his related achievement of having spoken at the League of Nations. He then added its significance: He spoke for the world. To speak for the world would be an achievement for nearly any leader. In just these few words, Selassie appears to develop footing with his audience.

Although footing is often facilitated by a speaker's personal achievements, it also may be furthered by those of one's country. For example, in successive UN addresses by a Mexican leader, they remind their audiences very early of Mexico's participation in the founding of that forum:

> I thank you, on behalf of the people of Mexico, for [granting] me the opportunity of reaffirming . . . Mexico's unshakable faith in the principles of the Charter which we signed at San Francisco. (Alemán, 1947, p. 45)

> Mexico, a founding Member of the United Nations, welcomes with enthusiasm any proposal to bring the affairs of nations under the rule of law. (Mateos, 1959, p. 163)

It is usual for heads of state or government to reaffirm their support of the UN but much less so, even for early members, to mention their country's historical tie. Mexico is rightly proud of its achievement. We merely wish to point out the possible footing function.

For further consideration of footing, observe in Box 2.3 how it is established and authority projected in an address at the UN. This example also provides opportunity for comparative analysis and insight to discourse differences.

Box 2.3: Footing: Lyndon B. Johnson's First UN Address as Head of Government

A. Compare Box 1.1 (A), the opening of John F. Kennedy's address, with the first two paragraphs of Johnson's in this box. How are the openings and the situation similar?

B. Comment on why *we* as an opener had special significance for the situation that both of these men had.

C. Read the rest of Johnson's address (abridged from the third paragraph) and identify how he establishes footing.

D. (Optional) Comment on (1) the differential use of *man, men,* and *women* in this speech; (2) the hidden irony about gender that possibly exists here; (3) whether gender could become a matter related to footing; (4) the comparison between alternative terms in the same sentences: Is there linguistic or stylistic justification for keeping LBJ's terms as they are?

1. We meet in a time of mourning, but in a moment of rededication. My nation has lost a great leader—this Organization has lost a great friend—world peace has lost a great champion.
2. But John F. Kennedy was the author of new hope for [human]kind—hope which was shared by a whole new generation of leaders, in every continent—and we must not let grief turn us away from that hope. He never quarreled with the past—he always looked at the future—and our task now is to work for the kind of future in which he so strongly believed.
3. I have come here today to make it unmistakably clear that the assassin's bullet which took his life did not alter his nations's purpose. We are more than ever opposed to the doctrines of hate and violence, in our own land and around the world. We are more than ever committed to the rule of law,

(continued)

in our own land and around the world. We believe more than ever in the rights of man, all men of every color—in our own land and around the world. And more than ever we support the United Nations as the best instrument yet devised to promote the peace of the world and to promote the well-being of [human]kind.

4. I can tell you today, as I told you in 1958, when I came as Majority Leader of the United States Senate to the First Committee of this great tribunal, that the full power and partnership of the United States is committed to our joint effort to eliminate war and the threat of war, aggression and the danger of violence. . . .

5. Like all human institutions, the United Nations has not achieved the highest of hopes that some held at its birth. Our understanding of how to live with one another is still far behind our knowledge of how to destroy one another.

6. But as our problems have grown, this Organization has grown. . . . We have seen too much success to become obsessed with failure. . . .

7. I know that vast problems remain: conflicts between great Powers; conflicts between small neighbors; . . . and all the rest. But men and nations, working apart, created these problems, and men and nations, working together must solve them. They can solve them with the help of this Organization. . . .

8. When I entered the Congress of the United States twenty-seven years ago, it was my very great privilege to work closely with President Franklin Delano Roosevelt. As a Member of Congress, I worked with him to bring about a profound but peaceful revolution. That peaceful revolution brought help and hope to the one-third of the nation that was then "ill-housed, ill-clad, and ill-nourished." We helped our working men and women obtain more jobs and we helped them obtain better wages. We helped our farmers to buy and improve their own land, conserve their soil and water, and electrify their farms. We harnessed the power of the great rivers, as in the Tennessee Valley and the Lower Colorado. We encouraged the growth of co-operatives and trade unions. We curbed the excesses of private speculation. We built homes in the place of city slums. And we extended the rights of freedom to all our citizens.

9. Now, on the world scale, the time has come, as it came to America thirty years ago, for a new era of hope—hope and progress for that one-third of [human]kind that is still beset by hunger, poverty and disease.

10. In my travels on behalf of my country and of President Kennedy, I have seen too . . . often the ravages of hunger, tapeworm and tuberculosis—and the scabs and the scars on too many children who have too little health and no hope. . . .

[*Paragraphs 11–14 are deleted here for present purposes.*]

15. President Kennedy, I am sure, would regard as his best memorial the fact that in his three years as President the world became a little safer and the way ahead became a little brighter. To the protection and the enlargement of this new hope for peace I pledge my country and its Government. . . .

Comment: Johnson appears to model his speech on Kennedy's, like none other found among the UN addresses examined. For example, both begin with the same initial expression: *We meet in [a time/an hour].* Both also use a contrastive theme, signaled by *but,* which contrasts a negative event with optimism for the UN's future. Kennedy's opening is particularly effective because of his metaphor, the personification of the UN, his apparent classical ritual call of "The king is dead; long live the king" (the successor), his parallel expressions that echo his contrastive theme (*but* expressions), and his brevity.

Johnson, too, uses personification and parallelism. However, he does so without echoing his contrastive theme, or without quite the flourish of his predecessor. Kennedy's address is particularly striking and the only one given such accolade by Prosser (1970) in his collection. "There is little doubt that John Kennedy's speechmaking was his presidential legacy" (Hart, 1984, p. 97). Partly for that reason, "Johnson labored under the semantic (and psychological) burden of being [Kennedy's] successor in office" (Hart, 1984, p. 109).

Another aspect that merits attention is their beginning with the collective *we* for the UN. Speaking for the audience and so early seems to require great standing and presence of mind. Perhaps for that reason, only one other world leader that we know of has begun with this *we* as the very first word after the salutation—Harry Truman. That was in dedication for the permanent UN headquarters in New York in 1949, still early in its history and easy for diplomats to rally around. To do so during height of the Cold War seems remarkable. Thus, it took a similar rallying event—the deaths of revered leaders—to allow Kennedy and Johnson to use the collective *we* in referring to the audience.

However, perhaps as a further measure of Kennedy's skill, he again used the same device in his other UN address but at a time absent of any like rallying event. This specific opening, however, was not to be used by Johnson again nor another American president. In passing, it may be worthwhile to mention another aspect of Kennedy's found very rare in UN addresses—wit or humor—like that in the salutation of his second UN address. So, if such aspects are any indication, Johnson did have a formidable act of succession to follow. This may explain his apparent emulation of Kennedy's first UN address, and also his need to show continuity in American leadership.

Johnson was suddenly thrust onto center stage in world affairs by an assassin's bullet. A man of plain tastes and beginnings, he had to become "presidential" and be among some of the world's elite, within just several weeks of time. As Hart (1984) explained, "if public presentations constituted the essence of the presidency for JFK, they were nothing but a colossal nuisance for a man who was a habitué of the Senate cloakroom" (p. 109). Besides the nature of the event and his possible emulation of JFK, Johnson also had the need to become diplomatic. Could he become "diplomatic" anymore quickly than by using the collective *we,* amidst the world's diplomats at the UN?

Kennedy may have had similar motivation. Despite his elite background, Kennedy carried a burden in the political world by being young and inexperienced. The UN may have especially made him aware of this. Still, Johnson may have had the comparatively heavier burden: As a senior politician, he had to play second fiddle to a young, upstart President Kennedy, and a popular one at that. Similarly, it may not be mere coincidence that this address of Johnson's registered the fourth highest frequency rate for the personal pronoun *I* among those studied. His frequency was nearly twice that for his two other UN appearances. His address was as much about himself as it was about Kennedy, his country, or the UN. He had to seize the reigns of his government to become presidential thus explaining his frequency of *I*.

Tie back, the final outer frame, is what we term a device for returning to the opening or early content of a discourse. Used at the end, a tie back signals closure. Examples arise in sample analyses found later.

Inner frames

Inner frames orient the audience about purpose, content, and organization. The *overview* functions that way early in a discourse. Academic presentations, spoken or written, are known for giving such overviews, especially about organization ("First, 'the subject' is viewed historically. Then the contemporary changes are considered. Third, my recommendations are given" . . . etc.). In contrast, UN speeches hardly ever contain an overview of the method of organization. "[Rhetorical] theory tends to advise" against such statements unless "listeners need special help in understanding" the speaker's way of treating the subject (Arnold, Ehninger, & Gerber, 1966, p. 314). A second type of inner frame is a *trigger,* a word or short phrase that triggers an organizational format or schema in the minds of the audience. "This is a story about . . ." triggers a narrative format, for example. A third type is *macrotheme,* which denotes the common meaning of "theme": ideational content that interconnects various elements and segments over extended text.

Formatting

As compared to *framing,* formatting is less broad in scope but more specific in form. Common formats found in discourse are presented later, such as narration or argumentation. Before doing so, "it is crucial to recognize—as many composition textbooks do not—that to 'tell a story' or alternatively to conduct an exposition of a subject do not constitute reasons for conducting discourse but rather *methods of conducting discourse*"

(Beale, 1987, p. 33). In other words, the emphasis on form over function puts the cart before the horse. This is unavoidable to some extent, as with the necessity to isolate formats for the instruction of writing, for example. However, if carried to an extreme, writing can become mechanical (Miles, 1976; Odell, 1981) and can obscure the nature of discourse as being rich in combination of forms (Beaugrande, 1984; Nida, 1984).

Narration

Narration is how a story or a series of events is told. Narrative events are typically related in chronological order, a universal across cultures (Hatch & Long, 1980; Hinds, 1980), although the "story" can differ cross-culturally in other features. A "natural narrative" model of organization is widely attributed to William Labov. His model is demonstrated in the discourse analysis at the end of this chapter. Narratives consist of such elements as the circumstances, conflict, and resolution. Contrary to traditional belief, narrative patterns "are one of the most common ways in which arguments are exemplified" (McCarthy & Carter, 1994, p. 63) and are frequently found in academic prose (Nicholas & Nicholl, 1985).

S(PR)E

Situation, **P**roblem, **R**esponse, and **E**valuation refer to the four parts in E. O. Winter's formulation of information (Hoey, 1983; McCarthy & Carter, 1994). His formulation is generally called *problem–solution;* however, *S(PR)E* (pronounced "spree") is the choice made here. We follow McCarthy and Carter (1994) in substituting "response" for "solution" in the formulation.

To illustrate the four parts of S(PR)E, consider this abbreviated account based on a technique of Winter's (1976):

1. I was working the lunch shift alone at Joe's Burgers.
2. Suddenly, a busload of hungry tourists burst through the door.
3. I emptied the freezer of burgers and grilled them.
4. Though I wasted some food, I got through the lunch hour.

These four sentences are identifiable in order as situation, problem, response, and evaluation. In actual discourses, each of these parts can range from phrases to pages. Also, the core problem–response may appear alone or in combination with one or the other two parts. Hence, we placed PR in parentheses. As seen later, the natural narrative and S(PR)E share close parallels, one essential being chronological ordering. Partly for this reason, S(PR)E will be reformulated in Chapter 5 but without contradicting its basic form.

Argumentation

Technically, argumentation may refer to a rhetorical use of formal logic. To uncomplicate matters, *argumentation* herein denotes informal reasoning, logical or otherwise. An argument offers certain propositions or ideas as evidence in support of a particular conclusion. Two common argumentation patterns identified by McCarthy and Carter (1994) are *hypothetical–real* and *general–particular.* The *hypothetical* presents a view for consideration, usually an opposing one, followed by the *real*—the view supported by the writer. The general–particular pattern presents "a generalization . . . followed by more specific statements, perhaps exemplifying the generalization" (McCarthy & Carter, 1994, p. 57). A third pattern is the "rank order."

The rank order pattern of argumentation places related ideas according to importance from high to low, or the reverse. Some rhetoricians seem to favor the high to low (e.g., Hart, Friedrich, & Brooks, 1975). However, a generally accepted psychological principle is that first and last positions in information orders are better remembered than others; this is known as the primacy and recency effects, respectively (e.g., DeVito, 1992). Consider this example of the low–high ranking:

> Of all the creatures on earth, dolphins seem the most likely to learn to talk with human beings. In relation to their size, their brains are as large as a human's. Like humans, they are mammals. They wander over all the oceans, much as people make their homes in many places on the land. Most importantly, dolphins have a tight social system, and seem to be able to speak to each other very well. (Pauk, 1983, p. 51)

One would have to agree that among these characteristics of the dolphin, the most "humanlike" to Pauk include tight social system and language, the final items mentioned. Therefore, he uses the low–high rank order pattern. The exercise in Box 2.4 consolidates information on framing.

Box 2.4: Exercise

Despite the deletions (for space purposes) in Box 2.3, consider Johnson's UN address from paragraphs 5 onward for its organizational elements. **Hint:** Paragraph 5 starts with what might be called a "State of the UN Report," and it and the next paragraph combine to form a part of the S(PR)E format and, at the same time, a pattern of argumentation.

Whenever applying the "spree" format in discourse analysis, it is probably best to first identify the related problem(s). To do so, look for terms such as *problem, difficulty, obsticle, failure, conflict* and so on. Consider if that is the "problem" of main concern. Once that is found, then the other part or parts usually come readily, though some reflective thought is required. Associated terms for the other parts of S(PR)E are much less prevalent.

Comment: In Johnson's address, if Paragraphs 5 and onward manifest the S(PR)E format, then Paragraph 7 represents the *problem* part because it includes various existing problems. Because they must develop in some way, problems have associated circumstances. Those mentioned by Johnson are on a world scale, so they are naturally provinces of the UN. It so happens that Paragraphs 5 and 6 discuss the UN's role and an assessment of its success. That assessment is of the then present *situation.*

Caution is needed with lines such as the first in Paragraph 6: "But as our problems have grown." Here, *problems* are of the past and help develop a historical context for the role of the UN—the situation. He, then, tells of UN success stories that grew out of them. These success stories are *particular* examples to the *general* in the Paragraph 5 and the top of Paragraph 6. The two paragraphs combine into a general-particular pattern of argumentation.

Present (remaining) problems call for a *response.* That response is partly the help by the UN, as explained by the end of Paragraph 7. An *evaluation* of the American response or solution comes in turn, which serves also as a platform for Johnson to establish footing as discussed earlier.

MIDLEVEL

Some elements that may assume a macrolevel proportion in one discourse can seem to contract to the midlevel or even lower in another. The S(PR)E format can range from phrases to pages. Similarly, some elements associated with the midlevel can be reasonably extended throughout a discourse. This flexibility of discoursal elements to contract or expand may explain the usual practice of restricting talk about discourse levels to two: macro and micro. As long as this flexibility of discourse is understood, the levels we have proposed ought to enhance the conception of discourse by adding further distinctions to the scope of discourse relations.

Sectioning

To help make discourse comprehensible, the speaker or writer will section the discourse, at least minimally, into paragraphs or even larger segments. Sectioning has a role in UN addresses because they become official diplomatic records and are later distributed as written discourse. Moreover, speakers may prepare their speech or address as written discourse to be read aloud. As such, they often may contain physical (orthographic) paragraphs and other sections.

The paragraph contributes to discourse analysis in providing convenient chunks of information to work with. It also can show shifts in topic. However, in terms of discourse organization, the paragraph mainly participates as part of a block. Blocks of paragraphs form the sections in a discourse that may manifest macrolevel organization. The discourse analysis made of an international speech by a Japanese at the end of this chapter shows well the integration of blocks to the framing and formatting of the speech.

Despite traditional views in composition, the paragraph (i.e., orthographically, physically speaking) is still not the intervening level between sentence and discourse (Beaugrande, 1984; Beaugrande & Dressler, 1981; Hoey, 1983, 1991; Morley, 1985; Nash, 1980; Phillips, 1985). Nida (1984), for example, did not include paragraph as an element in his taxonomy of discourse. Kaplan (1987), originator of "contrastive rhetoric," reversed his previous view of paragraph as the unit of discourse. For school compositions, their nature and short length may make paragraphs a reasonable vehicle of instruction. Otherwise, paragraphs are best seen as convenient chunks of information that follow rather than lead the organizational thrust of discourse.

Exercise: Read this extract and determine its type of sentence ordering used [previous paragraphs discuss a "Food-for-Peace" program]:

But man does not live by bread alone—and the Members of this organization are committed by the Charter to promote and respect human rights. Those rights are not respected when a Buddhist priest is driven from his pagoda, when a synagogue is shut down, when a Protestant church cannot open a mission, when a Cardinal is forced into hiding, or when a crowded church service is bombed. (Kennedy, 1963, p. 949)

Exercise: Besides the general–particular ordering (from *But man does not live . . .*) Kennedy also ranked ordered his examples, each initiated with *when.* Which rank order did he choose and why was it probably most effective?

Chaining

Chaining involves word repetition that connects stretches of discourse. The field of rhetoric has advocated repeating a key term from one paragraph to another to achieve unity in writing (e.g., Warriner & Griffith, 1977). Chaining, however, involves repetition of a far greater degree than solely at paragraph boundaries. It was functional linguists like Hasan (e.g., 1984) who brought attention to word chains to show how a discourse "hangs together." Chains are formed by repetitions and near repetitions (e.g., synonymy) of words whether key terms or not. Whereas repetition, in the field of rhetoric, is treated as a conscious strategy by the writer or speaker, chaining is largely the result of nonconscious processes. The reason is that chaining can be so extensive: It potentially functions at the macrolevel (Hoey, 1991). Whether chaining operates fundamentally at the macro or midlevel is beyond our present scope. It seems reasonable, however, to suggest that chaining as a macro function may be sensitive to topic consistency. Discourses of multiple topics may provide less opportunity for words to chain across an entire discourse.

For a brief example of chaining, though space limits the choice, an extract from a Lyndon Johnson address follows. Although this chaining realizes midlevel connections, it also contributes to discourse formatting:

> (7) But men and nations, *working* apart, created these problems, and men and nations, *working* together must *solve* them. They can *solve* them with the help of this Organization. . . .
> (8) When I entered the Congress of the United States twenty-seven years ago, it was my very great privilege to *work* closely with President Franklin Delano Roosevelt. As a Member of Congress, I *worked* with him to bring about a profound but peaceful revolution. That peaceful revolution brought *help* and hope to the one-third of the nation that was then "ill-housed, ill-clad, and ill-nourished." We *helped* our *working* men and women *obtain* more jobs and we *helped* them *obtain* better wages. (Johnson, 1963, p. 1031)

The words highlighted form some, but not all, of the lexical ties. Johnson suggests the genesis of world problems and their solution: *working* apart and then together to *solve* them. At the same time, *work* brings up his association with FDR, an important figure to the then UN members, for it was he who helped establish that very forum. In the final sentence of this segment, *help(ed), work,* and *obtain* converge together in the function of evaluation.

The "bud" of evaluation emerges here and blossoms in the 9th paragraph, for he proposes the American solution for the whole world because of its evaluated success. However, he must show that a world problem exists to merit this kind of response. He does so by his personal observations made around the world. Besides the general–particular pattern (generalization + examples), he also reinvokes his association with a revered leader—John F. Kennedy—in recalling his world travels made in service to JFK.

Several paragraphs later, he refocuses on JFK to signal closure by taking the perspective of JFK in evaluating improved world peace as his "best memorial." This perspective taking can signal closure because it is a spatio–temporal departure from the halls of the UN to the spiritual world; and because JFK's name also functions as a tie back to LBJ's opening lines of the address. Concurrently, JFK's presumed evaluation serves as further evaluation of LBJ's proposed response (the "American solution"), the final part of the S(PR)E format.

Transiting

Moving from one section of discourse to another can be aided by *discourse markers* (Schiffrin, 1987). One common discourse marker in UN addresses is *now.*

Discourse marker: organization

Note how *now* and *finally* function in the following UN address:

[Salutation ends]

1. I wish *now* to speak of the present Assembly. . . .
2. I shall *now* say a few words on the Congo. . . .
3. I turn *now* to . . . the subject of colonialism. . . .
4. I wish *now* to say a few words on East–West relations. . . .
5. [I have this to say about] aid and assistance. . . .
6. Finally . . . we [have yet to agree on] peacekeeping. . . .
7. I have spoken for Canada [thereafter the conclusion]. (Diefenbaker, 1960) (Canada)

Each numbered utterance introduces a major topic or perspective. *Now,* in bold, helps to signal this organizational change.

Technically, it can be argued that rather than a discourse marker, *now* is functioning as a temporal adverb. This possibility would be accepted, were it not for the fact that a major topic change occurs. Unquestionably, *now* does have a temporal sense in those utterances. However, compare those with a clear temporal meaning of *now* from the same address: "My hope is that . . . [Chairman Khrushchev] will give the lead toward [implementing free elections] here and *now*" (Diefenbaker, 1960, p. 306). A subtle difference appears. In the same way, consider how *now* functions as a temporal adverb in these extracts from UN addresses:

> We are *now* reaching a crucial point in the development of the United Nations. (Prado, 1961, p. 732) (Peru)

> I shall not dwell *now* on the reasons [for this action]. (Kasavubu, 1960, p. 654) (Congo)

> [T]he time is *now* ripe for a drive forward on disarmament. (Wilson, 1965, p. 1080) (United Kingdom)

> I referred just *now* to the new hopes [about better super-power relations]. (Ould Daddah, 1963, p. 974) (Mauritania)

> *Now,* after many thousands of years, man-made machines are cruising through space among the stars. (Ahidjo, 1963, p. 996) (Cameroon)

> Genuine discussion of disarmament, within this body, and based upon a real desire for success, is essential *now.* (Sukarno, 1960, p. 517) (Indonesia)

These examples clearly show the temporal function of *now.* Each did not signal a change in topic or segmentation of the discourse. These examples were also selected to show the various positions that *now* can assume within a sentence—front, middle, or end. Although the examples of *now* as a discourse marker of organization had medial positions in their respective sentences, a more common position is at the front, especially in informal speech. The prevalence of the medial position appears attributable to the high formality of UN addresses.

Discourse marker: orientation

Another discourse function of *now* is orientation (Schiffrin, 1987), though found uncommon in UN addresses. Consider these examples:

> *Now* you all know that the Suez Canal under Arab administration performs its role in the service of world economy more ably and efficiently than was the case [under its previous administrators]. (Nasser, 1960, p. 409) (United Arab Republic)

> *Now,* when we are going to discuss [colonialism] it may perhaps be appropriate to remind the United States delegation about [their] Declaration of Independence . . . a document which proclaimed . . . liberation from the British yoke. (Gheorghiu-Dej, 1960, p. 383) (Romania)

Both orients or cues the audience that a particular interpretation is required of the speaker's words. Specifically, the speakers appear to seek solidarity with the audience by which a common orientation is assumed toward ideational content. At such times, the discourse appears to switch from an informational focus to a focus on the audience. Such switches can offer the discourse analyst special insight into the view of the speaker and by that his or her strategies of discourse.

A JAPANESE BRIDGES AN INTERNATIONAL CONFLICT

To demonstrate discourse frames and formats within one speech, as well as in the context of international conflict, the case is taken up of a Japanese speaker at a Black church in Harlem. Reasons for choosing this case include the nature of the conflict, the organization of discourse, and the genre. (For a demonstration using UN speeches, Chapter 5 is fully devoted.) "Outside" genres provide a necessary and important function as reference points from which to compare UN speeches. This case also offers the compelling example of one individual's quest to bridge international misunderstanding between his own culture and another.

International tension has emerged between Japan and the African American community because of alleged racist remarks by Japanese politicians and the presence of racial caricatures about Blacks in Japanese popular culture (Anton, 1991; Covert, 1992; Walker, 1991). Such Japanese behavior does not reflect an animosity, but rather a social ignorance about non-Japanese. Because of Japan's historical self-imposed isolation and its island status, the Japanese, even today, have a strong sense of "we-ness." They very naturally are sensitive to *gaijin* (foreigners; literally, "outsiders" [Jeremy & Robinson, 1989:29]) of any kind. However, they can be extremely gracious, and Black students and professionals in Japan are warmly received. To repeat: The Japanese are not hostile to Blacks. However, misunderstanding has existed, which merits attention.

This case involves a Japanese Christian minister who addresses a church in Harlem, not only to share his spiritual message but also to bridge the cultural gap between his country and African Americans. Most Japanese surveyed say that this speaking task would be unusually difficult. Yet, this Japanese minister does exceptionally well and is given great approval by his Black audience.[1] His speech/sermon shows not only effective framing and formatting of the discourse, but also the combining of these features and their transitional devices as well.

Introduction

Imagine that you are a Japanese Christian minister researching African American culture, yet your home politicians have reportedly made racist remarks against Blacks, amid known Japanese popularity of "sambo" dolls

[1] Evidence for this comes from listening to the audio tape of the actual speech (courtesy of Kajiwara) and observance by the church members of an African American custom: In appreciation the church members collected money to give Kajiwara as a present. The gesture (not the money) made Kajiwara feel touched (Kajiwara, personal communication 1995).

and similar comic book characters (Anton, 1991; Covert, 1992; Walker, 1991). Such conditions, therefore, "place a great strain and tension on relations between [Japanese nationals and African Americans]" (Walker, 1991, p. i). To make matters worse, misunderstandings arise between certain Asians and African Americans within the American inner city. Just before you are to address a congregation in Harlem, old wounds are opened by a press report that the Japanese mass media recently ignored the confrontation of the Japanese emperor by an African American about such matters. The situation obviously would pose a special challenge for any public speaker, let alone one in a second language.

The purpose of this discourse analysis is to identify how this Japanese minister manages to do so admirably well, as well as showing the integration of various features of discourse organization. Sermons, moreover, may help in the appreciation of genre, a needed development in contrastive discourse studies (Donahue, 1990), for sermons make rich combinations of genre: narrative, dialogue, poetry, argumentation, hortatory and so on. To give shape to this discourse analysis, discussion begins with the probable tasks that faced the minister/professor in making his speech/sermon.

Overview of the Speech

This speech/sermon was delivered at the Canaan Baptist Church, New York City, on July 10, 1994, by Hisashi Kajiwara, minister and professor at Nagoya Gakuin University. We thank Professor Kajiwara for his kind permission to use his sermon.

Dual roles of the minister

According to Smith (1993), "the sermon is a complex, highly ritualized discourse genre made up of the specialized performance tasks of [interpreting] a fixed sacred text, illustrating it with narratives or poems, and exhorting the audience to change their behavior on the basis of its message" (p.147). These tasks may be subsumed under the role of *spiritual mediator.* Another role that the Japanese minister assumes is that of *cultural mediator* by his explaining Japanese culture and exemplifying cultural sensitivity.

Textual self

To fulfill the role of spiritual mediator, at least, requires developing a textual self (Smith, 1993) and applies no doubt to the second role of cultural mediator as well. As mentioned earlier, the "textual self" can help project a speaker as having authenticity, giving his or her statements authority, and amounts to speaker credibility (Smith, 1993). One can see how a textual self of credibility would especially be vital to the function of cultural mediator, in the context of cultural conflict. This textual self does not depend, as pointed out earlier, on oral delivery as it does on matters of experience and accomplishment. For that reason and the fact that the written text was followed closely by the spoken, the written version became the basis of the present discourse analysis. Another reason for using the written version is the original paragraphing that it contains.

Textual organization

Very broadly, the Japanese minister's sermon consists of five main sections: salutation, introduction, spiritual mediation, cultural mediation, and conclusion. Within these sections, his sermon utilizes the rich variety of discourse forms generally found in that genre. Complexity is further evident by the added role of cultural mediation. These sections, roles, and varieties of discourse must be woven together by the minister within the consistency of a sermon for cross-cultural speech.

Procedures of the Discourse Analysis

This discourse analysis focuses primarily on macrolevel and midlevel discourse elements, the terms of which correspond to the contents of Box 2.1. Once that the primary discourse units were in mind, the text of the speech was reduced into paragraph kernels (e.g., Donahue, 1990) of one sentence each. Each kernel attempted to summarize the paragraph or present an essential idea. The goal was to reduce the total word count of the speech by 90%, which was achieved. Next, the kernels were grouped to form blocks of paragraphs, making analysis more manageable. The result of this kerneling and blocking follows in Figure 2.1.

Another reason for having prepared this "discourse schematic" is that space limitations prevented the speechtext from being reproduced here. Consequently, the reader may wish to consider closely this schematic. Paragraphs are numbered in order and separated into associated blocks. Major transitions in organization, to be discussed later, are shown by letters (A, B, C, etc.). These major transitions mark changes in discourse topic or pattern and are integral to discourse organization. Also shown in the figure are the main sections of discourse (salutation, introduction, etc.). Discussion takes each of these main sections in turn.

SALUTATION		1 The Japanese minister gives acknowledgements.
	A	
INTRODUCTION		2 He begins a story about his son, a professional musician. 3 The son, while recording in New York, became deeply inspired by that church's gospel music; a spiritual is recited about the Holy Spirit reviving one's soul.
	B	
		4 The minister had a similar experience much earlier and remembers a hymn about Jesus' caring in time of trouble.
	C	
SPIRITUAL MEDIATION		5 Affluent societies, like Japan's, require a spiritual fountain; a related spiritual is quoted. 6 The minister's wife and daughter, in attendance, also drink from the church's spiritual fountain.
	D	
		7 He states the subject of his sermon: "the coming of morning," a theme of Martin Luther King's. 8 A King example of the theme is presented. 9 A related point by King about music is made. 10 The minister tells of the King text's significance. 11 He interprets King's morning metaphor.
	E	
CULTURAL MEDIATION		12 Japan has the illusion of day when actually at night; a related scripture is quoted. 13 Japanese wartime atrocities and treatment of minorities exemplify the illusion. 14 Japanese racial slurs about African Americans is another. 15 Japanese neglect of Black theology is another again.
	F	
		16 Japan's illusion requires an unveiling of the truth. 17 Japan's emperor received an unveiling about Japanese racism. 18 The Japanese mass media's ignoring the incident is explained.
	G	
CONCLUSION		19 The emperor's bowing to King's memory shows hope for Japan. 20 Thus the study of Black theology is encouraged; a scripture is quoted. 21 Prayers are asked for the perseverance to continue the struggle. 22 Morning is surely coming by the encouragement given to Japanese Christians by the emperor's incident; a spiritual ends the sermon.

Figure 2.1. Discourse Schematic of the Japanese Speech

Salutation

Guest speakers commonly begin by acknowledging their hosts and this Japanese minister is no exception. How he does so is especially effective:

> (1) The Reverend Dr. Wyatt Tee Walker, Mrs. Theresa Ann Walker, officers, and my beloved brothers and sisters of Canaan Baptist Church. (2) I am so excited and fascinated to be privileged to preach to you this morning from this honorable pulpit.

These utterances waste no words in addressing his hosts and establishing a footing with his audience. He quickly indicates his role or purpose (preaching), pays respect to the church, and explicitly identifies with his audience ("my brothers and sisters"). *Brother* and *sister* function as terms of kinship in the African American community and can act as code of identification. For example, during the Black Power Movement of the 1960s, the same terms were used in public address between members of the Black community, thus aiding social cohesion. For the Japanese minister to observe this custom suggests that he had a prior relationship with the same church. It would have been pure folly otherwise. Alternatively, he could have meant a religious kinship entirely. Either way, he expressed identity with his audience.

Another point is his having encapsulated much of this in a self-disclosure of here-and-now emotion ("I am so excited . . ."). Self-disclosure, with certain qualifications, is integral to intimate relationships, a notion well supported in social psychology. The same notion appears applicable to intercultural/cross-cultural relations (Gudykunst & Kim, 1992). The Japanese minister's self-disclosure seems prudently exercised and with the previous strategies help him in a most auspicious way. *Strategy* simply refers to communicative choices and intends no ulterior meaning.

Introduction

The introduction section, in miniature, shows how complex sermons can be by combining narratives, poetry, and argumentation. The Japanese minister, at transition Point A (see Table 2.1), commences the introduction of his speech with the simple but effective expression, *first of all.* This is commonly used for sequencing discourse elements and may activate a related cognitive schema for agenda-making in the mind of the listener. It also helps to trigger a narrative format:

> (4) First of all, I want to tell you a story . . .

This utterance, thus, marks a departure from issuing acknowledgments (the salutation) into the actual speech.

First narrative. The introduction section of the speech contains two successive narratives. The first narrative appears "fully developed," based on William Labov's model for "natural narratives," for it contains the first five of the model's components (Pratt, 1988):

Abstract:	(4) I want to tell you a story about my son. . .
Orientation:	Jun, who is a guitarist now with the world-renowned Japanese musician Sadao Watanabe. (5) It happened several years ago that
Complicating Event:	Jun was somehow really depressed in his heart and did not know which way to go as an artist. (6) As you know, this kind of thing sometimes happens to musicians and artists. (7) Jun was in the depth of his agony.
Resolution:	(8) In such a situation he had an opportunity to attend your worship service on a Sunday of 1989 with his friends while they stayed in New York for their recording. (9) And at that time he encountered a real live gospel music for the first time in his life. (10) Oh, he was moved!
Evaluation:	(11) He was shaken from the bottom of his heart. (12) Jun later told me how deeply he was moved, so much so that "tears ran down his cheeks and he could not check himself." (13) Since then he told me that his music changed. (14) And people around him appreciated it a great deal.
Coda:	(15) Isn't it a great thing?

The story contains an *abstract* by indicating it is a *story about his son.* The *orientation* sets the stage by identifying the participant or protagonist, time, and place. Perhaps because the story is short and the place is so central to the resolution, the minister delays giving that particular until later. The *complicating event* is what it suggests: a complication or problem. Jun was a depressed musician without direction, artistic presumably.

By entering this church and experiencing its service and gospel music, the son achieved a *resolution* of his problem: artistic inspiration. That a resolution was achieved seems valid by the son's emotional response—a catharsis—and his report that people around him appreciate the changes in his music. Thus, *evaluation* was fulfilled.

The final component, *coda,* merges the story events back to the real world of the present (McCarthy & Carter, 1994). This coda (*Isn't it a great thing?*) is not part of the story proper, for it concerns the view of the audience and not that of the protagonist. Most telling is the change of tense from the past for the story events to the present for the coda.

Lest the minister lose his spiritual role to that of a storyteller, he states:

> (16) I want to bear witness to his [son's] experience as a work of the Holy Spirit.

Clearly, this is an interpretive act most within the realm of a spiritual leader. In keeping with this role, he recites poetry from a spiritual popular among the congregation. A transition from utterance (16) to the next discourse section (B in Table 2.1) arises in the final lines:

> (20) Sometimes I feel discouraged and think my work's in vain. (21) But then the Holy Spirit revives my soul again.

Here, lexical linkage provides the transition with the words *Holy Spirit* and *revives my soul again.* The former ties with a previous use of the same term; the latter, with the minister's next utterance:

> (22) Yes, this is really a blessing that my son was given in your service.

This appears most likely to refer to the therapeutic effect of the church on his son—a revival of his soul. Utterance (22), a repetition of content, adds further transitional links between discourse parts and is boosted by the emphatic *yes* functioning as a discourse marker.

Second narrative. The repetition and lexical linkage in (22) provide the opportunity for the minister to tell another story—this time about himself. It is rather short, but it need not be otherwise because it is nearly identical to the son's: The church provided both people a moving experience. These two narratives strengthen the minister's bond with the audience and are understandably placed early in his speech. Why should he be concerned with such bonds? It is certainly relevant to explain his association with the church. Moreover, at his first visit at the church, quite sometime before this sermon, he was asked why he was interested in the Black church (as he relates in Paragraph 4). A natural question and one that gives impetus to his narratives. Finally, these narratives should leave no doubt about the appropriateness of his calling the congregation his brothers and sisters earlier in the speech.

In telling the second narrative, the minister recites poetry from a spiritual heard at his first visit, *Nobody knows the trouble I've seen.* This recitation builds commonality with the audience and provides a transition (Point C) to the next section of discourse—argumentation.

Preview to argumentation. Just as agenda and narrative schemata were seen cued by the expressions *first of all* and *I want to tell you a story,* so too schema for argumentation is cued to help facilitate comprehension of this form of discourse. That schema is cued by a preview of the related propositional content.

The preview is organized deductively and consists of two paragraphs—5 and 6, respectively. Paragraph 5 presents the minister's essential argument as stated in the initial sentence:

> (34) One of the pathological syndromes we fall in such an affluent society as Japan is dried-up-ness in spirit.

Pathological links with *trouble* (troublesome), the theme of the previous recited poetry.

Note also the collective *we*, which is used three times in the paragraph. Such use, both collective and quantitative, is found in only one other paragraph—19. In both paragraphs, *we* has the important function of drawing application to the audience concerning the minister's main message. One can see the necessity of creating bonds with the audience as discussed earlier. The paragraph previews not only his argumentation but also his spiritual mediation, which begins two paragraphs away.

The rest of the 5th paragraph explains his notion and instantiates a religious metaphor from the Bible, a metaphor with a thematic function for this speech: Water drunk from the well of Jesus provides eternal quench of thirst (= belief in Jesus Christ provides eternal spiritual life). This metaphor relates to *dried-up-ness in spirit* in utterance (34) and helps to tie together the earlier narratives and the next paragraph (6) to the church itself.

Paragraph 6 represents specific content in relation to that of the general as developed in the previous paragraph. In the sixth paragraph, the minister says that

> (39) Now I am very excited to tell you this morning that my wife . . . and daughter . . . are drinking of the same water that my son and I drank before with you Canaan brothers and sisters.

This implies that people from affluent societies (e.g., Japan) do need spiritual water, a corollary of Paragraph 5. Note the continued bond making with the audience through self-disclosure, direct address, and use of kinship terms, brothers and sisters.

Finally, the minister uses *now* as a discourse marker to show a transition, a device commonly found in sermons (Smith, 1993). Here and elsewhere in the sermon, transitional *now* appears at or near boundaries between major sections (but not all) in the discourse. Rather than its usual midsentence position for an adverb, transitional *now* occurs at the front of the sentence. A good example is found in the next paragraph, which initiates the minister's primary section of spiritual mediation.

Spiritual mediation

The minister inaugurates the sermon proper, that section consisting of Paragraphs 7 to 11 and that which is devoted to delivering his main spiritual message:

(45) Now I am going to preach to you this morning on the subject: "He knew that morning was coming."

Now functions to mark off this new major unit of discourse and is aided by his direct intention to preach, a trigger for that genre of discourse. Utterance (45) also introduces the major thematic metaphor of the speech: morning. Metaphor is a common device used in international speechmaking at the UN (Prosser, 1970). The term morning is found in each paragraph of the section, except the 10th. This thematic metaphor connects these paragraphs. It also connects the 10th paragraph by associated terms: *Martin Luther King* (the originator) and his *sermon* (about morning). As seen next, the counterpart of this morning metaphor is used in an interesting way by the Japanese minister to contrast the present state of Japan.

Cultural mediation

Cognitive cultural sensitivity. This major section, cultural mediation, emerges because the Japanese minister attempts to explain Japanese behavior and culture, as well as improving the international situation. There are two dimensions involved: cognitive and affective. Both are interrelated, but they are separated for analysis. The cognitive dimension relates to the organizing of discourse to facilitate its comprehension.

This cognitive section is marked off by what should come as no surprise—the discourse marker *now*:

(90) Now I want to extend to you this morning my particular perspective about this point as a Japanese Christian minister.

He explicitly states a change in perspective to one focused on Japan:

(91) I think that the decisive problem we Japanese are trapped in today is that we do not know it's midnight.

This utterance begins a chain of the midnight metaphor, a counterpart of the morning metaphor, which recurs at major points of transition: F, G, and at the end of the speech. Cultural mediation consists here of three paragraph blocks (from Paragraphs 12–22) corresponding, respectively, to *problem, response,* and *evaluation* using the S(PR)E model. (*Situation* can be seen as indirectly developed in Paragraphs 5-11.)

Problem: The problem section is identified straightforwardly enough by that same term as found in utterance (91) of Paragraph 12. This block of paragraphs is further organized in general to specific relation with

Paragraph 12 stating the problem in generalized form and successive paragraphs representing the specific instances.

Response: Propositional content readily identifies the response section and consists of Paragraphs 16 to 18. To start, the minister asks in Paragraph 16,

> (109) So what is, or should be, the gospel message that we Japanese Christian preachers deliver to our fellow people?

He answers his own question by saying that the solution (response) is presenting an antithesis—the illusion of midday versus the reality of midnight. By these associated terms, lexical chaining is reinforced for the morning metaphor and, as pointed out before, this metaphor appears at a major discourse boundary.

The other paragraphs in the response section are specific instances in relation to the general proposition in the first paragraph of the same block. Again, the minister appears to maintain consistency in adhering to general–particular ordering of content, an ordering that tends to exploit the discourse principle of expectancy. In this section also, the minister explains why the Japanese mass media generally ignored a racial incident in Atlanta involving the Japanese emperor and an African American minister.

Conclusion of the speech

Because the *evaluation,* the final part of the S(PR)E model, coincides with the conclusion in this speech, it becomes necessary to discuss this without delay. Consequently, the affective dimension of cultural sensitivity will be postponed until this section is completed.

Evaluation. The evaluation section coincides with conclusion as broadly envisioned and extends from Paragraph 19 to the end of the speech. The first utterance of this section bears markings of organizational change:

> (123) Now let me conclude my sermon.

Now functions again to mark off a major transition of discourse (G), and the minister makes emphatic his intention to finish. Interestingly, the midnight metaphor reappears in this same paragraph demonstrating again its possible discourse function similar to *now.*

> (124) It is true that it is still midnight in our Japanese situation.

This metaphor, then, disappears only to reappear again in the last paragraph of the speech, possibly suggesting closure—a continued discourse function.

The next two paragraphs (20 and 21) contain traces of dialogue—barely couplets. They occur between the minister and (a) his fellow Japanese and (b) God. In the first instance, the minister reports dialogue about why he studies Black theology and he replies that it is "like treasure hidden in a field."

The second dialogic matter does not contain an explicit reply by the minister, perhaps because humans are subordinate to a supreme being. A similar explanation is made by the minister why the Japanese mass media had ignored the emperor incident above. Despite that the emperor is no longer believed to be a deity, he is still accorded great, great respect. For that reason, according to the minister, the Japanese mass media generally ignored the related racial incident—a kind of silence.

The second dialogue has significance for another reason: its contribution to the textual self. Here it is probably least, but its occurrence raises interesting questions for research. Dialoguing with God would have to be the ultimate for a spiritual leader. How much would spiritual leaders differ in acknowledging such dialogues? If differences were appreciable, factors of culture, religious sect, congregation, and leader would no doubt have bearing. Finally, how would such differences affect the spiritual leader's textual self? Such questions could have important ramifications for the discourse analysis of sermons and other spiritual discourse.

The minister then goes on to juxtapose the morning and midnight metaphors. He shows that the morning metaphor is in ascendancy by the emperor's visit to the King Memorial (*Morning* also functions as a tie back here). He then ends the sermon by reciting poetry from a popular spiritual, "This little light of mine, I'm going to let it shine." The light for him comes from the emperor's visit, not only because he is Japanese but also because he is a leading scholar of Martin Luther King. For him, the visit, therefore, has deep and multiple meanings.

Affective Cultural Sensitivity

Thus far, the discourse analysis has primarily been concerned with cognitive strategies of the discourse. However, there is an important affective dimension running throughout, which has only been partly considered. In various ways, the Japanese minister manifested affective sensitivity for African Americans and, by doing so, could further Japanese—American relations even more.

At least two of these ways were seen: He shared how truly significant worship at the church was for him and his family and he actively appreciated one of the church's unique contributions to religious worship—its gospel music—by reciting some of its important poetry. Obviously, the

Japanese minister has immersed himself in African American culture and that fact may be highly appealing to his audience.

Another manner of appreciating the culture was his obvious admiration for one of the culture's great leaders and how he again involved his audience:

> (46) The biblical text for this morning is Luke 11:5–8. (47) The reason I selected this subject and this text for my sermon is that the late Reverend Dr. Martin Luther King, Jr. preached his sermon "A Knock at Midnight" for Dr. Walker's [the present pastor of the same church] installation service on March 24, 1968 at this Canaan Baptist Church by using this text. (48) I happened to find a copy of his sermon at the King Center in Atlanta, Georgia, in 1987. (49) You can imagine how excited I was then.

His audience was probably excited also by his deep passion for his subject.

Just as he displayed sensitivity for the church community, he also showed it in kind for the African American culture at large. For one, he explained the silence of the Japanese media about the emperor incident, a silence that had probably raised questions in the minds of African Americans. For another, he took up the topic of racial slurs and turned the tables on the apparent racists by pointing out their own ignorance:

> (99) [Some Japanese officials][2] are now notorious in the world. (100) But what is a deathblow to them is that they are not aware of its being a deathblow. (101) They have almost forgotten what they said. (102) It is just what I mean by the illusion we are trapped in. (103) We take neon signs for sunshine.

Another way again he showed cultural sensitivity was his acknowledgment of Eurocentrism in some religious thought to the detriment of indigenous Christian theology:

> (105) Oh how many times I have been asked, "Why are you engaged in such a marginal theology as Black theology? (106) Why don't you devote yourself to the mainline theologies in Europe? (107) Is there anything good in Black theology?" (108) I have always been reminded of what Nathanael said to Philip, "Can anything good come out of Nazareth?"

The minister understands African Americans at a depth that, perhaps, may only be perceived by close reading. At least his audience feels understood, we believe. True understanding of another human being is

---

[2] Karatsu (1992) points out that some Japanese officials have been mistranslated by the American press, which has caused needless furor over their comments. For this reason, caution is required until this matter is clarified.

more a premium than ever. Such attainments are what will bridge our cultural conflicts today and tomorrow.

CONCLUSION

Discourse analysis has revealed the richness of genre for the sermon. In the context of international conflict, genre provided various discourse patterns by which the Japanese minister could develop rapport, credibility, and a clear message. Macrolevel organizing in the form of triggers (or advance organizers) and well-crafted formats exploited the discourse principle of expectancy. Once primed, the audience was presented with thematic metaphors that further organized the speech and helped form the message as well.

In using this speech/sermon as a case study in international communication, it ought to be understood that discourse strategies observed here are not recipes. The essential learning is not the form, but the spirit. What made the minister so successful was the depth of his own participation in African American culture. He participated to the extent that he could use kinship terms with others whom he had studied. That was a privilege that could only be earned by long apprenticeship. It takes an attitude as much as effort. He was not afraid to get "wet" as it were.

APPLICATION

Prime Minister of Japan, Yasuhiro Nakasone, *spoke before the General Assembly in New York, in 1987. Read his address (abridged here) and identify patterns, strategies, and other features of discourse. This address was originally given in Japanese.*

I should like first to express my sincere congratulations to Your Excellency on your election as President of the General Assembly at its forty-second session. I am confident that, with the wealth of your experience in the conduct of United Nations affairs, your superior wisdom and able leadership, you will guide this session to a successful and fruitful conclusion.

. . . At the outset I should like to welcome most heartily the agreement that was reached in principle last week between the United States and the Soviet Union on the total elimination of intermediate-range nuclear forces and on holding a third summit meeting between the two leaders this autumn. I wish to pay a high tribute to them for the political determination that has made this possible.

[Two years ago at this same podium], I stressed that a new global ethic, together with the systems to support it, is necessary if we are to save the earth from the gravest perils of destruction it has ever faced. . . . To that end, I expressed

(continued)

the need for an attitude whereby we acknowledge the diversity and value of the world's cultures and civilizations. . . . I argued that the United Nations must become a vehicle for creating, on the basis of that attitude, a global civilization for all [human]kind.

Encouraged by the favorable response to my remarks, I should like today to share with you some of my thoughts about the practical means for pursuing my ideas, as well as Japan's position and the role it can play in this regard.

We are now little more than a decade away from the twenty-first century. And as we look back, the twentieth century has been a tumultuous age, full of dramatic events and upheavals, unprecedented in human history.

In the first half of the century, [human]kind endured two world wars and experienced the tragic explosion of nuclear weapons. Since then, we have suffered and agonized over the existence of growing stockpiles of nuclear weapons. The two nuclear Super-Powers have each now deployed an enormous number of intercontinental ballistic missiles, to the extent of overkill which could strike directly at the other's vital areas. . . . [I]nherent in their quest for security through deterrence is the danger of catastrophe. . . .

On the economic front, less than three decades into the century the world gave way to a rampant protectionism, inviting the disastrous Great Depression that preceded the outbreak of the Second World War. The world economy recovered from the ravages and impoverishment caused by the war, and subsequently attained unparalleled growth and prosperity. However, it was again thrown into turmoil by two oil crises—turmoil from which it has yet to fully emerge. The global economic problems we continue to face, particularly the disparities between North and South, global trade imbalances and instability in international finance, are extremely serious.

On the other hand, the scientific and technological advances of this century truly dwarf those of the Industrial Revolution in the latter half of the eighteenth century, and have ushered in a new historical era. From the vast outer limits of the universe to the microscopic matter from which life itself originates, advances in human knowledge . . . have contributed greatly to improving [human]kind's material well-being. Applied wisely, this knowledge can dramatically advance the information age and tremendously benefit human society. Applied unwisely, and not properly controlled, it could imperil the dignity of human life or irreversibly destroy the earth's environment, upon which all [human]kind depends.

This century has also witnessed the birth of many independent countries as peoples everywhere, and particularly in Asia and Africa, have sought to exercise their inherent rights and freedom. One after another, these new nations joined the United Nations. The number of independent countries world-wide doubled almost overnight, imbuing international politics with new vitality and marking in world history a new era in which the ideals of freedom, equality and universal brotherhood are pursued. [Human]kind has not, however, eliminated poverty and hunger in some of those new countries, nor has it done away with regional conflicts.

. . . As this eventful century of tragedy and hope draws to a close, and we look ahead to a new century, we must ask ourselves what we have learned from the traumas of the Great Depression and the two world wars, as well as subsequent experiences, and what are the lessons we should pass down to succeeding generations.

(continued)

Has humanity no choice but to live constantly under the threat of nuclear weapons—a sword of Damocles suspended by a single, slender thread? Have we no choice but to bequeath to posterity a planet that, in an increasing number of regions, is being stripped of its precious air and its verdant foliage, which have evolved over the course of four billion years? Can we really do no better than to pass along to the next generation a world with a burgeoning population and with countries of extreme poverty, untouched by science, technology and modern industry?

If we are to resolve these fateful issues confronting [human]kind, I believe it is necessary for all of us, all the countries and peoples represented here today, to reaffirm basic principles for joint action. . . .

. . . Maintaining and managing peace, and ensuring that it is lasting, will of course be an extremely complex and difficult task. But is it not the obligation of today's states[people] to confront squarely such epochal challenges? The United Nations is, after all, a hall of peace, where states[people] gather and, with the establishment of lasting peace as their common goal, work together . . . to nurture and preserve diverse values and cultures, and to enhance the dignity of [human]kind.

On this occasion I pledge that, together with representatives here, I shall shoulder the grave responsibilities placed upon me as one of the states[people] gathered here at the United Nations.

The current session of the General Assembly, in anticipation of the United States—Soviet summit for the reduction and elimination of nuclear weapons, is filled with hope for the future of [human]kind. Indeed, this is the most significant session in the history of the Organization for ensuring peace and coexistence. Let us work together in the earnest hope that rich blessings will be bestowed upon our children and upon the Earth in the twenty-first century.

[Nakasone ends by reciting in English the last stanza of Henry Wadsworth Longfellow's poem, "A Psalm of Life," the point of which Nakasone states is "to act so that each tomorrow finds us farther along the road than today."](Nakasone, 1987)

1. How does Nakasone explicitly frame his address?
2. In his survey of historical events, Japan goes unmentioned but still figured prominently in some of them. Identify at least two events that he could have had Japan in mind.
3. How does Nakasone order problematic issues of the world?
4. He suddenly shifts from Japanese to English at the very end. What significance is this shift, if any? How does this shift possibly reflect upon some of his earlier words?
5. Labov based his natural narrative on conversational speech (everyday talk). What implications may this have for its application in discourse analysis of UN speeches?

3

CONTRASTIVE DISCOURSE ANALYSIS: GENRE AND CULTURE

A genre is a category of discourse that has a particular audience, purpose, form, content, and style (see Swales, 1990). Because UN addresses have distinctive features, they may be reasonably considered a genre. Although sometimes part of the "general debate," the addresses in the General Assembly are "a series of monologues in which each head of delegation, usually the foreign minister, undertakes a *tour d'horizon* of the current state of the world's problems as seen in the light of his [or her] government's policy" (Kaufmann, 1980, p. 27). This description is in general, for some speakers may devote their attention to an issue in particular. The reverse proportion seems the case for addresses in the UN Security Council. Because Prosser's (1970) collection happens to have come from the General Assembly, that is the primary UN forum in mind here.

Such addresses contain the following distinguishing features: (a) congratulations to the current President of the proceedings, or at least addressing the speech toward him or her or similar officer; (b) an affirmation of the importance or necessity of the UN and one's allegiance to its aims; (c) the use of highly polite and formal language; and (d) observations on regional or world issues. At least one speaker at the UN has acknowledged the "genre" quality of such addresses:

> On coming to this rostrum, Mr. President [of the General Assembly], I take great pleasure in conforming to the tradition of this Assembly by offering you first all my own congratulations and those of my country on your election as President of the eighteenth session. (Ahidjo, 1963, p. 981) (Cameroon)

Recognition of a "tradition" or an expected way by an "expert" member of the related discourse community is significant evidence for a genre (Swales, 1990).

Exercise: Find instances how Ahidjo's statement exemplifies Points (a) and (c) about the genre features of UN addresses.

Despite the monologic character of General Assembly addresses, that still does not stop the participants from perceiving them as debate. For example, Harold Wilson, the former prime minister of the United Kingdom, had this to say about the General Assembly:

> It has been a year of debates, of critical and sometimes cynical analysis, and of searching examination. . . . What has dominated the lives of those who have met and debated and argued and worked here has been the great compelling crises and conflicts that have rocked the world, and, because this great edifice is the center of the world, every tremor, every seismic disturbance, every hurricane has been registered and sometimes amplified here." (Wilson, 1965, p. 1076).

Perhaps because world crises and conflicts do reverberate at the UN, addresses there are monologic and generally follow an expected level of propriety. Otherwise, UN addresses may be certain to hasten conflict rather than control it.

The genre characteristics of the UN address to be considered here concern two essential features: the salutation and level of formality. Coupled with its tendency to be a tour d'horizon, these aspects give much shape to the UN address.

SALUTATION

What is being called "salutation" is that section of a speech by which the speaker gives acknowledgments to his or her host and to the audience. These acknowledgments include gratitude for services received, appreciation of achievement, or recognition of personal or professional association. Identifying the area of the salutation is important to the discourse analyst for at least several reasons. First, the salutation, generally unrelated in content to the speech proper, can complicate the segmenting of a text into the respective parts of the S(PR)E format, if so formatted for example. Second, speechtexts may or may not be distributed with their salutations intact. Thus, comparative or contrastive studies could be compromised because the addresses had been unequally treated. Third, the special function of the salutation can provide additional information about the speaker or his or her situation.

Exercise: Consider the contents of Box 3.1 and decide where the salutation ends and the body of the speech begins.

Box 3.1: Determine the Saluation in Tito's UN address

Marshal Josip Tito, the President of Yugoslavia from 1953 to 1980, is credited with "free[ing his country] from the external control of the USSR, and ma[king] it the most liberal Communist nation in Europe" (The Concise Columbia Encyclopedia, 1983).

Mr. President, on behalf of the Yugoslav delegation and in my own name, I wish to congratulate you on your election to the high and responsible function of President of this important session of the General Assembly.

May I be allowed to express my gratification at having the opportunity to attend the fifteenth session of the General Assembly here at the United Nations Headquarters. The peoples and the Government of Yugoslavia have always attached an exceptional significance to the United Nations. . . .

I also wish to express, on behalf of Yugoslav delegation and in my own name, our satisfaction that the fifteenth session of the General Assembly is being attended by a large number of representatives of new Members of the United Nations, particularly of the African countries that have only recently attained their independence. . . .

We hope that the United Nations will achieve real and complete universality in the near future through the attainment of independence by all the peoples now under colonial rule. . . .

The fifteenth session of the General Assembly acquires special significance for more than one reason: above all because this Assembly is confronted with highly important and difficult tasks, and because it is taking place in an international atmosphere which causes grave concern, in an atmosphere marked by a revival of the "cold war" and by complete uncertainty as to where all this may lead in the future. . . .

There is little difficulty, we believe, in tracing the causes of the present situation, a situation which, unless the utmost efforts are made within this international Organization and already at the present session, might lead the world into a new catastrophe greater than any it has known in the past. (Tito, 1960, pp. 197–198)

Based on its definition here, the salutation would be most appropriately seen as consisting of the first four paragraphs in Tito's address. In the first two paragraphs, he acknowledges the President of the General Assembly and the UN as a whole. This line continues in the third paragraph by his acknowledgment of the new members of the UN notably from Africa. The fourth paragraph states a related but final thought: The wish that any who are under colonial rule can also attain their independence. Note how the term *to express* links the second and third paragraphs, which in turn links the fourth. The fifth and sixth paragraphs depart sharply from the previous topic of Africa, independence and colonialism and appear directed toward the speaker's main purpose.

One curious note is how Tito refers to himself as "in my own name."

This seems to have the ring of authority, surely a characteristic he must have had, for he achieved uncommon autonomy from the Soviet Union (*The Concise Columbia Encyclopedia,* 1983). Consider that other speakers may merely say "myself" or even go unmentioned.

LEVEL OF FORMALITY

UN addresses follow a high level of formality, a level manifested by language related to politeness, respect, and modality.

Politeness and Respect

An illustration of politeness and respect is provided by a self-reference made by Joseph Kasavubu, former president of the Congo (Leopoldville). In mentioning the members of his UN delegation, he referred to himself in a detached (polite) and respectful way: "Mr. Joseph Kasavubu, President of the Republic of the Congo [among others]" (Kasavubu, 1960, p. 655). This is notable for two reasons: (a) the fact that he was Joseph Kasavubu, the President of the Republic of the Congo was already known by the audience and (b) Kasavubu's address had the highest frequency rate of direct self-reference among all UN addresses examined for that element. Even compared to academic research articles, discourse also highly detached and formal, Kasavubu's self reference appears particular. Consequently, it seems safe to say that Kasavubu, in being so detached and respectful, was likely conforming to UN conventions of diplomatic discourse.

Modality

Other conventional aspects of politeness and respect are found with the frequent use of the modal verbs *may* and *should* and related adverbs:

- "May I express the hope that my exchange of views with President Eisenhower will be fruitful?" (Khrushchev, 1959, p. 148) (Soviet Union)
- "May I respectively express my complete agreement with what the President [Eisenhower] has said?" (Nehru, 1960, p. 569) (India)
- "If I may be permitted to strike a personal note, I should like to quote from a book—*New Zealand, a Working Democracy*—which I wrote." (Nash, 1960, p. 583) (New Zealand)

- "May I, in conclusion, summarize our views" (Tito, 1960, p. 215) (Yugoslavia)
- "I should like to cite a few figures" (Khrushchev, 1960a, p. 257) (Soviet Union)

Modality, an attitude toward a message, need not be restricted to modal verbs or adverbs. Other types of words may have similar function as with the following extract:

> Today, in addressing this session of the United Nations General Assembly, I feel oppressed by a great sense of responsibility. I feel a humility in speaking to this august gathering of wise and experienced statesmen from east and west, from the north and from the south, from old nations and from young nations and from nations newly reawakened from a long sleep. I have prayed to the Almighty that my tongue will find those words which are adequate to express the feelings of my heart, and I have prayed also that these words will bring an echo from the hearts of those who listen. (Sukarno, 1960, p. 506) (Indonesia)

These words came from an Asian, people for whom politeness is a way of life. Of course, politeness is a quality appreciated and practiced by westerners as well. The difference is at least one of degree. This is not to preclude the speaker's own characteristics. That possibility must be considered. However, the degree to which Sukarno elevates his audience appears unmatched by the UN addresses made by western speakers. It may be the case that cross-cultural differences in politeness and respect will show up in UN addresses. At least, it should be considered.

A forum that promises equality is especially important to the newly developing nations, so a leader of such a nation may place much in store for the UN. Yet, the UN is just as important for those in the First World, too. As the world seems to shrink by ever-advancing technology, global interdependence develops more and more. Issues from atoms to zebras crucially depend on the world's cooperation. To be without the UN is unthinkable. Thus, hearing such words of Sukarno's might remind us of the UN's importance.

AN EYE FOR AN *I*

To further show how discourse may differ across cultures, this section provides the results of a study of UN addresses concerning use of the personal pronoun *I*. "A number of researchers have argued that one of the most important factors in a culture is the relative emphasis placed on individualism and collectivism (Hofstede, 1980; Triandis, 1990; Triandis, Brislin, & Hui, 1988)" (Brislin, 1993, p. 47). Individualist cultures emphasize the individual over the social group; collectivist cultures, the reverse. Myers (1994) cleverly distinguished these two characteristics in terms of what he called "me" or "we" thinking. Individualism is principally predominant in "North America and Western Europe, and countries strongly influenced by these areas, such as Australia and New Zealand"; collectivism, in most others (Brislin, 1993, p. 48).

An example of this contrast from a UN context is how the sudden death of the popular Secretary General Hammarskjöld was treated. Typically, speakers at the UN made eulogies about his greatness. However, among all those who mentioned his death, only one speaker, Margai (1961) of Sierra Leone—an African—expressed sympathy to Hammarskjöld's family. Margai, as a member of presumably a collectivist culture, may have had a greater sensitivity for the collective. As such, he merged the "private" (the family) with the "public" (the workplace), matters usually separated in industrialized societies. He was more likely to do so, perhaps, because his nation was newly inducted into the UN membership and, therefore, he, his nation, or both were less experienced than others about international affairs.[1]

One must be careful about overgeneralizing from such examples. Individualism and collectivism are not necessarily opposed (Berry, Poortinga, Segall, & Dasen, 1992). Berry et al. (1992) suggested that both elements are present in cultures and may be independent factors in the human personality. Japan is considered collectivistic but still has its individualistic features as well. Japanese company benefits may include assistance in marriage betrothal, home loans, and liberal maternity leave. However, executives hardly ever involve their spouses in company socials, to preserve a strict separation of public and private. The higher value for the Japanese is the precedence for the larger collective—the company over the family. Separating or merging the public and private spheres depends on how this higher value is served. Thus, context plays an important role whether individualism or collectivism becomes manifest. In other words, culture is far more complicated than the generalized rules.

Given a basic feature of culture as the individual—collective divide, some related differences may be expected to occur in UN speeches. One such example was provided. For another, it was decided to investigate on

[1] Here one could argue that an international standard is unclear. However, western industrialized countries were largely responsible for the UN's founding and hold, so far, most of the permanent seats in the Security Council. For these reasons, it is likely that UN meetings are influenced by western concepts and styles of communication.

a larger scale for the extent of individualism—"me" thinking—manifested in the speeches. Noting that the formal equivalent of *me* is *I* (RHWCD, 1991), the appropriate choice for UN addresses, the question became: Would UN addresses differ according to their frequency of using *I*?

METHOD

The UN addresses in Prosser's (1970) collection became the basis for this study. Spanning the first 25 years of the UN, the addresses were given by heads of state or government and are unabridged. For our purposes, the addresses were classified into national, regional, or associated groupings, using *The Concise Columbia Encyclopedia* and *The World Almanac* for geographical references. It was decided that these groupings had to have at least four addresses to be considered for this study. Consequently, addresses from Barbados, Cyprus, Greece, Jamaica, Malta, Mongolia, and the Vatican City were eliminated. Four other addresses were dropped but for a different reason. These addresses came from Harry Truman, the American president who appeared to play the role of "host" to the UN in its early history. To offset any possible effects, one of his later three UN addresses—his fourth—was included by random selection. These actions left 120 addresses for the study.

Each address was then read and had its salutation marked off to exclude it from the calculations. Salutations were excluded because they are likely to contain personal references due to the introduction of the speaker and his or her acknowledgments. This exclusion was also necessary because some addresses have only bare salutations either by original purpose or by later editing.

Next, the addresses, excluding the salutations, were read to locate occurrences of *I* and circled. They were counted for each address and an "average frequency per published page" computed. The published page was defined as that of Prosser's (1970) hardbound edition and consisted of 40 lines of print. Salutations, footnotes, quoted lines, and dialogues held with the moderator of the Assembly were not counted. Less than 40 lines of text was expressed by a fractional amount of a page. A total amount of pages, including any fractional amount, was calculated for each address. This amount was divided into the total number of *I* occurrences to determine the rate of personal referencing for an address. (So a speech, minus the salutation, of 2½ pages with 10 occurrences of *I* has a rate per page of 4 personal references.) Then, the average frequency per page was calculated for the various national and regional groups. Finally, the groups were arranged in rank order from the highest frequency rate to the lowest (see Box 3.2).

Box 3.2: Personal Reference in UN Addresses—the First Twenty-five Years

Anglo States (5)	4.16
United Kingdom (4)	3.86
Africa (31)	2.99
United States (11)	2.92
Western Europe (9)	2.43
Southwest Asia (8)	2.33
Southeast Asia (7)	2.28
Arab States (13)	1.86
Latin America (13)	1.58
Soviet Union (4)	0.99
Eastern Europe (15)	0.68

Note: The numerical rate indicates the average number of first person singular references (I) per published page by a head of state or government at the UN during its first twenty-five years. Parentheses indicate the number of addresses included. Anglo States include the countries of Australia, Canada, Ireland, and New Zealand. Western Europe does not include the UK or Ireland for present purposes. SE Asia does not include China or Japan: Neither nation had yet made a UN address by a head of state or government during the related period here. The total number of addresses is 120.

RESULTS

These results appear consistent with previous findings that individualism is principally found in western industrialized countries. One obvious result is the opposite rank held by the western industrialized countries (Anglo States, United Kingdom, United States, and Western Europe) and that of the Soviet Union and Eastern Europe. For example, the Anglo States have a personal reference rate of more than four times that of the Soviet Union. Interestingly, the frequency rate for Eastern Europe is even much lower. Could this be a reflection of its then subordinate status to the Kremlin? Also noticeable is the prominence of English-speaking countries. The "Anglo connection"—United Kingdom, United States, and Anglo States—scored 3.42, a score above all other regions. In line with this, all but two speakers (the Congolese) with the highest rates of personal reference in Box 3.3 gave theirs in English. The Congolese spoke in French.

African speakers were nearly equally divided between the use of English (15) and French (16) for their addresses. Their rates for personal reference were also similar, though the English speakers had a slight edge (3.05 vs. 2.93). Could this near-identical result be related to the reputation of the English and French for valuing independent mindedness? Perhaps. Insufficient data prevent us from answering more affirmatively, but the results of this study do point in that direction. English and French,

Box 3.3: Individual Rates of Personal Reference

Joseph Kasavubu, Congo (Leopoldville)	9.87
D. K. Jawara, Gambia	7.98
Jawaharlal Nehru, India	6.27
Lyndon B. Johnson, United States	6.02
Walter Nash, New Zealand	5.67
King Hussein I, Jordan	5.66
John G. Diefenbaker, Canada	5.45
Robert Gordon Menzies, Australia	5.24
Achmed Sukarno, Indonesia	5.17
Harold Wilson, United Kingdom	5.15
Kenneth D. Kaunda, Zambia	5.12
Fulbert Youlou, Congo (Brazzaville)	4.92

Note: The individual rate for personal reference (I) here is the highest for one address. The addresses were the speakers' first given to the UN as a head of state or government except for Nehru. All but two of the addresses were originally given in English; those other two were in French by the Congolese.

as compared to Arabic, Russian, and Spanish may tend to have higher frequencies of first-person reference (*I*). This difference can undoubtedly be explained, in part, by political reasons. Other reasons are sure to involve linguistic and rhetorical factors. To tease all these factors apart requires a much larger data base.

An apparent anomaly in Box 3.2 is the rank of Africa, a continent whose cultures are mainly collectivistic (Brislin, 1993). A possible explanation is that these addresses were given by many who had experienced recent national independence. In this euphoria, a speaker at the UN may be especially spontaneous with personal feelings, thus being more likely to make personal references.

Consider the situation of an African leader who would say something positive about colonialism: "[Besides the] humiliations and injustices . . . it has also enriched us, both materially and spiritually" (Youlou, 1960, p. 659) (Congo-Brazzaville). Taking a balanced view toward a foreign culture or element can risk one's standing in his or her native culture, as this speaker seems to recognize: "In expressing myself spontaneously . . . today I do not have the feeling that I am betraying African culture" (Youlou, 1960, p. 659).

To take such risk seems to require strong individualism. In this regard, Youlou happens to have ranked among the leaders in making personal references. It is possible that if he had not taken a balanced approach, then he might not have made as many personal references as he had. Not all the African speakers mentioned colonialism. As already pointed out, individualism and collectivism are not necessarily opposed. Perhaps,

Youlou enculturated more of the foreign culture than other African leaders. Indeed, he was an ordained priest (Prosser, 1970), which suggests that he was not the usual Congolese. This also explains his attributing colonialism as providing spiritual advantages.

By immersing himself so deeply into a foreign culture (French, by virtue of the former colony), his immersion is likely to have threatened both his own native identity and his social relations as well. Such conflicts are likely to foster personal individualism, an attribute indicated by his high frequency of personal references. Even more significantly, of those personal references, he was found to have a high proportion of self-disclosures, a proportion higher than all but two of the speakers investigated. (Self-disclosures are discussed in the next section.) This fact gives further credence that Youlou may have possessed an exceptionally high degree of individualism.

PERSONAL REFERENCES: SELF-DISCLOSURES

Because cultural differences appeared in the frequency of direct personal reference (I), it became interesting to see how such references were used. This interest was held largely in relation to the speakers with the highest frequencies of personal references. Various functions come to mind for using I statements, such as:

1. stating a policy of government;
2. reporting on the condition or result of policy;
3. arguing ideas or principles;
4. hedging or modifying the intensity of statements;
5. making a direct appeal to the audience;
6. facilitating a comprehensible presentation;
7. accepting responsibility for an action or program;
8. reporting a personal feeling;
9. identifying a personal attribute, trait, or state of mind; and
10. indicating a fact or belief about one's personal background, experience, or role.

Among these functions, the last several appear to tap individuality the most, for they distinguish us in some way. For that reason, they are called self-disclosures. Self-disclosures can be divided into several types: affective (8), cognitive (9), and biographical (10).

Exercise: The several types of self-disclosures are exemplified by the following extracts. As an exercise, the reader ought to try classifying each I statement (whether sentence or phrase) according to its type. Such tasks should help in developing sensitivity for the multiple functions of language, especially for affective behavior.

Please read the following extracts and consider which of the three types of self-disclosure apply:

A. "[T]he people of Cuba have learned much; they are, and I say this with pride, equal to the task [undertaken]." (Castro, 1960, p. 347) (Cuba)
B. "I am a realist . . ." (Wilson, 1965, p. 1082) (United Kingdom)
C. "I can state with full authority that [if the Headquarters of the United Nations were moved to the Soviet Union], we would guarantee the best possible conditions for its work. . . ." (Khrushchev, 1960a, p. 275) (Soviet Union)
D. "[T]he shadow of nuclear annihilation [exists]. I am a soldier." (Khan, 1962, p. 857) (Pakistan)
E. "I wish to betray my simplicity and naiveté . . . since I am a novice [in international diplomacy]." (Busia, 1969, p. 1392) (Ghana)
F. "I was dismayed at the resumption of nuclear tests after a voluntary moratorium of three years. . . ." (Tubman, 1961, p. 781) (Liberia)
G. "I am confident that, if [our security were ever breached], Lebanon could always count on the solidarity and help of the Arab countries. . . ." (Salaam, 1960, p. 574) (Lebanon)
H. "I belong to a country which [is] part of [the] "held back" section of humanity." (Frondizi, 1961, p. 745) (Argentina)

Comment

Biographical information tends to be more easily determined than the other types of self-disclosure. We can probably agree that Statements C and D are classifiable that way. (Statement C asserts, in part, that he is the leader—a biographical aspect.) Statement D, incidentally, requires a *bridging assumption* (term, Haviland & Clark, 1974) to comprehend it. We assume that some connection exits between nuclear war and being a soldier beyond the obvious similarity in field (military). We bridge the gap by assuming that President Khan means his "soldierhood" affords him greater insight into the seriousness of warfare by his military expertise.

Statement H presents an interesting question of classification. For our purposes, Statement H would be classified as biographical, although we do recognize the affective component present. In such cases, the more obvious choice is taken. In other words, fewer bridging assumptions are required. This does not necessarily mean that that is correct. However, in President Frondizi's case, his statement seems more "factual" to mean that his country is one that has yet developed the power to put people on the moon and so forth. This becomes so known by examining the surrounding sentences, which are provided in abridgment:

> The same act that enables [humankind] to journey to the stars is a sure instrument for reconciling the hopes of people. . . . And yet, on this earth, where such a miracle has been performed, two-thirds of the people are living in poverty and ignorance. . . . I belong to a country which is part of this "held back" section of humanity.
>
> At this moment, my people [are] making a tremendous sacrifice to overcome [their] difficulties and to build up a community. (Frondizi, 1961, pp. 744–745)

Of course, some affect runs throughout this passage, but Statement H seems more "cognitive" or "detached" than the simpler alternative of "I live in a(n) ______ country." The blank would contain a word more basic or colloquial than "held back." Colloquial language is not necessarily absent in diplomatic discourse. For example, a British prime minister, in a speech at the UN, referred to a prior British government in history as having been "stupid" (Wilson, 1965, p. 1088). Of course, Frondizi intended to be polite. Politeness tends to be realized through lengthier and more complex sentences (e.g., "Pass me the salt" vs. "I was wondering if you would consider passing me the salt"). His politeness avoids strong feeling that is associated with colloquial language.

Comparisons require a common basis or standard. If these statements were not limited to one function, theoretically they could have infinite possibilities (see chap. 1), making comparative studies difficult to control. The analyst, therefore, attempts to judge each statement for its "dominant" function. Although some statements may seem to get "penalized" that way, the same limit is applied equally for all. For this chapter, this issue is made mute because all three types are counted as self-disclosures. The fine distinctions made in type could be used for other purposes, however.

Returning to our main discussion, Statement E is another similar case. Despite the affective dimension of being a "novice," it, too, seems best classified as biographical. Statement A is classified here as affective; Statements B and G, cognitive. For Statement F, a case can be made either way. Because "dismay" is less colloquial and more literary in use, Statement F probably has a stronger cognitive component than affective. However, the speaker makes a decidedly emotional appeal concerning the subject of nuclear testing:

> We are all agreed that all nuclear devices should be devoted to peaceful purposes; we *stand four-square* by this commitment and will continue to *denounce* such tests as being *diametrically* opposed to peaceful intentions.
>
> I was *dismayed* at the resumption of nuclear tests after a voluntary moratorium of almost three years, which we had welcomed *most heartily*. . . . We had *fervently hoped* that voluntary moratorium marked the beginning of an epoch in which we would see the great Powers *shoulder* more and more of that primary responsibility for keeping the peace. . . . We *dared* to hope that the moratorium [would lead to a] disarmed world—a world in which the *awesome* powers of the atom were employed for the enrichment of [human]kind. . . . I take this opportunity to *appeal* to, *implore* and *call upon* the great Powers to reverse this *most unfortunate* trend. (Tubman, 1961, pp. 781–782; italics added)

Tubman's word choices make clear that he feels deeply about the issue. His intensity is reflected in his sense of melody, metaphor, and modality (e.g., *denounce, diametrically, dismayed, four-square, shoulder,* and *most heartily, fervently,* etc.). Finally, he sums up his view by an emphatic directive to the "great Powers" by the repetition of ideas (*appeal* . . . upon and *most* . . . *trend*) and sounds (/p/, /l/ and /t/). Besides the intensity, the repetition of ideas and sounds helps to make memorable and comprehensible, a speaker's words.

"Dismay," then, seems to be part of a strong affective pattern and reasonably could be classified as an affective self-disclosure. Such classifications become a matter of personal interpretation, for "creation and perception of [discourse] is not exact or fully determined" (Sinclair, 1993, p. 20). What separates informed interpretation from mere whim is the identification of "regularities and patterns in language" (Nunan, 1993, p. 7). By having shown that "dismay" was part of a common semantic network, a basis emerged for the classification made. This example also conveniently showed discourse analysis at the micro and clause levels: Sentential elements became part of microlevel interconnections, which contributed to a macrolevel or overall message of the discourse. Finally, here was an example of quantification used for cross-cultural comparison.

Individual Case Analysis

Similar data can be used for individual case studies. Lyndon Johnson needed, as seen earlier, to project himself as "presidential" on his sudden ascendance into the presidency. He was shown to engage much footing with his UN audience to exercise his leadership. Understandably, he ranked first in personal references among speakers from countries whose native tongue was English; and fourth overall. By examining self-disclosures more closely, this tall Texan was found to have had the highest rate for self-disclosures: 42%.

In doing this "proportional analysis" of how speeches/addresses are proportioned according to function, we have concentrated on those addresses with the highest frequencies for personal references. Our main interest was with self-disclosures. It should be noted that self-disclosures were computed in proportion to the amount of personal references, not the whole speech. If a speaker had a self-disclosure rate of 35%, it meant that one third of his or her personal references were self-disclosures. Such analysis may be useful for comparing the relative emphases between addresses.

As stated in Chapter 2, Lyndon Johnson's address was really about himself. It comes as no surprise that all of his self-disclosures were of the biographical type, related to role or experience, such as:

- "I can tell you today, as I told you in 1958, when I came as Majority Leader of the United States Senate to . . . this great tribunal."
- "When I entered the Congress of the United States twenty-seven years ago, it was my very great privilege to work closely with President Franklin Delano Roosevelt."
- "As a Member of Congress, I worked with him to bring about a profound but peaceful revolution."
- "In my travels on behalf of . . . President Kennedy, I have seen too much of misery and despair in Africa, in Asia, and in Latin America."
- "I have seen too often the ravages of hunger, tapeworm and tuberculosis."

Next in the highest frequencies for self-disclosures were several Africans. They, like Johnson, had an apparent need to project themselves as leaders, and so had high proportions devoted to biographical self-disclosures. Unlike Johnson however, they all made some affective self-disclosures, most likely due to the speech situation. The Africans were there for a joyful event—induction into the UN; Johnson, for a sad one—the mourning of President Kennedy.

The most interesting finding, perhaps, was that three out of the four Africans studied devoted higher proportions of personal references to administrative policy as compared to Johnson. Although Johnson was surely under pressure to develop policy, he proportionately directed more of his personal references on biographical statements than anything else. This differential can be easily explained. The Africans had probably more to gain by policy statements than Johnson could. It was no secret that—as the Africans themselves often stated—they needed UN assistance. Policy statements would likely weigh heavily on the minds of those giving such assistance. Because Johnson became the US leader so suddenly, he could be forgiven for any shortcomings in policy. As pointed out before, he had the larger job of seizing the reigns of leadership. To do that, it was natural to reveal his own experience for the job.

CULTURAL LOGICS

Diplomatic discourse being cross-cultural by nature will inevitably involve "cultural logics"—different patterns of thought or logic. Cultural logic means here not the formal system (rules) for reasoning but the informal. This logic can range from everyday thoughts and common sense to behavioral patterns. A different cultural logic is not necessarily illogical, although people have tended to view those in other cultures as being just that. This appearance of illogic is not due to inherent processes of thought but to different premises (Steinberg, 1982); for "anthropologists have never found a group of humans who were not rational or logical" (Steinberg, 1982, p. 116).

Cultural logics differ according to their underlying assumptions, beliefs, and values. The Japanese, compared to Americans, are quite flexible about religion. A devout Japanese Christian may still follow Buddism without compunction. Indeed, in Japan, many people, Christian or otherwise, are known to follow Shintoist ritual at birth, Christian, at marriage, and Buddhist, at death. This condition, even if only for ritual, would be unthinkable to most Americans. However, given a traditional belief in multiple deities and a unified cosmos, one can well imagine following multiple religious practices. The premises are simply different, not the mental process: One allows multiple gods; the other does not.

Cultures may also differ in communicative style. For formal speeches, North Americans try to begin with a joke; Japanese, with an apology or excuse. For personal letters, Japanese find it almost mandatory to start by mentioning the present season or weather. For narratives, this sensitivity for nature may emerge sometimes as a literary signal for an abrupt close and reliance on the reader to finish the ending.[2] For conversations, listeners are expected to provide frequent encouragement to continue, both nonverbal and vocal. The Japanese receiver may, therefore, carry a relatively heavier burden communicatively. In international situations, the difference in style may result in the Japanese being misconstrued as "inscrutable."

Different cultural logics are inevitable given our different histories and backgrounds. A visitor to the troubles in Belfast or Tel Aviv would be terribly naive, if he or she were to believe that the combatants ought to just forget the past and make up. That is what they should do, but the world was never ideal. For them, the past still holds special meanings that the visitor cannot appreciate. In another vein, a conflict emerges internationally between the United States and the Soviet Union. In the UN, the Russians appeared to violate their own principles by frequently vetoing proposals, an action that they had previously agreed to limit. Such contradictory behavior might appear illogical. In a similar way, Eisenhower violated his own by lying about an American spy plane over the Soviet Union.

Illogical or immoral as such behavior may be, one ought to temper this with the awareness of an additional premise: the condition of conflict of interest. Nations may perceive themselves fighting for survival. At such times, extreme measures are sometimes taken to gain an advantage. The point being made is not to excuse such measures. Rather, it is to caution concluding that such behavior reflects an inherent national trait. Before doing so, it would be wise to consider how frequent and under what circumstances such behavior was made.

Cultural Logics: Further Exploration

Three additional cases related to cultural logics are shown. The first two consist of addresses made to the Security Council in 1992 by Li Peng of China and Miyazawa of Japan. The third one is a General Assembly address by Sukarno.

Li Peng of China

Chinese premier Li Peng, "closely linked to the ordering of the 1989 massacre" at Tiananmen Square (*The Reuter Library Report*, 1992 [Online]), spoke at a 1992 Security Council summit amid much controversy

---

[2] This about the narrative comes from Kitagawa and Kitagawa (1987); other observations here find support, for example, in Gudykunst and Nishida (1994); Neustupný (1987); Nishida and Gudykunst (1982); and Tatematsu, Tateoka, Matsumoto, and Sato (1992). Exceptions do occur, so these points are made in general.

concerning human rights. John Major, the organizer of the summit, was criticized by "*The Independent,* a London newspaper, for compromising human rights issues in exchange for" Li Peng's presence (*The Daily Yomiuri,* 1992 [Online]). The summit's Joint Statement was reported to have "sidestep[ped] the issue of human rights largely at the insistence of China" (Kamiya, 1992 [Online]). Protestors could be heard outside UN headquarters, "the most vocal and active [being] exiled Chinese students who erected a replica of the Goddess of Democracy to protest . . . Li [Peng's] presence . . . and his role in the Tiananmen crackdown" (Leopold, 1992 [Online]). Nevertheless, this summit meeting was a chance for him "not only to seek better relations with the west but also to overcome his status as an international pariah for" his connection with the Tiananmen massacre (McFadden, 1992 [Online]). How did Li Peng treat the issue? Complete the activity in Box 3.4 to find out.

Box 3.4: Li Peng of China Speaks (an extract)

Read this speech extract and answer the questions below:

Li Peng (1992): The human rights and fundamental freedoms of all [human]kind should be universally respected. Human rights cover many aspects. They include not only civil and political rights but also economic, social and cultural rights. As far as the larger number of developing countries is concerned, the rights to independence, subsistence and development are of paramount importance. In essence, the issue of human rights falls within the sovereignty of each country. A country's human rights situation should not be judged in total disregard of its history and national conditions. It is neither appropriate nor workable to demand that all countries measure up to the human rights criteria or models of one country or a small number of countries. China values human rights and stands ready to engage in discussion and cooperation with other countries on an equal footing on the question of human rights on the basis of mutual understanding, mutual respect and seeking consensus, while reserving differences. However, it is opposed to interference in the internal affairs of other countries using the human rights issue as an excuse. (Li Peng, 1992: pp. 92–93)

1. How do you think a UN audience would greet his statement?
2. How well organized is this passage?
3. What do "human rights" mean to Li?
4. How likely would there be international misunderstanding with his message?

According to Mouat (1992b [Online]), "Li [Peng's] point on sovereignty as off-limits to the UN struck a chord that runs deep for many UN members." Mouat does not identify who these members are, but the less powerful, non-western ones seem likely. Indeed, Li Peng takes the perspective of developing countries early on.

About criticism of China, recall Mead's (1995) caution about our neglect of its history. The apparent double standard of ignoring American social ills was not lost on the Chinese, and it is not today. Hardly can a tragedy like Tiananmen Square be condoned; nor would one want to. However, the Chinese leadership has its own view that must be reckoned with regardless of merit. Recognizing that view may help us to understand why Li Peng's speech struck a chord with his audience, as well as, how our views do differ.

Different cultural perspectives may result in radically different interpretations of meaning and discourse organization. A western perspective views human rights at the level of the person; the Chinese leadership, the nation perhaps. Although Li Peng begins with an apparent universal belief (to us), his actual belief becomes clearer when he says that human rights also include the economic, social, and cultural. These aspects go undefined, however. A definition is necessary because they could apply more on the national level (e.g., national achievement) than on that for the individual. In his fourth sentence, his terms again appear conflicting as to which level is meant. Unless he has a different priority in mind (the collective), then his fifth sentence seems unnecessary. The collective view gains further credence with Sentences 2 through 4. They simply make better sense that way.

For some nations, such as the developing ones as he seems to say, the collective good is more important. Economic development and subsistence come at the price of civil order or obedience. He argues this by saying that (individual) human rights are not universal; rather, they depend on the particular conditions or circumstances of a nation. Obviously, if his meaning of human rights and ours were the same, then differences would cease to exist.

If we were to agree with this analysis, then even Li Peng's use of *[human]kind* bears attention. In the context of human rights, *[human]kind* may differ in meaning according to perspective. To the westerner, it refers to human beings (collectively) (RHWCD, 1991); to Li Peng, perhaps, less broadly to mean only certain collectives or groups. Compare *humankind* with *people* (or *human beings*). Humankind is more abstract, as it has a secondary meaning of "the quality or condition of being human: human being" (RHWCD, 1991). It is this abstractness that could be used to blur individuals into a mass. That transformation, paradoxically, could remove the element of humanity present. For example, the racist cop might be unable to tell Blacks apart, a common complaint heard by inner city dwellers. By failing to distinguish Blacks individually, the racist cop may end up denying them both their humanity and their rights. A similar process could have been involved in the tragedy of Tiananmen Square. Li Peng's sense of *humankind* may be quite different from our own.

Again, if this were not so, then his fifth sentence (*In essence*. . .) would appear misplaced. Rather than speaking about individual human rights as we think, he is entirely concerned with national sovereignty. And this coincides with his insistence that human rights be excluded from the summit's Joint Statement. Finally, his talk never gets to the subject of individual Chinese; instead it ends at the level of the collective, the nation of China. Rather than the "universal" message that we think we first started to hear, he may have been speaking entirely about China's sovereignty.

Cultural concepts, if not shared, could lead foreign observers astray about contrastive discourse styles. By not realizing Li Peng's subtle difference in meaning, westerners may view his passage as lacking coherence. Sentence 5 would seem misplaced and the ending of the passage, too abrupt. That is, his ending would come without sufficient orientation or triggers (advance organizers).

Miyazawa of Japan

Read the extract from Miyazawa's address in Box 3.5 and answer the question given.

Box 3.5: Miyazawa of Japan Speaks (an extract)

Read statements A to D and decide which one that Japan's Prime Minister (Miyazawa) most advocates in the passage below:

A. The General Assembly should adopt Japan's previous proposal for the Declaration on Fact-Finding.
B. The UN should admit Japan as a permanent member in the Security Council.
C. The UN Charter should be changed to better deal with the Cold War.
D. The Secretary General's transmission of information to other offices requires more advanced technology.

First of all, I believe that, in securing a peaceful world order, the ideals and purposes of the United Nations Charter, which represent fundamental and universal values, will be of even greater relevance than ever before. It is incumbent on Member States to strive, constantly, to ensure that each of these values is respected in practice. At the same time, it is also necessary for the United Nations to evolve while adapting to a changing world. For example, certain sections of the United Nations Charter are based on the realities prevailing in 1945, when the United Nations was founded, which predate even the Cold War.

In addition, since the Security Council is at the center of United Nations efforts to maintain international peace and security, it is important to consider thoroughly ways to adjust its functions, composition and other aspects so as to make it more reflective of the realities of the new era. This is a process in which Japan is prepared to take an active part.

(continued)

> Secondly, it is important to consider concrete measures to strengthen the functions of the United Nations so that it can work more effectively to secure a peaceful world order. The importance of peace-keeping activities does not need to be repeated here, but I should like to comment on the need to strengthen the functions of the United Nations in the area of conflict prevention. It is essential that the Secretary-General, who plays a crucial role in the United Nations mediation efforts and good offices, be given sufficient information concerning tensions that could escalate into international conflicts. An important step in that direction was made last December with the adoption by the General Assembly of the Declaration on Fact-Finding by the United Nations in the Field of the Maintenance of International Peace and Security, which was proposed and sponsored by Japan and other countries. It would also be useful if countries with sophisticated information-gathering capabilities would provide the Secretary General with relevant information, as appropriate. I hope that this issue will receive due consideration. (Miyazawa, 1992: pp. 105–106)

Comment: Choice A seems likely but is not correct. The General Assembly, according to Miyazawa, had already adopted the proposal mentioned. If Choice A was chosen, the passage ought to be reread before continuing.

Choice C is also incorrect. The Cold War was surely over by 1992 by the breakup of the Soviet Union, and Miyazawa mentions it merely as a historical reference. The correct answer is Choice B but requires explanation.

Here is a case in which the language is clear mainly to insiders—the players themselves and their confidantes. For that reason, media reports are especially helpful guides. Japan, among other hopefuls, was widely reported to have its sights on a permanent seat on the Security Council. The Japan Economic Newswire (Johnson, 1992) reported 2 days before the Summit that the Japanese and Indian prime ministers were expected to press for reorganizing the Council. Because Japan had been elected for "a record" seven 2-year terms (since its admission to the UN in 1955), as an economic superpower, and has been the second largest contributor in funding the UN, "Japan is quietly campaigning for a permanent Council seat by 1995, when the 50th anniversary of the Charter's signing is celebrated" (Johnson, 1992 [Online]).

Primed with this knowledge, we can appreciate the reporting by *The Christian Science Monitor* on Miyazawa's speech:

> Japan and Germany, for instance, are often mentioned as potential permanent Council members. Since any change would require Charter revision and open up other problems in the process, there is now a virtual consensus that making changes by the UN's 50th anniversary in 1995 will be soon enough. (Mouat, 1992b, [Online])

Prime Minister Miyazawa, citing the date, noted diplomatically that the Council should be made "more reflective of the realities of the new era" (Mouat, 1992b, [Online]). This report makes clear Miyazawa's intention. *The New York Times* helps as well: "[S]ome countries also aired *pet grievances* about the way the Security Council works now that it is becoming more influential in world affairs. Japan, Venezuela, India and Zimbabwe all said that the Council was unrepresentative of the present-day world" (Lewis, 1992, [Online]; italics added).

Lest it be thought that the Japanese are unique for making understatements, consider the next speech extracts from Venezuela and India. Which is more similar to Japan in understating its pet grievance?

> **Venezuela:** "The Organization must restore the basic principle underlying its validity: that of equality of rights and obligations. The Security Council reflects political realities as they existed at the end of the Second World War, and not current realities. The General Assembly is repetitive in its resolutions and weak in providing political guidance to humanity" (Perez, 1992, p. 56).

> **India:** "The actions by the Security Council must flow from [the] collective will and not from [that] of a few. A general consensus must always prevail. . . . As the composition of the General Assembly has trebled since its inception, the size of the Security Council cannot remain constant any longer. Wider representation in the Security Council is a must, if it is to ensure its moral sanction and political effectiveness" (Rao, 1992, p. 97).

Why did the Japanese prime minister so understate his country's cause for a permanent seat? Certainly, Japanese collectivism and related etiquette offer an explanation. One does find that Japanese officials tend to state that certain negative events are "regrettable" without much more comment. However, one must also consider the emphasis that Japan places on its economic power rather than political or military. Assertive involvement in international politics might risk its economic relations. After all, Japan had to completely rebuild itself after its near annihilation in World War II, a focus given impetus by its limited natural resources. Japan must also be cautious not to offend its Asian neighbors, who suffered under war-time Japanese occupation. For such reasons, Japan was reluctant to involve itself in the Gulf War despite its reliance on imported oil, a stance incomprehensible to the United States at the time.

Finally, one must also consider an apparent reluctance of the permanent members—the "Big Five" powers—to allow Japan into its realm. A joint statement drafted by Britain before Miyazawa's speech (Japan Economic Newswire, 1992), and subsequently approved by the Summit members, did "not refer to the structure of the [Security Council], meaning that the UN leaders ha[d] decided to ignore [Japan's] quiet campaign to become a permanent member of the decision-making body" (Kamiya, 1992 [Online]). Perhaps Japan's campaign was too quiet. However, the Big Five powers doubtless exert much influence on UN policies and would naturally be reluctant to relinquish it.

Although the idea of Japan becoming a permanent member of the Council was first proposed by US president Nixon, the then US president Bush held apparent reservations (*The Daily Yomiuri,* 1992). His reservations were partly rooted in the awareness that other countries would be encouraged also to seek a permanent seat and that some Asian countries, remembering World War II, might become fearful of Japan (*The Daily Yomiuri,* 1992). After tacitly agreeing to the organizational status quo, Miyazawa hardly could be expected to forcefully raise the issue later in his speech address. Venezuela similarly sidestepped the issue, and India, somewhat as well.

UN members belong to a "world community" of nations. The very notion of community is a social one. By definition, a society involves a social hierarchy. Some members will have more status than others. Higher status usually carries more power than others. So despite the wish for "sovereign equality," nations are ultimately treated unequally. An example was found in the case of differential respect given to North and South Korea, as seen in Chapter 1. Another is the permanent veto power invested exclusively with the Big Five Powers. Each nation member has its place or status in the international community. Japan, like most other nations, must weigh itself in this light. Becoming a permanent member of the Security Council would surely disrupt the status quo in international affairs. Miyazawa's understating his country's wish for a permanent seat is hardly unreasonable given the realities at the time. Discourse may manifest indirectness but for different reasons. That is precisely why context plays a major role in analysis. Determining how the situational and cultural factors are involved serves well both the analysis and intercultural relations.

Sukarno of Indonesia

In the section on modality, we observed the words of Sukarno, a former president of Indonesia, who elevated his audience in a way rarely seen, even in UN addresses. His Asian background was suggested as one possible explanation. His address is examined again for its possible link to culture. This inquiry merely intends to be suggestive and hopes to lay groundwork for further study of discourse across cultures.

In making *I* statements, Sukarno tends to repeat them in his address. For example:

> I believe, yes, I firmly believe that the adoption of those five principles and the writing of them into the charter would greatly strengthen the United

> Nations. I believe it would bring the United Nations into line with the recent development of the world. I believe that it would make it possible for the United Nations to face the future refreshed and confident. Finally, I believe that the adoption of Pancha Shila [five ideals of Indonesia] as a foundation of the Charter would make the Charter more whole-heartedly acceptable to all Members, both old and new. (Sukarno, 1960, p. 530)

Is Sukarno's purpose here to state his personal convictions or his suggestions? He repeats *I believe* so much that it may put undue focus on himself at the expense of his suggestions. Contrast this extract with one from Martin Luther King's acceptance speech for the Nobel Peace Prize:

> I refuse to accept the cynical notion that [nations must end up in nuclear war]. I *believe* that unarmed truth and unconditional love will have the final word in reality. That is why right temporarily defeated is stronger than evil triumphant.
>
> I *believe* that even amid today's mortar bursts and whining bullets, there is still hope for a brighter tomorrow. I *believe* that wounded justice . . . can be lifted . . . to reign supreme.
>
> I have the audacity to *believe* that peoples everywhere can have three meals a day . . ., education and culture for their minds, and dignity, equality and freedom. . . . I *believe* that what self-centered men have torn down men other-centered can build up. I still *believe* that one day [human]kind will bow before the alt[a]rs of God and [triumph] over war. . . . And the lion and lamb shall lie down together. . . . I still *believe* that we shall overcome. (King, (1964/1986, p. 226; italics added)

King's repetitious use of *believe* appears effective because the matter is precisely his own personal beliefs. Rather than making suggestions, King states his rationale or his faith. The very fact that King can still believe in the goodness of humankind, despite the struggle for civil rights, uplifts us all.

In contrast, Sukarno's tentativeness of *I believe* makes his suggestions sound weak. On the contrary, he probably had the opposite intent. Nonnative speakers of English sometimes mistake the expression *I believe* for one of strong assertion. Asians, in particular, impressed with the apparent assertiveness found in English, overgeneralize their image of western individuality. Ironically, *I believe* or *I think* in English may act as a constraint. Suggestions are unconfirmed beliefs, at least from the receiver's perspective. If couched weakly, suggestions may receive little notice. If in an international context, westerners must attune themselves to this possible Asian "rhetoric."

This point about suggestion making is made in passing, for a larger interest lies with Sukarno's repetition of language. Functional expressions used with *I* were repeated in succession more than 37% in the same address. Some examples found in Sukarno (1960) follow:

- "I know my people; I know their unquenchable thirst . . . and I know their determination."
- "I speak of China. I speak of what is often called Communist China."
- "I use strong words, and I use them deliberately, because I am speaking for my nation and because I am speaking before the leaders of nations."
- "I share their horror, I share their fear. I share that horror and that fear because . . ."
- "I think you have forgotten something. I think you have forgotten about more than 1,000 million people, the people of Asia and Africa . . . who followed neither the *Communist Manifesto* nor the Declaration of Independence. Mind you, we admire both, and we have learned much from both, and we have been inspired by both."
- "I bring to you the greetings of ninety-two million people, and I bring to you the demand of that nation."

Repetition has an important role in the comprehension of discourse. However, the frequency that Sukarno uses it with *I* statements appeared unmatched by other UN addresses examined. Is this a matter of personality or culture or, is it a case of mistaken propriety in English?

In Sukarno's case, his repetitions seem to operate in this way: Introduce a topic and then amplify it. By doing so, it may arouse the audience by the inherent delay of the informational climax. On the other hand, it could have a deadening effect if overused. Alternatively, he may have wanted to be indirect in keeping with his earlier respect shown to his audience. Or, perhaps, for the opposite reason this enabled him to emphasize one's personal self by using *I*, presumably his image of the "individualism" of English, the language he spoke in.

Repetition, however, is not directly related to the personal pronoun *I*. Repetition of other forms can be found on nearly every page of Sukarno's address. Several early examples follow:

- "*Here is the proof that* generations of struggle have been justified. Here is the proof that sacrifice and suffering have achieved their end. Here is the proof that just justice has begun."
- "I speak also *to those* you represent, to those who have sent you here, to those who have entrusted their future to your hands."
- "I speak to you on behalf of my people, *those ninety-two million* people of a distant and wide archipelago, those ninety-two million who have lived a life of struggle and sacrifice, those ninety-two million people who have built a State upon the ruins of an empire."

We recognize these repetitions as parallel expressions but the great frequency by which Sukarno uses the technique appears unusual. It so happens that the Indonesian language could be at play here.

Reduplication or repetition of lexical base forms for generating words is "very characteristic for Indonesian and related languages" (Prentice, 1990, p. 199), as with *duduk (sit) → dukuk-dukuk (sit around "doing nothing"); cabik (tear) → cabik-cabik (tear to pieces);* or *habis (finished) → habis-habisan ("all-out, total")* (Prentice, 1990, p. 200). Whether Sukarno's discourse was, indeed, a reflection of this lexical process is unknown. Ultimately, for any of these proposed factors, extensive inquiry and observance of other cases would be required. The mention of Sukarno is merely to suggest the possibility for cross-linguistic or cultural influence on discourse. The next chapter further explores such issues related to contrastive studies of discourse.

CONCLUSION

UN addresses are distinguishable by certain genre qualities, such as formality, modality, and topical content. These features provide an established framework by which consistency in discourse inheres across political and cultural boundaries. By their formality and modality, diplomats can maintain intelligent and respectful debate, even if sharply conflicting. However ritualistic UN salutations may seem, they do function vitally in helping to establish a genre and to preserve orderly diplomatic debate. Genre is considered further through rhetorical analysis in Chapter 8.

Although consistent in genre, UN addresses still can differ in relation to culture. One way is with politeness and respect; another way is modality. Still another, is with the dimension of individuality—collectivity. An intriguing example was the frequency of the personal pronoun *I*: Western countries, particularly those English-speaking and the Soviet Bloc countries were opposite in frequency. Except for Africa, frequency scores appeared to follow the individualist—collectivist dimension. These findings suggest that even if the UN were to edit the related speechtexts (e.g., for spelling), certain distinctive characteristics still remain. This possibility was demonstrated with several cases of Asian diplomatic discourse under the rubric of cultural logics. Possible cultural differences were found in the use of concept, qualification, and repetition.

Suggestions were also made in this chapter for conducting both quantitative and qualitative studies of UN addresses. The quantitative was illustrated by amounts of frequencies; qualitative, by the study of self-disclosures, for example. For a rough distinction: The quantitative approach essentially summarizes information into numerical form; qualitative, into verbal. The mere use of such forms does not necessarily make one's work quantitative or qualitative. Mention of these approaches is made solely to suggest their potential use.

Whatever approach, however, a more primary concern rests with genre and culture in relation to choosing what discourse to study. In making cross-cultural comparisons, a correct alignment of genre is necessary. Contrasting American off-track betting with Japanese temple worship, in order to say that Americans were irreligious in comparison would be highly misguided. A central issue in contrastive discourse analysis concerns the concept of discourse structure. Familiarity with this issue will greatly aid contrastive discourse analysis and is explored in the next chapter.

APPLICATION

1. The following speech extract from Eisenhower (1960) is used, not only to balance our view of his performance, but also to illustrate some effective strategies of discourse. Read and try to identify them:

> If the United Nations system is successfully subverted in Africa, the world will be on its way back to the traditional exercise of power politics, in which small countries will be used as pawns by aggressive major Powers. Any nation, seduced by glittering promises into becoming a cat's paw for an imperialistic Power, thereby undermines the United Nations and places in jeopardy the independence of itself and all others.
>
> It is imperative that the international community protect the newly emerging nations of Africa from outside pressures that threaten their independence and their sovereign rights. To this end I propose a program which contains five major elements. (Eisenhower, 1960, p. 188)

2. Consider again the extract from Martin Luther King's speech. Try to determine the logic for arranging his sentence order. Specifically, why were the *believe* statements so ordered? Why did he indent his paragraphs where he did?

A Study of Personal References

Use the UN speech of Nakasone's at the end of Chapter 2, which was originally delivered in Japanese. Follow the procedures for the study of personal references in Chapter 3 and determine how closely Nakasone's speech mirrors the average for Southeast Asia. At the outset, we wish to state that this exercise was created without prior knowledge of Nakasone's performance in this regard. Moreover, his speech was abridged before the related study was performed or the creation of this exercise.

For the purposes of this study exercise, it was estimated that an average line of print in Prosser's (1970) publication contained 12.4 words. As was reported in this chapter, a page had 40 lines. A computer count of Nakasone's abridged speech totaled 1,049 words and an additional 4,417 words for the discarded portion of his address. (Salutatory segments were subtracted from the latter word count.) Among the discarded portion of the address, 31 personal references (*I*) were counted. Conduct your study by including these steps: (a) plan and decide your procedures, (b) determine Nakasone's relative frequency of *I* statements, (c) categorize them in several ways in looking for self-disclosures, (d) analyze your data, and (e) consider the validity of the study and formulate any recommendations.

Consider Nakasone's address again, but for its universal aspects of discourse, as well as possible reflections of Japanese culture. Why is genre an important concept in communication studies? Why does genre have special significance for UN speech addresses both for the participants and for who study them?

4

FUNCTIONAL VERSUS STRUCTURAL APPROACHES TO DISCOURSE ANALYSIS

Functional and structural views of language and discourse represent a fundamental division in linguistics (Schiffrin, 1994). Neither side monopolies the truth, for both have their place in linguistic studies. However, present concern is with extreme structuralism that would treat discourse as if it were a "super sentence." That is, a discourse would be seen as rigidly structured as that of a sentence. Such a view may treat paragraphing as only correctly done if initiated by a topic sentence, for example. Discourse, though, defies such strictures. The multiple functions of language make it so. Accounting for those functions, as this chapter attempts to show, is an important purpose of discourse analysis.

THE CONCEPT OF STRUCTURE

Allerton (1979, p. 12) stated that the term *structure* in linguistics has "a fairly literal meaning, akin to its original sense in the sphere of building." He went on to say that

> The different parts of a window, for example, the uprights, cross-pieces, hinges, panes, and so on, must be of the correct number and of the right size and shape as well as being in the proper relative position, and together they must form a unified whole, a window: only then do they form a structure. These requirements—number of elements, type of elements, ordering of elements—are precisely those of a linguistic [sentential/grammatical] structure. (Allerton, 1979, p. 12)

Although this kind of structure may fit the sentence, its application to discourse is a another matter. The structural view of discourse assumes that language is invariant "but [as] Beaugrande (1985) correctly observes . . . this invariance is essentially a fiction" (Horowitz, 1987, p. 121).

> In real communication, an element is classified not by what it is in the linguist's scheme, but by what it does, that is, by its function in the processing of the participant. A single element may have several functions, and a single function may be assigned to several elements. (Beaugrande, 1985, p. 49; quoted by Horowitz, 1987, p. 121)

The sentence grammar of English has rigid requirements about what goes with what. Discourse, however, is not governed by such rigid rules as seen in this example by Widdowson (1983):

A: I have two tickets to the [movies] tonight.
B: My examination is tomorrow.
A: [Too bad.] (quoted in Nunan, 1993, p. 74)

What first appears as random utterances becomes immediately coherent, not by knowledge of grammar but that of semantics. Yes, structural relations contribute to understanding these utterances individually but not collectively as a discourse. The decisive element is our background knowledge of everyday affairs. Structural relations of the sentence simply do not apply.

Because "structure" does have a tightly bound sense in linguistics, like a building, some specialists like Hoey (1983, 1991) avoid applying the word to discourse. Nevertheless, "discourse structure" is so widely used both inside and outside of linguistics, that it is exceedingly hard to avoid. In an attempt to show why it may be prudent to do so, we will contrast a structurally based cross-linguistic study of English and Japanese from a functional perspective.

A FUNCTIONAL REANALYSIS OF A CROSS-LINGUISTIC STUDY

As background, Kaplan (1966/1988) proposed that cultures differ in preferred discourse styles based on his study of essays written in English by students from various foreign countries. His proposed "Oriental" style of circularity was in marked contrast to his "linear" style of English. Although Japanese formed his largest sample group, he excluded it from his Oriental classification for unspecified reasons. It was left to Hinds

(1980) to provide the first major study in linguistics to purport that Japanese "expository" writing predominantly follows a circular style. However, such characterizations require caution because of the historical tendency in the west to view the Japanese as irrational or illogical (Donahue, 1994). Despite evidence for a Japanese indirect speaking style, the case for written prose in Japanese appears quite different (Donahue, 1990; Karatsu, 1992; Kubota, 1992; Ludden, 1994; Uzawa & Cumming, 1989).

Based on Donahue (1990), the following will attempt to show how characterizing Japanese prose as circular in style becomes problematic. One problem is that a structural metaphor may have influenced Hinds (1980) to ignore important contextual factors. His study compared bilingual articles on the same topic from a publication on popular entertainment in Hawaii. From this, the researcher concluded that Japanese discourse follows a "return to baseline theme" (hereafter *baseline theme*) each time before taking a new perspective. So, for example, in reporting about the life of a Hawaiian (Japanese American) singer in Japan, the article touched base with her "foreignness," the baseline theme, before advancing its story.[1] The effect was a spiraling of content around the baseline theme, rather than the assumed straight line approach in English. Baseline theme, however, is not unique to Japanese, and other problems were found as well. These problems, we propose, derive from an overemphasis on structure to the neglect of context. Before continuing, the articles (Boxes 4.1 and 4.2) ought to be compared. How many differences in content can you find between the English and Japanese texts? (Boxes 4.1 and 4.2 ought to be read now to find out.)

A problem with this cross-linguistic study was the absence of a comparison of differences in content. Instead, Hinds (1980) simply assumed that they were negligible. By assuming so, the researcher, then, believed that contextual factors, such as purpose, topic familiarity and location of the audience, were the same for both articles being compared. If they were the same, then any differences in style could be attributed to culture.

On the contrary, the May Yokomoto articles differ considerably in content, using Hinds's (1980) own translation. These differences form two patterns: *depth of description* and *spatio-temporal relations*. These two patterns also show that the audiences were not in the same place (Hawaii) as assumed by the researcher. Instead, the Japanese audience was actually perceived to be in Japan, if not outright located there. Different locations,

---

[1] We have chosen for analysis the largest of two Japanese specimen texts in Hinds's (1980) study. We also take Hinds at his word that, "due to the brevity of [the other] article, it is difficult to offer any strong evidence for [his] analysis." (1980, p. 134). This present analysis, like Hinds's, relies on the article about this Hawaiian singer.

Box 4.1: *ENGLISH* Version, *May Yokomoto*

*May Yokomoto: It's a Lot of Fun**

(1) May Yokomoto returned to Hawaii recently to appear in the Star-Tanjo. (2) In addition, the friendly eighteen-year old was kept busy by photo sessions with Sakiko Ito. (3) They had numerous pictures taken of them on the beach for *Myojo* magazine in Japan.

(4) She is having a good time in Japan doing commercials, television, and radio work. (5) For example, she appeared on the TV game show "*Kekkonshimashoo*" (Let's Get Married), where she won two trips to Hawaii, which she is saving for future use. (6) May also appears on "*Sekai no* Circus" with her favorite actor, Masaaki Sakai. (7) On this program, May had to dress up like a clown and (8) even swung on a trapeze. (9) She also had a radio program on Radio-KANTO called "Teach Japanese to May."

(10) May has her own apartment in Tokyo, (11) but still has a hard time getting around on trains. (12) Recently, though, people have begun to recognize "May-chan" and (13) help her find her destination. (14) She says living in Japan is not easy, (15) but is fun most of the time.

(16) May's parents are pleased that her Japanese has improved so much, (17) but she says she still has a hard time understanding some of the songs.

(18) May says, "While in Hawaii, my teacher Harry Urata always explained everything to me. He made it seem easy."

(19) May has traveled all over, from Hokkaido to Kyushu. (20) In the process, she has learned all about Japanese gourmet foods.

(21) Two years ago May was the winner of the "Star Tanjo." (22) Last year, she made her debut in Japan and (23) is already a popular talent.

(24) May began studying hula at the age of five, and (25) started music lessons with Harry Urata at the age of seven. (26) She was a runner-up in the Miss Teenage Hawaii contest in 1974. (27) Her real name is Cid Akemi Yokomoto. (28) She is a graduate of Roosevelt High School.

*"May Yokomoto: Japan, it's a lot of fun." *Kokiku*, May 1977, p. 7.

therefore, suggest that the audiences could have differed in topic familiarity by virtue of exposure to different mass media. Furthermore, because the discourse events occur between Hawaii and Japan, differences in spatio-temporal relations reverse some of the ideational content. The Japanese discourse organization is further affected by sociolinguistic factors that compel its author to seek acceptance of the Hawaiian character by the audience of Japanese nationals. (We adopt *Hawaiian* here in view of its dictionary definition: "any native or inhabitant of the Hawaiian Islands" [RHWCD, 1991].) Finally, these differences in audience and purpose result in different organizational patterns apart from the purported circular nature of Japanese discourse.

Box 4.2: *JAPANESE* Version, *May Yokomoto*

*May Yokomoto**

(1) "I hosted a program called "World Circus" with Masaaki Sakai. The film of the show came from London, and I had to do things like dress-up like a clown, and fly on a trapeze in a large studio. I'm happy."

(2) The parents of May Yokomoto keep a close eye on this modern girl who speaks Japanese fluently. (3) She is fresh as a young sweet-fish splashing on the water.

(4) When she speaks of Japan, she continually uses the word *tanoshii* (happy). (5) Some examples of her happiness are . . . (6) When she appeared twice on Sanshi Katsura's program "Let's Get Married," she was paired with two of her fans, and she ended up winning both times; and now she has two tickets for a Hawaiian vacation.

(7) She now lives in an apartment near [Toritsu] University by herself, and since she cannot read Japanese, she has difficulty with the trains. (8) However, many strangers recognize her on the street and help her.

(9) She has traveled in her work from Hokkaido to Kyushu, and has been able to sample a variety of local foods. Etc . . .

(10) "Well, there are bad things too, but I forget those." (11) She is perfectly open and friendly. (12) Because of this she is loved by everyone.

(13) "However, when I don't grasp the meaning of the songs I sing it's terrible. There are lots of words that don't appear in the dictionary. At those times I think back on all the help with the language I used to get from Mr. Urata when I was in Hawaii."

(14) She began hula lessons at five, and at seven she began singing lessons with Harry Urata. (15) She began with a song called something like "The Doll with Blue Eyes."

(16) The TV programs she appears on frequently are singing shows like Star-Tanjo. (17) Last year she had a 2½ hour radio program on Radio Kanto called "Teach Japanese to May." (18) The last program at the end of March was done via international telephone from Hawaii.

(19) This time she has returned home in conjunction with an appearance on Star-Tanjo in Waikiki, and for a magazine frontispiece picture session with Sakiko Itoh.

(20) May Yokomoto, who was elected two years ago as Hawaii's new star on Star-Tanjo is a lucky girl whose looks and talents were noticed, and who has been sought after for commercials for leading companies, for magazines, and for TV after her debut in May of last year. (21) She has released her third record called "*Anata* chance *yo.*"

(22) Her real name is Cid Akemi Yokomoto.

(23) She graduated from Roosevelt High School. (24) She is a pure Hawaiian product, and was a runner-up in the Miss Teenage Hawaii contest in 1974.

---

*This translation is Hinds's (1980) but has been adjusted in its paragraphing to follow the original Japanese as found in *Kokiku* (May 1977, p. 7). One other change was transliterating rather than translating the name of the Japanese university mentioned in the article.

Depth of Description

That the audiences did differ in location appears clear from the content of the articles. Observe Table 4.1 how this is so.

As seen in Table 4.1, the Japanese text is specific in a way that residents in Japan would appreciate. The greater detail about her apartment hardly can be significant for those without direct experience in Japan. Moreover, the Japanese text treats the item about food differently: It uses the concept of *local* versus that in English, *gourmet.* There is a subtle difference that only people very familiar with Japan would know: Regional cuisines can be quite different in Japan. For example, marriages between those who come from different regions are expected to have some "friction" about different tastes for *miso* soup. "White" (*shiro*) is favored in the west (e.g., Kyoto, Osaka); "red" (*aka*), in central Japan (e.g., Nagoya); and mixed in the east (e.g., Tokyo). *Gourmet* food hardly can suggest the potential regional conflict that *local* can. Thus, the English and Japanese audiences appear to be treated as though they possess unequal familiarity about Japan. One reason is that the Japanese article could have originated in Japan but later reproduced in Hawaii. The audiences may well have been in different countries, a factor left uncontrolled by Hinds (1980).

Assuming that most Japanese Americans have yet to travel to Japan, it is unlikely that a writer knowledgeable about Japanese Americans would write "over their heads." Consequently, it seems more likely that the text was written for Japanese nationals. Whatever doubts there are seem to retreat once it is noticed how differently May's Hawaiian background is handled by the English and Japanese versions.

Residents of Hawaii, especially Japanese Americans, would not need information about the ethnicity of one of their community's own heroes; consistent with this expectation, the English text makes no explicit mention of May's ethnicity. In contrast, the Japanese version does mention her ethnicity, raising the question of why the Japanese text seems uncharacteristic for Hawaii. The best answer seems to be that the text is not

Table 4.1. Depth of Description Between English and Japanese

Item	English	Japanese
May's apartment is	in Tokyo [10]	near Toritsu University [7]*
May samples Japanese	gourmet food [20]	local food [9]
May's background is	ø	Hawaiian [24]

***Note:** The university mentioned, *Toritsu* (lit. "metropolitan," *Kenkyusha's New Collegiate Dictionary,* 1987) is not particularly renowned and is probably familiar only to residents of Tokyo. Gourmet food probably refers to the standard fare found in Japanese restaurants abroad but does not recognize local specialties in Japan.

meant for Hawaiians at all, but for Japanese nationals. (As suggested earlier, Hinds's methodology does not appear sensitive to having an audience of Japanese nationals.) However, a question would still remain as to whether those Japanese nationals are in Japan or Hawaii. The answer to this question is "in Japan," as the next section attempts to show.

Spatio-Temporal Relations

The English text begins with May's return to Hawaii; conversely, this information appears near the end of the Japanese text (sentence numbering is Hinds's):

English: May Yokomoto returned to Hawaii recently [1]
Japanese: This time she has returned home [19]

The difference is all the more striking if the Japanese readers are also Hawaiian; they would presumably share the same anticipation of May's return as evident in the English version, even more so because May is also a member of the Hawaiian (Japanese American) community. One possible explanation is that the Japanese readers are in Japan (at least psychologically) and have been aware of only May's presence, unlike the Hawaiians waiting for her return. Consequently, time frames are reversed depending on whose perspective is adopted in reference to May's coming and going.

Additional support for different spatio-temporal frameworks arises from a choice made between the temporal conjunctions *when* and *while*. These two words differ respectively in reference between a point in time and duration. Although they overlap in meaning, *while* may impart a greater emphasis on duration (Quirk, Greenbaum, Leech, & Svartvik, 1985). It is this function of duration that seems to be exploited in the English version reporting May Yokomoto's past music lessons in Hawaii:

English: . . . while in Hawaii. . . . [18]
Japanese: . . . when I was in Hawaii. [13]

The English version seems to affirm May's Hawaiian identity; the Japanese, to underplay it. (Both writers had similar linguistic options in their respective languages.) The choices made also appear consistent with spatio-temporal frameworks related to May's absence from Hawaii (for Hawaiians) and to May's presence in Japan (for Japanese nationals). If we were to agree that the Japanese text was for an audience of Japanese nationals rather than Hawaiians, we may further agree that some differences in text organization resulted from variations in spatio-temporal relations and perceived information gaps. Whereas the former accounts for a reversal in propositional orders between the Japanese and English texts, the latter, as will be shown next, anticipates a similar result.

Information Gap Between Audiences

Why did the Japanese text open with excerpts from an interview dialogue about May's regular participation on a weekly television show? To be sure, various reasons are possible. If the readers are really avid fans of hers, however, they would already know about her television appearances. It could be that the writer anticipates reader lack of familiarity here. Although the Hawaiian television station on whose behalf the text was distributed[2] knows its viewers' background by virtue of the station's programming, no such knowledge would necessarily exist for an audience made up of Japanese nationals. Consequently, reference to May's television show, which is not devoted to her singing, may function to bridge perceived information gaps of the average Japanese reader. He or she might be unfamiliar with May as a pop singer, but being a television viewer, know her from the television show. In contrast, the English-language counterpart is on more knowledgeable grounds, and so the opening sentences can dispense with this information about May.

The early occurrence of dissimilarity in spatio-temporal relations and topic familiarity may profoundly affect the short text's overall organization. How significant the effects could be is unknown; nevertheless, because these differences were not included in Hinds's analysis, this oversight may weaken the conclusions his study makes. His conclusions seem less than convincing because his analysis ignores possible differences in purpose between the texts.

That the Japanese text does differ in purpose from the English seems apparent from how certain content differences relate to sociolinguistic factors between Japanese Americans and Japanese nationals. Before we demonstrate how sociolinguistic factors may have prompted different purposes for the Japanese text, a brief sketch of Japanese society may prove helpful.

Sociocultural Factors

Japanese social relations display high degrees of homogeneity, hierarchy, communality, and conservatism. These social aspects, conditioned by the country's island status, high population density, and centuries of self-imposed isolation from the world, cause the Japanese to be overly sensi-

---

[2] This information is based on the recollections of two Hawaiians who recalled that the *Kokiku* publication was produced in conjunction with the KIKU (Hawaii) television station.

tive to ethnic and physical differences. Because of this sensitivity to difference, it is virtually impossible for *gaijin* or foreigners ("best translated as 'outsider' "; Jeremy & Robinson, 1989, p. 29]) to enter "into full membership in Japanese society" (Reischauer, 1988, p. 399). Foreigners are so strongly associated as outsiders that some Japanese abroad may even refer to the native people there as *gaijin,* suggesting that it means more broadly *non-Japanese.* In effect, the foreigner in Japan is kept at "arm's length," and this distancing from the outsider, in turn, reinforces Japanese insularity. Although the forebears of the Japanese Americans of Hawaii came from Japan, they were mainly from the peasant class in the south of Japan (Yoshida, 1978/1909, p. 26)[3] and therefore were probably speakers of a low-prestige dialect. Japanese sense of social class and region, even today, may make it difficult to gain social acceptance on the Japanese mainland. It is thus very likely that a Hawaiian publication would assume the role of May Yokomoto's advocate when addressing Japanese nationals about this prized "hometown girl."

Professional entertainers, of course, are regularly promoted by their agents. In May Yokomoto's situation, however, it may require more than the usual promotion. Regardless of how lucrative or respectable her profession is in the west, to the traditional Japanese, May is a female engaged in less than esteemed employment. In this regard, it is not uncommon for young Japanese female pop stars to retire soon after marriage.[4] Besides her "problems" of gender and occupation, May is also an offspring of Japanese emigrants. Thus, the most effective promotion would most likely seek to offset May's negative status. Curiously enough, her promotion does not begin by announcing her musical achievements, but by establishing the following points:

1. May comes from a respectable family.
2. May comes from good stock (ethnic or national).
3. May is young and virginal but still sophisticated.
4. May likes Japan (a great deal).
5. May can be trusted as a foreigner.

To establish these points tactfully and in a few paragraphs is a formidable task indeed! Bearing this in mind, let us observe how it is done.

---

[3] Thanks go to Dee Yamashita, who pointed this out and provided the reference as well.

[4] Gundersen (1990) reports how Seiko (Matsuda), a Japanese popular female singer, after her marriage and a 5-year retreat, is trying to make a comeback not in Japan but in the United States. Seiko is quoted as saying: "I stayed home for two years and did house work and had a baby (Sayaka, now 3). Then I tried to come back. But Japan is very traditional. Women stay home after they are married." In her actions, Seiko, as the article notes, has "become the unwitting leader of a women's movement."

In a society stressing collectivist social interactions, one's responsibilities to others are ever paramount. In the Japanese text, May's parents seem respectable because they adhere to their parental duty:

English: [May's] parents are pleased that her Japanese has improved so much . . . [16]
Japanese: [May's parents] keep a close eye on this modern girl who speaks Japanese fluently. [2]

Such duty, being virtuous, is accorded high prominence in sentence rank. Furthermore, close parental supervision suggests that May is young and a "sweet thing" (*kawaii-mono* in Japanese), qualities consistent with a traditional female role:

Japanese: [May] is fresh as a young sweet-fish [*ayu*] . . . [3]

A principle of social psychology says that we tend to like those who like us. The author of the Japanese text, as compared to the one in English, tries to use this principle in May's favor. One can discern this subtle difference in what follows:

English: [May] is having a good time in Japan doing commercials, television, and radio work. [4]
Japanese: When [May] speaks of Japan, she continually uses the word tanoshii (happy). [4]

The Japanese version focuses on Japan as the source of May's happiness; whereas in English, Japan's contribution seems only coincidental. The choices made by the Japanese writer seem rather predictable, given the issue of foreignness for the Japanese nationals.[5]

This last item, along with the positive moral values that parental supervision, family cohesion, and virginity convey, serves the same social function as, for example, a *meishi* (calling card) does as a means of social introduction in Japanese society. Japanese social interaction crucially depends on a *meishi,* for the card informs one about another's occupation and thus his or her place in society. This information elicits the correct

[5] Hinds also recognized the Japanese foreignness syndrome, but he ignored the apparent attempt made by the Japanese (Hawaiian) text to counter this syndrome. Under Hinds's analysis, some of his "foreignness" items also appear in the English text, which means that the items may not be distinctive to Japanese culture. Consequently, this analysis has an advantage because its foreignness items appear only in the Japanese text, suggesting distinctive Japanese cultural features.

behavior relative to the hierarchical status (superior or inferior) of interlocutors, and more meaningfully, it evokes the appropriate stylistic level of Japanese (*keigo*) to be used. A *meishi* then can engender respect and deference from others, important social lubricants in Japanese society. As a result, in mainstream society, social interaction between strangers only properly begins with the presentation of one's *meishi*.

The next item engenders May's trust as a foreigner by stating overtly that she is extremely well liked:

Japanese: [May] is perfectly open and friendly. Because of this she is loved by everyone. [11–12]

On the other hand, the English text ignores her many possible friends in Japan and only perfunctorily mentions her personal characteristic of friendliness:

English: the friendly eighteen-year-old was kept busy by photo sessions . . . [2]

Finally, the Japanese text asserts that May comes from good stock, and therefore gratifies the Japanese desire for purity (Reischauer, 1988) or a Hawaiian author's ethnic pride:

English: ϕ
Japanese: [May] is a pure Hawaiian product . . . [24]

The last two items from the Japanese text could have been placed earlier, but they seem to function as reinforcers of the positive image of May. Moreover, tactfulness may dictate that these points be dispersed throughout the text.

The more one considers these contextual differences and realizes that both texts may have come from the "same set of notes" (Hinds, 1980, p. 124), the more the Japanese text appears to have ulterior motives. It is almost as if the Japanese writer exhorts the reader to accept May, a change from a focus on content to a focus on the addressee. Therefore these texts differ in purpose, which makes their comparison invalid for demonstrating culture-specific rhetorical patterns.

Because audience and purpose were insufficiently treated, the very factors that most determine patterns of discourse (Cooper & Matsuhashi, 1983; Odell, 1981), the researcher ended up trying to match noncomparable texts. An important point was missed: "Many [texts] employ one mode to fulfill the functions of another" (Britton, Burgess, Martin, McLeod, & Rosen, 1975, p. 5). Rather than a single type, most actual texts combine various genres (Beaugrande, 1984; Nida, 1984). This adds up to a flexibility of discourse that may be incompatible with a strict structural view.

Would it be unreasonable for the Japanese text to be nonlinear, assuming that it seeks May's social acceptance on the Japanese mainland? Who has not been tactful, indirect, or roundabout with emotional topics? The rhetoric of nearly any politician is a prime example. What is more, the "discovery" that Japanese writing may proceed along a baseline need arrest our attention only momentarily, because a full range of straight-line to circular discourse is possible in any language (Kaplan, 1987, p. 10). Examples of baseline theme in English can be found in advertising by which a product's value is reiterated throughout. Another example is Governor Cuomo's speech at the Democratic Convention in 1992 endorsing Bill Clinton for president. His speech, read as written discourse the next day in major newspapers, strategically used the phrase *We need Bill Clinton* or its derivatives as a baseline theme to promote his endorsement. Toner (1992, p. A1) reported that Cuomo endorsed Clinton "with far more spirit and passion than many had expected." It was Cuomo's rhetorical baseline theme that we contend helped make the speech impassioned and neutralized anxiety about Clinton's character.

Because *baseline theme* in English discourse was ignored entirely, it hardly can be assumed unique to the Japanese. Reviewers of cross-linguistic studies such as Clyne (1994) also ignore these vital points. He accepts too uncritically research purporting that Japanese written discourse is circular in style. He explains that baseline theme in Japanese is due to the lack of "advance organizers." Advance organizers, an author's early orienting statements about how the text is organized, even if rare in Japanese, are absent in the English version of the May Yokomoto article. Clyne (1994) similarly erred in accepting later cross-linguistic studies by Hinds that had mistaken a Japanese genre of poetic prose (term, Gray, 1990) for "exposition" (Donahue, 1990; Kubota, 1992). In such a genre, advance organizers are rare, as they would be in English, as well.

Cultural differences exist, but that fact does not lessen concern for the effects of bias on research results. Unless researchers are able to assume the frame of reference of those whom they study, and unless they attempt comprehensive discourse analysis (Hill & Larsen, 1983) whereby form and function are linked within their context of situation, efforts in contrastive studies of discourse analysis are likely to be inadequate. Without accounting for author intent and other factors through "rhetorical profiles" (Larson, 1984) or text subtypes (Grabe, 1987), contrastive rhetoric is likely to match noncomparable texts, as the May Yokomoto texts appear to demonstrate. Cultural differences are bound to occur considering that discourse consists of a multitude of features (e.g., Nida, 1984). However, a serious problem emerges when the matter involves logic or thinking patterns. Thus cautioned, one may avoid the potential pitfalls associated with classifying cultures according to their presumed discourse style, from linear to circular in form.

CONCLUSION

Continuing the theme of contextualism, this chapter endeavored to contrast functional versus structural approaches to language. A reanalysis of a previously published cross-linguistic study of Japanese and English revealed a confounding of variables. Moreover, a social tension between Japanese Americans and Japanese nationals was suggested to offer a more compelling account of the "structure" found in a related Japanese news article. At the same time, the value of a functional or sociolinguistic analysis over a structural one appeared manifest. In order to understand cross-cultural logics, their premises must be ascertained and that requires understanding the related context.

APPLICATION

Obtain Nida's (1984) journal article (at your library or through interlibrary loan) and determine his pattern of the use of *discourse structure* or *rhetorical structure* and its significance. The terms are traced for you and is summarized by the discourse schematics in Boxes 4.3 and 4.4. His use is unusual. (A suggested analysis is provided in Box 4.5 and is best understood after considering Nida's actual article.) Would his use of the terms support or contradict the view of structure developed in this chapter? Why?

Box 4.3: Discourse Schematic of Nida's Main Headings

[TITLE] "Rhetoric and Styles: A Taxonomy of Structures and Functions" (Nida, 1984)

[MAIN HEADINGS]

INTRODUCTION

> ". . . As a means of putting the various elements of this approach to rhetoric and style in proper perspective it seems best to treat the **structures** and then their **functions.**"

RHETORICAL FEATURES

FUNCTIONS OF DISCOURSE

STYLE

[end]

Box 4.4: Discourse Schematic of Lexical Links

The paragraphs in Box 4.4 are numbered sequentially and are separated by dotted lines. Space limitations required including only the most essential paragraphs—those at the beginning and at the end. Related terms appear in the order as they did in the original source and are placed in the schematic to form "chains."

"Rhetoric and Styles: A Taxonomy of Structures and Functions" (Nida, 1984)

Abstract	rhetorical structures		
	rhetorical structure		
			rhetorical features
1			features of rhetoric
			rhetorical features
			such features
	discourse structure		
2			
3			features of rhetoric
4			rhetorical features
			rhetorical features
			these features
			such features
	structures		
Heading			Rhetorical Features
5			rhetorical features
6			rhetorical features
			rhetorical features
65	rhetorical structures		
		rhetorical devices	
		rhetorical devices	
		rhetorical devices	
66		rhetorical devices	
71 (last)			rhetorical forms
	rhetorical structures		

APPLICATION (CONTINUED)

1. How does grammatical structure differ from discourse structure?
2. How does the issue of *discourse structure* have special importance to cross-cultural studies of discourse?
3. Why does topic familiarity of an audience impact a study in contrastive discourse that compares a news article written in two different languages?
4. What important variables are related to a cross-linguistic study of a news article, or actually, any writing?
5. How did discourse analysis reveal a strategy of discourse followed by Nida (1984) in his research article?
6. Why can we say that that is a strategy of discourse?

Box 4.5: The Semantics of the Term *Structure*

Analysis reveals that Nida restricted the term *discourse* (or *rhetorical*) *structure(s)* to the margins of his study. *Feature(s)* is then substituted for the meat of it. Box 4.3 shows how *structures,* a key term found in the title of the research paper and one used at the juncture between the Introduction and the body of the paper, is substituted by *features* for use in a main heading of his paper, unlike that of his other key term, *functions.* This instance suggests that Nida treats *structures* and *features* synonymously. At such a main juncture point, one must wonder why the substitution is made. The answer seems related to the issue of linguistic *structure* as a metaphor for discourse. This reason gains support from the apparent pattern that emerges in the use of Nida's terms.

Box 4.4 traces some, but not all, of the relevant lexical (word) chaining indicating the restriction placed on *rhetorical structure(s)* or *discourse structure.* The paragraphs in Box 4.4 are numbered sequentially and are separated by dotted lines. Space limitations required including only the most essential paragraphs—those at the beginning and at the end. Related terms appear in the order as they did in the original source and are placed in the schematic to form "chains." *Rhetorical features* is actually synonymous with *rhetorical structures* in Nida's paper. Their visual separation is integral to the point being made about the avoidance of *rhetorical structure* or *discourse structure.*

Perhaps because *structures* appears in the title, it also starts off the Abstract. (The abstract of a research paper should not be confused with that part of the same name in Labov's natural narrative, as met previously.) However, *structure(s)* seems to skirt the main discussion. It reappears at the end of the Introduction only to be substituted until the very end of the paper. Interestingly, the substituted words *features, devices,* and *structures* appear to be used in ascending order of rigidity or concreteness. Although *features* could denote both abstract and concrete aspects of discourse, Nida does appear to use *features* in a more restricted sense,

(continued)

that having a sense of concreteness—*structures* (see Box 4.3). Another notable item is the absence of *rhetorical features* in the last paragraph despite its prevalence throughout the main discussion of the research paper. *Devices* can be seen as a transitional item to return smoothly back to reuse of *structures,* initial term of the paper. Because Nida's substitution for *structure* follows a pattern, it appears motivated.

Nida does use the term *discourse structure,* and which also appears synonymous with *rhetorical structure.* Moreover, he makes clear that he is involved with discourse by virtue of his first sentence of his abstract ("A satisfactory study of discourse calls for . . .") and the first sentence of his introduction ("Recent linguistic analyses of discourse . . .").

In Nida's defense, it is hard to resist applying the term *structure* to discourse. A discourse, at first, may appear to be loosely grouped sentences (or utterances) but can reveal through analysis tightly knit networks of internal elements. Such revelations resonant with beauty to the analyst. *Structure* may best mirror such feeling. However, linguistics is already steeped in talk about *structures* related to grammar and the sentence. To apply the term *structure* to discourse could lead one to unwittingly assume far more about discourse than what is actually allowed. That may not necessarily apply in Nida's case because of his apparent strategy of keeping the term outside of his main discussion.

Could the mere use of *discourse structure* lead to overestimating how much discourse is actually structured? Already this suggestion has been made herein and elsewhere (e.g., Donahue, 1990). As all things are relative, research crucially depends on the standard upon which comparisons are made. If the standard style of English is viewed as heavily "structured," then obviously matching language/discourse will be that much harder to find. For example, model paragraphing in traditional rhetoric (= written composition) has fallen in disrepute for that very reason (Donahue, 1990). The seriousness of the matter will become more apparent by considering the functional reanalysis made in this chapter of a previous cross-linguistic study of English and Japanese.

5

ASIAN CONFLICT: NORTH AND SOUTH KOREA FACE OFF AT THE UN

Korea is the "Cold War's last divided country" (Hammes, 1992, p. 4), a divide created by settlements after World War II (Eberstadt & Banister, 1992) and by the two sides never having completed peace accords for the Korean War. Because one or both nations have near-nuclear capability and their combined area is nearby to three major power centers—China, Japan, and Russia—the Korean question could strain or even rupture the "new world order" (Eberstadt, 1992). Aggravating this situation is North Korea's reputation as the "hermit kingdom," a seclusion that continues even today after a change in leadership (NHK News, 1995).

"North Korea has been one of the most closed societies on earth. Foreigners had been [once] barred from entering the country and North Korea's people have had virtually no exposure to the outside world" (Manning, 1992, p. 6). Even the South, though ever vigilant about reconciliation, forbids its citizens from communicating to their relatives in the North (Hammes, 1992), and had sanctions in the past against reading and talking about the North (Gittelsohn, 1992). As a result, some Korean married couples have been tragically separated since 1950, the start of the Korean War (Breen, 1992). The prime ministers of the two countries did not meet again until 1990, while the then North Korean president still refused to meet his counterpart from the South (*The Economist,* 1992). Hence, both countries' admission into the UN in 1991, after long-held opposition by China and North Korea, marked an important new chapter in this story.

A Case for Discourse Analysis

A turning point in the Korean conflict came in 1988 when, for the first time, both sides spoke at the UN together (Lewis, 1988, p. A6). Their speeches, therefore, offer an intriguing study concerning international communication at the UN. Those who spoke there were Roh Tae Woo, President of South Korea (Republic of Korea) and Kang Sok Ju, Foreign Minister of North Korea (Democratic People's Republic of Korea). (Hereafter the official country names are dispensed in favor of their common appellations.)

The fact that the North's top leader, Kim Il Sung, chose not to attend suggests continued conflict. How would the North and South present its views and that of the other? What emphasis would be placed on reunification if any? Would they concentrate on the so-called Korean Question or take up other issues instead? What political bloc would they align themselves with, or would they simply project independence? Would either of them seek leadership of other developing countries? These are just a few of the questions that spring to mind about the situation.

Probably, no two discourse analyses will be identical in procedure or content. Each discourse must be treated in its own uniqueness. The infinite combinations of language make this so. Different purposes of the analyst will also contribute, such as that for instruction. Toward an instructional purpose, an excerpt from the South Korean president is read first and then responses are made to questions that follow. Let us begin by reading the content of Box 5.1.

Box 5.1: South Korea: President Roh Addresses the UN

1. Forty-three years ago, as the Second World War came to an end, the world was taking steps towards the creation of the United Nations, with great hope for lasting peace. The new body was to be entrusted with charting a new international order of peace and stability.
2. In my country the end of the Second World War gave rise to overwhelming jubilation and hope as the Korean people were liberated from the yoke of colonial rule and recovered the land which had been theirs for thousands of years. The joy of liberation, however, soon turned to despair over the tragic division of our homeland.
3. As a matter of convenience, in the process of disarming the defeated colonial forces, a line of artificial division was drawn through the mid-section of the Korean peninsula along the 38th parallel. The decision to divide our land was made against the will of the Korean people, dictating the fate of the nation in the decades to come. Overnight, this cruel division turned brother against brother and plunged the Korean peninsula into a violent storm of the Cold War.

(continued)

4. On a peaceful Sunday morning in June 1950, war broke out on the Korean peninsula, and soon the whole nation was in flames. Over the next three years, tens of thousands of young people from 20 countries entered the war, and eventually over three million lives fell victim to the clash of ideologies. The war also reduced nearly everything on the peninsula to ashes.
5. Experiencing battle as a volunteer soldier still wearing my high-school uniform, I saw the young and innocent die in the flames of war and came to long for peace and reconciliation. I also came to believe that we must make all possible efforts to end the division and confrontation which were causing such great suffering in our nation.
6. The conflict ceased in 1953 with the signing of an armistice, but this did not bring about genuine peace. A state of tension and confrontation between the two parts of Korea has persisted ever since. Even though many seasons have come and gone and the world has changed dramatically over the decades, this hostile confrontation along the Korean Armistice Line has remained frozen in time and continues to be a source of danger which could trigger hostilities involving the whole world.
7. Beyond these political and strategic implications, the human costs of this stand-off have been enormous. Millions of family members—fathers and mothers, husbands and wives, brothers and sisters—have remained separated between the North and the South since the war and have been unable to exchange even letters or telephone calls. The emotional strains caused by this situation run deep in both the North and the South of Korea.
8. Is there no way out of this impasse? I stand here today to answer this question with a message of hope. We must henceforth do everything possible to hasten the coming of the springtime of peace and reconciliation on the Korean peninsula.
9. In this connection, I wish to welcome, on behalf of the Government and people of the Republic of Korea, the timely decision of the General Assembly to adopt the agenda item entitled "Promotion of peace, reconciliation and dialogue in the Korean peninsula."
10. I should also like to congratulate you, Sir, on your election as President of the General Assembly. I hope that this session of the General Assembly will produce fruitful results.

Questions

1. How do you feel toward Roh after reading this passage?
2. How would you explain your feeling?
3. How effective was the passage to you? Why?
4. How is the passage organized by using Labov's narrative model?
5. What word or words in the address function as a trigger for the narrative format?
6. Why may Labov's narrative format be more applicable than S(PR)E in the present case? Or is it?

7. Paragraph 5 could be eliminated without disruption to the narrative. Why does the speaker use it and how does it function?
8. If the entire address consisted of only Paragraphs 1 through 7, what segment could be said to function as a frame for the discourse?
9. Why do you think Roh did not begin his address with Paragraphs 9 and 10, if allowing for a change in wording? (In which case, he may have begun with the words *I wish to welcome* or something to that effect.)
10. Who do you think was the colonialist power referred to in Paragraphs 2 and 3? Why do you think that country is unnamed?
11. What difference in meaning is there between the words *country, nation,* and the speaker's choice of *homeland*?

THE CRUCIAL BEGINNING

Framing and Formatting

The beginning of a communication may be the most crucial, for a message requires attention if it is to be understood. Some college professors refuse to read a thesis any further if begun incoherently (Easton, 1982). In Roh's case, he uncharacteristically begins with the matter at hand—not with ritualistic or ceremonial statements often found in UN speeches. His first words are "Forty-three years ago," obviously meaning 1945. Thus, he begins with a temporal frame, a universal at least as a progression in time. Chronology underlies two basic formats—narrative and S(PR)E (Jordan, 1984). In the present case, however, Labov's natural narrative appears more applicable. It not only seems more like a "story," but it also contains an *abstract* in the form of the first two paragraphs.

Besides indicating that this story, a form triggered by "forty-three years ago" (and other elements), is about the UN and Korea, the first two paragraphs appear to achieve three important objectives by (a) distinguishing two sets of experience (the UN's and Korea's), (b) reminding the audience of the UN's purpose, and (c) stating the most significant attribute of Korea—its division. Note how tactfully these points are established within the framework of this story. In other words, they do not call undue attention to themselves. This abstract, then, establishes a remarkable beginning for the speaker.

The *orientation* follows in Paragraph 3, in giving further detail about the division of Korea, a convenience for the Big Powers but a tragedy for the Koreans themselves. After that, the *complicating event* of war (Paragraphs 4 and 5), its *resolution* and *evaluation* (Paragraph 6) occur. However, evaluation shows that a true resolution did not occur, for the war's end did not have the desired result. Thus, a new *complicating event* was created (a persistent state of tension), the extent of which is mentioned in Paragraph 7. Just before, a tie back occurs by focusing on the whole world, the subject of how he first began his speech.

Refocusing on the world reinstates his prefatory point: The world cannot assume that Korea has enjoyed the same experiences (dramatic changes). This tie back also signals a possible closure and a switch in perspective from Korea to its people. Switching to the Korean people helps him explain the extent of the (new) complicating event. Psychologically, we desire a resolution. Roh uses this expectation by asking rhetorically, "Is there no way out of this impasse?" to effectively involve the audience.

A Reformulation of S(PR)E

A question arises about the applicability of S(PR)E to the present speech address. The opportunity is now taken to reformulate S(PR)E. S(PR)E and the natural narrative, as mentioned before, are both chronologically based. What separates them is that the natural narrative has an *abstract* and an optional *coda.* (Some specialists would also treat the abstract optionally). However, if the remaining four parts are aligned with S(PR)E, they appear essentially identical. Consequently, we will reformulate S(PR)E to have an optional *preVIEW* in this way: V[S(PR)E], pronounced "vee-spree." V functions as a "viewer" not only to preview or frame content but also to gain attention through titles, opening lines, or summaries. By this change, we can come closer to a universal format model. This new format could apply to news report articles by which V includes the function of the summary lead. Other types of writing also may have a kind of summary lead or preview. Research articles, for instance, often begin with an "abstract," a segment distinguished from its namesake under the natural narrative. The former is far more complex and involved than the latter. Some "expository" writing also may preview its content early on. As for Roh's address, V[S(PR)E] has the same applicability. Lastly, note again that V, S, and E are optional depending largely on the genre and knowledge of the audience.

Word Choices

To help Roh further capture the attention of his audience, he makes apt word choices, most notably in terms of *human interest* (term, Hart, 1984) and *natural phenomena.* Human interest is "an adaptation of Rudolph Flesch's notion that multiple reference to human beings gives discourse a lively, down-home quality" (Hart, 1984, p. 17). In this category, Hart includes vocabulary related to kinship terms and personal pronouns. Adapting further than this, we also add entities or objects closely associated with their owners, such as a child's toy or a grandparent's rocker. Let us observe Roh's word choices, the numerals of which refer to the paragraph:

Human Interest

2. in *my* country
2. land that had been *theirs;* division of *our homeland*
3. turned *brother* against *brother*, divide *our* land
5. wearing *my high school uniform*
5. the *young* and *innocent* (= children)
7. *family* members—*fathers* and *mothers*; *husbands* and *wives*, *brothers* and *sisters*
7. *letters* or *telephone calls*

Natural Phenomena

3. a violent *storm* of the cold war
4. nation was in *flames*
4. peninsula to *ashes*
6. many *seasons* have come and gone
6. the Korean Armistice has remained *frozen* in time
8. We must . . . do everything [for a] *springtime* of peace

By these terms, Roh weaves a human commonality theme that emerges in Paragraph 7:

> the human costs of this standoff have been enormous. Millions of family members have remained separated. . . . The emotional strain caused by this situation run deep in both the North and South of Korea.

The costs are not in terms of material goods but in terms of people: Families have been torn apart. This description can speak to everyone, for we all have a sense of family. We also have a sense of country that gains expression in how Korea was put into "flames" and the "peninsula into ashes" at the cost of many "young and innocent" lives. Roh reports as a first-hand witness having volunteered for service while "still wearing [his] high school uniform." Roh then not only utilizes cognitive and affective devices for audience appeal but also the appeal of an eyewitness account by a man of character (one who volunteered for service).

After getting the audience to ponder the Korean impasse, Roh then situates his UN presence as timely and purposeful by asserting that he has the answer, "a message of hope." At this crescendo, Roh curiously brakes his stride by giving thanks to the UN and paying tribute to the President of the General Assembly. He surely is sincere but no doubt these remarks are strategically placed. First, by applying the brakes, the speaker asserts control over his pace of delivery. Having taken the audience up and now down, he sets them in store for those points he may consider climactic. Second, creating a lull when the audience least expects it may engender continued interest. Finally, there are no easy solutions for the Korean Question. If he were to unveil his "message of hope" after an early audience build up, disappointment may likely result. He needs to put his message in perspective and will need time to do so. By gaining audience attention early, he can build up his case in a measured way. For the rest of Roh's address see the contents of Box 5.2.

In terms of framing and formatting, Roh's address appears complex; however, once it is broken down, discernable patterns emerge. One way to proceed is first by grouping the paragraphs into blocks. You can soon see that Paragraphs 11 through 15 and 16 through 22 form two blocks: the first, a preview of sorts; the second, the situation of South Korea. Paragraphs 23 through 26 form the problem, although problematic elements do not emerge until the block's last segments. Paragraphs 27 through 38 form the response of various proposals. Finally, a two-layered evaluation is found consisting of Paragraphs 39 through 47 and Paragraphs 48 through 51. The first of these layers concerns how Korean unification is tied up with relations with the outside world. The second layer evaluates world problems at large. The parts of V[S(PR)E] are indistinct due to some conformity to the genre of UN discourse, the elaborate story early in the speech, and the Korean conflict itself. For example, Roh appears to proceed gingerly on the topic of North Korea, for he does not mention that nation by name until Paragraph 7 and then not again until the 27th. This appears diplomatic. The effect is rather roundabout, but the V[S(PR)E] format, interestingly, still seems evident. Especially in such a case, the V[S(PR)E] format aids coherency and forward thrust. Further comment is curtailed by space. However, we trust that macrolevel organization, such as V[S(PR)E], has received sufficient attention thus far. Discussion now goes on to other discourse strategies, some of which will relate to this overall formatting. Box 5.2 ought to be read before continuing.

The Image of South Korea

As Roh established his "credentials as an eyewitness" in the first part of his address, he similarly attempts to establish his country, South Korea, as meritorious of UN help. After indicating peaceful trends around the world (Paragraphs 11–15), he suggests that South Korea is peace-loving, open, and even inspirational (Paragraphs 16–21), as well as harmonious (Paragraphs 22–23). In short, Roh creates trust in himself, South Korea, the UN, and world conditions upon which to build his plans for the reunification of Korea. However, even before he presents his plans, he seeks optimistic thinking (Paragraphs 25–26) and argues for exchange and cooperation (Paragraph 27). Therefore, he is led to reiterate his past calls for ceasing hostilities and other proposals (Paragraph 28), actions that cast him as a peacemaker.

Box 5.2: South Korean President Roh, Part 2

11. In the world today we can see movements towards openness and reconciliation. The cold-war conflicts which have dominated the international scene since the end of the Second World War have begun to surrender to the power of human reason and common decency. [Human]kind's expectations are changing from confrontation to coexistence, from antagonism to reconciliation. I join all the members of this Assembly in welcoming these trends.
12. I should also like to express my gratitude and respect to the Secretary General, Mr. Perez de Cuellar, for his insight and leadership, which have helped achieve a cease-fire in the eight-year-old Gulf war.
13. Thanks to the Secretary General's role, all of us have greater confidence and expectations regarding this bulwark of peace. The Nobel Peace Prize just awarded to the United Nations Peace-keeping Forces is a testimony to this.
14. In Afghanistan, Cambodia, Namibia and the Western Sahara, steps are being taken towards peaceful resolution of outstanding conflicts.
15. Furthermore, it is highly encouraging that, through their summit meetings, President Reagan and General Secretary Gorbachev have been able to reduce this number of deadly weapons capable of annihilating [human]kind.
16. I have come here in the spirit of "harmony and progress," the theme for the Seoul Olympiad, which ended exactly two weeks ago. The 24th Olympic Games were a great festival of co-operation and understanding in which young people from 160 countries gathered together despite differences of ideology, race and religion. Furthermore, the East and the West met in sporting arenas for the first time in 12 years at the Seoul Olympiad.
17. As one of the most successful Olympiads ever, the Seoul Games have instilled in all of us the hope that at last peace and reconciliation are beginning to spread throughout the world. Still, it is ironic that that wonderful festival of peace should be held in a land where the danger of conflict still looms large. But this also gives us great hope for the future. In fact the historical drama I am referring to must be seen as a part of the larger global development that is emerging from [human] aspirations for peace and common prosperity.
18. I should like to take this opportunity to express my gratitude to the peoples of all the countries whose participation and support helped make the Seoul Olympiad a successful and safe festival for all [human]kind.
19. Only a generation ago the Korean nation lay in ruins and was shackled with great suffering, hunger and poverty. We have overcome these adversities and made great progress through diligent work mixed with blood and tears. We are quite proud of our achievements, which we believe have contributed to releasing the well-springs of harmony among diverse peoples. It is also our sincere wish that these achievements offer hope and courage to all people in developing nations who are struggling against similar circumstances.
20. Only three decades ago we were a poor, agrarian society dependent on other nations' help for survival. We were able to transform ourselves into a

(continued)

newly industrializing nation only through our people's great desire to achieve, together with a passion for education.

21. We also took advantage of an open and competitive political and economic system which allows individuals to achieve their highest potential. [Human]kind's inviolate rights and inborn creativity are essential elements for making societal progress.

22. International trade also has played an important role in our rapid economic growth. As the 12th largest trading nation in the world, we are keenly aware of the fact that the growth of world trade has helped promote the rise in income and employment of trading partners. In this, the Republic of Korea has been especially fortunate. So, although the world brought national division and other trials to Korea, it also made it possible for us to grow and make substantial progress in many areas.

23. There are undoubtedly many problems facing [human]kind today. But it can be discerned, nevertheless, that progress is being made towards reconciliation, peace and prosperity.

24. In order for [humankind's] hope to survive and progress to be realized, we must spare no effort to promote openness and mutual exchanges, co-operation and reconciliation. There is no alternative. Isolation and confrontation will bring only calamity and suffering to every corner of this global village.

25. As far as the Korean people are concerned, we believe we have been able to progress through international co-operation and openness toward others. That is why we are looking to the future with optimism and confidence that we will eventually achieve democracy, prosperity and national reunification for all Koreans on the peninsula. There is vitality in every corner of the Republic of Korea today as well as in every individual, thanks to the freedom protected by our social system. I am sure that this new vitality will accelerate our progress and bring nearer the springtime of peace and reconciliation on the Korean peninsula.

26. Today our world stands at an important turning-point that delineates one era from another. It has been said that the only thing that does not change is the inevitability of change itself. The world of confrontation and conflict is giving way to a world of détente, a trend which is taking place right here at the United Nations. Serious efforts are also commencing to bring peace and the relaxation of tension to the Korean peninsula, one of the last vestiges of the cold war.

27. The distrust left behind by the Korean war gave rise to the confrontation between North and South Korea. During the 35 years since the Armistice Agreement, enormous military forces have continued to confront each other across the armistice line. In order to put an end to this hostile stand-off, there is no alternative but to build mutual trust by engaging in exchange and co-operation, and destroying the wall that separates us. To achieve this, we need a fresh approach. And that is precisely what I unveiled on 7 July this year.

28. I have declared that the North and the South of Korea should immediately end all forms of hostile, confrontational relations. For instance, we should im mediately cease publicly attacking each other. I have made it clear that we are determined to pursue a relationship of partnership with North Korea. Our cultural and historical unity demands that we devote ourselves to the pursuit

(continued)

of common prosperity and mutual well-being for all Koreans. In the same declaration, I proposed that we allow not only the reunion of millions of separated family members but also free exchanges among political, economic and religious leaders as well as ordinary citizens. Also, I have taken concrete steps to pave the way for free trade between the northern and southern parts of Korea.

29. We must transform the North-South Korean relationship so that we can reconnect every roadway, whether a major highway or a little path, linking the two sides which remain disconnected now. Then we could be enabled to go on to develop our common land by combining our human, technological and financial resources.

30. If there may be any difficulties for North Koreans in opening their doors just now, I believe that we could work together towards this by building a "city of peace" in the demilitarized zone. Within such a city, family members who have remained separated for more than three decades could freely reunite. Broad trade and other kinds of exchanges could also be facilitated by establishing in the new "city of peace" such venues as a home for national culture, a center for scholarly exchanges and a trade center.

31. Similarly, I stated in the same 7 July declaration that we are determined to end confrontation with North Korea in our external relations. It is our sincere hope that North Korea will participate fully in the international community. Doing so can only benefit the North Korean people, not harm them. Within the world community, the North and the South must recognize each other and co-operate to promote the common interest of the entire nation.

32. It is our wish that our allies and friends will contribute to the progress and opening of North Korea by engaging Pyongyang in expanding relations. It is also our position that those socialist countries with close ties to North Korea continue to maintain positive relations and co-operate with North Korea even as they improve their relations with us.

33. The pursuit of mutual respect and prosperity through increasing co-operation, however, is not our ultimate goal. It is a requisite process we must go through in order to build the relationship of trust necessary for the nation's reunification. When such a relationship is firmly established, we can look forward to realizing peaceful reunification.

34. On the anniversary of our national liberation last August, I proposed to North Korean President Kim Il Sung that we hold direct talks. Since the peninsula became divided, both sides have put forth many different proposals concerning peace and reunification. But what is necessary now is that the leaders of both sides who hold the ultimate responsibilities in their areas meet together without setting any pre-conditions. We must initiate discussions with a new spirit of openness and explore together possible avenues of compromise acceptable to both sides. We must find a common ground to build institutions for peace and create a single national community.

35. Hence, I have taken particular notice of the fact that President Kim Il Sung has reacted to my proposal for a North-South summit meeting. I hope I can visit Pyongyang as soon as possible. When the summit meeting does take place, I would like to propose that we agree to a declaration of non-aggression or non-use of force in order better to construct a framework for mutual trust and security.

(continued)

36. In order to end the military confrontation which has lasted for more than three decades now and build a new relationship dedicated to shared peace and prosperity, we need to create a new basic framework for progress. Creating such a framework, of course, can be accomplished only at the level of direct contact between the leaders of the North and the South.

37. In this connection, I want to make it absolutely clear that even before a nonaggression declaration is made with the northern side, the Republic of Korea will never use force first against the North. We cannot expect durable peace on the Korean peninsula without ending the current military confrontation.

38. I propose that at our summit meeting, we discuss sincerely and resolve all the problems raised by either or both sides with regard to disarmament, arms control and other military matters. We must also explore institutional structures for peaceful relations, mutual contacts and co-operative ventures and, of course, ways of bringing about reunification. We can at the same meeting also search for concrete ways to transform the Armistice Agreement into a permanent peace arrangement.

39. Clearly, the problems between the northern and southern Korean sides must be dealt with and resolved by the independent efforts of the Korean people themselves. But due to Korea's geopolitical situation, the problem of durable peace on the Korean peninsula cannot be considered in total isolation from its relations with the surrounding nations.

40. In order for durable peace to prevail on the Korean peninsula, it is necessary not only for the northern and the southern Korean sides to reach rapprochement, but for both of them to build and maintain more rational and normal relations with all the nations that have an interest in peace on the Korean peninsula.

41. The Republic of Korea will continue to maintain and expand close cooperation with its traditional allies and friends, including the United States. In particular, we will continue our consultations and common efforts for the maintenance of peace and stability on the peninsula. In parallel with such efforts, we are also taking positive steps to improve our relations with countries such as the People's Republic of China, the Union of Soviet Socialist Republics, and many Eastern European nations with which we have had only remote relationships due to our ideological differences.

42. By conducting normal relations with one another under the principles of equality and mutual respect, all the nations of the world will contribute to mutual prosperity. This also serves the cause of world peace because, through dialogue and mutual understanding, nations can work to eliminate sources of conflict while cementing friendship and partnership.

43. It is from this perspective that I welcome as an encouraging development the fact that socialist countries such as China and the Soviet Union are showing a forward-looking attitude in recent months concerning mutual exchanges and co-operation with the Republic of Korea in a number of fields. I find it significant that China, a nation which traditionally was a good neighbor of Korea, is moving to overcome the wall of separation that has lasted for nearly half a century and is expanding its mutual exchanges and co-operation with the Republic of Korea. I have also taken careful notice of the positive signals being made by General Secretary Gorbachev of the Soviet Union.

(continued)

44. At the same time, we will continue to deepen our co-operative relationships with developing countries and, in fact, we intend to strengthen our political, economic and cultural ties with many nations to the third world and the Movement of Non-Aligned Countries. It is our intense desire to do all that we can to share our developmental experience and technical resources with the developing nations. To be able to contribute to the development of the third world nations would give immense satisfaction to the Korean people who are themselves a developing nation.

45. The Asia-Pacific region is marching forward towards a new era of prosperity. This is taking place thanks to the strengthening of international co-operation as well as the strong will of the region's peoples to achieve progress based on their infinite potential and dynamism. Within the Pacific Rim, north-east Asia constitutes the seat of age-old oriental civilization. Yet that region has challenged world peace as it has endured a century of conflicts, namely the Sino-Japanese War, the Russo-Japanese War, the Pacific War, and the Korean War. It is my belief that without peace in north-east Asia, there cannot be peace in the world, and that without co-operation among the area's nations, there cannot commence an era of Pacific prosperity.

46. Therefore, I take this opportunity to propose a consultative conference for peace among the United States of America, the Union of Soviet Socialist Republics, the People's Republic of China and Japan as well as North and South Korea, in order to lay a solid foundation for durable peace and prosperity in north-east Asia.

47. Such a conference can deal with a broad range of issues concerning peace, stability, progress and prosperity within the area. To be sure, it may not be easy to gather these States together at the same table because of the outstanding differences in ideology, social systems and policies among them. But I am sure we can overcome such difficulties if we all acknowledge the fact that we are inseparable partners in the pursuit of peace and prosperity. The realization of this proposal will certainly create an international environment more conducive to peace in Korea and reunification of the peninsula.

48. Looking forward to the twenty-first century, I sense that a new chapter of human history is unfolding. Indeed, changes are taking place in this global village, and [human]kind is increasingly guided by tenets of reason and wisdom rather than by ideological obsessions. Nonetheless, there is no guarantee that [human]kind will not some day be plunged into the whirlwind of global conflict. If we are to avoid this tragedy, openness, peace and co-operation are the only options left to us.

49. I look forward to this new chapter of history wherein peaceful efforts towards co-operation and progress will be the norm rather than the exception. Likewise, the time will certainly come on the Korean peninsula when the brotherhood of all Koreans, North and South, will triumph over our differences, leaving the Korean nation free of tension, conflict and the threat of war. I believe that the present ordeal will finally come to an end and the blessing of peace and reunification will be bestowed upon the Korean people who, incidentally, have never attempted invasion of a foreign country throughout their five millenniums of history.

(continued)

50. Upon the day when swords are beaten into ploughshares on the Korean peninsula, the opportunity for lasting world peace will be strengthened. Believing that this day will come, I will continue my efforts, together with my 60 million compatriots, in seeking lasting harmony in our nation. This is a solemn responsibility of my generation and the dream and passion of our younger generations in Korea. Through concerted efforts, we are determined to overcome whatever difficulties we may encounter. As the most successful Olympics ever held just concluded in a land once dominated by conflict and poverty, so too the day will come when the wall of separation on the Korean peninsula will fall and harmony will prevail.

51. Lastly, I earnestly appeal to you all to support and encourage the aspirations of all the Korean people who, as expressed by the theme song of the Seoul Olympics, so strongly desire to go "hand in hand over the walls" and realize the goals of peace and reunification. May I also assure you that the Korean people will demonstrate that they are worthy of your support, as we build a unified, peaceable nation on the peninsula.

PROPOSALS BY A PEACEMAKER AND STATESMAN[1]

Roh had recently been elected president and was making his first presidential speech abroad. His speech already seems to have projected himself as a leader knowledgeable of his people while establishing his character and intent. He now can focus on proposals for solving the problem of the two Koreas. His proposals appear systematic and well conceived for both domestic and international affairs. Making such proposals displays good statesmanship.

A pivotal point for the South is trust between the Koreas. Having been once invaded by the North, trust is a reasonable issue to expect. Roh proposes to develop a relationship of trust by (Paragraphs 28–32):

- reuniting separated families between North and South,
- exchanging political and other kinds of leaders,
- trading freely between the Koreas,

[1] Ironically, Roh, the "father of democracy" for South Korea, was indicted in 1995 for political graft on immense scale (CNBC Asia News, 1995). Regardless of his culpability, that has little to do with most of this analysis, particularly related to speech and language skills such as delivery, organization, and so on. Where it could have bearing is in the evaluation of his proposals regarding North Korea. And even there, it would have to be shown that the graft in question was already committed, appreciably affected the "Korean Question," and was known by the North Koreans at the time. Finally, we are most interested in the relation between speech, speaker, and audience. How Roh's projected audience reacted cannot be undone by later events. That some of the elite media reacted positively is historical fact and unchangeable.

- building a "city of peace" in the demilitarized zone as a trial run of reunification, and
- recognizing each other in the outside world.

These items seem to follow chronologically the order in which Roh proposed them previously. Yet, it is only later that Roh proposed holding direct talks between himself and Kim Il Sung, the then North Korean president. As Kim refused to meet a South Korean president, one must wonder how Roh's previous proposals could ever be actualized.

Parallel to his roundabout approach to North Korea mentioned earlier, Roh's proposals appear particularly so. As if part of a mammalian mating ritual, Roh seems to encircle his counterpart closer and closer until springing his proposal about direct presidential talks. As Roh states, "We must find a common ground to build institutions for peace and create a single national community" (Paragraph 34). At the same time, Roh acknowledges that "both sides have put forth many different proposals concerning peace and reunification" (Paragraph 34). Here, Roh also displays both sincerity and generosity by his series of proposals and his acknowledgment of efforts by the North as well.

Roh also shows vision in that he already knows his next move if direct talks were to happen: proposing a nonaggression pact with the North (Paragraph 35). This proposal mirrors the leader's methodical steps of before and is a natural progression. He is also careful to say that South Korea would "never use force first against the North" (Paragraph 37) nevertheless. He shows further thinking by revealing his proposed agenda at such direct talks to include disarmament, arms control, and completing unfinished peace accords of the Korean War (Paragraph 38). Thus, both Roh and the South appear sincere in having well-developed plans and peaceful intent.

Acting the astute leader, Roh shows sensitivity to the effects of reunification on international relations. He recognizes that reunification "cannot be considered in total isolation from . . . relations with the surrounding nations" (Paragraph 39). Of course, it could not be without the agreement of China, whose Security Council veto had long squashed moves by South Korea to have its own UN seat. He reiterates South Korea's alignment with the United States and its allies but also intends to improve ties with the communist world (Paragraphs 40–43). He then shifts attention to the Third World, offering South Korea's expertise and technical resources to them. At this point, Roh has covered the entire world except one entity—Japan.

DIPLOMATIC EUPHEMISM

Relation with Japan is a sensitive topic, owing to past conflicts. First, he kindly left unmentioned Japan's identity as the colonialist power in Paragraph 2. Later, he seems to speak euphemistically about that nation, as part of Northeast Asia (Paragraph 45). This region "challenged world peace [for a] century" (Paragraph 45), a point that the expansionist Japan figured most prominently. Indeed the first mention of Japan is war related in Roh's naming of the Sino–Japanese War, the Russo–Japanese War, and the Pacific War. Finally, we can fathom his reason for caution: His proposed peace conference between the United States, the Soviet Union, China, the two Koreas, and Japan (Paragraph 46).

Nevertheless, no other mention is made of Japan despite its economic dominance of the region. Because of its explicit absence, its inclusion in the peace conference seems sudden. Yet, Japan's inclusion is apparently for its past transgressions: The Asia–Pacific region has been the site of past war. World War II memories of Japan are still fresh in the minds of Southeast Asians, who sometimes peer suspiciously at their island neighbor across the Japan Sea. Moreover, Japanese relations are complicated due to past enslavement of Koreans, their discrimination in Japan, and certain terrorist attacks launched by North Koreans from Japan. Roh must have felt ambivalent toward Japan as shown by this euphemistic treatment in the speech. Still, their future destinies appear bound up together, a realization that may inspire reconciliation.

CLOSURE

In closing his speech, Roh appears as ever the optimist by expressing enthusiasm for the 21st century and hope for a union of all Koreans (Paragraphs 48–50). He finishes by dedicating himself toward reunification and by appealing for UN support in remembrance of the Seoul Olympics theme song of peace and harmony.

One cannot help being moved by Roh's speech. (Mortimer [1988] of the *Financial Times,* for example, called it "eloquent.") He spoke concretely of the human suffering in Korea. He did so using universal forms, metaphors, and concepts, as well as presenting himself and his country as sincere and peace loving. Although impassioned, he steers away from ideology and speaking ill of his opponents. Finally, against all odds, he remains optimistic and celebrates the joy of being Korean.

KANG, THE NORTH KOREAN

Speaking at the UN on the Korean Question was an opportunity treated differently between North and South Korea. The South sent their highest ranking official; the North, a senior official. This difference had possible effects on how the event was staged at the UN. These effects are considered part of the social situation as shown next.

UN SPEECHMAKING: A SOCIAL SITUATION

Due to the different ranks of the speakers, the Korean Question could not be approached equally. One example of the social effects is the different treatment received by the Korean speakers at the UN, as we recall from Chapter 1 (see Box 1.4). The words of greeting and departure by the then UN chair of the meeting appear quite remarkable. In effect, the North Korean was ignored. Was such different treatment simply due to the speakers' relative diplomatic positions? Their diplomatic positions had a large bearing. Lewis (1988) reported that "North Korea's decision to send a much lower level official than President Roh to address the General Assembly had already been interpreted by diplomats as a sign that it would have little encouraging to say about its tense relationship with the South on this occasion" (p. A6). However, as seen in Chapter 1, the presiding UN official (Caputo of Argentina) did not thank North Korea for the address as he did for the South. Whatever the cause, this shows that even speech communication at the UN does not begin (or end) with a clean slate. Given this different social recognition, we must consider the possible effects on the audience (the General Assembly).

Do audiences become more predisposed to one speaker than another because of different treatment received? This consideration is beyond the present scope, but as pointed out in Chapter 1, even the slightest social differences can predispose negative evaluations of others. We would at least think that, at a momentous occasion of bringing two opposing camps together for talks, they could be equally welcomed. This factor may be crucial for a nation like North Korea, which would likely view the UN as too influenced by the United States. After all, the United States had sided with the South in the Korean War. Any slights received may then be misperceived as American inspired, encouraging North Korea to disparage the UN.

Incidentally, our attention in this chapter is placed on Roh, the South Korean. Reason for that is simple: He was a head of government. That the North Korean was a lesser official requires different attention in comparative analysis. Because they were under different constraints by their office, their addresses cannot be compared in the same way. Chapter 4 attempted to show how noncomparable situations can undermine research results in a contrastive study between English and Japanese. Of course, the Korean speeches can still be contrasted, but our conclusions must be tempered by knowledge of their different situations.

Having raised the caveat about comparison, let us go on to read the North Korean's address. Please note that later discussion will be more focused on content than organization. We wish to note how we feel about Kang's address, the North Korean official. What is the North Korean view? Will he be as cautious or roundabout as Roh was? How conciliatory will he be? Roh used the word *peace* 38 times and *reconciliation* 9 times. He also used the word *North* 20 times. Roh's address totaled approximately 3,498 words and Kang's 4,699. How may this information be used?

Box 5.3: North Korea: First Deputy Minister for Foreign Affairs Kang Addresses the UN

1. Let me first of all congratulate you, Sir, on your election as President of the General Assembly at its forty-third session and express my profound thanks to you, and to the Secretary General for giving an opportunity to the delegation of the Democratic People's Republic of Korea to take part in the discussion of the Korean question, which has been placed on the agenda of the current session of the General Assembly. I also express my gratitude to the representatives of many countries for their strenuous efforts to have included in the agenda of the General Assembly the item entitled "Promotion of peace, reconciliation and dialogue in the Korean peninsula," which my delegation has initiated.
2. I am pleased and honored to speak in this forum to focus world public opinion on clarification of the position of the Government of the Democratic People's Republic of Korea on agenda item 146.
3. The United Nations has again formally placed the Korean question on the agenda of its General Assembly for discussion 13 years after it was last considered. The General Assembly, at its thirtieth session, in 1975, adopted the resolution on dissolving the "United Nations Command" and withdrawing all foreign troops stationed in south Korea, replacing the Armistice Agreement with a peace agreement and drastically reducing the armed forces of the north and the south to an equal level. That reasonable resolution adopted by the United Nations, however, remains unimplemented. Tension is still acute and the danger of war is constantly hovering over the Korean peninsula.
4. Today the Korean people are faced with a grave choice: peace or war, reunification or division. We have now an immediate duty to resolve this difficult situation; terminate the division, which spells untold misfortune and suffering for the Korean nation; and achieve peace in the Korean peninsula.
5. To link the severed national ties of blood and reunify the divided country is a sacred struggle to achieve the coordinated development and prosperity of the entire Korean nation.
6. As is well known, Korea is a homogeneous nation which had lived in harmony for 5,000 years in the same territory with one and the same language and culture. Forty years have already passed since our compatriots, who had lived as part of the same stock throughout history, were separated into the north and the south. New generations that were born in the divided territory have grown up without knowing the reunified motherland.
7. The split of the territory and nation brings about distrust and confrontation within the country and wastes enormous energy and wealth of the nation. It is for that reason that our people's aspiration to reunification is so strong and fervent.

(continued)

8. Although the territory and nation are divided into two and a barrier of division stands across the territory, the national spirit of the Korean people is as united as ever. There can be no barrier in the hearts of the countrymen, who long for reunification. There is no internal reason for the Koreans, who have lived as a homogeneous nation for thousands of years, to be severed into two parts in our time.
9. Unfeeling objects can be mechanically divided, but no force can divide the reunification aspiration of our nation of 60 million. That is why the South Korean people are crying out that reunification is the only way of survival. In South Korea today, youths and students and other people are rising up as one in a broad struggle to oppose the country's division and achieve national reunification; they are shouting "Let's go to the north. Come to the south. Let's meet at Panmunjom." This nation-wide struggle against territorial and national division clearly indicates that there are but a handful who seek national division. The absolute majority of the people in south Korea are longing for reunification.
10. The Korean people have never wanted and will never want our country to be bisected into "two Koreas." The division must be ended, and the reunification will inevitably be accomplished.
11. Because of its very nature Korean reunification should be achieved on the basis of the three principles—independence, peaceful reunification and great national unity—already agreed upon between the North and the South. The three principles for national reunification are reasonable ones to meet the independent requirements of the Korean nation and the aspirations of the world's people as reflected in resolutions of the United Nations General Assembly.
12. The Democratic People's Republic of Korea holds that the realistic method of settling the question of national reunification is to establish a Democratic Confederal Republic of Koryo on the basis of the three principles of independence, peaceful reunification and great national unity. There exist two different social systems in the north and the south of the Korean peninsula. The existence of these two different social systems should not be a pretext to divide our country into two.
13. We oppose any attempts to create "two Koreas" to perpetuate the division of Korea. The aim of dividing Korea into two on the pretext of the different social systems in the north and the south of Korea is to keep south Korea as a permanent estate of some foreigners. The attempt to freeze the division of Korea runs counter to the ardent aspirations of the Korean people to reunification and the desire of the world's peoples for peace. It is said that peace will be settled in Korea if the existence of "two Koreas" is legally fixed by methods of "cross contacts," "cross recognition" and "admission into the United Nations." But this is an incorrect and unrealistic way of thinking.
14. We have suffered much pain for nearly half a century because of State and national division. On what grounds, then, should we allow legalization of a division into "two Koreas" now? The legalization of "two Koreas" will never bring a peace settlement on the Korean peninsula but, on the contrary, will further aggravate the situation, deepening the danger of war. The historical facts show that if a country and nation remain divided—no matter in what form—distrust,

(continued)

misunderstanding and confrontation will ensue and will end in conflict, instead of peace. The only way for our nation to live peacefully without being divided and fighting against each other is to achieve national reunification, leaving the two social systems in the north and the south as they are.

15. It is our view that we can achieve the unity of the nation and the reunification of the country even if the different ideas and systems exist in the north and the south. We consider it reasonable to form a unified State by federating the two autonomous governments, leaving the two systems as they are on the basis of the principle of coexistence, each refraining from conquering the other or from overwhelming the other in order to reunify the country, since different ideas and systems really exist in the north and the south of Korea.

16. The great leader Comrade Kim Il Sung, President of the Democratic People's Republic of Korea, put forward in October 1980 the proposal on establishing a Democratic Confederal Republic of Koryo; he reiterated the proposal this September in his report to the National Meeting to celebrate the fortieth anniversary of the founding of our Republic. Our proposal to found a confederal State envisages the establishment of a supreme national confederal assembly with an equal number of representatives from the north and the south, the organization of a confederal standing committee in the assembly and the setting up of a unified government to guide the regional governments in the north and the south, to discuss and decide on common affairs connected with the country's overall interests and to carry forward the uniform development of the nation. In this proposal of ours there is no hidden attempt to insinuate "unification through communization" and no intention to impose our ideas and system on the southern side.

17. In view of the present situation and conditions on the Korean peninsula, the most reasonable way to achieve national reunification is by bringing the existing two social systems in the north and the south together in a confederation through coexistence.

18. The purpose of our proposal on establishing the confederal republic is to achieve the cause of national reunification. It is also intended to put an end to the war on the Korean peninsula forever and to protect the peace and security of the Asia-Pacific region from any possible conflict that could result because of the Korean question. Only when the confederal State is established can a durable peace be ensured on the Korean peninsula and the desire of the nation be put into effect.

19. We have already clarified the program to be enforced by the unified confederal State. This is the 10-point policy of the Democratic Confederal Republic of Koryo (DCRK).

20. The Democratic Confederal Republic of Koryo should adhere to *Chajusong*—that is, independence—in all State activities and follow an independent policy as a fully independent, sovereign State and nonaligned, neutral nation which is not a satellite of any other nation. The Democratic Confederal Republic of Koryo should effect democracy throughout the north and the south and develop a democratic social and political system in all spheres of society.

21. The Democratic Confederal Republic of Koryo should bring about economic cooperation and exchange between the north and the south and ensure the development of an independent national economy. The authorities or enterprises

(continued)

in the north and the south would set up and run joint companies, common markets and the like. The Democratic Confederal Republic of Koryo should realize north-south exchange and co-operation in the spheres of science, culture and education, reopen transport and communications, including now closed motor roads, railways and air and shipping lines, and ensure a stable livelihood for the entire people.

22. The Democratic Confederal Republic of Koryo should completely remove the source of military confrontation between the north and the south, amalgamate the armies in both parts to form a single combined national army followed by the massive reduction of military strength, abolish the military demarcation line and dissolve militia organizations.
23. The Democratic Confederal Republic of Koryo should defend and protect the national rights and interests of all Koreans overseas, handle properly the foreign relations established by the north and the south prior to reunification and coordinate the foreign activities of the two regional Governments in a unified way. The Democratic Confederal Republic of Koryo is to repeal all treaties with other countries detrimental to national amity, including military treaties concluded separately by the north and the south prior to reunification.
24. The Democratic Confederal Republic of Koryo should permit the north and the south to co-operate economically with other countries irrespective of their social systems, and not only leave intact the capital invested by other nations in south Korea prior to reunification and continue to ensure their concessions but also promote new investments of foreign capital.
25. The Democratic Confederal Republic of Koryo should, as a unified State representing the entire Korean nation, develop friendly relations with all countries of the world and pursue a peaceful foreign policy. The Democratic Confederal Republic of Koryo should be the only representative of the entire Korean nation in foreign relations. The Democratic Confederal Republic of Koryo should represent the entire Korean nation in the United Nations and other international organizations and would have to send a single delegation to all international meetings and gatherings where the whole nation is to be represented. The Democratic Confederal Republic of Koryo should adhere to a line of neutrality, follow a policy of non-alignment and not threaten in any way the adjacent countries.
26. Neither side of Korea should be a satellite of other nations during the present state of division, and Korea should not be a satellite of any other country even after it is reunified.
27. The Democratic Confederal Republic of Koryo should make the Korean peninsula a permanent peace zone and nuclear-free zone. To this end, it should prohibit the presence of foreign troops and the establishment of foreign military bases on its territory and ban the manufacture, introduction and use of nuclear weapons.
28. Thus, our proposal for the establishment of a confederal State is acceptable to everybody as the most reasonable and practical peaceful reunification program. To establish a Democratic Confederal Republic of Koryo is the most

(continued)

correct way to settle the question of Korea's reunification independently and peacefully by the united efforts of the entire nation to meet the common desire and will of the nation.

29. In order to reunify the north and the south of Korea into a confederal State, north–south dialogues and negotiations must be developed. We want the north–south dialogue to be a dialogue for reunification, for détente and for reconciliation, and have made sincere efforts to achieve this. It is true that north–south dialogues through different channels have been held on several occasions, but they have borne no fruit.

30. Why have these dialogues failed? Because the dialogue was not a dialogue for reunification. The dialogue cannot be fruitful as long as the other side intends to use dialogue to freeze in place the national division no matter how great an effort we make to hasten reunification through dialogues.

31. The north–south dialogue should be in any case a catalyst for national reunification, not a means for division. No dialogue can be productive but will only lead to fruitless and empty talks, as in the past, if the parties concerned do not take an attitude and stance of true reconciliation, of unity for reunification. This is one of the important lessons we have experienced through our previous north–south dialogues.

32. Another reason for the failure of the north-south dialogue is the continuation of the serious political confrontation and military tensions which create deep-rooted misunderstanding and distrust between the north and the south. It is very clear that no progress can be expected unless the political and military confrontation is removed and the tensions eased between the north and the south.

33. For nearly half a century since our country was divided, we have advanced various reasonable initiatives and proposals to remove the political and military confrontation through dialogue and to realize national reunification, and we have made all efforts to implement them.

34. After the cease-fire in Korea the Government of the Democratic People's Republic of Korea proposed discussing how to ease tension and remove the source of war as a priority for national reunification. The problems of distrust and misunderstanding cannot be settled, nor can an atmosphere of trust be created between the north and the south in our country, simply through the solution of humanitarian problems or exchanges in other irrelevant or subsidiary areas. Trust can be ensured only when the political and military confrontation is removed.

35. The north–south dialogue must address itself first of all to solving the fundamental questions related to reunification. The regaining of confidence and the fundamental question of reunification cannot be achieved only through trade or mutual visits, especially if the discussion of the political and military questions for creating preconditions for reunification is ignored.

36. The dialogue should be a wide-ranging dialogue that can reflect the requirements and will of the entire people in a democratic manner. The dialogue for reunification must not be monopolized by the authorities or by any particular party or group. The north–south dialogue must be participated in

(continued)

not only by the authorities of the north and the south but also by different parties, social organizations, people from all walks of life and overseas compatriots. They should actively promote different forms of bilateral and multilateral contacts and negotiations.

37. Early this year we set forth a proposal for a north–south joint conference attended by authorities of both sides, representatives of the political parties and social organizations and people from all walks of life in the north and the south. On 20 July last the Standing Committee of the Supreme People's Assembly of the Democratic People's Republic of Korea sent to the National Assembly of south Korea a letter requesting a north–south parliamentary joint conference to adopt a joint declaration on non-aggression.

38. Because of our positive initiative, talks are now being held for the convening of a north–south parliamentary joint conference in our country. We are exerting patient efforts in the hope of making great progress in paving the way to reunification through the north–south parliamentary joint conference now under discussion.

39. We also wish to hold top-level north–south talks to further the north–south dialogue. Such top-level talks have already been proposed by us.

40. The respected leader President Kim Il Sung made clear once again our stand on the north–south top-level talks at the national meeting to celebrate the fortieth anniversary of the founding of the Democratic People's Republic of Korea, held this September.

41. The north–south top-level talks must discuss and decide, first of all, the matter of adopting a non-aggression declaration between north and south by which neither side is restrained or guaranteed by anyone else, as well as the question of the founding of a confederal Government of the unified State or establishment of a committee for peaceful reunification and the like for the setting up of such a Government. They must not discuss the matter of keeping the country divided into "two Koreas" while forever turning their faces away from the discussion of such fundamental questions. From such a point of view, we welcome a visit to Pyongyang by the highest authority of south Korea in order to adopt a non-aggression declaration and discuss the problems of national reunification.

42. The point in question is to develop the conditions for the holding of north–south top-level talks in order to produce the desired results. Today in south Korea, those who study the reality of the north and read books on the *Juche* idea are arrested and imprisoned on charges of violating the law. In such a situation, we are afraid that even the highest authority of south Korea could be charged with violating the law if he were to come to Pyongyang.

43. Laws that create obstacles to dialogue and reunification must be repealed. Without abrogating such laws it will be difficult to bring into effect any dialogue for reunification and true reconciliation between the north and the south. And furthermore, in south Korea large-scale military exercises against us are constantly being conducted. This is also spoiling the atmosphere of reconciliation and dialogue between the north and the south.

(continued)

44. Under such conditions, when they are rudely filling the air with the sound of war exercises against the north while hiding a dagger in their breast pocket, how can we talk about reconciliation between the north and the south and have an open-hearted exchange of views? If the south Korean authorities really want reunification, they should turn their words into deeds, participate in mutual travels and contacts and take substantial steps from creating a fresh atmosphere for realizing reconciliation and dialogue.

45. If the south Korean authorities are not able to take such steps at the moment, there could be high-level political and military talks between the north and the south aimed at easing acute political confrontation and military tensions on the Korean peninsula; these could be an intermediate step towards creating the necessary conditions for top-level talks between the north and the south of Korea.

46. We wish that the proposed north–south top-level talks will bear good fruit to put an end to the tragedy of the territorial split and the national division and open up the door to reunification so as to fulfill the expectations of the entire nation.

47. The removal of the war danger and the easing of tension on the Korean peninsula are the most urgent and important question and provide the indispensable conditions for the peaceful reunification of Korea. A peace agreement should be concluded between the Democratic People's Republic of Korea and the United States of America and a non-aggression declaration be adopted between the north and the south to arrange for a firm guarantee of peace on the Korean peninsula. The foreign troops and nuclear weapons should be withdrawn from south Korea, a drastic phased reduction of arms be effected in the north and south, and the Korean peninsula be converted into a nuclear-free peace zone.

48. We have long proposed to hold talks between the Democratic People's Republic of Korea and the United States to replace the Armistice Agreement with a peace agreement to settle these problems. We set forth proposals on several occasions in the 1980s alone and left no stone unturned to implement them. In January 1984, the Government of the Democratic People's Republic of Korea proposed the holding of tripartite talks between the Democratic People's Republic of Korea, the United States of America and south Korea to conclude a peace agreement between the Democratic People's Republic of Korea and the United States and to adopt a nonaggression declaration between the north and the south.

49. In April 1985, the Supreme People's Assembly of the Democratic People's Republic of Korea proposed to hold north-south parliamentary talks to discuss the problem of détente, including the problem of making a public joint declaration on nonaggression between the north and the south.

50. We also put forward a proposal for north–south high-level political and military talks to discuss such problems as refraining from slandering one another, realizing multilateral collaboration and interchange, reducing the armed forces, stopping an arms race, turning the demilitarized zone along the Military Demarcation Line into a peace zone, refraining from large-scale military exercises, increasing the authority of the Neutral Nations Supervisory Commission and organizing a neutral nations inspection force.

(continued)

51. In order to open up a decisive breakthrough in easing tension on the Korean peninsula, the Government of the Democratic People's Republic of Korea put forward on 23 July 1987 an epoch-making proposal that the north and the south of Korea should reduce their armed forces in three stages, so that by 1992 each side should maintain a level of less than 100,000 troops respectively, and that along with this phased military reduction by the north and the south, the United States should withdraw all its forces, including nuclear weapons, from south Korea.
52. In order to bring into effect these phased military reductions, the Government of the Republic proposed to hold tripartite talks between the north and the south of Korea and the United States, and also to proceed with two channels of bilateral talks, namely, between the Democratic People's Republic of Korea and the United States of America, and between us and south Korea, in case the United States and south Korea do not immediately accept the tripartite talks.
53. With a view to effectuating the possibility of a military reduction on the Korean peninsula, the Government of the Republic unilaterally demobilized 100,000 men of the Korean People's Army by the end of 1987. The meeting of the Standing Committee of the Supreme People's Assembly of the Democratic People's Republic of Korea held on 20 July this year proposed parliamentary talks between the Democratic People's Republic of Korea and the United States to discuss the question of the conclusion of a peace agreement.
54. In fact, there is no reason or condition today why an arms reduction should not be effectuated on the Korean peninsula. They allege that foreign troops are stationed in south Korea to curb a so-called southward invasion. However, no "southward invasion" has ever happened for the last decades, and it will never happen in the future either. No one can justify the stationing of foreign troops in south Korea by invoking the "ghost" of a so-called southward invasion.
55. The United States should adopt an earnest stand for dialogue and negotiations with us, be it tripartite talks or bilateral talks, to replace the Korean Armistice Agreement with a peace agreement.
56. When the peace agreement between the Democratic People's Republic of Korea and the United States is concluded and a north–south nonaggression declaration is adopted, this will provide excellent pre-conditions for peace and peaceful reunification on the Korean peninsula.
57. The Government of the Democratic People's Republic of Korea also considers the question of United Nations membership in view of our striving for reunification. We think that it is quite natural for the Democratic People's Republic of Korea to have its own seat in the United Nations. Who on earth thinks that we are rejecting the idea of United Nations membership? On the contrary, we are eager to become a Member State of the United Nations.
58. However, we must seriously handle the question of Korea's United Nations membership because we are a direct party concerned and responsible for the country's reunification. If the north and the south of Korea enter the

(continued)

United Nations separately, it will fix the division of Korea and legalize the existence of "two Koreas" internationally. This will only bring about the grave result of perpetuating the division of our country. We demand that the question of entry to the United Nations by the north and the south of Korea be discussed first between the parties concerned. Peace has not been settled and misunderstanding and mistrust have not been removed on the Korean peninsula today. This is because of the failure to reunify Korea, not because of the non-United Nations membership of the north and the south of Korea.

59. I am authorized to reclarify on this rostrum the stand of the Government of the Democratic People's Republic of Korea that Korea must enter the United Nations under the designation of one reunified confederal State, after its establishment through the desire for reunification of the Korean nation. Once the confederal State is established on the Korean peninsula the entire Korean people will naturally have their full-fledged seat in the United Nations.

60. The Government of the Democratic People's Republic of Korea since the first day of its founding has respected the purposes of the United Nations and the principles of its Charter and will continue actively to co-operate with the United Nations. The United Nations is now playing an important role in resolving regional conflicts and disputes, and confidence in the United Nations is increasing. We believe that the United Nations should pay deep attention to the solution of the Korean problem as one of its priority issues, in conformity with the purposes and principles of the Charter of the United Nations.

61. The United Nations should, first of all, take appropriate steps aimed at getting the foreign troops wearing the helmets of "UN Forces" withdrawn from south Korea, an action which will help the United Nations fulfill its obligation and contribute to paving the way for settling the problems by the Korean people themselves in accordance with the Joint Statement of 4 July 1972 agreed to by the north and the south.

62. We will always spare no wisdom and power for peace, not war, for reunification, not division. The Korean people who underwent the disaster of the war and are still suffering from the pain of division treasure peace more than anybody else and wish to live in peace and harmony together with all the peoples of the world.

63. The Government of the Democratic People's Republic of Korea in unity with the peace-loving United Nations Member States will wage an ever more active struggle to build a peaceful and independent new world and to materialize the long-cherished desire of the 60 million Korean people for reunification.

64. I would like to take this opportunity to express deep appreciation to the Governments of various countries for their deep attention to the development in the Korean peninsula and for their support to my Government's stance towards the independent and peaceful reunification of the homeland. At the same time I also express my gratitude to those delegations which expressed their strong solidarity with our people's cause of reunification in their deliberations in the general debate of the General Assembly.

65. Last but not least, I wish the current forty-third session of the General Assembly all success.

MEDIA REACTION TO KANG

Compared to previous North Korean declarations, Kang's speech was more conciliatory (Shannon, 1988, p. 11), but some American diplomats complained that the speech included "the same old arguments" (Lewis, 1988, p. A6). In the words of Vernon A. Walters, "[w]hen you have a problem with your neighbor, you should talk to your neighbor" (Lewis, 1988, p. A6). That may say more about Americans than anything else. Nevertheless, it suggests how dissatisfying Kang's speech must have been for many at the UN. After Roh's masterful oration, Kang's apparent unworkable solution—a federation of two separate systems—must have been doubly irksome. In sum, the North downplayed the need for trust and instead pushed its federation idea, as well as demanding the withdrawal of American military and nuclear weapons from the South.

The North appears too demanding and thus less intent on reunification. Although the North frequently suggested a nonaggression pact (Shannon, 1988), the South was understandably cautious. It was the North that invaded the South in their last war. The South naturally requires much trust between the governments. To scorn that need may suggest that the North has something other in mind than reunification. And that they do—a less than full reunification, a move characteristic of a "hermit kingdom."

KANG'S ADDRESS COMPARED

Kang's address lacks the worldliness of Roh, as it ignores relations with the rest of the world. The essential issue is reunification, an issue that surely affects Korea's neighbors and others. Also, unlike Roh, he neither appears as a "man of the people," for not speaking of personal sufferings like that of his people, nor does he seem to understand the depth of Korean feeling to the extent that Roh does. For instance, Kang ignores how thousands of Koreans suffer being split from relatives on the other side. His approach is so top heavy that activities from the grass-roots level are all but dismissed.

This top heaviness is particularly evident in how Kang refers to Kim Il Sung as the "great leader Comrade Kim Il Sung" (Paragraph 16) and the "respected leader President Kim Il Sung" (Paragraph 40): Note the laudatory expressions and full name usage throughout. Kang seems to pay homage to Kim, which reminds us of observations that Kim had "created a vast 'cult of personality' around himself" (Manning, 1992, p. 7). One wonders, then, from a democratic point of view, to what extent North Koreans really support Kim's thinking on reunification. One further wonders if Kang can be critical about the very words he speaks and if he has any concern for his audience. To proclaim his own leader as great and respected suggests uncritical thought. He hardly can assume that his audience feels the same way about his leader. Consequently, the audience could become distrustful of Kang and loose their receptiveness in the process.

If Kang were to be perceived as uncritical of his government, the audience may wonder about to whom does the North Korean government owe allegiance, to the people or to itself? In this regard, a telling difference exists between the speakers' relative awareness of suffering by their peoples. Roh appears more acutely aware than Kang. This difference in awareness is clear by comparing the early paragraphs in both speeches. Whereas Roh treats Korean disunity through humanism, Kang does so primarily through economics: "The split of the territory and nation brings about distrust and confrontation within the country and wastes enormous energy and wealth of the nation. It is for that reason that our people's aspiration to reunification is so strong and fervent" (Kang, Paragraph 7). Comparative mention of national division is revealing in itself: Roh's "tragic division of our homeland" versus Kang's "split of the territory." Kang focuses on Korean suffering more as a *nation* (a country) than its *people*, and economic waste is the reason given for reunification. So, Roh develops an early relative advantage in their speeches by projecting positive personal qualities.

However, this apparent edge for Roh ought not to mean that Kang's speech is altogether wanting. On the contrary, the speech is coherent as much as others of the UN genre and forcefully argues that division is not a Korean wish. The North does seem to want reunification. One can understand the wish not to legitimize the division by establishing separate UN seats. That wish, however, seems to vanish in importance when North Korean demands are understood. The North wants to maintain two separate systems but still have some sort of interdependence.

A CONTRADICTION

Two disparate systems could hardly be maintained in tandem in the usual sense of "one country." That would keep a separate mentality resulting in what the North claims to be against—a legitimizing of separateness. So, Kang's speech appears contradictory about its most central point: its proposal to create a confederation of two systems. This contradiction may be symptomatic of the failure to consider the view of the audience, a problem similar to falsely assuming commonality with the audience as noted earlier. By ignoring the possibility of contradiction, the communicator does not seem focused enough on the needs of the audience.

Kim could not allow themselves to be so focused, for that would require facing their biggest fear: dissolution of their cult. That fear, of course, is driving their hard demands. To demand that the South forget the preliminary steps, throw away their defenses, and instead join a confederation with the North seems absurd. This explains, though not condones, the kind of treatment received by Kang at the UN. He did not receive the pomp that one may expect for the occasion: the first time for both sides to speak at the UN. Given the "hermit kingdom" mentality though, such slights could become an excuse to continue their isolation from the world. (Although the North eventually halted its objection to two Korean seats in the UN, that does not mitigate the importance of social factors related to speaking at the UN. Some practical matters came into play in that turn around: changed views in China and the Soviet Union, the latter's breakup, and worsening economic conditions for the North. This is not to say that social factors at the UN determine international affairs. Rather, it is merely to suggest the possibility.)

CONCLUSION

In summary, Roh made an effective speech at least as viewed in western media. In accounting for his effectiveness, this chapter identified several reasons: Roh's metaphors, content, and organization. Significantly, he combined all these elements effectively where it is most crucial—in the opening of the speech. By doing so he could seize and maintain attention while offering systematic thinking on the subject. At the same time, he projected an image of being a man of the people as well as an astute statesman. Both attributes can help build trust and confidence in the audience for the speaker. Kang's speech, on the other hand, utilized little of these elements. Although orderly and coherent, it lacked an important element—"voice." The speech seemed too "top heavy" to allow Kang to project his own personality or voice. A lack of criticalness and focus on the audience by the speaker appeared evident. The most central part of its content was found to be contradictory. As a result, Roh's speech appears far more effective than Kang's.

APPLICATION

1. *A study of personal references:* Study personal references as used in Kang and Roh's addresses, which were originally made in Korean. Follow the procedures found in Chapter 3 and determine how closely Kang and Roh mirror the average for Southeast Asia.

For the purposes of this study exercise, it was estimated that an average line of print in Prosser's (1970) publication contained 12.4 words and had 40 lines per page. Refer to the word counts for Kang and Roh's addresses reported elsewhere in this chapter. Conduct your study using the information given here: (a) plan and decide your procedures, (b) determine the speakers' relative frequency of "I" statements, (c) categorize them in several ways in looking for self-disclosures, (d) analyze your data, and (e) consider the validity of the study and formulate any recommendations.

2. What may have motivated the North and South Korean speakers to take their apparent early perspectives, namely economic and humanistic, respectively?
3. How may the different perspectives affect our view of the speeches?
4. What purpose or purposes may there be for Roh's establishing separate perspectives between the UN and South Korea?
5. What aspects of V[S(PR)E] potentially give it wide applicability?
6. *A study of language and thought:* Roh and Kang differ in the capitalization of *South Korea(n).* Roh capitalizes South; Kang does not ninety percent of the time.
    a) How does this difference in capitalization parallel the two men's position on Korea?
    b) How do the two also differ in the use of *North Korea(n)*? Discuss its significance, if any.
    c) Recall the information in this chapter on their use of *peace* and *reconciliation* and use that in making an overall analysis of their views and their speech performance.

PART II

RHETORICAL ANALYSIS

6

CLASSICAL ANTECEDENTS AND THEIR SUCCESSORS

The last several chapters have developed the concept of *discourse analysis* as a means of understanding the *descriptive* nature of messages, both oral and written, primarily from a sociolinguistic perspective. Chapter 5 provides a specific example of the application of discourse analysis. In this chapter, and those immediately following, the emphasis is on the contributions of rhetorical theory, criticism, and practice as a means of understanding the *prescriptive* nature of messages, both oral and written and their applications.

This chapter primarily introduces classical Greek antecedents, but includes some Roman contributions as expansions of Greek antecedents, as well as neoclassical and other rhetorical developments up to the 20th Century. Our treatment is far from exhaustive and is synoptic. Roman authors such as Cicero, Quintilian, and Augustine greatly enriched the study of classical rhetoric; much of their work returns to the Greek antecedents for their own departure points. The postclassical and medieval authors of rhetoric worked from fragmented manuscripts until the great discoveries of the classical corpus in the early 1400s. Although the Renaissance rediscovered the riches of classical antiquity, very little added rhetorical contribution occurred from Augustine (354–430 CE—Common Era) with his *De Doctrina Christiana* (*On Christian Doctrine*) until the 18th Century, and more particularly until considerable developments occurred in contemporary 20th Century periods.

For the purposes of this chapter, we first identify the linkages between the ratio of the human senses and culture and the stages of communicative development through culture and time. We briefly explore the Platonic views that rhetoric must either be ignoble, without consideration for the truth, or noble, and based in the truth. Aristotle's counter argument is that rhetoric is neither moral nor immoral, but amoral. For Aristotle, his perspective is that rhetoric, finding all of the available means of persuasion, is the counterpoint of dialectic or philosophical enquiry, which is connected directly to philosophical but not necessarily practical reasoning.

Aristotle isolated three genre of rhetoric: (a) *epideictic* or *ceremonial,* which finds its subject matter praise or blame and is largely present oriented; (b) *deliberative,* which is future oriented and moves people to agreement on policies or action; and (c) *judicial* or *forensic,* which stresses past guilt or innocence and frames the substance of legal rhetoric. These three genres are illustrated with an application of UN examples of such rhetoric.

We introduce the Greek concept of *stasis,* later developed by Quintilian as *status* or *basis* of the case at hand. Essentially, this means the clash point between two opposing views on an issue and is of interest as we approach international conflict situations. Although Aristotle wrote of many aspects of rhetoric, we stress his views on proof: logical reasoning and proof or *logos,* emphasizing basic premises, syllogisms, enthymemes, examples, and refutation; ethical proof or *ethos* which deals with character and credibility especially of the speaker or writer; and emotional appeals or *pathos* linking the speaker or writer directly to the audience through emotions.

Finally, in this chapter, we provide a synthesis of developments in rhetoric from the classical period to the 20th Century, where its dimensions take different directions than the earlier heavy emphasis primarily focusing on persuasive rhetoric.

THE RATIO OF THE HUMAN SENSES IN THE DEVELOPMENT OF CULTURE

Walter J. Ong, in *The Presence of the Word,* indicated that during all of history, societies have been shaped by completing and complementing a full ratio of the human senses. Ong (1967) suggested:

> Man's sensory perceptions are abundant and overwhelming. He cannot attend to them all at once. In great part a given culture teaches him one or another way of productive specialization. It brings him to organize his sensorium (or sense ratio) by attending to some types of perception more than others, by making an issue of certain ones while relatively neglecting other ones. The sensorium is a fascinating focus for cultural studies. Given sufficient knowledge of the sensorium exploited within a specific culture, one could probably define the culture as a whole in virtually all its aspects. (p. 6)

The sense ratio is the way that each culture combines its attitudes and uses both verbal and nonverbal communication. The senses operate on each other to communicate within or between races, ethnic groups, cultures, or societies (Prosser, 1989, pp. 117–118). "Humans are rooted in 'speaking silence'" (Ong, 1967). Silence is sound's polar opposite. People who are blind accentuate other senses more than sight, such as touch and sound; people who have impaired hearing or are deaf stress other senses than sound, such as sight and touch. Ong (1967) called touch a bridge between sight and sound because it tends to annex itself to both. Sight does not carry sound, smell, or taste with any of the directness with which it conveys touch.

STAGES OF HUMAN DEVELOPMENT THROUGH COMMUNICATION

Ong (1967) identified three stages of societal development relating to human communication: "the unrecorded word," which was *oral–aural*, "the denatured word," which was *script* oriented, and "*electronic* with a new ratio of the senses." The third stage split sound from sight and later reunited them. In the first stage of clearly identified history, "The unrecorded word" was the dominant medium from about 3,000 BCE (Before the Common Era) until the full development of the alphabet. Even then, the number of persons who could read and write was very limited. Ong argues that words were primarily oral, as seen in the tradition of the story teller such as Homer in predominantly oral-aural societies.

Sound had different emphases in different cultures. Ancient Hebrews saw understanding as hearing; the ancient Greeks saw it as a kind of seeing (Ong, 1967). The Hebrew Testament of the *Bible* was developed over a 1,500 year period and was strongly a part of the oral-aural tradition of the ancient Middle East. Even the Christian Testament was not written by the evangelists until long after the death of Jesus, and in the case of the last Gospel, by John, nearly 40 years later. Koinei Greek for the scriptures, formal Latin for Roman literature, politics, education, and diplomacy, and other learned languages, such as classical Arabic, for an understanding of the *Koran*, split sound and sight. However, both Cicero and Saint Jerome wrote many letters apologizing for their delay in writing because they had sore throats. The meaning of this was that they could neither pen the words of the letter without speaking the words simultaneously nor could other writers of those periods. We could argue that the Medieval period, feudal in nature, and largely controlled by the Holy Roman Empire which replaced the Roman Empire, with its forced conversions by Catholic monarchs and clergy, represented the full flowering of the oral–aural stage in

Europe. The oral–aural stage of Western history was thereby dominated by sound as the leading component in the ratio of the senses.

The second overlapping stage in Western societies began to dominate with the flourishing of the great European universities in the High Middle Ages, and the rediscovery of long lost classical treatises at the beginning of the 1400s (Benson & Prosser, 1969). The script stage, and a more visual period in Western history began in the mid 1400s with the invention of movable type, which McLuhan (1962) called "The Gutenberg Galaxy." Ong (1967) suggested that in comparing the oral–aural versus the script society, "words fly away; what is written remains." Latin, the language of the Roman Empire, gradually had become the language entirely of the church, education, and diplomacy. The vernacular (e.g., Middle French) was becoming more and more the actual language that the common people spoke and understood. With Gutenberg's movable type, and the emerging education of those who were not elite by prospects in government, diplomacy, or the church, increasing potential occurred for new developments and freedom of thought. In Western societies, this later period of development was represented by the Protestant Revolution, the break up of the feudal system, an emerging middle class, and the overseas conquests and invasions by Columbus and others. The script stage was dominated by an emphasis on sight or the visual as it related to the ratio of the senses.

The third stage, which Ong (1967) called "electronics and a new ratio of the senses," includes the telegraph—electronic processing of alphabetized word; the telephone—electronic processing of the oral word; sound pictures—electronic sound added to electrically projected vision; and television—electronic vision added to electronic sound. Eastern Europe remained essentially a feudal and oral–aural system until the early 1900's, where print and electronic media developments were slower to penetrate. In Africa, many societies leapfrogged from the oral–aural stage over the script stage directly to the electronic stage, particularly in relation to radio, which again had an oral–aural component. In some African countries, where illiteracy can range from 40 to 90 percent among persons without running water, electricity, or plumbing, the portable radio becomes the focus of the new oral–aural tradition.

Since Ong wrote his book, *The Presence of the Word* in 1967, and alluded to the future which we already have seen and heard, we can clearly establish a fourth stage: the computer and satellite age. Computers initially silenced words once more and completely reorganized thought processes by extreme quantification. The Tiananmen Square protest in Beijing in 1989 had much success before the massacre by the soldiers, partly due to the widespread availability of fax machines and directories of persons or institutions with fax machines in western countries. Western media were allowed to televise and broadcast the protest efforts and even the massacre by the Chinese soldiers in early June of 1989. CNN was especially active.

Now, we have a fifth stage, called by some cybernetics, by others, cyberspace, and perhaps best by digital communication, with interactive computers, especially through the Internet, the World Wide Web, and interactive television. Well before the Millennium, much of the world had received 50 to 500 television channels. Active Internet users throughout the world receive and send hundreds, or even thousands, of instantaneous messages daily. These advances, however, remain the province of elite, educated, and frequently linked individuals in industrial and developing countries. Multinational organizations tenaciously expand their communications outward—especially as businesses and industries, for example, strive to reach billions of new customers in the People's Republic of China, India, and elsewhere.

The computer and satellite age, and now cybernetics, have already made such countries as Japan, Korea, Singapore, and the Republic of China major industrial players in the world market. New treaties such as the GATT, the European Economic Union (EEU), and North American Free Trade Agreement (NAFTA) treaties have already made the world economy vastly different than a few years earlier. Presently, most of the benefits continue to be realized by elite members of these societies, but hopefully it will even out over time.

Even more advanced stages in the development of communication as an organizing principle of culture are forthcoming. Temporally, the time frame has shortened dramatically as we move with alacrity toward the future: about 4,500 years of identified time for the flourishing of the oral–aural stage; about 400 years for the advancing script stage (but bypassed by a large number of countries and cultures); about 100 years for the expansion of the electronics stage; less than about a half century for the development of the fourth stage—computers and satellites. The fifth stage represents a still far shorter stage in the passage of time.

EARLY GREEK CONTRIBUTIONS TO RHETORICAL THEORY AND ANALYSIS

In approximately 900 BCE, the tradition of the Homeric hymns, plus Homer's two great epics, *Iliad* and *Odyssey*, became a highly popular genre through their development by various oral story tellers in Greece. This "blind" Homer, or more likely, various story tellers over an extended time period, went from place to place in Greece, gathering audiences of men, embellishing the heroic 10-year conquest of Troy (1,200 BCE), and Odysseus's long 10-year wanderings in his effort to return home.

Enos (1993) argued:

> If we consider the notions of discourse evidenced in Homer's work and if we examine what the characters in the *Iliad* and *Odyssey* say and think about discourse, we may consider the *Iliad* and *Odyssey* the first important steps in the history of writing and rhetoric. . . . In brief, even the earliest Greek writing indicates an emerging awareness of the relationship between human thought and the processes by which such thoughts and sentiments can be symbolically expressed. (pp. 2–3)

Because much of *Diplomatic Discourse* deals with discourse analysis and rhetorical analysis of communicative conflict, primarily but not solely in the UN, it is interesting to note that many of the stories of Homer dealt with strife and wrangling. Enos commented:

> Homer often combined strife and wrangling. On some occasions, strife provoked wrangling, while in other instances, the opposite happened. Yet, just as Greeks later bonded concepts of the true and beautiful together, so also did Homer equate strife and wrangling. This coexistence of strife and wrangling forged a unity of reciprocal relationships. . . . Athena characterizes taunting words as a reproachful attack. . . . Man has the power to generate strife through discourse, as do gods. Man has the power to resolve strife through discourse, as do gods. Man, like the gods, has the capacity to generate discourse which will create and mitigate violent words and create and mitigate violent acts of "strife and wrangling." (pp. 6–7)

The stories of Homer and other bards were based on certain stylistic formulas and commonplaces which exploited conflict because the oral–aural society of that period wanted to hear such stories.

At the same time, because many different story tellers were treating the same saga hundreds of years after such events might have happened, sometimes having heard it differently from other older story tellers, there are many contradictions both in the *Iliad* and in the *Odyssey*. These epics are an early example of both the oral–aural tradition and historical fiction, as is the later famous "Funeral Oration" of Pericles during the period of 500 to 429 BCE, which Thucydides apparently invented for him to have delivered orally some time between 457 BCE and 401 BCE, well after the actual event and long after Pericles' death. Abraham, Isaac, Moses, Solomon, and David all contributed to the Hebrew development of epic heroes. *Beowulf* was among the first great epics in early English. The Norse had their legendary epic heroes. In fact, most cultures developed their oral–aural traditions built around epic heroes.

Major Greek dramatists, such as Sophocles, Aristophanes, and Euripides, flourished from about 500 BCE to 450 BCE and contributed greatly to Greek life by developing the tragedy and comedy, which Aristotle describes and for which he prescribes correct practices in *Poetics.* Much later, toward the end of the first century in the Common Era, Virgil the Roman poet, retold the stories of the Greek epic hero, Odysseus, as Aeneas, for his Roman audience through his *Aeneid.* The whole pantheon of Greek gods was appropriated by the Romans, as well as most other cultural aspects which they considered positive. The Roman dramatists and later Shakespeare retold and expanded the Greek dramas, both the tragedies and comedies. Shakespearean and much modern drama have their starting point directly in early Greek drama and dramatic theory. Many scholars, in looking at the development of Western civilization, cite the emerging influences of the Graeco–Roman, Judeo–Christian periods as the foundations for contemporary western society.

Several hundred years before the Common Era, the young Greek male citizen's prescribed educational goal was to become a citizen orator, learning to engage himself in public discussions in the Agora or marketplace, participating in massive jury trials, acting both male and female parts in the Greek dramas, engaging in the Olympic sports, and becoming a brave military leader for his city state. Isocrates (436–338 BCE) identified this goal as follows:

> We are in no respect superior to other living creatures; nay, we are inferior to many in swiftness and in strength and in other resources; but, because there has been implanted in us the power to persuade each other and to make clear to each other whatever we desire, not only have we escaped the life of wild beasts, but we have come together and founded cities and made laws and invented arts; and generally speaking, there is no institution devised by man which the power of speech has not helped us to establish. (Isocrates, cited in Benson & Prosser, 1969, pp. 47–48)

Women, foreigners, and slaves were essentially excluded from the civic oral life of the community in ancient Greece and later in imperial Rome.

Political and military developments such as the Persian Wars (499–449 BCE), the supremacy of Pericles (462–429 BCE), the Peloponnesian War (431–404 BCE), the Spartan supremacy following the surrender of Athens (404–371), the supremacy of Alexander the Great (336–323 BCE), the First Punic War (264–241 BCE), the four Macedonian Wars (215, 200–196, 171–167, 149–148 BCE), the Roman Civil War between Marius and Sulla (92–88 BCE), the conspiracy of Catiline in 63 BCE, Caesar's conquest of Gaul in 58 through 51 BCE, his civil war with Pompeii in 49 through 48 BCE, Caesar's assassination in 44 BCE, the Second Civil War, and the assassination of Cicero in 43 BCE all indicate that the periods of ancient Greek and Roman history were turbulent times. In

Homer's earlier period, they may have been called times of "strife and wrangling."

Aristotle, ancient Greece's premier encyclopaedist of all then known human knowledge, served as the tutor of Alexander when Alexander was 16 years old. Aristotle's *Rhetorica* begins with his protesting against the technical writers of rhetoric of his time. Nonetheless, the pseudo *Rhetorica ad Alexandrum* is considered by some scholars as a technical treatise on rhetoric, or persuasive discourse, written as a guidebook for Alexander by Aristotle. Perhaps it aided Alexander in some of his diplomatic persuasion of other cultural despots, either as a prelude or epilogue to his military achievements. Whether Aristotle's admiration for his young student continued during Alexander's conquests is unclear. However, in *Nicomachean Ethics,* Aristotle takes great pains to demonstrate all of the components in a man's life which lead him to ultimate happiness, such as good birth, a good family, good friends, good education, a good disposition, good health, and sufficient wealth, but adds that with all of these components, the final great achievement for the ultimately happy man is to die gloriously for his country on the battlefield.

It is important to note that for both the early Greeks and Romans, only one group had the rights to education as citizen orators or to expect ultimate happiness: men who were or would become citizens through birth. As we have noted, women, slaves, and foreigners had essentially no rights either in Greek or Roman societies. Even the Hebrew societies out of which the Hebrew Testament of the *Bible* developed had little regard for women, except as child bearers and mothers. A woman caught in adultery could be stoned, but not the man. It was not until Jesus preached his "good news" to the poor that he made equality of the sexes a potential counter view in Hebrew life. Many African societies today still consider women to be the property of their parents, or if married, of their husbands. *Lobola* or bride price is paid for them by the men, who believe that they then have the right to do whatever they wish with their property, whether cattle or women.

THE ROLE OF RHETORICAL TRUTH IN ANCIENT GREECE: PLATO'S VIEWS

Corax probably wrote the first Greek treatise on rhetoric (sometimes called the "bad egg of the bad crow"; i.e., Corax) in the 5th Century BCE. Gorgias of Leontine (496–388 BCE), a Sicilian rhetorician and sophist, is often credited with bringing the art of practical rhetoric to Athens, perhaps in the year of Plato's birth (429, 428, or 420 BCE). Plato's Socratic dialogue, *Gorgias,* with Socrates and Gorgias the Sophist, as two major interlocutors, plus two of Gorgias's supporters, pits the distinguished but aging practical trainer of orators and speaker on any subject, Gorgias, with two of his disciples, against the urbane and witty, but falsely modest, philosopher Socrates in an argument about the value of rhetoric (*persuasive discourse*) versus the value of dialectic (*philosophical discourse*).

Plato casts Gorgias and his supporters into a devastating investigation and rejection of rhetorical, as opposed to philosophical, culture. As a well-known sophist, Gorgias was prompted to argue that the content of rhetoric was less important than its style of presentation. Socrates sums up his perception of Gorgias' definition of rhetoric: "You say that rhetoric is a producer of persuasion, and has therein its whole business and main consummation." Gorgias replied: "Socrates, your definition seems to me satisfactory; that is the main substance of the art." Gorgias continued, under sharp questioning from Socrates: "I mean that kind of persuasion, Socrates, which you find in the law-courts and in any public gatherings . . . and it deals with what is just and unjust" (Plato, cited in Benson & Prosser, 1969, pp. 3–19). Gorgias's implication that rhetoric is the most powerful of all arts, almost supernatural in character, leads Socrates to refute his arguments:

> Then the case is the same in all the other arts for the orator and his rhetoric: there is no need to know the truth of the actual matters, but one merely needs to have discovered some device of persuasion which will make one appear to those who do not know to know better than those who know. (Plato, cited in Benson & Prosser, 1969a, pp. 3–19)

In a later Platonic dialogue, *Phaedrus,* Plato had Socrates say: "If a speech is to be good, must not the mind of the speaker know the truth about the matters of which he is to speak?" He reminds Phaedrus that "a real art of speaking . . . which does not seize hold of truth, does not exist and never will." He further warned Phaedrus that unless he became a student of philosophy, he would never be able to speak properly about anything (Plato, cited in Benson & Prosser, 1969b, p. 25).

Gorgias's statement in Plato's *Gorgias* that the rhetorician could never be guilty of wrongdoing, prefigures the statement several centuries later of the first state teacher, the Roman Quintilian (35–95 CE or 40–118 CE), that the rhetorician is always "the good man speaking well" and that the "orator at all times must study morality." Unfortunately, Quintilian's subservience to the Emperor Domitian, as tutor of rhetoric to his grand nephews, who were later exiled by their Grand Uncle, led John Quincy Adams to write:

> If any thing could be wanting to complete our abhorrence of arbitrary power, it would be sufficient to behold a man of Quintilian's genius and in-

> dustry prostrate in the dust before a being, like Domitian. In the midst of this degradation, it is however some consolation to observe gleams of unquenchable virtue, still piercing through the gloom. (Adams, cited in Benson & Prosser, 1969, pp. 116–117)

Socrates, in *Gorgias* (but less so in *Phaedrus,* if rhetoric deals in truth) dismisses rhetoric as nothing more than and in the same category of a knack, such as flattery, cookery, or personal adornment. He argued that rhetoric is a

> semblance of a branch of politics. . . . A base one, I call it for all that is bad I call base. . . . I refuse to give the name of art to anything that is irrational. . . . As self-adornment is to gymnastic, so is sophistry to legislation; and to cookery is to medicine, so is rhetoric to justice. . . . Well now, you have heard what I state rhetoric to be—the counterpart of cookery in the soul, acting here as that does on the body. (Plato, cited in Benson & Prosser, 1969a, pp. 19–21)

Plato's denunciation of rhetoric in *Gorgias* continues to resonate negatively in modern society, when politicians routinely say: "Let's be done with this mere rhetoric," or "We don't need any more rhetoric; we need action."

ARISTOTLE'S RHETORICA: DEFINITIONS

Unlike Plato who required that for rhetoric to be noble, it must deal with the truth, Aristotle defined rhetoric as the speaker (writer) discerning

> in every case the available means of persuasion. This is the function of no other art. . . . Rhetoric appears to have the power of discerning the persuasive in regard (one may say) to any given subject; and therefore we describe it as having the quality of Art in reference to no special or definite class of subjects. (Aristotle, cited in Benson & Prosser, 1969, p. 56)

Thus, his view of rhetoric, but not of the rhetorician, was that rhetoric was neither moral nor immoral, but amoral. He believed, in contrast to Plato, that rhetoric is the counterpart of dialectic since both are concerned with things that are common to all, and belong to no definite science. In Aristotle's view, dialectic, or philosophical reasoning, was also neither moral nor immoral in itself. He may have used an analogy such as this one: "Here is a knife. Is it moral or immoral? A knife can be used to cut bread or to kill an animal for food. It can also be used to kill someone in defending one's family or property. It can also be used to kill in anger or through greed. Is the knife doing a good or bad act? No, the credit or blame must be put on the person doing the act, and this person is moral or immoral, but not the knife." Aristotle may have been a charter member of the United States National Rifle Association for their slogan: "Guns do not kill people. People kill people."

He argued as well that if the rhetorician teaches his students to use rhetoric for noble purposes, he cannot be blamed if the students should happen to use rhetoric for ignoble purposes. Aristotle wrote:

> If it is objected that an abuser of the rhetorical faculty can do great mischief; this, at any rate, applies to all good things except virtue, and especially to the most useful things as strength, health, wealth, generalship. By the right use of these things a man may do the greatest good and by the unjust use, the greatest mischief. (Aristotle, cited in Benson & Prosser, 1969, p. 56)

Aristotle's statement about rhetoric as a means of arguing the truth was adopted by early American presidents such as Thomas Jefferson and John Quincy Adams, among others. Thomas Jefferson's "Free marketplace of ideas, where truth will win over dishonesty," is reminiscent of Aristotle's statement:

> One should be able to persuade, just as to reason strictly, on both sides of a question, not with a view to using the two-fold power—one must not be the advocate of evil—but in order, first, that we may know the whole state of the case; secondly, that if anyone else argues dishonestly, we on our part may be able to refute him . . . that which is true and better being naturally, as a rule, more easy to demonstrate and more convincing. (Aristotle, cited in Benson & Prosser, 1969, pp. 55–56)

Later, we see that "the whole state of the case" refers to the Greek concept of *stasis* or the clash point of an issue between two opposing viewpoints.

This statement of Aristotle also rejected the sophistic tendency for Greek orators to tell their audience to pick either side of an issue, that they would debate the value of that side, and then at a moment's notice, would switch to the other side. Toward the decline and end of the Roman Empire, called the Second Sophistic period, this sort of disputation, typically on meaningless subjects, was all that the corrupt emperors would allow speakers to attempt. To do otherwise could mean execution. Where authoritarian governments exist today, representing slightly more than half of the countries in the world, speakers or writers may be restricted to expounding on meaningless issues in relation to the life of their countries' critical issues, especially if they offend the monarch, dictator, or ruling government.

Aristotle's Rhetorica: Three Major Genres

Plato's student, Aristotle (384–322 BCE), identified three kinds or genres of public discourse: (a) *epideictic or ceremonial,* dealing with current praise and blame; (b) *deliberative,* dealing with important, and often political, policy decisions that are possible for the audience to adopt in the future; and (c) *forensic or judicial,* dealing with past actions often relating to justice and injustice and part of legal rhetoric. Aristotle wrote:

> The species of Rhetoric are three in number, for the hearers of speeches belong to that number of classes. The speech has three elements—the speaker, the subject, and the person addressed; and the end proposed has reference to this last, that is, to the hearer. . . . It follows that there must be three kinds of rhetorical speeches, the deliberative, the forensic, the epideictic. (Aristotle, cited in Benson & Prosser, 1969, p. 61)

Aristotle defined these three genres further:

> The elements of counsel are exhortation and dissuasion; since both private advisers and speakers in the public interest always either exhort or dissuade. The elements of litigation are accusation and defense; since the parties to a suit must be occupied with one or the other of these. The elements of an epideictic speech are praise and blame. The times which belong to these classes severally are—to the deliberative speaker, the future; for he offers advice, exhorting or dissuading, about things to be;—to the litigant, the past; for the subjects of accusation on the one hand and defense on the other hand are always things past;—to the epideictic speaker, properly the present; for all men praise or blame in accordance with existing conditions, though they often avail themselves also of reminiscences from the past and conjectures about the future.
>
> For these three classes there are three distinct ends, namely:—for the counselor, utility or harm (since the exhorter advises a thing as being better, and the dissuader opposes it as being worse), and it is in reference to this topic that he uses the subsidiary topics of justice and injustice, honor and shame;—for litigants, justice and injustice,—and these, again, use subsidiary topics in reference to this one;— for those who praise or blame, the honorable and the shameful; and these, too, refer their other topics to this standard. (Aristotle, cited in Benson & Prosser, 1969, p. 61)

These three genres of discourse were considered the standards of oral discourse until Saint Augustine (354–430 CE) added a fourth genre, *preaching.* He engaged in vigorous arguments with other Church Fathers about whether such persuasion in God's service would be aided or tainted by the classical authors. Charles Sears Baldwin wrote:

> A clean break is made by St. Augustine. The fourth book of his *De Doctrina Christiana* has historical significance in the early part of the fifth century out of all proportion to its size; for it begins rhetoric anew. It not only ignores sophistic; it goes back over centuries of the lore of personal triumph to the ancient idea of moving men to truth; and it gives to the vital counsels of Cicero a new emphasis for the urgent tasks of preaching the word of God. (Baldwin, cited in Benson & Prosser, 1969, p. 133)

During the Medieval period, *letter writing, or dictamen,* was identified as a fifth genre of rhetoric. Although nearly devoid of content as practiced in medieval periods, and with their antecedents in classical Greece and Rome, some of the practices of this genre exist still today, notably in greetings and endings of letters. When you end your letters "Sincerely," the question of truth versus dishonesty again comes to the fore. The Latin words, "Sine Cere" mean "without wax" or an authentic signature. If you sign your letter, "Cordially," it comes from the Latin term "cor" heart, or from the heart.

In the neoclassical period of George Campbell (*The Philosophy of Rhetoric,* 1776, reprinted 1823), Hugh Blair (*Lectures on Rhetoric and Belles Lettres,* 1783), and Richard Whately (*Elements of Rhetoric,* 1828), psychological and philosophical trends dominated British and Scottish rhetorical thought. *Argumentative rhetoric* developed from mainstream deliberative rhetoric. Aristotle, of course, may have been among the first persons interested in the psychology of audiences, and argument itself, as seen through his many prescriptions for winning the opinions of young, middle-aged, and older audiences, as well as in the emotional appeals to make in connection with the different genre of speeches.This genre, *argumentative rhetoric,* is a basis for courses in argumentation and debate in contemporary universities, and modern academic and cross-examination debate in the United States, Canada, and the United Kingdom. Japanese and Korean students in their own countries have a particular interest in learning debate, partly as a means of adapting the more aggressive Western styles of persuasion, rather than their more typical harmony based rhetoric, and partly as a means of becoming more efficient in the English language in a thrust and counter-thrust situation.

Entertainment has been added as still another genre of practical rhetoric. An example is the luncheon or dinner speech, usually given after dinner in the United States, but before dinner in Japan. There are still other types, such as business and industrial speaking, but these three, *epideictic* or *ceremonial, deliberative,* and *judicial* or *forensic rhetoric* remain from the period of Aristotle to the present as major genres of rhetorical or persuasive discourse, whether oral or written.

Many of the addresses made before the UN General Assembly, especially by heads of state and government, are ceremonial in nature. The three week "General Debate," which opens each annual three-month General Assembly session in late September, and many of the addresses by heads of state and government given at various other times, have more of a ceremonial quality than a deliberative one. Even then, most heads of state or government speaking to the General Assembly seek to convince their diplomatic audience and more broadly to agree to certain principles, to accept certain argumentative proposals, and to take specific action. Thus, their addresses also have a deliberative content. Legislative bodies, such as the US Congress, the British and Canadian Parliaments, and the UN Security Council tend toward deliberative rhetoric. Judicial rhetoric develops mostly in court systems throughout the world such as the International Court of Justice, or in various countries, where attorneys, lawyers, or solicitors argue the merits or demerits of a case before the court. It is good to recognize that all three genres have overlapping goals and time frames. At the same time, Aristotle argued that all rhetoric has a judge, in the audience members who have the potential for applause or disdain, agreement or disagreement, action or inaction, and acquittal or declaration of guilt.

THE GREEK CONCEPT OF STASIS AND ROMAN CONCEPT OF STATUS, OR BASIS AS THE CLASH POINT OF AN ISSUE

Plato's Socrates enjoys challenging Gorgias, although reasonably respectfully because of the latter's age and reputation. He is much less kind with one of Gorgias' supporters, a young man named Polus (which has the meaning in classical Greek of a "young colt"). Socrates and Gorgias are discussing the meaning of rhetoric when Polus interjects rather impetuously. Socrates says that Polus is "so young and fresh"—with the semantic meaning that Polus is acting like a "Polus," a young colt. Gorgias tells Socrates "not to mind him," but to continue the dialogue. When Polus finds it necessary to speak for his mentor, Gorgias, Socrates's remarks suggest a minor clash point on the issue between the impertinence of youth and the wisdom of age.

Earlier in the dialogue, however, Socrates has asked Gorgias:

> Will you be utterly unable to teach him (the orator) rhetoric unless he previously knows the truth about these matters? Or what is the real state of the

> case, Gorgias? For Heaven's sake, as you proposed just now, draw aside the veil and tell us what really is the function of rhetoric. (Plato, cited in Benson & Prosser, 1969a, pp. 15–19)

In this case, the focus of the central point at issue in the entire dialogue between Socrates and Gorgias lies in the question—is rhetoric ignoble or noble, a base semblance of the truth, or actually a true art?

In *Phaedrus,* Plato has Socrates define the organization of a speech: "like a living being, with a body of its own, as it were, so as not to be headless or footless, but to have a middle and members, composed in fitting relation to each other and to the whole" (Plato, in Benson & Prosser, 1969b, p. 28). Aristotle, rejected the sophistic tendencies toward seven or more parts of a speech with a very simple organizational pattern: "The speech has two parts:—it is necessary to *state* the matter which is our subject, and to *prove* it. . . . The *necessary* parts of the speech, then, are Statement and Proof. These are proper to all" (Aristotle, cited in Benson & Prosser, 1969, pp. 191–192).

Stasis a Greek term, is said to have been adapted from Isocrates by Hermagoras (160?–110? BCE) to define the central point at issue in legal rhetoric, whether *legal questions* (as formed by written laws) or *rational questions,* which for him are formed by the skill of the orator. These definitions are similar to Aristotle's inartistic and artistic proofs. Hermagoras modified the Aristotelian parts of rhetoric by dividing political questions into two classes: *theses* (controversies not involving precise individual persons) and *hypotheses* (specific controversies involving specific persons and events). He called the crucial point at issue *stasis,* which was later called *status* by Cicero, and *basis* by Quintilian (Benson & Prosser, 1969, p. 309).

The Roman rhetorician, Quintilian, writing about the concept of *basis* of cases, indicates that the chief form of providing the definite basis of cases, or the clash point of an issue, is best developed by definition, but can also be argued by inference, differentiation, resolution of ambiguity, distinction, and classification (Quintilian, cited in Benson & Prosser, 1969, 127). Quintilian, referring directly to legal rhetoric, wrote: "There are three things on which enquiry is made in every case: we ask *whether a thing is, what it is,* and *what kind it is.* . . . One or more of them is discussed in every demonstrative, deliberative or forensic theme" (Quintilian, cited in Benson & Prosser, 1969, p. 144). He argued that three major *bases* for a legal situation are *definition, conjecture,* and *quality* of the case. Quintilian indicated that every legal case contains a cause for bringing the case to court, a point for the decision of the judge, and the central argument, about which the accuser and the defendant disagree. We need to point out that the Roman legal system of hiring a person to represent the accused person is an advance over the Greek system, where the accused provided his own defense, often with the aid of a hired logographer, or ghost writer. The rhetorician Isocrates was a frequent ghost writer for such defenses.

Later, we see the modern neoPlatonic rhetorician Richard Weaver making the same point—that definition is the highest form of coming to the clash point on an issue with the potential of two opposing sides. Weaver also argues that there are several other arguments which bring an understanding of the truth of the matter, similar to those developed through classical rhetorical authors, both Plato and Quintilian.

ARISTOTLE'S DEFINITIONS OF PROOFS AS A FORM OF PERSUASION

Aristotle stressed that there are both artistic proofs, those created by the speaker or writer, and inartistic proofs, those supplied from outside the speaking or writing situation, such as witnesses, depositions under torture (a practice coming from classical antiquity to the present). Aristotle identifies three kinds of proofs provided by the speaker or writer or speech or written message: "one kind depending on the character of the speaker (writer); another, on disposing the hearer (reader) in a certain way; a third, a demonstration or apparent demonstration in the speech (message) itself" (Aristotle, cited in Benson & Prosser, 1969, p. 57).

These are more clearly identified as *ethos* or *ethical proof,* spoken or written in such a way as to make the speaker or writer credible through personal character, trustworthiness, truthfulness, reputation, or all of these; *pathos or emotional appeals,* when the hearers (readers) themselves become the instrument of proof because their emotions are stirred in them by the speaker or writer and connected to those emotions; and *logos* or *logical proofs.* Aristotle argues: "Proof is wrought through the speech (written message) itself when we have demonstrated a truth or an apparent truth by the means of persuasion available in a given case" (Aristotle, cited in Benson & Prosser, 1969, p. 57). In other words, we may ask: Is this speaker or writer reliable for us by establishing his or her own authority as an honest, trusted, or experienced person (*ethos*)? Is he or she able to move us as an audience to agreement or action because we find our emotions, such as pain or joy, anger or pleasure, or liking or hatred, connected to those stirred by the speaker or writer (*pathos*)? Has the speaker or writer been able to convince us that his or her basic premises, arguments, and refutation are true or have the appearance of truth and are sound? Is the evidence offered to support these arguments both reliable and valid (*logos*)? Reliability and validity are tests for any field or laboratory study conducted by honest researchers.

Aristotle's Logical Proofs: Basic Premises, Arguments by Examples and Enthymemes, and Refutation

The artistic logical proof of which Aristotle wrote, leads, he believed, the skilled speaker or writer to become a master of enthymemes, or truncated sylogisms, built on deductive reasoning, or implied deductive reasoning, whereby he or she has demonstrated the real or apparent truth on a question. For Aristotle, there are two kinds of evidence to support one's basic premises: the *inductive example* and the *rhetorical demonstration* or *enthymeme* which Aristotle claimed is the most authoritative of the logical proofs.

Consider this use of examples that Ambassador Adlai Stevenson utilized in a June 22, 1962, Security Council statement in which he condemned the Soviet Union for its flagrant misuse of the veto. The veto had the effect of halting all Council action on a question before it. Stevenson's basic premise in this statement is that the Security Council veto had been given to the permanent Security Council powers in 1945 (France, Republic of China, Soviet Union, United Kingdom, and United States) because it would be "their military and economic power which would have to be used to sustain and enforce Security Council decisions directly affecting vital world interests." As a second basic premise, however, Stevenson stated that from the beginning the big powers had agreed: "It is not to be assumed . . . that the permanent members, any more than the nonpermanent members, would use their veto WILLFULLY to obstruct the operation of the Council" (Stevenson, cited in Prosser, 1969, p. 471).

Utilizing examples to show that the Soviets had broken their own commitments, Stevenson said:

> Before the first year was out the Soviet Union had cast nine vetoes. The Soviet member of the Council has today cast its 100th veto. . . . The Soviet Union has used the veto lavishly to prevent states from assuming their rightful place in the United Nations. In fact, fifty-one of these vetoes were cast on applications for membership in the United Nations. . . . The Soviet Delegate used the veto thirteen times to assist Soviet bloc activities against the territorial integrity and the political independency of other states.

These and other inductive examples by Stevenson, in a frequently interrupted speech about points of order by Ambassador Morozov of the Soviet Union, were intended to support Stevenson's basic premise that the Soviet Union was now violating its own agreement made at the beginning of the UN (Stevenson, cited in Prosser, 1969, pp. 469–483). It is, however, possible that Stevenson was simply using an analogy to embarrass the Soviet delegation.

Aristotle wrote that proving a proposition by a number of like instances consists of *inductive examples,* such as those seen above in Stevenson's statement. It is likely that Aristotle would agree that Stevenson had proven his proposition that while the Soviet Union had agreed not to misuse the veto, as had the other four veto powers in the Security Council, these examples, and others which Stevenson introduced, clearly showed that the Soviet Union had misused the veto.

The standard classical *syllogism* has a major premise, a minor premise, and a conclusion: "All men are mortal. Socrates is a man. Socrates is mortal." If both the major premise and the minor premise are accurate, then the conclusion, in Aristotelian logic, must also follow. Linguistically, we could say that: "All cows are green. Elsie is a cow. Elsie is green." We could also say linguistically: "All cows sing furiously. Elsie is a cow. Elsie sings furiously." From a grammatical perspective, these last two major premises, minor premises, and conclusions are linguistically correct. However, unless there is a hidden analogical or metaphorical meaning, most people would not agree that they carry a clear semantic meaning.

A contemporary enthymeme (a truncated syllogism) is the political slogan: "John Doe: too liberal for too long." The full Aristotelian syllogism may read: Major Premise: "Long term liberal politicians are dangerous." Minor Premise: "John Doe is a long term liberal politician." Conclusion: "John Doe, a liberal politician, is dangerous." A final enthymeme develops: "Do not vote for John Doe—too liberal for too long." A familiar enthymemic political slogan is the statement with which most American presidents end nearly all of their speeches: "The United States is the greatest country on earth! God bless America!" and the popular slogan, particularly when the United States is involved in overseas military action, has often been: "America. Love it or leave it." The first can be seen as this sort of syllogism: Major Premise: "God blesses the greatest countries." Minor Premise: "The United States is the greatest country." Conclusion: "Because America is the greatest country, God blesses it." In the second case, the syllogism may go like this: Major Premise: "Disloyal Americans despise their great country." Minor Premise: "Jane Doe is a disloyal American." Conclusion: "Jane Doe despises her country."

In an earlier chapter, we saw an example from President Kennedy's address to the UN in 1961, mourning the recent death of Secretary General Dag Hammarsjkold, by saying enthymemically: "Dag Hammarsjkold is dead. But the United Nations lives." A well-recognized historical enthymeme is paralleled in this statement: "The King is dead. Long live the King." If you were to build a rhetorical syllogism from these enthymemes, how would it develop? Perhaps it would be: Major Premise: "Even with the death of one king (leader), the monarchy (institution) lives on," or "A new king (leader) emerges." Minor Premise: "Dag Hammarsjkold has died." Conclusion: "The institution continues," or "A new leader emerges."

Aristotle discussed *demonstrative syllogisms* and *enthymemes* which he claimed are of two kinds: "The demonstrative syllogism consists in drawing a conclusion from consistent propositions; the refutative, in drawing a conclusion from conflicting propositions" (Aristotle, cited in Benson & Prosser, 1969, p. 163). Benson and Prosser argued that at least three kinds of topics appear in *Rhetorica:* special topics related to the subject matter of various fields of knowledge; *universal, general,* or *common* topics, called commonplaces; and special forms or lines of argument used to construct enthymemes (Benson & Prosser, 1969, p. 154).

Such syllogisms or enthymemes can be used either to develop one's argument, or to refute the arguments of another. Aristotle identified the major *commonplaces:* possible or impossible, greater or smaller, and past or future. He listed 28 topics from which to construct enthymemes, either for one's own speech (message) or for refuting another's speech (message). Some examples include: opposites, relative terms, comparison by degree, considerations of time, various senses of the same word or phrase, comparison by division, previous decisions on the same points; separating the parts; arguing from consequence; paradoxes; symmetry of results, arguing identity of cause to identity of effect, events that have happened but are incredible, noting previous inconsistencies, and so forth. (Aristotle, cited in Benson & Prosser, 1969, pp. 163–170).

One example of such refutative topics is used by Soviet Ambassador Morozov during the speech by Stevenson on June 22, 1962. The question before the Security Council was an explanation of the vote on the Kashmir situation. Stevenson should only have explained the US vote on the question of Kashmir. Ambassador Morozov's interruptions included many refutative topics that he applied both to the statement of Ambassador Stevenson, as well as to the rulings of the June 1962 Council President's statements related to Morozov's points of order. In one of his several interruptions of the Stevenson speech, Morozov called a point of order and said:

> We are obviously hearing a very interesting lecture, no doubt; it is a survey of all the occasions when the veto was used, the veto of the Soviet Union. I would be quite ready to listen to this lecture and to this summing-up if it were on the agenda. But the item on the agenda is not entitled "Summary of the utilization of the veto by the Soviet Union in the Security Council since the inception of the United Nations." (Morozov, interrupting Stevenson, cited in Prosser, 1969, p. 472)

Several of the topics identified by Aristotle could be applied as illustrative of refutative syllogisms or enthymemes.

SYNOPSIS OF RHETORICAL TRENDS TO THE 20TH CENTURY

As we have already identified, the Greek classical rhetoricians, especially Plato through his Socratic dialogues, Isocrates through his training of the young male citizen orators of Athens, and Aristotle through his *Rhetorica,* set the framework for much of the rhetorical theory and analytical criticism which followed. As adapters of the best of Greek wisdom, myths, and customs, the Romans were less original than imitative. Cicero, a leading Roman citizen–orator–politician, outstanding legal advocate, and prolific writer on many subjects, contributed to the field of rhetoric especially through his *De Oratore (On Oratory),* written in 55 BCE after he had been driven from public affairs, and his last work, *Orator* (46 BCE), a slightly disguised praise of himself as the ideal orator. Even so, only a fraction of his rhetorical contributions were new. Cicero's *Orator* suggests that the ideal orator reaches true eloquence, both in thinking and in expression, "so as to prove, please, and persuade" (Cicero, cited in Benson & Prosser, 1969, p. 232).

Quintilian (35–95 CE or 40–118 CE) a Spanish Roman, the first state paid teacher of rhetoric in Rome, who despite his groveling before the Emperor Domitian, served as an important transitional writer on rhetoric between the greatness of the Roman empire and its gradual decline. He was the first major writer on rhetoric in the Common Era. His major rhetorical contribution of 12 books, *Institutio Oratoria (The Institutes of Oratory,* about 95 CE), was the first full text book for the early training of the future orator, and contains his famous expression that the orator "is the good man speaking well." It had considerable influence during the early Common Era, but the volumes were lost until 1470 CE, when its influence became extensive during the Renaissance.

Saint Augustine (354–430 CE), originally a teacher of pagan rhetoric, before his conversion to Christianity, developed the first Christian rhetoric in his *De Doctrina Christiana (On Christian Doctrine):* "He who seeks to teach in speech what is good, spurning none of these three things, that is, to teach, to delight, and to persuade, should pray and strive that he be heard intelligently, willingly, and obediently. When he does this well and properly, he can justly be called eloquent, even though he fails to win the assent of his audience." Following Aristotle's view on the amorality of rhetoric, Augustine proposed:

> While the faculty of eloquence, which is of great value in urging either evil or justice, is in itself indifferent, why should it not be obtained for the uses of the good in the service of truth if the evil usurp it for the winning of perverse and vain causes in defense of iniquity and error? (St. Augustine, cited in Benson & Prosser, 1969, pp. 134–135)

Augustine's contributions centered the Christian Fathers' debate on whether or not pagan literature and writings could be utilized in support of the church. His thinking on rhetoric was a major influence on the Christian preaching of the Medieval Ages, which became the dominant form of rhetoric, with *dictamen* or letter writing as the second most important rhetorical development during that period.

During the Medieval Ages, the roots of modern day university colleges of liberal arts developed, with the trivium consisting of grammar that was concerned with meanings (for boys), rhetoric that was concerned with convincing the will (for young men), and dialectic that was concerned with understanding (for mature men) and the quadrivium, including music and scientific subjects (Miller, Prosser, & Benson, 1973). We keep in mind, of course, that education was still primarily male-oriented.

The Renaissance Rhetoricians

The rediscovery of Greek texts in the beginning of the 1400s and the Roman texts later in the century, plus a new interest in architecture, art, sculpture, literature, philosophy, and poetry generated a major new interest in rhetoric. Peter Ramus (1515–1572 CE) in his *Dialectique* (1555 CE), defined rhetoric as the study of style and delivery, and dialectic as content and subject matter which the classical authors had listed under the rhetorical heading of invention and arrangement of arguments, thus separating rhetoric and logic. Golden, Bergquist, and Coleman in *The Rhetoric of Western Thought,* suggest that this division remains the patterns in contemporary university education, with logic being taught primarily in philosophy programs and what remains of rhetoric being taught in communication and English programs (Golden et al., 1989, pp. 125–127). There is, of course, the additional fragmentation of the Medieval trivium, where grammar, poetry and rhetoric as composition are taught in English programs, rhetorical theory and criticism in communication programs, logic in philosophy programs, and linguistic structure in programs in linguistics.

Peter Ramus had a significant influence on later university education, by his identification of three laws: the Law of Truth, which "required any principle in any liberal discipline to be universally true"; the Law of Wisdom, which "required the principles of any liberal discipline to be ordered in relation to their generality or particularity"; and the Law of Justice, which required that "each liberal discipline must keep to its own subject matter, must share no doctrine with a sister discipline" (Ramus, cited in Golden et al., 1989, pp. 127–128). This disciplinary fragmentation became a major force in university education as it progressed to contemporary periods. Even today, university students in European and former European colonial African or Asian educational systems follow very rigid and narrow disciplinary programs. Leaving secondary education, such students in law or medicine beginning at the age of 18 or 19, for instance, have very little additional crossover into the broader subjects that contribute to liberal arts programs in North American university systems.

The Enlightenment Rhetoricians

The end of the 16th Century, especially in British thought, was still classically oriented and was called neoclassicism or the Augustan Age. Neoclassicism was dominant from 1700 to 1740 in Britain under the prevailing influence of Jonathan Swift (1667–1745) with his "Battle of the Books," a satirical criticism of the futility of modernist forces in literature; Alexander Pope (1688–1744) and his "Essay on Criticism"; and John Dryden and his extensive contributions to criticism (1631–1700). All three authors, and a number of others in the neoclassical mode, stressed imitation primarily of classical genius rather than originality, except in the mode of expression. All of these authors pointed backward to the classical Greeks and Romans rather than to those who were then considered "the moderns" for their views of literary and rhetorical criticism. However, Golden, Bergquist, and Coleman indicate that "With dramatic suddenness, revolutionary scientific, philosophical, and psychological developments modified traditional theories of knowledge, thereby creating the demand for a 'new rhetoric' rooted not only in the past but in modern epistemology" (Golden et al., 1989, p. 131). They suggest that the 18th Century's major rhetorical developments interacted for the next 200 years: neoclassicism, belle lettres, epistemology, and elocution, a rather sterile movement located almost entirely in an interest in delivery.

The eclectic method of the belletristic scholars such as Joseph Addison (1672–1719), Edmund Burke (1729–1797), known also for his speeches in the British Parliament on the American Revolution, and Hugh Blair (1718–1800), the most noted of the group, emphasized an Aristotelian communication model, still utilized today: the *source, the message,* and the *receiver.* Today, this particular model adds the *channel.* The belletristic scholars also stressed the three major classical modes of proof, *logos, ethos,* and *pathos,* a recognition of the importance of occasion on a speaker's choice of material and development of themes, and an appreciation for appropriate style. They endorsed Cicero's and Quintilian's five canons of rhetoric: invention, arrangement, style, delivery, and memory; accepted their separation of the ends of discourse to instruct, please, and move an audience; and praised the role of nature, imitation, and the use of models in the formation of an orator or writer. Longinus's (200–273 CE) *On the Sublime,* which some modern scholars argue was not his, when it appeared in 1674 in translation and with commentary, still caught the imagination of French and English scholars. The belletristic scholars, extolling *On the Sublime,* combined rhetoric and poetry in what may be a forerunner of contemporary literary criticism. From then "modern" works, they adapted principles of faculty psychology, the function of reason in criticism, insights into oratorical and literary genius, and examples of actual eloquence in the native idiom as models for their speakers and writers.

One of the leaders of this movement, Hugh Blair, became a Professor of Rhetoric at the University of Edinburgh in 1760 and in 1762 its Regius Professor of Rhetoric and Belles Lettres. His *Lectures on Rhetoric and Belles Lettres,* mostly a reproduction of his earlier oral lectures on rhetoric, literature, and criticism, was printed in many editions in England, in America, and on the continent for the next 100 years and was translated into several European languages. Part of his success was attributed to his ability to blend classical themes with modern examples and developments (Golden et al., 1989, pp. 133–159).

Golden et al. identified the third group as the psychological–philosophical or epistemological school of thought whose principal concern was to relate communication theory to the basic nature of man. Their goal, through the natural and social sciences as they were then developing, was to unravel the mystery of the human mind and soul. Among the innovators from 1600 to 1725 were Francis Bacon (1561–1626), René Descartes (1596–1650), and John Locke (1632–1704).

Francis Bacon, recognizing the importance of recent discoveries—printing, gunpowder, and the compass—called for a "total reform of human knowledge, a true advancement of learning, and a revolution in the conditions of life." From his discussion of the *faculties of the mind: history* to the human memory, *poesy* to one's imagination, and *philosophy* to the human reason, and adding *will* and *appetite,* Bacon drew the rhetorical prescription that "the duty and office of Rhetoric is to apply Reason to Imagination for the better moving of the will." His development of invention related less to the role of discovery of arguments, than to the ability to reach back in memory to summon forth knowledge that one already knows, and then to apply it to the rhetorical situation at hand. He recommended that orators should observe the world around them, converse freely with others to gain insights, and study widely, especially in the area of history. All of these methods are recommended by contemporary public speaking texts today.

Moving away from the Aristotelian *deductive logic* of general principles to specific examples, and rejecting the growing tendency in his time to utilize *inductive logic,* in which one starts with examples and moves to general premises, and then to judgment and the discovery of middle axioms, Bacon argued for establishing progressive stages of certainty both in the balanced ratio of the senses and in particulars, "rising by a gradual and unbroken ascent, so that it arrives at the most general axioms last of all." He rejected the *syllogism* as a productive means for establishing principles because he believed that it had little relevance to the actual nature of things, again preferring a modified induction, as it upholds the sense, and closes with nature, and comes to the very brink of nature. Finally, he rejected the concept of grand style, recommending instead for scientific enquiry a clear and unadorned style (Golden et al., 1989, 160–166).

Golden et al. indicated that René Descartes's parallel influence in France on the nature of the human and methods of study was initiated in 1637 with his publication of his partly autobiographical *Discourse on Method.* Descartes regarded "eloquence highly and was in raptures with poesy," believing however that "both were the gifts of nature rather than the fruits of study." He believed that both great orators and poets were born, not trained, though training could polish what nature had provided. He argued that the *syllogism* "was incapable of investigating the unknown and separating truth from error" and was thus useful in communicating only what one already knows. He praised mathematics because of its certitude and evidence of its reasonings. The power of reason to determine truth and to discipline the imagination led him to his famous conclusions, such as, "I think, therefore I am," "Cogito, ergo sum," or "God exists," "Deus est." According to Golden et al., he was unique and prophetic:

> In arguing that experiment takes precedence over disputation, inquiry over communication, and action over speculation, he broke with the logicians of the past . . . to make bold predictions "which became the assumptions of nineteenth century science." . . . It is a dividing line in the history of thought. Everything that came before it is old; everything that came after it is new.

Golden, Bergquist, and Coleman argued that according to Descartes and some of his contemporaries, because rhetoric cannot produce truth, it is, at best, relegated to the simple task of communicating principles that logic and experimentation can discover (Golden et al., 1989, pp. 166–167).

John Locke's *Essay of Human Understanding,* written in 1690, had a major influence on the Fathers of the American Revolution, especially in Thomas Jefferson's "Declaration of Independence," his Virginia "Statutes for Religious Freedom," and in his founding of the University of Virginia—his three achievements which he wished placed on his tombstone. Locke made major statements related to the treatment of the *faculties of the mind, association of ideas, pathetic proof,* and the *syllogism.* He saw the mind as having two faculties: the *understanding* and the *will* because the mind has the power to perceive and to prefer. His development of *psychological–philosophical* theories of discourse had a direct influence on George Campbell's (1719–1796) 18th Century *Philosophy of Rhetoric* particularly in relation to his treatment of the faculties of the mind, the association of ideas, pathetic proof, and the syllogism. Like earlier writers, Locke rejected the syllogism because it neither demonstrates nor strengthens the connection that two ideas may have with each other. He believed that syllogisms do not advance an argument or lead to moral truth. The human begins with a "tabula rasa," ("blank slate"), but God's gift, the power of inference, Locke argued, makes it possible to perceive associations and to determine whether or not ideas are coherent or incoherent. The rational process, itself, must be reinforced by a pathetic appeal that ultimately becomes the major determinant of action. The will may be influenced when the passions are stirred. There is, however, little opportunity for persuasion if the mind is at ease, because the desire for happiness has already been achieved (Golden et al., 1989, pp. 167–168).

The writings of Descartes and Locke had an influence on a variety of writers and thinkers in England and France, including David Hume (1711–1766), Adam Smith (1723–1790), Francois Voltaire (1694–1778), and Jean Jacques Rousseau (1712–1778), and in America, Thomas Paine (1739–1809) and Thomas Jefferson (1743–1826). Golden et al. (1989) indicate that as rationalism fully developed in the 18th Century, there were three clearly delineated features: a heightened consciousness for the need of logic in the study of humans and their institutions, an absolute belief in the attainability of reliable knowledge, and a faith in the capacity of humans to make things better. Reason had moved beyond the domain only of philosophers, and had become a weapon for social improvement, thus invoking certain new elements of persuasion. Rationalism also had a major effect in secularizing society in terms of religious belief, and as an influence in governmental and social affairs. The scientific revolution continued to develop, as we have discussed much earlier in relation to the third stage of communication—the electronic media. The rationalist effort to study human nature convinced the epistemologists of the human power to engage in abstract thought and to communicate on the level of symbolism. "To understand the [human mind], they came to believe, was to recognize the nature and function of discourse. Consequently, writers of diverse orientation developed a considerable interest in rhetoric. This interest combined classical and modern scientific and social value" (Golden et al., 1989, pp. 173–175).

David Hume, of Edinburgh, a city described then as a "hotbed of genius," and "the Athens of the North," wrote *A Treatise on Human Nature* in 1739, and later, *An Enquiry Concerning Human Understanding,* and *An*

Enquiry concerning the Principles of Morals. Golden et al. traced his intellectual heritage to Cicero and Locke, and Cicero was frequently quoted in all of his works, including his *De Oratore,* and *De Natura Deorum (On the Nature of gods).* Hume was most enchanted, however, by Locke's *compartmentalization of the faculties,* his *theory of association,* and his belief in the *primacy of the emotions.* Golden et al. called him "the first to put the whole [of human science] upon an empirical footing, and to appeal to experience exclusively and systematically in reaching results" (Golden et al., 1989, p. 176). Hume saw the mind as subdivided into two faculties: *impressions* and *ideas.* Like Locke, Hume held that human motivation stems from the human emotional nature, and that appeals to the passions of pleasure and pain are necessary to persuade the will to act. Going farther than Locke, Hume wrote: "reason is and ought only to be the slave of the passions, and can never pretend to any other office than to serve and obey them." This caused him, like Bacon and Locke, to reject the *syllogism* as an effective tool in exploring human nature. Whereas Aristotle had made inartistic proofs such as oaths, witnesses, and documents a subordinate position in rhetoric, Hume elevated testimony to a high status (Golden et al., 1989, pp. 176–177). Hume was frustrated in his own life time, as he believed that several of his works "had fallen deadborn from the press," but he had a major influence on intellectual thought both during and after his life.

As Aristotle was a student of Plato, and found himself in disagreement with his mentor, so did George Campbell, a student of David Hume, disagree with his teacher who was a skeptic. Both Campbell, a Scottish Presbyterian minister, and Richard Whately, an Archbishop of the Church of England, made major contributions to the progressive tradition of rhetoric, especially *epistemologically.* Campbell's 1776 *Philosophy of Rhetoric* "more than any preceding volume devoted exclusively to rhetoric, brought together the best knowledge available to 18th Century scholars" (Golden et al., 1989, p. 186). He was devoted to the classical rhetoricians, but also saw rhetoric as a dynamic and developing process, including contributions from *faculty psychology, the laws of association, sympathy, moral reasoning,* and what the Scottish philosophers and theologians called *"common sense."* The work of Bacon, Locke, and Hume all assisted him, as he further developed the categories of imagination and the passions in a hierarchical pattern, ranging from the elementary *faculty of the understanding* to the more complex *faculty of the will.* For Campbell, persuasion is the final result of a four step process that starts with *instruction, imagination,* and *passions,* and then motivates the *will.* Because of his interest in imagination, he included fables, parables, allegories, and poetry as appropriate rhetorical devices, allowing the speaker or writer to use "vivid and compelling language" which then leads to the passions, and finally to motivation of the will to act. Campbell argues that the most difficult component is for the communicator to influence the will. First, the communicator must convince the audience, and then persuade it to act (*conviction–persuasion duality*). This idea was also endorsed by rhetoricians for decades after. Campbell defined eloquence "as that art or talent by which the discourse is adapted to its end" (Golden et al., 1989, pp. 187–188).

Richard Whately's *Elements of Rhetoric,* published in 1828, limited the scope of rhetoric to *argumentation,* as contemporary philosopher–rhetoricians, the British Stephen Toulmin (1922–) and the Belgian Chaim Perelman (1912–1984) have also done. "The orator approaches the process of rhetorical invention not as an investigator but as a communicator, already armed with a general proposition he will advance and with a knowledge of the substantiative resources, factual and inferred, by which that proposition may be established" (Whately, cited in Golden et al., 1989, p. 204). Two major classes of argument for Whately were *a priori* and *sign.* The first, Whately believes, is reasoning from cause to effect, which includes a sufficiently strong cause to establish plausibility. The second, sign, moves in the direction of an "effect to a condition," which may include testimony. Like Augustine, Whately saw the development of the argumentative thrust as critical to the progressive support of Christianity. His view of presumption and burden of proof both continue to be supported in contemporary texts on argumentation and debate (Golden et al., 1989, pp. 205–206).

CONCLUSION

In this chapter, we have isolated some important concepts in Greek and sometimes Roman rhetoric that form the basis for understanding the role of the orator or writer. Additionally, we have provided a synopsis from the classical period to the 20th Century of major rhetorical developments. Plato, Isocrates, Aristotle and others among the Greek rhetoricians and Cicero, Quintilian, and Saint Augustine provide the major developments of early classical rhetoric—many of which continue to be both reliable and valid today as methods of rhetorical analysis and criticism. Classical rhetoricians were very interested in the role of dialectic or philosophical enquiry, which Plato championed, and rhetoric or enquiries about how a speaker (writer) wins over a listener or audience with which Aristotle was very concerned. Plato questioned whether rhetoric can be noble, if it provides only the semblance of the truth rather than the actual truth, whereas Aristotle neutralized it, but not the speaker or writer who bears the responsibility for utilizing good rhetoric. Plato, Aristotle, and especially the Roman Quintilian argued that for every kind of rhetoric, deliberative, epideictic, or judicial, one can identify where the central point of agreement or disagreement occurs. Hermagoras later called this *stasis,* Cicero called it *status,* and Quintilian called it *basis.* Today, we speak of the clash between opposite points of view.

Over time in Roman rhetoric, but probably not fully in the consideration of Plato and Aristotle, five classical canons of rhetoric emerged: *invention* (where one locates arguments, for example in common places), *arrangement* (of one's arguments after having identified which ones to use), *style* (how one clothes arguments to please the listener or audience, using as Cicero, Quintilian, and Augustine recommended, either grand, middle, or simple style), *delivery* (how one presents these arguments for the listener or audience), and *memory* (how the speaker or writer is able to work with specific commonplaces or devices which can be called forth particularly in an oral speech). In the Greek consideration of genres of rhetoric, it is made clear that one may locate arguments differently for deliberative, epideictic, or judicial rhetoric; similarly, one may arrange arguments differently for each genre of rhetoric; clothe the arguments differently for various genres; deliver or present the arguments differently; and call on different memory devices for each genre. We have not discussed these five classical canons in any detail in this chapter, but because contemporary rhetoric has its wellsprings from classical rhetoric, some of these canons are implied in the classical concepts of rhetoric which we have considered and will reappear later.

We have identified what Aristotle considered the most important proofs for *logos,* arguments, or rational reasoning, consisting of basic premises, logical arguments, evidence, and refutation; *pathos,* or emotional appeals made to the listener or audience, which link that person or judge to the speaker or writer; and *ethos,* which are the appeals by which the speaker or writer develops personal character, truthfulness, and reputation. We have noted that as time progressed, many different interpretations of rhetoric developed, including efforts to separate dialectic from rhetoric more strongly, with new views by the Enlightenment rhetoricians—who were often writing more directly about then current societal changes, and rhetoric as it contributed to such changes.

Later, continuing to use Aristotle's three genres as an organizing pattern for analysis, examples of *epideictic, deliberative,* and *judicial* rhetoric are provided, as well as contemporary perspectives on rhetoric. In the next chapter, we move directly to consideration of a number of 20th Century contributions of rhetoric, where we see that the identified authors become more and more interested in language and its rhetorical impact. This feature will continue to link both discourse analysis and rhetorical analysis.

APPLICATION

1. Why did Plato and Aristotle disagree on the morality of rhetoric? How did each agree?
2. Which would you consider the most important genre for contemporary life, epideictic, deliberative, or judicial rhetoric? Why?
3. Why did Aristotle consider rhetoric the counterpart of dialectic? What does this mean in contemporary society? Are there implications for discourse analysis?
4. Which proof, *logos*, *ethos*, or *pathos*, would you consider most important in contemporary life for the speaker or writer? Why?
5. In the last chapter, speeches by South Korean Roh and North Korean Kang were compared through discourse analysis. How would you compare their use of rhetorical proof in their speeches?
6. As we move beyond the classical periods, how did writers on rhetoric move from the concept of rhetoric as *persuasive* discourse to rhetoric as *philosophical* discourse?
7. What comparisons can be made between rhetorical analysis and discourse analysis? What are the social points of each? How do they differ?

7

CONTEMPORARY WESTERN PERSPECTIVES

In this chapter, as we move fully into the present, we consider several North American and European rhetoricians. We provide a synopsis of contemporary developments in rhetoric. We are heavily indebted to two major sources: Golden, Berquist, and Coleman's *The Rhetoric of Western Thought,* and Conley's *Rhetoric in the European Tradition,* both of which provide their own very useful synopsis of several major authors. Golden et al. indicate that contemporary rhetoric moves beyond the Aristotelian concept of "finding all of the available means of persuasion" as a rhetorical definition to new rhetorics such as "meaning-centered" rhetoric, "value-centered" rhetoric, "motivational/dramatistic-centered" rhetoric, and "argument-and-knowledge centered" rhetorics all of which have made major contributions to the development of modern rhetorical theory, criticism, and practice. These developments also move us closer to linkages with discourse analysis as we have demonstrated them in earlier chapters. We briefly consider the work of such seminal authors as I.A. Richards, Marshall McLuhan, Richard Weaver, Kenneth Burke, Stephen Toulmin, Chaim Perelman, Michel Foucault, and Jurgen Habermas.

CONTEMPORARY NORTH AMERICAN RHETORICIANS

There are many contemporary American writers on rhetorical theory, practice, and criticism, including a number who will not be discussed in our synopsis. Those rhetoricians selected are illustrative for our purposes in considering rhetoric practiced diplomatically in the UN. For the student in rhetoric, two of the more popular texts in the recent past have been Hauser's *Introduction to Rhetorical Theory* (1986 and its later editions) and Andrews' *The Practice of Rhetorical Criticism* (1990). In Hauser's work, one sees both the influences of classical and neoclassical rhetoricians, and also of the 18th Century epistomological rhetoricians. Besides many of the standard chapters in contemporary public speaking texts, Hauser includes chapters on "Making Commitments Through Rhetoric," "Acting with Language," "Experiencing Meaning in Rhetoric," "Rhetorical Form as Strategy," and "Strategic Forms of Argument Structures." We have already discussed language as strategy in an earlier chapter in our study of discourse analysis. Andrews discusses not only the nature of criticism and the constituents of the rhetorical act, through its context (also discussed in an earlier chapter), but also the audience, speaker, and rhetorical texts. Andrews also provides a series of critical case studies, such as Lincoln's "Second Inaugural Address," Nixon's "Address to the Nation on the War in Vietnam," and various other critical examples as written by authors in the field.

Golden et al. suggest several contemporary approaches to theory building and critical applications of rhetoric: *meaning centered* as an inherent communication problem in social relations, highlighted by such authors as Marshall McLuhan (1911–1980) and I. A. Richards (1893–1979); *value centered* as demonstrated by neo-Platonist Richard Weaver (1910–1963); *motivational and dramatistically centered,* as exemplified by Kenneth Burke (1897–1993), author of *A Grammar of Motives* and *A Rhetoric of Motives;* and *argumentative-and-knowledge centered* rhetoric, as demonstrated in the writings of Chaim Perelman (1912–1984) and Stephen Toulmin (1922–) (Golden et al., 1989, p. 234). Authors McKeon (1900–1985), Richards, McLuhan, Weaver, and Burke are discussed briefly in this section on North American contemporary rhetoric. Toulmin and Perelman are discussed in the section on Contemporary European rhetoricians with Michel Foulcault (1926–1984) and Jurgen Habermas (1926–1984).

What is the difference between meaning-centered rhetoric, value-centered rhetoric, motivational-and-dramatistic-centered rhetoric, and knowledge-centered rhetoric? All can be traced back in a general way to the classical Greek and Roman authors, as the foundations for later thought during the Enlightenment, and more directly to the 20th century, especially as World War II and its aftermath affected several of these authors in various ways.

It is important to note that just as in the Enlightenment period, the contemporary period, both in North America and in Europe, has generated many efforts at creating or explaining "the new rhetoric." Wayne Booth, in an address to the Modern Language Association of America in 1964, stated a paradox, "ours is a rhetorical age without a rhetorical theory—and calls for a revival of rhetoric as a discipline—not a revival of old rhetorics, but creation of a new rhetoric, a comprehensive theory that will take account of both the pervasiveness and the peculiar character of modern rhetorical practice" (Booth cited in Steinmann, 1967, p. 1). Martin Steinmann's book is titled *New Rhetorics*. We also see that the Belgian author, Chaim Perelman's major contribution to the study of rhetoric, *Traité de l'Argumentation* is more popularly known in North America as *The New Rhetoric*.

Robert Scott and Bernard Brock in their *Methods of Rhetorical Criticism: A Twentieth Century Perspective*, provide several characteristics of critical perspectives of the contemporary emphasis on "New Rhetorics." First, the notion of the new rhetorics stresses society as being in a continual state of process with the focus on interaction and change (like communication or culture themselves). Second, the belief in stable relationships, a factor in the first concept, potentially leads to a critical consensus on a method flexible enough to enable the critics to analyze rhetorical patterns typical of the social process. Third, the "word–thought–thing" relation is reciprocal, so that the nature of the object or relation affects the selection of words, but the use of the symbol system itself affects a person's perception of reality. Scott and Brock isolate two basic approaches within the general perspectives of the new rhetorics: the *semantical–grammatical*approach and *the dramatistic* approach. The first approach or meaning–centered rhetoric starts with the assumption that the rhetorical critic should begin her or his rhetorical analysis with the speaker's or writer's use of language. Scott and Brock recommend Richard Weaver's essay "Some Rhetorical Aspects of Grammatical Categories" as an effective illus-tration of how a critic can analyze diverse materials in the semantical–grammatical framework. Both the *syntax of grammar* and the *semantics of meaning* are appropriately utilized in this type of semantical–grammatical method of rhetorical analysis (Scott & Brock, 1972, pp. 262–265). The dramatistic approach incorporates the dramatic and poetic nature of conflict both in oratory and in writing.

Richard McKeon: A New Rhetoric

Thomas Conley, in *Rhetoric in the European Tradition*, indicates that Richard McKeon (born in 1900 and a later professor of the University of Chicago Program of Ideas and Methods), saw the complexity of a world community faced in the period after World War II both with conflict and interdependence and was stung by his extensive negative experience with UNESCO. He sought a philosophy that could illuminate the human problems of freedom, and its absence, as well as of life and death. He called in 1966 for a new rhetoric: "the method of a new rhetoric, transformed to philosophic uses, is needed to bring invention to bear on innovation of insights rather than on repetition of verbal forms and to bring judgment to bear on issues of causes rather than on adjustments to formed habits, characters and prejudices" (McKeon, cited in Conley, 1990, p. 289). In 1971, he moved the argument farther from dialectic to rhetoric, as did Kenneth Burke, and recommended the need of a universal rhetoric:

> an art of producing things and arts, and not merely one of producing words and arguments. . . . Rhetoricians and philosophers might today make rhetoric an architectonic art which relates all things by means of science and [human experiences]. Rhetoric in all its applications is focused on the particular, not the universal—particular questions or constitutions in law, particular works or compositions in art, or particular facts or data in experience and existence. In an age of technology . . . we seek to produce it in concrete experience and existence by rejoining reason and sense, cognition and emotion, universal law and concrete occurrence. (McKeon, cited in Conley, 1990, pp. 289–290)

Essentially, Conley argues, McKeon attempted to create the basis for a new rhetoric, suitable for the discussion and resolution of problems peculiar to the age of international conflict and cooperation, technological innovation, and rapid change: a rejoining of wisdom and eloquence (Conley, 1990, pp. 190–191).

MEANING CENTERED RHETORIC

I.A. Richards and Marshall McLuhan are identified with meaning-centered rhetoric, or the semantical–grammatical method of rhetoric. Richards and McLuhan both considered an inherent communication problem in social relations the nature of meaning and its relation to the reality of life. The neoPlatonist, Richard Weaver, was most interested in investigating rhetoric as an emerging value system as values impact on language systems. Scott and Brock also place him in the semantical–grammatical perspective. Obviously, there is considerable overlapping. Kenneth Burke based his rhetorical system primarily on human motivation, as expressed in dramatism, in two of his major works: *A Grammar of Motives* and *A Rhetoric of Motives.* Stephen Toulmin and Chaim Perelman both approached rhetoric as an instrument for the creation and advancement of knowledge (Golden et al., 1989, p. 234).

Meaning-Centered Rhetoric: I.A. Richards

I.A. Richards (1893–1979), a professor at Cambridge University, Tsing Hua University in Bejing, China, and Harvard University, authored several important books in the early part of the 20th century, including *The Meaning of Meaning,* coauthored with C.K Ogden in 1923; *Principles of Literary Criticism* (1924); and *The Philosophy of Rhetoric* (1936). These books had a rippling effect for most of the 20th century on the study of *semiotics* (the logic of meanings), *syntactics* (the branch of semiotics that deals with the formal properties of signs and symbols), *semantics* (the study of meanings in language forms in linguistics and the relation between signs and symbols and what they represent in logic), and *pragmatics* (the branch of semiotics that deals with the relation between signs or expressions and their users).

Conley describes Richard's belief:

> Conflict arises from misunderstanding, and misunderstanding arises in large part from misplaced expectations and less than conscious presumptions about language," Richards argues. "What is required is a 'new rhetoric.' Unlike the 'old rhetoric'—'the theory of the battle of words . . . dominated by the combative impulse'—the new rhetoric 'will be a study of misunderstanding and its remedies,' one that explores the conditions of understanding discourse by studying how language does what it does. (Richards, cited in Conley, 1990, pp. 262–263)

Conley explains Richard's "Proper Meaning Superstition,"—the belief that each word has a meaning, ideally a single meaning of its own, independent of and controlling its use and the purpose for which it should be uttered," and his "Proper Usage Superstition," the doctrine that there is a correct or commendable use for every word and that "literary virtue consists in making use of it." Richard's difficulty with the superstitions is that they have no bearing to the reality of actual language usage.

Richard's cure is his "Context Theorem of Meaning," which clusters events that fit together within a single *context* and in which the *metaphor* is the very essence of language and of thought. Conley identifies Richards and his colleague Ogden in *The Meaning of Meaning,* as delineating that the explanation of "meaning" must begin with:

> the consideration that, as human beings, we respond to sensory data in our environment. Every stimulus we receive through the senses leaves a trace or impression. . . . In every perception, a context is formed made up of the sensations experienced and stored in the memory. Whenever any part of a context is experienced, the missing parts of that context are recalled; so

> when part of the context is experienced, that part affects us as though the entire context were present. (Conley, 1990, p. 264)

Richards hopes that as we develop our skills in comprehension by understanding the meaning contextually, and by being able to supply the missing parts of the context from which it draws its usefulness, or "delegated efficacy," it thus leads "to a new era of human understanding and cooperation in thinking" (Conley, 1990, p. 264).

Basically, Richards is saying, as do later semanticists, that meaning does not reside in the word, but in people's minds and in specific contexts. Meaning is not just a matter of linking a word to a thing, but encompasses the relation between the word, its referent, and the cluster of perceptions we associate with both. Words, by themselves, are open to ambiguity (Conley, 1990, pp. 264–265). Conley indicates that Richards' view of the new rhetoric, which no longer calls for persuasion as its core, is much closer to the study of rhetoric as composition than the Aristotelian concept of rhetoric, or is a rule book for composition of discourse distinguished on one side from poetry and on the other side from scientific writing—"that is, purely referential discourse," and thus has the ability to subject communication to empirical scrutiny (Conley, 1990, pp. 267–268). Because the metaphor shows the relation between "two different thoughts of different things active together and supported by a single word, or phrase, whose meaning is a resultant of their interaction" (Richards, cited in Conley, 1990, p. 266), Conley argues Richards's statement of the metaphor is the essence not only of language but also of thought itself, makes sense:

> since thought is also a transaction between contexts as thought works about in its activities of sorting, comparing, and abstracting. Command of metaphor is essential in the interpretation (the apprehension of the meaning) of all discourse, and of poetry in particular. But it can do more, Richards argues, for (it) can help us understand how our minds work and thus help us 'control . . . the world that we make for ourselves to live in' . . . and "restore life itself to order." (Richards, cited in Conley, 1990, p. 266)

Golden et al. (1989) made this assessment of I.A. Richards:

> Perhaps no one in the last generation has exerted more influence upon literary criticism, both theoretic and applied, than has I.A. Richards. His distinction (made in *The Meaning of Meaning*) between the "referential" aspect of words and the "emotive" seemed to split in two, not merely the world of words, but the universe itself, wrenching asunder fact and fiction, science and poetry, thought and emotion. (In some quarters, his use of the distinction was hailed as a necessary liberation of science; in others as a ruthless amputation of poetry)

As Richards's view is that rhetoric is a study of misunderstandings and its remedies, "understanding and cooperation in thinking" (Richards cited in Conley, 1990, p. 264), it would seem highly applicable to the UN and to our efforts in *Diplomatic Discourse.* Secretary-General Boutrous Boutrous Ghali wrote in 1994:

> At this moment the first words of the Charter, "We the Peoples of the United Nations" convey a meaning originally intended but perhaps never before fully comprehended. We—all of us—*are* the United Nations. Unique in its universal character as the world Organization, the United Nations is not a substitute or surrogate for individual, community, national or international action. The United Nations is now and increasingly will be what we choose to make of it. (Boutrous-Ghali, 1994, p. 1)

Meaning-Centered Rhetoric: Marshall McLuhan

One of the 20th Century's most curiously interesting rhetorical or communication theorists, and identified by Golden et al. as having a meaning centered-rhetoric was the Canadian University of Toronto Professor, Marshall McLuhan, born in Alberta in 1911. McLuhan's rhetorical and communication developments spanned erratically over his more than 12 books, including *The Mechanical Bride: Folklore of Industrial Man,* a little noted 1951 publication; perhaps one of his most serious ones, but at the same time, chapterless: *The Gutenberg Galaxy: The Making of the Typographic Man* (1962). It was strongly influenced by the Canadian economist, Harold Innis, and his *The Bias of Communication.* McLuhan's The *Gutenberg Galaxy* began to develop a type of "communication cult" around McLuhan, his *Understanding Media: The Extensions of Man* (1964), his and Quentin Fiore's *The Medium Is the Massage: An Inventory of Effects* in 1967, and his and Harley Parker's *Through the Vanishing Point: Space in Poetry and Painting* (Parker created a museum of "McLuhanisms," 1968) all spiraled him into international prominence.

Like Walter Ong's *The Presence of the Word,* McLuhan's *The Gutenberg Galaxy* identified stages of cultural development through communication which he designates somewhat differently than Ong: the preliterate oral–aural stage, the manuscript stage extending from the invention of the alphabet to the development of the Gutenberg printing press and movable type, and the fourth stage, electric circuitry. McLuhan argues: "A theory of cultural change is impossible without knowledge of the changing sense ratios effected by various externalizations of our senses," and "when technology extends one of our senses, a new translation of culture occurs as swiftly as the new technology is interiorized" (McLuhan, 1962). As Edward Hall's books, *The Hidden Dimension, The Silent Language, Beyond*

Culture, and *The Dance of Life* remarkably popularized anthropological linkages with intercultural and nonverbal communication, so did McLuhan's many books popularize communication and media theory.

Although *Understanding Media* begins to explore the human's extensions—in all sorts of media in a rather standard academic format, *The Medium Is the Massage* boldly and graphically announces these extensions: "All media are extensions of some human faculty-psychic or physical," "The wheel is an extension of the foot," "The book is an extension of the eye," "clothing, an extension of the skin," and "electric circuitry, an extension of the central nervous system" (McLuhan & Fiore, 1967).

McLuhan describes himself:

> CASTING MY PERILS BEFORE SWAINS
>
> I am an investigator. I make probes. I have no point of view. I do not stay in one position.
>
> Anybody in our culture is regarded as invited as long as he stays in one fixed position. Once he starts moving around and crossing boundaries, he's delinquent, he's fair game.
>
> The explorer is totally inconsistent. He never knows at what moment he will make some startling discovery. And consistency is a meaningless term to apply to an explorer. If he wanted to be consistent, he would stay home.
>
> Jacques Ellul says that propaganda begins when dialogue ends. I talk back to media and set off on an adventure of exploration.
>
> I DON'T EXPLAIN—
>
> I EXPLORE. (McLuhan, cited in Stearn, 1967, p. xii)

Golden et al. called him an important figure in the rhetoric of western thought because of his provocative insights on communication media—which he described very broadly—as any human extension. He was among the early proponents that the human image of his or her world is significantly changed by various media, dominant at the time. They centered him firmly in the meaning-centered rhetoric with I.A. Richards (Golden et al., 1989, p. 259).

Kenneth Boulding summarizes the major points of *The Gutenberg Galaxy* and *Understanding Media* by three points:

> 1. A social system is largely structured by the nature of the media in which communications are made, not by the content of these communications. . . .
> 2. Media can be divided into "hot" media, which do not involve much participation on the part of the recipient, and "cool" media, in which the process of communication involves a great deal of participation on the part of the recipient. The effect of a medium on the structure of society depends very much on its temperature. . . . McLuhan argues that by far the most important thing that has happened in the twentieth century is the development of television, which is a cool medium of communication, involving a

> high level of participation on the part of the viewer. . . . We have on the one hand the dimension of involvement of the recipient, which is the one on which McLuhan concentrates, and this is indeed important. . . . Some media are demanding, some are undemanding. . . . A second dimension . . . is the range of a medium. This is closely related to the ability of the medium to develop a system of feedback from the communicatee to the communicator. . . . A third dimension of media is their information density. . . . The concept here is close to the information theorist's concept of capacity . . . the human's capacity is limited by the capacity of his sense organs. . . . Print created an "explosion" resulting in the breakup of an old integrated order into individualistic, differentiated, atomistic, mechanical human particles, producing classical economics, Protestantism, and the assembly lines. Electricity creates an "implosion" which unifies the nervous systems of all mankind into a single contemporaneous whole, bringing us back to the tribal village, this time on a world scale. (Boulding, cited in Stearn, 1967, pp. 68–75)

One of McLuhan's most famous statements is first that the "medium is the message," and later that the "medium is the massage." Content is obviously less important in McLuhan's thinking than what channel or medium conveys the content. Henry Gibson's one line poem on "Laugh-In" in 1968: "Marshall McLuhan, what are you doin?" has been widely quoted when referring to him as a larger than life and rather comical influence in the 1960's. *Life's* proclamation of him as "The Oracle of the Electric Age," *The New York Herald Tribune's* statement about him that he was "the most important thinker since Newton, Darwin, Freud, Einstein, and Pavlov," and *The Nations's* label, "the media guru from Toronto," are counterbalanced by Arthur M. Schlesinger, Jr.'s depreciation of him as: "an intelligent man who, for reasons of his own, prefers to masquerade as a charlatan." Schlesinger, who held the Albert Schweitzer Professorship of the Humanities at the City University of New York at the same time that McLuhan held the Albert Schweitzer Professorship at Fordham University, questions the nature of McLuhanism:

> What then is McLuhanism? It is a chaotic combination of bland assertion, astute guesswork, fake analogy, dazzling insight, hopeless nonsense, shockmanship, showmanship, wisecracks, and oracular mystification, all mingled cockily and indiscriminately in an endless and random dialogue. It also, in my judgment, contains a deeply serious argument. . . . One may read McLuhanism as perspective or prophecy. The perspective enables him to say many things—some subtle and impressive, as on privacy or on the generational conflict, some forced and dubious, as on TV commercials—about contemporary culture. The prophecy is less lucid and, I think, entraps him in inherent contradictions. . . . One suspects, indeed, that he is indulging his vision of the future primarily for the shock of the thought and the plea-

> sure of the scandal. Underneath the hyperbole and the vaudeville there remains a significant and fertile truth. . . . we . . . stand in debt to McLuhan for a marvelously stimulating insight into the dynamics of change. (Schlesinger, cited in Crosby & Bond, 1968, pp. 190–193)

On the one hand, McLuhan appeared not to take himself too seriously, calling some of his own communication theories "difficult," or "nonsense." McLuhan's dialogue with an interviewer, suggests the eclectic nature of his rhetorical development:

> Goldman: How is it, Professor McLuhan, that you should be so concerned with media? Here you are the son of Baptist parents, convert to Catholicism, a Canadian student of English literature, formerly an engineering student and now . . .
>
> McLuhan, Oh don't bother about that data.
>
> Goldman: Why?
>
> McLuhan: It's all wrong! And, in any case quite unnecessary! (McLuhan, cited in Stearn, 1967, p. xv)

On the other hand, McLuhan would not infrequently keep very expensively funded events waiting while he finished grading his student's papers so that he could return them on time. With his sweep of history from the Greeks to the present, he not only offered metaphors which when taken literally seemed senseless, but also could correctly quote a whole range of historical and literary authors when he turned from comic one-liners to serious scholarly thinking. He was a paradox and a master of paradoxes.

Just as I.A. Richards argued that the metaphor is the essence both of language and thought, McLuhan was a master of metaphors, many of them appearing absurd if taken as literally meaning what they suggest. This is of course the value of metaphors. From *The Gutenberg Galaxy,* we see examples of metaphors about the senses and print such as: "Civilization gives the barbarian or tribal man an eye for an ear and is now at odds with the electronic world," "The new time sense of typographic man is cinematic and sequential and pictorial," "Print, in turning the vernaculars into mass media, or closed systems created the uniform, centralizing forces of modern nationalism," "Typography cracked the voices of silence," and "The interiorization of the technology of the phonetic alphabet translates man from the magical world of the ear to the neutral visual world." From *The Medium Is the Massage,* McLuhan has a whole range of metaphors, including the title itself, as well as "The medium is the message" as one of his most important, whether or not right, statements. We have already cited his "extensions of man" metaphors. A major metaphor for which he became very famous, in addition to "The medium is the message," and "The medium is the massage," is his statement: "The new electronic interdependence recreates the world in the image of a global village."

Jonathan Miller in *Marshall McLuhan,* believes that his best book is *The Gutenberg Galaxy,* and that all of his other books were simply glosses of this earlier work, which McLuhan laid out as a mosaic, precisely to demonstrate the unreliability of a strict linear precis, placing ideas and quotations side by side in suggestive juxtaposition, and leaving the reader to draw his or her own conclusions. Miller indicates that McLuhan's claim that human experience is both plural and voluminous, and that in the very act of being conscious of ourselves, we are in the receipt of a rich manifold of simultaneous sensation, makes sense. For McLuhan, the larger the number of senses involved, the better the chance of transmitting a reliable copy of the sender's mental state. McLuhan claims that spoken language exerts an irresistible power over the listener's imagination and that words have acquired the status of "momentary deities." Challenging McLuhan's arguments systematically, although giving him credit for his contributions which Miller finds often highly exaggerated, Miller ends his book: "Perhaps McLuhan has accomplished the greatest paradox of all, creating the possibility of truth by shocking us all with a gigantic system of lies" (Miller, 1971, pp. 123–124).

However, Golden et al. although noting discrepancies and inconsistencies throughout his works, believed that McLuhan had four major strengths as a rhetorical and communication theorist: (a) We are indebted to him for alerting us to the great extent in which a medium affects the message and its reception; (b) because the nature of the medium affects the message reception, speakers should either choose that medium most suitable to their natural style or modify the style so as to make it appropriate to the medium; (c) the resurgence of the oral mode of communication has been due to the influence of the electronic media, and according to McLuhan, has gained so much popularity during the age of television that it has contributed to the retribilization of humans; and (d) the structure of public discourse and the modifications that may have to be made in our conception occur as we move more and more into the electronic age. Golden et al. concluded:

> McLuhan, despite his frequent excesses and unsupported claims, has gone far beyond most of his predecessors and peers in describing the relationship between the medium and the message, and in challenging traditional views regarding the canons. More than any other rhetorician analyzed in this book, he helps us understand and appreciate the reciprocal relationships between rhetoric and the mass media and the influence of the latter on our sensory perceptions. (Golden et al., 1989, pp. 263–265)

McLuhan sums up the dilemma for understanding messages in contemporary society:

> Stearn: "The communications expert," one of your detractors has remarked, "cannot communicate," underlying Jonathan Miller's observation: "McLuhan opens many doors, including the doors of chaos."
>
> McLuhan: Communication in the conventional sense, is difficult under any conditions. People prefer *rapport* through smoking or drinking together. There is more communication there than there ever is by verbal means. We can share environments, we can share weather, we can share all sorts of cultural factors together but communication takes place only inadequately and is very seldom understood. . . . There is a kind of illusion in the world we live in that communications is something that happens all the time, that it's normal. And when it doesn't happen, this is horrendous. Actually, communication is an exceedingly difficult activity. (McLuhan & Stearn, cited in Stearn, 1967, p. 283)

VALUE-CENTERED RHETORIC: RICHARD WEAVER

Richard Weaver (1910–1963) was a "Southern Agrarian," seeing the South, "a rooted culture," as the new Athens which Plato had called for in Greece, as well as morally superior to the northern United States. He associated himself with the "New Criticism" that developed in southern American universities. Weaver taught humanities and English at the University of Chicago from 1944 until his death in 1963. He developed into a neoPlatonist, calling for an honest rhetoric, preceded by dialectic as a method of inquiry

> for the establishment of truth about doubtful propositions on the basis of categorization, definition, implication, and exposure of contradictions. But dialectic, since it is concerned only with the meaning of propositions in discourse, cannot establish truth or compel belief by itself. It cannot *move* individuals to action or change of attitude. Thus dialectic must be supplemented by rhetoric in the world of action. (Conley, 1990, p. 280)

Conley (1990) indicated that

> deeply troubled by the world around him, a world in which "(we are) confronted not only by evil practioners, but also, and probably to an unprecedented degree, by men who are conditioned by the evil of others," Weaver revived the idealism of Plato in his search for social and personal salvation. (p. 280)

Conley indicated that Weaver saw himself as a "true conservative" and offered major critiques of the radical left, radical egalitarianism, progressive education, cultural relativism, materialism, and degenerate forms of art and music (in which he included impressionism and jazz). Conley stressed that although Weaver, like Richards and Kenneth Burke, was moved by the conflicts of the age to find some cure, it was quite unlike Richards' "study of misunderstandings and its remedies," and Burke's "the use of language as a symbolic means of inducing cooperation in beings that by nature respond to symbols." Instead, Weaver saw an ideal Platonic rhetoric in which the "noble rhetorician's" arguments are grounded in dialectic that allow him or her to construct a hierarchy of argumentative modes which approach the ideal—starting with the most noble argument from definition (Conley, 1989, pp. 280–281).

Weaver's first book in 1948, which he wanted to call *The Fearful Descent*, became instead *Ideas Have Consequences.* Its cover calls it "an unsparing diagnosis of the ills of our age, with a realistic remedy based on the right use of [a person's] reason, acceptance of an absolute reality, and the recognition that ideas, like actions, have consequences." As a reaction to the evils generated by World War II, its destruction, the weakening of cultural values and ethical principles, and the Cold War that it had already generated immediately after the war, Weaver writes that his book is

> an intuition of a situation. The intuition is of a world which has lost its center, which desires to believe again in value and obligation. . . . It seems to me that the world is now more than ever dominated by the gods of mass and speed and that the worship of these can lead only to the lowering of standards, the adulteration of quality, and, in general, to the loss of those things which are essential to the life of civility and culture. (Weaver, 1948, p. vi)

Citing directly what he considered the contemporary conflict of 1948, Weaver wrote:

> Now, in the first half of the twentieth century, at the height of modern progress, we behold unprecedented outbreaks of hatred and violence; we have seen whole nations desolated by war and turned into penal camps by their conquerors; we find half of [humankind] looking upon the other half as criminal. Everywhere occur symptoms of mass psychosis. Most portentious of all, there appear diverging bases of value, so that our single planetary globe is mocked by worlds of different understanding. (Weaver, 1948, p. 2)

Although Reinhold Niebuhr wrote that "*Ideas Have Consequences* is a profound diagnosis of the sickness of our culture," his solutions were somewhat limited. They included endorsing the defense of the right of private property—"the last metaphysical right remaining to us"; the purification of the language, so that the power of the word could be used for good and not evil; an attitude of piety towards nature, other humans, and the contributions of the past; support of true justice; a reinvigoration of intellectual culture; a return to civility; and a revival of religious belief.

Weaver asked in his conclusion whether modern humans really want to get well from the morass affecting them, or whether they wish to destroy the world. If modern humans really want to get well, he asks, are they willing to pay the price? Are they willing for deep reforms? Are they willing to speak of duties rather than just freedoms? Weaver concluded:

> We are all in this together. Practically, no one can stand aside from a sweep as deep and broad as the decline of a civilization. If the thinkers of our time cannot catch the imagination of the world to the point of effecting some profound transformation, they must succumb with it. (Weaver, 1948, pp. 186–187)

Many of the addresses, speeches, and statements given by world leaders in the UN during its first 50 years offered a similar theme—a choice of world-wide survival or world-wide destruction.

Weaver's *The Ethics of Rhetoric* expanded his concepts in the earlier book. Conley notes that in the first book, Weaver had laid down a tripartite analysis of knowledge and a general theory of culture consistent with that analysis:

> There are three levels of "conscious reflection" at which we perceive, order, and evaluate our world: ideas, which are thoughts about particular empirical things; beliefs, or concepts that order the world of facts; and the "metaphysical dream," an "intuitive feeling about the immanent nature of reality." Truth resides at the level of the metaphysical dream and is determined by the degree to which facts and ideas conform to their archetypal essences. Every culture revolves around some metaphysical dream embodied in a "tyrannizing image" that acts as the principle of coherence society imposes on the morass of things. (Weaver, cited in Conley, 1990, p. 279)

This is highly similar to Plato's ideal world.

Developing this concept of the "tyrannizing image" of culture further, Weaver in *The Ethics of Rhetoric,* argued that rhetoric stands at the center of social order, for, formed by dialectical questioning, it provides advice about how humans can cooperate in promoting a better society. Like Plato, Weaver stressed the need for the rhetorician to be preoccupied with truth, justice, and the best good for society, starting with definition and first principles as the highest form of knowledge.

A concept that he developed has become a standard ultimate term in rhetorical criticism: "god" and "devil" terms, both of which he criticizes because they tend to be used irrationally and often in violation of ethical precepts. A "god" term represents a universal value that is good, desired, or recommended, whereas a "devil" term represents a negative universal or near universal concept that is considered unfavorably. At the UN before the collapse of the Soviet Union, both the Charter and the Universal Declaration of Human Rights were almost always god terms for both the east and west; the term *the United Nations* and *democracy* frequently were god terms for most of its member delegations; the Bible and Quran were both god terms; the Declaration of Independence and the *Communist Manifesto* both served as god terms for different delegations; *freedom, justice, progress, disarmament,* and *the will of the people* all served as "god" terms. *Imperialism, colonialism, Zionism, Apartheid, communism, racism, underdevelopment, superpowers, the Cold War, captive nations, the Iron Curtain,* and *the bamboo curtain* were all devil terms for one delegation or another.

Before 1972, when the People's Republic of China was admitted to the UN, and for some time after, American media regularly called it "Red China," whereas Chinese officials and media referred to the United States and the west as "the running dogs of imperialism." In the 1967 Fifth Emergency Special Session of the General Assembly related to the 6-day Middle East War, the Israelis were particularly offended when the leaders of several Eastern European countries used the devil term "Hitler's blitzkrieg," to refer in their addresses to the Israeli attack on Jordan, Egypt, and Syria. A recent god term has become *sustainable development.* A "devil" term found on signs outside the UN in protest of Li Peng's presence at the Security Council at the level of heads of state and government in 1992, was "Butcher of Tiananmen Square."

Richard Weaver's speech at the University of Oklahoma in 1962, "Language Is Sermonic," a year before his death has been widely reprinted and is considered his most important statement on rhetoric. Based on this speech and his chapter in *The Ethics of Rhetoric,* "Some Rhetorical Aspects of Grammatical Categories," Scott and Brock placed Weaver in the semantical–grammatical approach to rhetoric with I.A. Richards because of his *Ideas Have Consequences, The Ethics of Rhetoric,* and his "Language Is Sermonic." Golden et al. placed him as a value-centered rhetorician. We can ask if Weaver can reasonably be identified in both ways. The answer is probably yes because he was seriously interested in the relationship of language and meaning in all three works to the decline of contemporary civilization, whereas at the same time in all three works he offered prescriptive suggestions for how rhetoric can help humans to move beyond their current decline, at least as he saw it as a true conservative in 1948, 1953, and 1962. Although his reputation was nowhere as high as McLuhan's or even later as high as Kenneth Burke, who outlived him by three decades, it was not an insignificant conservative voice in the last 16 years of his life, and beyond. It is not clear if he informed the conservative thrust generated by Senator Barry Goldwater in the 1964 presidential campaign and election, but if he was political, it would not seem unlikely.

In "Some Rhetorical Aspects of Grammatical Categories," in *The Ethics of Rhetoric,* Weaver spent considerable time speaking of grammar, the sentence, and parts of speech. He wrote:

> In total rhetorical effect the sentence seems to be peculiarly "the thing said," whereas all other elements are "the things named." And accordingly the right to utter a sentence is one of the very greatest liberties; and we are entitled to little wonder that freedom of utterance should be, in every society, one of the most contentious and ill-defined rights. The liberty to impose this formal unity is a liberty to handle the world, to remake it, if only a little, and to hand it to others in a shape which may influence their actions. (Weaver, cited in Scott & Brock, 1972, p. 271)

Breaking up parts of the sentence, he called the noun and verb forceful, with the noun having special dignity and expressing things whose being is completed, and the verb, with the noun, creating phenomena: actions or states of being; the adjective has secondary force and status, as the noun can exist without the adjective but not the reverse; the adverb has superior mobility within the sentence because of its ability to be placed with different parts of speech, and is often judgmental; the conjunction enables the speaker or writer to express relation, which Weaver considers very important when considering definitions as the highest form of argument, precisely because definitions express relationships of a comparative or contrastive nature (Weaver, cited in Scott & Brock, 1972, p. 271).

"Language Is Sermonic" begins with Weaver's views of decline in the contemporary period, as did *Ideas Have Consequences.* He included rhetoric itself, the teaching of literature, a cultural event in the changing human image of other humans, the method of scientific inquiry, the decline of religion, and the decline of civility. Weaver said that although logic is increasingly becoming "symbolic logic," rhetoric is always addressed to humans in their humanity, as every speech intended to persuade others is directed toward a special audience, even a radio address appealing "to the world." We could note that for many decades, the Roman Pontiff gives an annual radio address, which is also widely televised in the more recent period, "ad urbis, ad orbis," "to the City (of Rome) and to the world." Weaver said the object of rhetoric is to appeal to the "whole" person, as it not only appeals to his or her reason, but also to a feeling being who also suffers:

> Rhetoric is intended for historical man, or for man as conditioned by history. . . . Just as man from the point of view of rhetoric is not purely a thinking machine, or a mere seat of rationality, so he is not a creature abstracted from time and place. If science deals with the abstract and the universal, rhetoric is near the other end, dealing in significant part with the particular and the concrete. . . . Rhetoric should be considered the most humanistic of the humanities. . . . Rhetoric always comes to us in well fleshed words, and that is because it must deal with the world, the thickness, stubbornness, and power of it. (Weaver, cited in Johannensen, 1971, pp. 163–168)

Giving credit to the classical writers, Weaver established four types of arguments: (a) defining its nature—which he considered the highest form; (b) cause–effect; (c) relation of similarity and dissimilarity, for example literal analogies and figurative metaphors; and (d) testimony, which is an external force. A fifth type of argument is an appeal to circumstance, which Weaver considered the weakest argument. Even in law courts, circumstantial evidence has an extra burden of proof. Weaver argued that unlike formal logic, the user of rhetoric has the responsibility to be realistic; he or she deals with specific questions rooted in a historical situation; she or he must always be concerned with what the audience needs or will respond to; the user of rhetoric has to make choices about which topics to incorporate; he or she has the ethical responsibility to be fair in these choices; rhetoric gives its users the potentials for leadership, as a human necessity, for good or ill; the language of the user is never entirely neutral, but because the human is a creature responding to purpose, his or her linguistic expression will be the carrier of tendency, and is predicative, and thus always sermonic or persuasive:

> As rhetoric confronts us with choices involving values, the rhetorician is a preacher to us, noble if he tries to direct our passion toward noble ends and base if he uses our passion to confuse and degrade us. Since all utterances influence us in one or the other of these directions, it is important that the direction be the right one, and it is better if this lay preacher is a master of his art. (Weaver, cited in Johannensen, 1971, pp. 168–179)

MOTIVATIONAL OR DRAMATISTIC RHETORIC: KENNETH BURKE

Kenneth Burke (1897–1993) was a major 20th Century social critic, neo-Aristotelian, and American leader of the "motivational" and "dramatistic" approach to rhetorical and literary criticism. Eventually, as he lived nearly a century, Burke's methods of dramatistic criticism found many followers, including a Kenneth Burke Society. Burke began working in 1921 as a critic and reviewer for a small Greenwich Village magazine, *The Dial*. During this period, he wrote a number of essays which he later gathered into his first book in 1931, *Counterstatement*. It was seen as a "new rhetoric." Later books dealing in one way or another with rhetoric included *Permanence and Change* (1935), *Attitudes Toward History* (1937), *The Philosophy of Literary Form: Studies in Symbolic Action* (1941), *A Grammar of Motives* (1945), *A Rhetoric of Motives* (1950), *The Rhetoric of Religion: Studies in Logology* (1961), *Language as Symbolic Action: Essays on Life, Literature, and Method* (1966) and an unfinished work "A Symbolic of Motives," which may have been intended to finish a trilogy on "motives." Even *The Rhetoric of Religion* had a thrust into motives.

Like other rhetoricians and communication theorists, such as Marshall McLuhan, I.A. Richards, and Richard Weaver, he was surprised to find extensive academic audiences outside of the range of his intentions. Richard Johannesen summarized Burke's theory of rhetoric: "as the conscious or unconscious use of verbal or nonverbal symbolic strategies to achieve identification between men. The function of rhetoric, urges Burke, is to induce cooperation and to transcend hierarchy and estrangement in achieving the Good Life." Man, Burke said, can be defined as

> the symbol-using (symbol-making, symbol-misusing) animal, inventor of the negative (or moralized by the negative), separated from his natural condition by instruments of his own making, goaded by the spirit of hierarchy (or moved by the sense of order), and rotten with perfection. (Johannesen, 1971, p. 75)

One of Burke's most active interpreters, Marie Hockmuth Nichols, said that "a good many people would classify Kenneth Burke as the most perceptive critic recently writing in America. . . . It would not be misleading to say that Burke has reached his present stature through singular devotion to a study of man and his language-using habits" (Nichols, 1971, p. 80). She suggested that Burke can be considered from five points of view: (a) the bases of communication, (b) the essence of rhetoric, (c) the scope of rhetoric, (d) the method of accomplishing communication, and (e) Burke's characteristic mode of analysis of motivation. Concerning the first point, Nichols proposed that the basis of communication lies in generic divisiveness, which, being common to all, is a universal fact about them prior to any divisiveness by social classes. Out of this divisiveness emerges the cause for linguistic communication; thus, communication is compensatory to division, noting that Burke sees all humans as having both an animal nature, which grounds them in physical property, and their rational property, or symbol using capacity, and the resulting differences. Burke believed that communication, involving verbal symbols to appeal to another, demonstrates three elements: (a) speaker, (b) speech, and (c) an appeal for a spoken-to person. The appeal, or the rhetorical use of language, becomes the essence of communication. The rhetorical use of language is "rooted in an essential function of language itself," namely "the use of language as a symbolic means of inducing cooperation in beings that by nature respond to symbols." Nichols pointed out that Burke would say whenever there is meaning there is persuasion, and wherever there is persuasion there is rhetoric. Burke would say that as long as humans use language symbols at all, they cannot help being rhetorical (Nichols, 1971, pp. 82–83). This is similar to Weaver's emphasis that all language is sermonic.

Nichols believed that Burke would say that one can place in terms of rhetoric all those statements by anthropologists, ethnologists, individual and social psychologists, and the like, that bear upon the persuasive aspects of language, the function of language as addressed, as direct or roundabout appeal to real or ideal audiences. Burke in 1951 summed up in one word the difference between old rhetoric—as *persuasion,* and new rhetoric—as *identification,* which can include a partially unconscious factor in appeal. Nichols believed that for Burke, identification is the central doctrine of his rhetorical perspective. For Burke, when people identify themselves with someone else, or with something else, they become *consubstantial*—thus the *doctrine of consubstantiality* may be necessary for any way of life. Substance, or "the thingness of a thing," involves for Burke the idea of identity, separateness, and uniqueness that gives coherence to the parts. There are various substances, both material and nonmaterial. Language has a property, or substance of its own, in that it transcends, through dialectic and for supporting identifications. A speaker or writer identifies with his or her audience through various means, structure of the message, style, and bringing consubstantiality out of division (Nichols, 1971, pp. 84–88).

According to Nichols, when Burke models the critical analysis for human motivation or action, he calls it his *dramatistic pentad* and the *dialectical substance.* There were many who sought, often unsuccessfully, to apply his *pentadic ratio* of five issues: *(a) act, (b) scene, (c) agent, (d) agency,* and *(e) purpose,* as though linked together in a drama. This method of rhetorical criticism parallels, more or less the standard of contemporary practical and daily journalism's basic questions (adding "when") which frame almost every Western news story: "who, what, where, how, and why" (Nichols, 1971, pp. 84–88).

Thomas Conley argued that correctly used, conflicting claims and rationalizations in a rhetorical endeavor can be mapped and brought into opposition with each other by consideration of Burke's "ratios" at work in their formation. The pentad thus becomes a tool for locating agreements and disagreements in rhetorical conflicts. Conley proposed that "put in proper use, the pentad can show the way toward 'creative conflict,' . . . Dialectic itself is less than perfect, as it is, ultimately, incomplete; yet we cannot afford to overlook its resources as an instrument of overcoming division" (Conley, 1990, pp. 274–275).

Nichols suggested that the dramatistic pentad is ontological, or a human's act, in which the language act itself is a substance: through the permanence of acts as seen by the act itself or a substance, the agent or agents who perform the act, an agency or means by which the act is performed, for example, language or drama, a scene, or background out of which the act develops, and a purpose for which the act is done (Nichols, 1971, p. 81). When Burke speaks of motive, he is actually concerned with the speaking or writing situation. Because language use for Burke is an act, a symbolic situation represents a coordination or interrelationship between the act, agent, agency, purpose, and scene. For Burke, symbolic action takes place in the drama of human relations. Burke said that one must constantly ask how language use obtains its ends. He believed that one can find out something about the nature of meaning, motive, human relations in general, through language used strategically. One of Burke's goals through all of his writing about motives and rhetoric is to promote "the good life" through a better understanding of the resources of language. Nichols stressed that although he saw language originally as a vehicle for his and other creative writing, he saw language break down in the depression of the 1930s and World War II, and that by the 1950s and later, he saw the purpose of rhetoric and language as a method for creating personal and ethical resources in this pursuit of "the good life" for more and more people (Nichols, 1971, pp. 88–92).

In the introduction to *Sow the Wind, Reap the Whirlwind: Heads of State Address the United Nations,* the point is made that the tension that exists between the human's peace-lovingness, and his or her divisiveness creates what Burke called the "universal rhetorical situation" which is the human's attempt to unite as a community, coupled with the fearful determination to maintain separateness. Burke said that as a symbol-inventing, symbol-using animal, the human wants not only survival, but security as well; the human wants the freedom to exist without anxiety and doubt; the human worries about his or her own survival. As an animal, the human wants to exist; as a symbol user, the human wants to exist as a human (Prosser, 1970, p. 4). To put it in the terms of Paulo Freire, the internationally known Brazilian adult educator: "The ontological vocation of humans is to be human; fully human and alive; fully human, alive and creative; fully human, alive, creative, and aware; fully human, alive, creative, aware, and free" (Freire, SIETAR International Congress, 1992).

There is considerable agreement among world leaders, heads of state and government, foreign ministers, and national representatives at the UN that it does transcend, as Burke would say, the human's separateness, his or her division, because the ideals of the Charter do offer common sacred elements and substance with which they can identify as they seek to promote the authentic spirit of their own people, and to motivate others in the international organization to identify their situation consubstantially with those whom they represent (Prosser, 1970, pp. 4–5). Followers of Burke's dramatistic method and dialectical situation and close observers of the UN for many years, Conor Cruise O'Brien and Felix Topolski suggest that the symbolic nature of the UN is its most important characteristic:

> It will be said that the assimilation of the United Nations to drama—sacred or not—is no more than a metaphor. It is a metaphor and yet more than a metaphor, because the United Nations itself is a structure of metaphors. It may be safer to approach this structure in terms of recognized metaphor—the relevance of which one must try to demonstrate at every stage—than in literal and legalistic terms which tend, by their ordinary associations, to shut out from our recognition the elements of fantasy, illusion and ritual which make up so large a part of the actual life and function of the organization. (O'Brien & Topolski, 1968, p. 18)

In the UN, one sees both verbal language as symbolism and nonverbal symbolism on a constant basis. Verbally, the language may be peaceful or warlike, boastful or humble, inclusive or exclusive, happy or angry. The cross-cultural archetypal metaphor pertaining to universal images such as nature, storms, the wind, floods, tides, and so forth is used frequently by speakers at the UN, particularly by representatives of cultures that are more traditional and orally–aurally rooted than script oriented. Michael Osborne postulated: "One could even consider questions such as whether the quantity of imagery varies according to rhythms such as crisis and calm of development and deterioration within a culture" (1967, p. 115). Although most heads of state and government speaking at the General Assembly are dressed in Western styles, many African leaders wear their tribal clothing; Popes Paul VI and John Paul II and Archbishop Makarios came to the UN in their religious clothing; Yassar Arafat, Fidel Castro, and other military leaders of countries came to the UN wearing military uniforms; early PRC delegates wore the Mao jackets still somewhat popular when the People's Republic of China entered the UN; Prime Minister Nehru of India wore a typical Indian jacket and hat; Muslim leaders wore the traditional Islamic clothing.

CONTEMPORARY EUROPEAN RHETORICIANS

Golden et al. spoke of such major contemporary European scholars in their futuristic consideration of rhetoric as: French philosopher and historian Michel Foucault, one of the most often quoted scholars of the 20th Century and the German critical theorist, Jurgen Habermas (1929–). Thomas Conley in his *Rhetoric in the European Tradition* discussed also the contemporary European writers: Toulmin, Perelman, both of whom Golden et al. placed within the argument-and-knowledge-centered rhetoricians, and Habermas. Although much of the contemporary discussion of rhetoric and its applications have been generated by Americans, Chaim Perelman and Stephen Toulmin have already been cited as examples of thinkers on rhetoric coming from outside the United States. Marshall McLuhan was Canadian.

Contemporary European Rhetoricians: Argument and Knowledge Based: Stephen Toulmin

Cambridge University's Stephen Toulmin (1922–) in his *Reason in Ethics* (1948), made a cogent case for ethics as a field of rational enquiry, as a practical philosophy and as a matter of survival:

> At times of crisis, when problems of particular complexity and importance are to be considered, the volume increases and the arguments offered become more wild and confused; until finally, when war or tyranny comes, reason is driven out into the wilderness, and the open discussion of general moral problems, even when completely abstract, is paralyzed by the dangers of lapsing into bad taste or treason. (Toulmin, cited in Conley, 1990, p. 293)

In Toulmin's 1958 book, *The Uses of Argument,* he proposed that a radical reordering of logical theory is needed in order to bring it in line with practical everyday logic. Toulmin distinguished between arguments and proofs—saying that arguments are not inferences but justifications. He said that argument begins when one party makes a claim or conclusion, and the other party disagrees or disbelieves it. It then becomes necessary for the claimant to show the grounds or proof for the claim. If the linkage between the claim and the support offered for it is unclear, then the claimant must explain what "warrants" the connection. One may need to move far closer toward probability rather than certainty. If there is a distinct contrary probability, one needs to introduce a qualification or disclaimer. Toulmin believed that the determination of whether an argument is sound varies from field to field.

Although Toulmin's redefinition of argument and proof was well accepted in the United States, his Cambridge and Oxford colleagues were brutally unsympathetic to his attempt to uproot formal Aristotelian logic. In the United States, Toulmin is frequently a subject in courses on rhetoric, argumentation and debate, and public speaking. Conley suggested that although both McKeon and Toulmin moved from a rather abstract philosophical base to a very practically oriented rhetorical base, McKeon focused on genre, stasis, and commonplaces, as in the rhetoric of Cicero, which is primarily a rhetoric of invention. Toulmin, with his concept of fields of rhetoric and the warrants that vary with them, is in the tradition of Aristotle, even while he moves away from the Aristotelian syllogism (Conley, 1990, pp. 291–295).

The method of analysis is seen from Toulmin's movement from accepted *data,* through a *warrant,* to a *claim.* The claim is the conclusion; the data answer the question about what evidence there is to support the claim and together these two concepts are the main proof line. The warrant provides the mental "leap" from the data to the claim. Toulmin showed the relation this way: *data* ≫ (therefore) *claim* ≫ *warrant,* (since) ≫ *backing,* (because) ≫ *qualifier,* (probably) ≫ rebuttal (unless). The development becomes more complicated with a *qualifier* and *rebuttal,* but the line of argument becomes more in tune with actual reality, Toulmin argued, than the Aristotelian syllogism which depends not only on the acceptance of the *major premise,* but also the *minor premise* for the conclusion to be valid. Although the Aristotelian syllogism is still useful in formal logic and in mathematical formulas, in rhetoric, where one deals with practical matters of recommending or advocating policy and action, Toulmin's system is more understandable and useful.

Golden et al. demonstrated the model with potentially reasonable information that they developed before the collapse of the Soviet Union as follows:

> (**Data**) Russia has violated 50 of 52 international agreements;
> (**Warrant**) Since past violations are symptomatic of probable future violations;
> (**Backing**) Other nations which had such a record of violations continued such action; Expert X states that nations which have been chronic violators nearly always continue such acts;
> (**Qualifier**) Probably,
> (**Claim**) Russia would violate the proposed ban on nuclear weapons testing.
> (**Rebuttal**) Unless the ban on nuclear weapons testing is significantly different from the violated agreements.
> (Golden et al., 1989, p. 358)

In a June 5, 1995, *US News and World Report* article "Pro and Con: Is the UN Beyond Rescue?" the headline is: "It's a bloated bureaucracy, say critics. It's fixable, insist backers. Here are arguments for and against reducing US funding for the United Nations," starting from the reverse position, with the claim first.

Pro Claim for Reducing US Funding to UN	**Con Claim Against Reducing Funding**
"Amid budget cuts and pressing domestic needs, the United States cannot afford to bear a disproportionate burden of the United Nations' costs."	The UN is the only multipurpose organization with global legitimacy. If the United States abdicates its leadership role, other countries will step in and tilt the international agenda to suit their interests."
"The UN is expensive and wasteful."	"Member states fail, not the UN"
"And it's unreformable."	"It's really a bargain."
"The United States already pays more than its fair share."	"There have been successes."
"The UN is ineffective."	"It can be fixed."
	"Global problems need global solutions."

We have not filled in all of the details of the one page article from *The US News and World Report,* but, utilizing Toulmin's method of argument, you can now develop his line of reasoning for both the pro and con side, with data, warrants, backing, qualifiers, claim, and rebuttal from the material supplied, with speculative details which you can fill in yourself for the purpose of the examples.

Contemporary European Rhetoricians: Argument and Knowledge Based: Chaim Perelman

The Jewish-born Chaim Perelman (1912–1984) and faculty member at the Free University of Belgium was heavily involved in the Belgian Resistance to the Nazis between 1940 and 1944. Although out of sight during this period, he completed a major article on the idea of justice that marked his own turn from philosophy to rhetoric. Perelman believed it was impossible to move from formal justice to concrete specific justice without some value judgment, and asks the question: "How does one reason about values?" He decided that he had no correct answer, and looked again at the complementary concepts of dialectic and rhetoric, which he had studied in the Belgian high school just before rhetoric was removed from the curriculum. In his university study, he thought that his instructors of rhetoric did not know what they were talking about and saw rhetoric, like Latin, as dead. After a decade of study, Perelman and his colleague Lucie Olbrechts-Tyteca, published *Traite de l'Argumentation (Treatise on Argument)* which Conley pointed out is recognized today as a landmark for the revival of rhetoric in Europe. Although Perelman least expected it, it became very popular in the United States. In English, it came to be called *The New Rhetoric.*

Perelman and Olbrechts-Tyteca defined argumentation as the discursive means by which an audience is led to adhere to a given thesis, or by which its adherence is reinforced. They treated the premises concerning facts, truths, and values that are basic to agreement, the choice of data and their adaption for the speaker's or writer's purposes, and the modes of presentation in discourse. There are some similarities to the work of Toulmin, both of which were developed independently of each other.

Conley stressed that the two authors were speaking about the entire range of discursive methods of argumentation, and not just "logical" forms. They returned to the concept of "places" or "commonplaces" which both Aristotle and Cicero developed from where one can find arguments, such as a premise of a general nature (Conley, 1990, pp. 296–299). They develop the notion of the "universal audience" (which we may develop as a concept for addresses and statements in an international forum such as the UN General Assembly and Security Council). Conley remarked that *The New Rhetoric* is a passionate book, as seen by its ending:

> Only the existence of an argumentation that is neither compelling (contraignant) nor arbitrary can give meaning to human freedom, a state in which a reasonable choice can be exercised. . . . The theory of argumentation will help to develop . . . the justification of the possibility of a human community in the sphere of action. (Perelman & Olbrechts-Tyteca, cited in Conley, 1990, p. 299)

Golden et al. placed Perelman in the argument-and-knowledge-centered" rhetorical trends of Europe, because Perelman proposed that practical argument, not formal reasoning, is the required tool for disseminating ideas: "In other words, practical argument is a way of knowing." Like authors such as Burke who have introduced their own vocabulary to establish a new rhetoric, Perelman has several, including "universal audience" that audience—either immediate or long range, which is comprised of rational men and women, who know how to judge and test the strength or weaknesses of an argument by applying the criterion of "experience." For Perelman, the very nature of practical argument in reality as contrasted with formal reasoning can be seen in the word *quasi-logical.* What Perelman called "the starting point of argument" resembles basic premises, as he said that it is impossible for an advocate to promote an adherence of minds, unless members of the audience are in agreement at the beginning with respect to the usefulness of facts, truths, presumptions, and values. "The rule of justice" refers to the advocate's requirement to give identical treatment to beings or situations of the same kind, and therefore to be fair in the use of analogies, such as comparisons and contrasts. Golden et al. indicated that in Perelman's own view, "disassociation of concepts" may be the single most important principle in his theory of argumentation, as it

> is always prompted by the desire to remove an incompatibility arising out of the confrontation of one proposition with others, whether one is dealing with norms, facts, or truths. When there is a pair: appearance and reality, the advocate has the ability to disassociate rhetoric from appearance, and to reassociate it with reality. (Golden et al., 1989, pp. 389–391)

Contemporary European Rhetoricians: Michel Foucault

One of the most quoted 20th Century authors in the humanities, French-born Michel Foucault, although not linked directly to the contemporary rhetorical tradition in terms of authors whom he cited, had a considerable interest in language and discourse. Among his many works, *The Order of Things* (1970), *The Archaeology of Knowledge* (1972), *Language, Countermemory, Practice* (1977), and *Power/Knowledge* (1980) all represent Foucault's explorations into language and discourse. Golden et al. indicated that three major themes develop from these works of his, and others: (a) his theory of discursive formations, (b) his archaeological/genealogical method of enquiry, and (c) his notion of power. Because Foucault was a historian, he was interested in what constituted knowledge at a particular point in history, and what type of discourse may have been used and acceptable at that point in time. He suggested that the expression of knowledge at one point or another in history is an articulation of propositional (persuasive) statements that conform to widely accepted rules, which may not be consciously followed, but which subconsciously dominate the influence on that historical period. Golden et al. identified several questions that are relevant to understanding his position on discourse: What rules permit certain statements to be made? What rules order these statements? What rules permit us to identify some statements as true and some as false? What rules allow the construction of a classificatory system? What rules are revealed when an object of discourse is modified or transformed? What rules allow us to identify certain individuals as authors? What rules give discourse "value and practical application as scientific discourse?" Why is it that one particular statement appeared rather than another? (Golden et al., 1989, pp. 439–440).

Golden et al. proposed that Foucault's answer to the question dealing with the making and prohibiting of certain statements "has far reaching significance for a student of contemporary rhetorical theory." What is excluded or silenced, either through external rules or cultural internal rules, may be as important as what is accepted as knowledge, particularly on such topics as madness and insanity, and sexuality in which Foucault had considerable interest as "rules of exclusion." His relativistic view of truth as what is considered true within a discursive formation makes truth dependent on discourse, Golden et al. claimed, and thus is highly controversial. They argued that Foucault insightfully sees authors as the product of discursive formation that is prevalent, within a specific historical or cultural perspective, rather than being in a superior position in terms of the text. Foucault saw a problem in authorship because an author's published works only reveal what was stated for public consumption, rather than what ideas the author develops outside of the published text. Additionally, Author 1 is not Author 2, as Author 1 may never be more than the author of a particular text, whereas Author 2 whose new discursive practice has the power to generate a different kind of discourse over a long period of time (Golden et al., 1989, pp. 441–442).

Foucault's methods of inquiry that he termed archaeological/genealogical were intended to "emancipate historical knowledges" that have been suppressed or ignored, to give a history to sentiments and instincts that have been motivating, and to cast doubt on traditional conclusions that had been presented with unchallenged finality. Foucault clarified the distinctions between the two methods:

> Archaeology would be the appropriate methodology of this analysis of local discursivities and genealogy would be the tactics, whereby, on the basis of the descriptions of these local discursivities, the subjected knowledges which were thus released would be brought into play. (Foucault, cited in Golden et al., 1989, p. 443)

Thus, such an effort involves strategy of action for those who have been excluded from being able to utilize significant discourse on a subject of importance to them.

The third element that Golden et al. cited as important to an understanding of Foucault's contribution to rhetorical/communication theory is power. His probes, unlike McLuhan's which allowed McLuhan to say he had no idea where they would lead, had the effect of implying for Foucault that power focuses on social relations and persuasive strategies. Because power has persuasive potential that may positively or negatively affect social relations, thereby determining what is viewed as knowledge and truth, with specific discourse, Foucault argued:

> The longer I continue, the more it seems to me that the formation of discourses and the genealogy of knowledge need to be analyzed, not in terms of consciousness, modes of perception and forms of ideology, but in terms of tactics and strategies of power. (Foucault, cited in Golden et al., 1989, p. 444)

Contemporary European Rhetoricians: Jürgen Habermas

Jürgen Habermas, born in Düsseldorf, Germany, in 1929, was a member of Hitler Youth. At the end of the war, when the war-ruined cities were everywhere in Germany and the Holocaust had become fully known to the German people, Habermas saw that "we had been living in a politically criminal system." He embraced the strongest form of antifacism, Marxism, and since receiving his doctorate in 1954 became one of Germany's most well-known philosophers. Conley called his Marxist critique of society central to his work, and the distinctively "dialectical" character of his thought is Marxist in nature. Conley (1990) wrote:

> The "dialectical" approach led him to conclude that no particular exchange of symbols (communication) can be understood without developing first a universal model of all communication [a model which shows how rationality—and irrationality—are manifest in ordinary social interaction; that is, ordinary communication between] speaking and acting subjects. (p. 301)

As neuroses impede the individual's progress toward self-fulfillment, socially distorted communication—or ideology—impedes progress toward full emancipation, which is the goal of any just society. Conley spoke of two of Habermas' notions of "communicative rationality," which includes the "consensus theory of truth," and "the ideal speech situation." Habermas argued that the validation of truth claims, then, is a function of grounded consensus, which derives exclusively from the dynamics of discourse itself, from the force of the better argument, and that excludes any external constraints and biases. Habermas endorsed Toulmin's "jurisprudential" model of argumentation, which argued that when claims are called into question, evidence must be offered through data and warrants, with defense from objections. This ensures freedom from bias, moving the communicative interaction toward an "ideal speech situation." All participants must be able to contribute to the argumentative assessment of truth claims.

Like the positive appeal of Toulmin and Perelman in the United States, Habermas has received a similar reception. At the same time,

Habermas does not express a specific interest in rhetoric, Conley speculated, because he had deep fears about the essential corruptness of language itself, so that one does not enter into another period of "systematically distorted communication." Habermas spoke to orient himself toward developing a universal principle of rationality that cannot be accomplished out of the old order which it was meant to overcome (Conley, 1990, pp. 299–302).

CONCLUSION

It is important to note that as we move forward in history from the classical period, where rhetoric and persuasion were synonymous, and where formal Aristotelian logic was the dominant form of reasoning, the Renaissance rhetoricians were becoming more interested in rhetoric as language, and were beginning to reject the formalistic logic of Aristotle as impractical in actual life. Although there were trends that rejected those perspectives then considered "modern," the essential rhetorical developments began to blend some of the positive constructs of the classical authors and to expand new ways of thinking about rhetoric. Argumentation during the Enlightenment, spurred by earlier authors such as Francis Bacon, began to separate more and more rhetorical argument from philosophical argument.

What we call the contemporary period, developments during the 20th century, demonstrated what Golden et al., Thomas Conley, and other authors have called "new rhetorics." Golden et al. designated some of these "new rhetorics" as meaning centered, value centered, motivational and dramatistically centered, and knowledge centered, and delineated such authors as I.A. Richards and Marshall McLuhan in the first category; Thomas Conley would have added Richard Weaver in the first category. Golden et al., however, placed Richard Weaver among the value-centered rhetoricians. They placed Kenneth Burke as motivational and dramatistically-centered, and Stephen Toulmin and Chaim Perelman as knowledge centered.

Thomas Conley concluded his discussion of continental rhetorical influences after World War II, where both Perelman and Habermas were deeply affected by that war and the hardening of ideological positions during the Cold War. Their view of truth is not that of the absolute truth possible to Plato which petrifies into dogma, that spawns ideology, which Conley argued impedes human freedom. He suggested that McKeon, Toulmin, Perelman, and Habermas all share a determination to combat dogma, to relate philosophy to everyday life, and to ground that philosophy in controversy. Although Ciceronian, their attempt is to make the new rhetoric a means of transforming society (Conley, 1990, p. 304).

Goldman et al. ended their discussion of Jurgen Habermas:

> As we think about a rhetoric of the future, we are convinced that Habermas' theories will play a fundamental role. His abiding belief that communication competence resulting from an instructive and persuasive use of speech act utterances and sound reasoning, occurring within an ideal speech situation, place him in the forefront of those who are interested in the theme of how rhetoric may perform the task of producing knowledge. (Golden et al., 1989, pp. 438–439)

Speaking of Foucault, they concluded that he

> has presented a challenge that we cannot easily ignore. In effect, he is saying that if we want a viable rhetoric of the future, we need to reexamine the past again and again to see what possibilities we have overlooked, or what potentially rich ideas have been silenced or excluded. (Golden et al., 1989, pp. 444–445)

One of the things that you may have noted as we provided a synopsis of major thrusts of discourse analysis and western rhetorical analysis, from the classical to the contemporary period, is that there are some striking differences between the two approaches to analysis. However, the closer that we get to the present, both methods of analysis share greater and greater similarities as a study of language, misunderstanding, and its remedies. This complementarity should be of assistance to you as you seek to understand how to apply various principles of discourse analysis and rhetorical analysis jointly to the understanding of messages.

APPLICATION

1. How do discourse analysis and rhetorical analysis parallel each other in their views of language/communication?
2. What has been a key departure from Aristotelian rhetoric taken by some contemporary rhetoricians? How does that departure appear to involve more of the actual language used in argumentation?
3. In what ways might written speechtexts fail to capture the full experience of the audience live at a UN address? Is this factor operative equally for all addresses? Why or why not?

8

THREE UN SITUATIONS

The previous two chapters have provided considerable information about major thrusts of classical Greek rhetoric, its importance to rhetorical criticism and analysis and successors, as well as contemporary western developments in rhetoric. In this chapter, we provide an analysis and guidelines for analysis for three Aristotelian genres of addresses, statements, or messages related to the UN. The first of these genres is *epideictic* or *ceremonial* in nature, present oriented, and emphasizing praise or blame. The second is *deliberative,* which assumes that members of the audience have the ability to strengthen or change their points of view, to establish policy, or to take action. Because it involves policies or actions to be undertaken, it has a future orientation. The third, *judicial* or *forensic* rhetoric, typically is legal in nature, and often centers its attention on finding a defendant innocent or guilty, and thus has a past orientation.

In this chapter, three longer examples will be utilized to demonstrate rhetorical analysis of their messages or statements about the issue itself. The first will be an *epideictic* address by Queen Elizabeth II to the UN General Assembly in 1957, four years after her coronation, and on the occasion of her first state visit to the United States. The second involves an analysis of *deliberative* rhetoric in the Security Council by Ambassador Adlai Stevenson in December 1961, in relation to a crisis called "The Goa Question" before the Council. Here, he calls for specific and urgent action both on the part of the Council and on the part of the Indian Government whose military forces have invaded Portuguese territories, Goa, Damao, and Diu, on the Indian border. Stevenson called this brief one day crisis and debate, in which he failed to achieve his objective, the most fateful day in the history of the UN. Moving closer to the present, we will consider the messages provided by major media surrounding the "Nicaraguan Complaint Against the United States for Mining its Harbors," before the International Court of Justice (ICJ) in the mid-1980s as an aspect of *judicial* rhetoric.

EPIDEICTIC OR CEREMONIAL RHETORIC IN THE UN GENERAL ASSEMBLY

We have noted that ceremonial rhetoric tends to deal with the present, although it may recall the past, and may sometimes point to the future. Basically, its role is to offer praise or blame. You are personally involved in such rhetoric on a regular pattern: "This movie is very good (bad); this food is excellent (terrible), this instructor is great (awful), this text book is interesting (boring)," and so forth. We move beyond these simple statements when we are called on to elaborate our praise or blame and to provide evidence for our views. We give toasts at weddings; we give eulogies for those who have died. We condemn atrocities. When we are in a worship service, our intention is to praise the Supreme Creator or Being and sometimes to condemn evil, sin, or the devil.

In some cultures, the content of a message is less important than that the message has been given. In Japan, it is customary for former teachers to come to their students' weddings to praise their accomplishments, whether or not members of the wedding party pay close attention. While lengthy epideictic messages may not move an audience to changes in policy or to take specific action there is high symbolism attached to the event itself. Faculty who march in North American academic processions for graduating students, as well as the graduating students themselves and their families, may find themselves tearfully moved when Sir Edgar Elgar's "Pomp and Circumstance" begins as the graduates and faculty process into the graduation setting, without any sense of precisely what Elgar was trying to convey. Elgar was certainly not writing his processional for North American graduation ceremonies.

Martin Luther King Jr.'s 1963 Lincoln Monument Address, "I Have a Dream," directly to 250,000 people, plus hundreds of thousands of others who heard or saw him on the electronic media, is more poetic than propositional. Most similar epideictic addresses, speeches, and statements generally do not engage in deliberating very much with the audience about specific policies or changes which they can help to bring about. The 1995 World Youth Day address in Manila by Pope John Paul II, potentially to 5 million persons in his direct audience, and to millions of others by live satellite transmission, carries very important symbolism, with a mix of a great religious leader and his superstar personality. John Paul II extols morality and condemns various moral excesses. His addresses, speeches, and encyclical letters may be an exception to the concept of ceremonial rhetoric over deliberative rhetoric because he also exhorts his crowds and readers to lead more moral lives and often he provides specific steps which they should take. Nonetheless, his ceremonial presence has extraordinary symbolic and ritualistic importance. Many of his visits to various countries have received almost full print and electronic media coverage both within the countries and more broadly internationally. He was named *Time*'s "Man of the Year" in 1994.

Many addresses by heads of state and government in the UN General Assembly also have considerably symbolic and ritualistic importance, beyond their possible impact in calling for policy changes or direct action. Many of the addresses in the annual 3-week General Debate at the late September start of each annual 3-month General Assembly session, by heads of state and government, and foreign ministers, as well as many other addresses by heads of state and government during the year in the UN, have extensive ceremonial significance. Typically, a head of state or government is symbolically and ceremoniously escorted to the podium by the current president of the General Assembly and by the secretary general, no matter how small or insignificant his or her country may be. Five-, 10-, 25- and 50-year anniversaries of the UN (as occurred in October 1995 for the 50th anniversary when approximately 140 heads of state and government spoke, praising its achievements and condemning its failures), often become the situation for special world renowned leaders to speak ceremoniously at the UN. Not all addresses by heads of state and government to the UN General Assembly have primarily epideictic qualities over deliberative aspects, but a great many have as their primary achievements such components.

Emperor Haile Selassie was the only head of state or government to speak at the League of Nations (1936 when Ethiopia was being attacked by Italy), and the only one to speak at both the League of Nations and the UN (1963). Though his addresses were deliberative in intent, high symbolism was attached to the fact that he spoke in 1936 to the League of Nations and in 1963 to the UN. President Harry Truman gave the first two addresses to the UN by a head of government. The one given in April 1945 by radio hook up to San Francisco where the Charter was to be debated was only weeks after becoming the American President because of the death of President Franklin Roosevelt. In this address, Truman said that the meeting to create the UN Charter was the most important conference in history. When the Charter was completed in June 1945, President Truman took a train from Washington to San Francisco to deliver an address on a "Charter for Peace," with high symbolism.

Since Truman's first addresses to the General Assembly, every American president has given an address at the UN during the autumn after election or succeeding a deceased president, as Truman and Lyndon B.

Johnson did. President Gerald Ford gave an address in the autumn immediately after becoming President when President Richard Nixon resigned in August 1974. President Ronald Reagan gave the most UN addresses of any American president. His were not the most by any head of state or government, which was accomplished by Prince Norodom Sihanouk, Head of State, of Cambodia and then later of Democratic Kampuchea, over more than a 30-year span. Many of the more than 1,000 addresses given by heads of state and government in the General Assembly during its first 50 years, and some few in the Security Council, have a mix of *epideictic* and *deliberative* rhetoric. When King George VI opened the first General Assembly session in war torn London in 1946, the symbolic impact of his address was very great as the delegates had to step over or around the rubble still in London's streets from the Nazi bombing to reach the Assembly sessions.

In 1955, President Eisenhower traveled to San Francisco for a 10th-anniversary address. In 1965, Pope Paul IV made a 24-hr trip to the UN in New York City to give his address "Never Again War! War Never Again!" Although we cannot note that his message was entirely successful in stopping wars, 75 foreign ministers traveled to the UN to hear his address, and American television carried live coverage for most of his one day visit to the United Nations and New York. Many addresses by heads of state and government command little media attention, except perhaps in their own countries, where their addresses are often broadcast live. President De Gaulle of France never spoke at the UN, perhaps because he had little respect for its importance. Most of the heads of government in Western Europe in the last few decades have spoken at the UN, some frequently. During the 1960 World Summit and 1967 Emergency General Assembly to consider the Middle East crisis, many Eastern Europe heads of government spoke in the General Assembly. With the changes in Eastern Europe, many new leaders have spoken at the UN as many countries have been admitted. Some African leaders make nearly annual visits to the UN to present their views to the assembled delegates.

Epideictic or Ceremonial Rhetoric of Queen Elizabeth II at the UN

Elizabeth II was born in 1926, married Prince Philip in 1947, and assumed the throne in 1952 at the death of her father King George VI. Her coronation was in 1953. This address was given to the General Assembly on October 21, 1957.

"The Goal of a World at Peace"
Queen Elizabeth II, October 21, 1957
United Kingdom

I THANK YOU, Mr. President, for your words of welcome.

I wish first to express to you, to the Secretary General, and to the General Assembly of the United Nations my great pleasure at being here today.

This Assembly was born of the endeavors of countless men and women from different nations who, over the centuries, have pursued the aim of the preservation of peace between nations, equality of justice for all before the law and the right of the peoples of the world to live their lives in freedom and security.

The Charter of the United Nations was framed with a view to giving expression to these great purposes and so forming a fitting memorial to the men and women whose toil and sacrifices turned those ideas into articles of faith for the nations of today.

Time has in fact made the task of the United Nations more difficult than it seemed when the terms of the Charter were agreed at San Francisco twelve years ago. We are still far from the achievement of the ideals which I have mentioned, but we must not be discouraged. The peoples of the world expect the United Nations to persevere in its efforts.

Ten Commonwealth countries are represented in this Assembly, countries which form a free association of fully independent States and which have widely different histories, cultures and traditions. Common ideals and hopes, not formal bonds, unite the members of the Commonwealth and promote that association between them which, in my belief, has contributed significantly to the cause of human freedom.

The countries of the Commonwealth regard their continuing association with one another and their joint service to their high ideals as still an essential contribution to world peace and justice. They add and will continue to add to the United Nations a tried element of strength and of accumulated experience.

The United Nations is an organization dedicated to peace, where representatives from all over the world meet to examine the problems of the time. In it men and women from all these countries—large or small, powerful or weak—can exercise an influence that might otherwise be denied to them. The United Nations also originates and inspires a wide range of social and economic activities for the benefit of the whole human race.

But the future of this Organization will be determined, not only by the degree to which its Members observe strictly the provisions of the Charter and co-operate in its practical activities, but also by the strength of its peoples' devotion to the pursuit of those great ideals to which I have referred.

(continued)

> When justice and respect for obligations are firmly established, the United Nations will the more confidently achieve the goal of a world at peace, law-abiding and prosperous, for which men and women have striven so long and which is the heart's desire of every nation here represented, I offer you my best wishes in your task and pray that you may be successful. (Queen Elizabeth II, in Prosser, 1970, pp. 117–118. The title was given by Prosser)

APPLICATION

1. As head of state of the United Kingdom, and other British Commonwealth nations, such as Australia, New Zealand, and Canada, Elizabeth II has no political power, only symbolic power. How do you think that this may have shaped her brief address? How does her symbolic connection to the British Commonwealth find expression in her address? Why do we call this an epideictic or ceremonial speech?
2. In the United States, the president is both head of state and head of government. In the United Kingdom, the sovereign is the symbolic head of state as a constitutional monarch, and the prime minister is the working head of government. In Swaziland, an absolute monarchy (or diarchy, as the Queen Mother shares some responsibilities), the king is both head of state and government. What would you consider the significance of an address given by a British monarch, versus a British prime minister, versus the king of Swaziland, versus the president of the United States? How would an address in the UN by the king of Swaziland be different from that of his prime minister? How would an address by the sovereign of the United Kingdom be different from that of the country's prime minister? If their addresses are epideictic or ceremonial, how would they all be different?
3. Because the British monarch delivers addresses from the throne, for example, to open parliament, for the ruling party, what is the likely influence of the prime minister and his or her staff in developing such an address as that given by Elizabeth II? Is it likely that her staff or the prime minister's staff wrote the address? What is the symbolic importance when the British monarch opens parliament in the United Kingdom or in one of the Commonwealth countries with an address? Are the ideas the monarch presents entirely those of the ruling party, or are personal ideas expressed—for example in Elizabeth II's address to the UN?

4. What are the basic premises of Elizabeth's address to the UN? What evidence is offered to support these premises? What efforts are made to establish *ethos*, *pathos*, or *logos* in the address? What is the source of authority which Elizabeth II calls on in her address? Is she able or likely to offer refutation of ideas with which she or her government disagrees?
5. Noting that her father, George VI, welcomed delegates to the first session of the General Assembly in war torn London in 1946, would a reference to her father have increased her own *ethos* for her address? or by being the Queen, does she create her own *ethos, sui generis* (or of her own person)?
6. When Elizabeth II spoke to the UN in 1957 and when King Hussein I of Jordan spoke there in 1960, both used the first person singular *(I, my, me)*, as did Pope John Paul II, in 1979. It was an ancient custom for monarchs to use the "royal we" and until John Paul II, for popes to use the "papal we." Pope Paul VI speaking to the UN in 1965, used the "papal we" consistently through his address, and also the more inclusive "we" for all of the delegates assembled and all people of good will. What importance do you attach to Elizabeth II, Hussein I, and John Paul II using the first person singular, whereas Paul VI used the first person plural in referring to himself? Which builds greater *ethos* for the world leader, the first person singular or first person plural?
7. Does Elizabeth II use any specific emotional appeals in her address to link her to her immediate or "universal" audience? Sir Leslie Monroe of New Zealand, President of the 1957–58 General Assembly, introduces her as his "own beloved Sovereign," and after her address, remarks: "I venture to say that there is not one among us who does not rejoice in the presence here today of a queen, a wife and a mother who is a symbol in her lovely person of the noblest ideals of womanhood." Do these statements enhance her *ethos* or *pathos* for her with her audience? If you were called on to introduce Elizabeth II today, how would you wish to introduce her? Would Sir Leslie's remarks be considered appropriate today?
8. If Elizabeth II's son Charles were to ascend to the throne, how would his probable address to the UN be similar or different today from that of his mother? Would he wish to give a more *deliberative* address than that of his mother? How much of his own personal *ethos* or *pathos* would he be likely to attempt to insert into his address?
9. Virtually all American presidents call on God as they end their addresses and speeches, including references by Presidents Truman,

Eisenhower, Kennedy, and Johnson in the UN, with such phrases as "We beseech almighty God," "divinely bestowed rights," and "the eternal blessing of God." Many other world leaders at the United Nations call upon God's or Allah's help. Elizabeth II, head of the Church of England, and "Defender of the Faith," however, ends her address to the UN with the words "I offer you my best wishes in your task and pray that you may be successful." As the British monarch, Elizabeth is also the official head of the Church of England and "Defender of the Faith," a title which King Henry VII ascribed to himself when he broke from the Roman Catholic Church. Is Elizabeth's "pray that you may be successful" comparable to references to God by American presidents noted earlier, or could one insert instead "hope that you may be successful," as her meaning? If the latter, how would this insertion differ symbolically from the explicit references to God by the American presidents cited? Would there be expectations for her as head of the Church of England which she has not met?

DELIBERATIVE RHETORIC OF AMBASSADOR ADLAI STEVENSON IN THE SECURITY COUNCIL ON "THE GOA QUESTION," DECEMBER 18, 1961

"The Failure of the Security Council Is a Failure of the United Nations" US Ambassador Adlai E. Stevenson Security Council of the UN Statements on the Goa Question, December 18, 1961

I SHOULD like to express the views of the United States at this fateful hour in the life of the United Nations. I will not detain you long but long enough, I hope, to make clear our anxiety for the future of this organization as a result of this incident.

When acts of violence take place between nations in this dangerous world, no matter where they occur or for what cause, there is reason for alarm. The news from Goa tells of such acts of violence. It is alarming news and, in our judgment, the Security Council has an urgent duty to act in the interests of international peace and security.

We know as the world knows, and as has been said countless times in the General Assembly and the Security Council, that the winds of change are blowing all over the world. But the winds of change are man-made and man can and must control them. They must not be allowed to become the bugles of war.

(continued)

Our Charter begins with the determination "to save succeeding generations from the scourge of war" and pledges its members to "practice tolerance and live together with one another as good neighbors."

In that connection it deserves to be said that all of us at the United Nations owe much to India. The largest contingent in the United Nations effort to establish peace in the Congo are the troops of India. India has also contributed of its resources in the Middle East. Few nations have done more to uphold the principles of this organization or to support its peacemaking efforts all over the world and none have espoused nonviolence more vehemently and invoked the peaceful symbolism of Gandhi more frequently. That nation is led by a man whom I regard as a friend, who has been a lifelong disciple of one of the world's great saints of peace, whom many have looked up to as an apostle of nonviolence and who only this year addressed this Assembly with a moving appeal for a United Nations Year of International Cooperation.

These facts make the step which has been taken today all the harder to understand and to condone. The fact is, and the Indian Government has announced it, that Indian armed forces early this morning, on December 18, marched into the Portuguese territories of Goa, Dameo, and Diu. Dameo and Diu have been occupied and there is fighting at this moment within the territory of Goa.

Here we are, Mr. President, confronted with the shocking news of this armed attack and that the Indian Minister of Defense, so well-known in these halls for his advice on matters of peace and his tireless enjoinders to everyone else to seek the way of compromise, was on the borders of Goa inspecting his troops at the zero hour of invasion.

Let us be perfectly clear what is at stake here, gentlemen. It is the question of the use of armed force by one state against another and against its will, an act clearly forbidden by the Charter. We have opposed such action in the past by our closest friends as well as by others. We opposed it in Korea in 1950, in Suez and in Hungary in 1956, in the Congo in 1960, and we do so again in Goa in 1961.

The facts in this case are unfortunately all too clear. These territories have been under Portuguese dominion for over four centuries. They have been invaded by Indian armed forces. The Government of India regards these territories as having the same status as the territories of Britain and France on the subcontinent from which those countries have voluntarily withdrawn. The Government of India has insisted that Portugal likewise withdraw. Portugal has refused, maintaining that it has a legal and moral right to these territories.

Mr. President, we have repeatedly urged both of the parties to this dispute to seek by peaceful processes the resolution of a problem which has its roots in the colonial past.

(continued)

I do not at this time propose to concern myself with the merits of this dispute. We are not meeting here today to decide the merits of this case. We are meeting to decide what attitude should be taken in this body when one of the members of these United Nations casts aside the principles of the Charter and seeks to resolve a dispute by force.

But, Mr. President, what is at stake today is not colonialism. It is a bold violation of one of the most basic principles of the United Nations Charter, stated in these words from Article 2 of paragraph 4: "All members shall refrain in their international relations from the threat or use of force against the territorial integrity of political independence of any State, or in any other manner inconsistent with the purposes of the United Nations."

We realize fully the depths of the differences between India and Portugal concerning the future of Goa. We realize that India maintains that Goa by rights should belong to India. Doubtless India would hold, therefore, that its action today is aimed at a just end. But if our Charter means anything, it means that states are obligated to renounce the use of force, are obligated to seek a solution of their difference by peaceful means, are obligated to utilize the procedures of the United Nations when other peaceful means have failed.

The Indian tradition of nonviolence has inspired the whole world, but this act of force with which we are confronted today mocks the faith of India's frequent declarations of exalted principle. It is a lamentable departure not only from the Charter but from India's own professions of faith.

What is the world to do if every state whose territorial claims are unsatisfied should resort with impunity to the rule of armed might to get its way? The Indian sub-continent is not the only place in the world where such disputes exist.

The fabric of peace is fragile, and our peace-making machinery has today suffered another blow. If it is to survive, if the United Nations is not to die as ignoble a death as the League of Nations, we cannot condone the use of force on this instance and thus pave the way for forceful solutions of other disputes which exist in Latin America, Africa, Asia, and Europe. In a world as interdependent as ours, the possible results of such a trend are too grievous to contemplate.

This action is all the more painful to my country because we have in recent weeks made repeated appeals to the Government of India to refrain from the use of force. This has included not only a series of diplomatic approaches in Washington and in New Delhi but also a personal message from President Kennedy to Prime Minister Nehru on December 13 indicating our earnest hope that India would not resort to force to solve the Goa problem.

As a culmination of these efforts, the United States Government last Saturday made an appeal to Prime Minister Nehru through the United States Ambassador in New Delhi and through the Indian Ambassador in Washington to suspend preparations for the use of force in connection with a

(continued)

direct offer of United States help in seeking a peaceful solution to the problem. This resort to armed action is a blow to international institutions such as our United Nations (and) the International Court of Justice, which are available to assist in the adjustment of disputes.

This is our principal concern. This body cannot apply a double standard with regard to the principle of resort to force. We appeal to India to recognize that its own national interests, as well as those of the entire world community, depend on the restoration of confidence in the processes of law and conciliation in international affairs. Indeed, Mr. President, this tragic episode reveals clearly—if nothing else—the need for urgent review of peaceful settlement procedures to deal with the problems of peaceful change. The United States will have more to say about this at an appropriate occasion.

The Council has an urgent duty, in our judgment, to bring this dispute back from the battlefield, so fraught with danger for the world, to the negotiating table. We earnestly urge the Government of India to withdraw its armed forces from the territories which they have invaded. We earnestly appeal for a cease-fire. And we earnestly urge the Governments of India and of Portugal to enter into negotiations to achieve a solution. We must ask for an immediate cease-fire, in our judgment; we must insist on withdrawal of the invading forces and we must insist that the two parties negotiate on the basis of the principles of the Charter.

The law of the Charter forbids the use of force in such matters. There is not one law for one part of the world and another law for the rest of the world. There is one law for the whole world, and it is, in our judgment, the duty of this Council to uphold it.

Stevenson's Second Statement
December 18, 1961

MR. PRESIDENT,

I am the only delegate, I think, at this table who was present at the birth of this organization. Tonight we are witnessing the first act in a drama which could end with its death. The League of Nations died, I remind you, when its members no longer resisted the use of aggressive force. So it is, sir, with a most heavy heart that I must add a word of epilogue to this fateful discussion, by far the most important in which I have participated since this organization was founded sixteen years ago. The failure of the Security Council to call for a cease-fire tonight in these simple circumstances is a failure of the United Nations. The veto of the Soviet Union is consistent with its long role of obstruction. But I find the attitude of some other members of the Council profoundly disturbing and ominous because we have

(continued)

> witnessed tonight an effort to rewrite the Charter, to sanction the use of force in international relations when it suits one's own purposes. This approach can only lead to chaos and to the disintegration of the United Nations.
>
> The United States appeals again to the Government of India to abandon its use of force, to withdraw its forces. We appeal to both parties again to negotiate their differences. This is the course prescribed by the Charter. It is the course of wisdom. The inability of the Council to act because of a Soviet veto does not alter this fact. We will consult overnight with other members of the Council about further steps which the United Nations might take and we reserve the right to seek a further meeting at any time. (Stevenson, 1961)

APPLICATION OF ANALYSIS BASED ON CLASSICAL RHETORIC: STASIS—THE POINT OF CLASH ON THE GOA QUESTION

Ambassador Stevenson, and specific American allies in the Security Council, the British, French, Republic of China, and Turkish representatives, identified the major issue as an international invasion by the Indian Government against the Portuguese enclaves of Goa, Damao, and Diu, situated on its borders, as against the prescriptions of the UN Charter, and one which should be condemned by the Security Council. Stevenson's statement defined one side of the issue: "Let us be perfectly clear what is at stake here, gentlemen. It is the question of the use of armed force by one state against another and against its will, an act clearly forbidden by the Charter." Stevenson called for a cease fire, a withdrawal of Indian troops from the Portuguese territories, negotiation between Portugal and India to settle the territorial dispute, and mediation efforts by the Secretary General. The resolution to this effect submitted by the United States, and cosponsored by the United Kingdom, France, and Turkey, won the seven votes required for passage, but failed because of the Soviet veto. The five permanent members, originally France, the Republic of China (the seat assumed by the People's Republic of China in 1972), the Union of Soviet Socialist Republics (the seat assumed by the Russian Federation in 1992), the United Kingdom, and the United States all were given the veto when the Charter was formed in 1945.

In contrast to the American, British, French, and Turkish co-sponsored resolution, the view of Ambassador Jha of India, and several Third World nations' representatives in the Council, was that the issue focused on "self-determination" of the Portuguese territories of Goa, Damao and Diu, that the Indian Troops had liberated these territories from the Portuguese, at the request of the Goans, Damaoans, and Diuans, and had returned them to the "motherland." Ambassador Jha denied even that an invasion had occurred, and argued that the issue was entirely a "colonial issue."

Because of the Soviet veto, Stevenson could have taken the issue to the General Assembly on December 19, 1961, under the "Uniting for Peace" resolution. The United States had gotten the "Uniting for Peace" resolution established as a precedent in the Security Council during the Korean War in 1951, in the midst of a Soviet walk out from the Security Council, when the Soviet delegate could not exercise his right of the veto. Ambassador Zorin of the Soviet Union, refuting Stevenson's statement that the decision had been the beginning of the end of the UN, said during the December 18, 1961 debate: "Today, there was no beginning of the end of the United Nations, but a demonstration of the will to defend colonial countries and peoples, the will to defend their right to freedom and independence. . . . Whoever does not understand this does not understand the substance of the problems that now stand before the United Nations (Zorin, cited in Prosser, 1964, p. 191).

Stevenson did not call on the "Uniting for Peace" resolution in relation to the Goa Question, saying that the Portuguese troops had already surrendered in Goa, and that the question of a cease-fire was now mute. More realistically, with the influx of new Third World members at the end of the 1950s and early 1960s in the UN, the United States probably would not have engineered enough support for its position in the General Assembly.

STEVENSON'S BASIC PREMISES IN HIS TWO STATEMENTS

As previously noted in discussing the center of conflict in the debate and resolution of the Goa Question, Stevenson's identification of the American view of the issue sharply differs from that of the Indian, Soviet, and other ambassadors speaking in the Council. "Invasion" or "self-determination" also became the foundation for Stevenson's basic premises. In his first statement, Stevenson argues: "When acts of violence take place between nations in this dangerous world, no matter where they occur or for what cause, there is reason for alarm. The news from Goa tells of such acts of violence. It is alarming news and, in our judgment, the Security Council has an urgent duty to act in the interests of international peace and security." Shortly after introducing his remarks, Stevenson clarifies the point of tension, as suggested in the discussion on *stasis.*

He denied the Indian claim of the central point at issue: "What is at stake today is not colonialism. It is a bold violation of one of the most basic principles of the United Nations Charter, stated in those words from Article 2 of paragraph 4: 'All members shall refrain in their international relations from the threat or use of force against the territorial integrity of political independence of any State, or in any other manner inconsistent with the purposes of the United Nations." Condemning the Indian actions, Stevenson insisted: "This resort to armed action is a blow to international institutions such as our United Nations (and) the International Court of Justice, which are available to assist in the adjustment of disputes." We see in our example of media reactions to the judicial rhetoric in the International Court of Justice, that his reference to the ICJ has a later interesting irony in the Reagan administration position on the US bombing of the Nicaraguan harbors, when the Nicaraguan Government has taken its complaint to the ICJ, and the US government has rejected the ICJ authority to make judgments in such a case, and subsequently withdrew from the case.

STEVENSON'S LOGICAL DEVELOPMENT OF ARGUMENTS AND EVIDENCE

Very early in his first statement, Stevenson developed a metaphorical analogy: "The winds of change are blowing all over the world. But the winds of change are man-made, and man can and must control them. They must not be allowed to become the bugles of war." This is an archetypal metaphor. Such a metaphor tends to have more influence as an emotional appeal or stylistic device than as a logical appeal. Both President Kennedy's 1961 and 1963 addresses to the UN Generally Assembly utilize such metaphors as part of his logical chain. Because Stevenson was Kennedy's UN Ambassador, and because many of Stevenson's UN statements were crafted by staff members in the US Mission to the UN, we could question whether this metaphor is really a part of Stevenson's standard deliberative rhetoric. Based on considerations of his earlier speeches and statements, however, it would appear to be his own pattern. Additionally, during the 1960 summit conference of heads of state and government during the general debate at the opening of the Fifteenth General Assembly, called by Premier Khrushchev of the Soviet Union, the "winds of change" and "bugles of war" metaphors were introduced as part of the logical development of arguments in the addresses of various heads of state and government.

Stevenson was fond of hypothetical syllogisms. Utilizing the Charter as a major reference source from which to draw conclusions, a very common practice in many of the addresses and statements in the UN on a nearly world-wide basis. Stevenson introduced a series of hypothetical syllogisms, for example: "If our Charter means anything, it means that States are obligated to renounce the use of force, are obligated to seek a solution of their differences by peaceful means, are obligated to utilize the procedures of the United Nations when other peaceful means have failed:" A major premise may be: "The UN Charter calls for State renunciation of force in international disputes, peaceful solution of differences, and utilization of the UN procedures when other peaceful means have failed." Minor premise: "Portugal and India are member States of the UN and subscribe to the principles of the Charter." Conclusion: "Portugal and India should renounce force, seek peaceful means of settling their dispute, and call on the UN procedures." Based on this syllogism, one could create an enthymeme, or truncated syllogism, which suggests: "The successful Indian invasion of Goa, Damao, and Diu will cause the UN to die." A counter syllogism by Ambassador Jha of India, and others supporting his position, would be: Basic Premise: "All colonial territories should now be liberated." Minor Premise: "Goa, Damao, and Diu are colonies of Portugal." Conclusion: "Goa, Damao, and Diu should now be liberated." An enthymeme coming from this syllogism may be: "Return Goa, Damao, and Diu, to the Motherland."

A second hypothetical syllogism is introduced by Stevenson: "If it is to survive, if the United Nations is not to die as ignoble a death as the League of Nations, we cannot condone the use of force in this instance (occupation of Goa, Damoa, and Diu by the Indian military) and thus pave the way for forceful solutions of other disputes." A syllogism might emerge: Major premise: "The United Nations, like the League of Nations, will die if it does not renounce the use of force." Minor Premise: "The United Nations has not renounced the use of force on the Goa question." Conclusion: "The United Nations will die."

Stevenson's major arguments were often based on analogies, testimony (most often from the Charter), and recent efforts by the UN and the United States to resolve the Goa Question in advance of the Indian occupation of Goa, Damao, and Diu. Based on the logic of the Charter, Stevenson appears to have proven that the American and Portuguese position on the issue, that the Indian occupation of these three Portuguese territories was a violation of the Charter, is the correct one. However, as we note shortly, Ambassadors Zorin and Jha, and others, rejected Stevenson's appeals to build the American and his personal *ethos.*

In Stevenson's first statement, he uses examples as evidence: the Indian efforts for peace, their troop contributions to the Congo, their troop contributions to peaceful settlements in the Middle East, and Prime Minister Nehru's dedication to peace. As evidence that the Indian Government had broken the peace in Goa, Damao, and Diu, Stevenson offers as examples the Indian announcement that its troops had marched that morning, December 18, 1961, into the three territories, and that Defense Minister Krishna Menon was on the borders of Goa inspecting his troops immediately before the invasion. Stevenson gives examples of the American efforts to end the crisis, through diplomatic approaches from Washington to New Delhi, through appeals to the Indian ambassador to the United States in Washington, through appeals from the American ambassador of the United States to India in New Delhi, and by a personal message from President Kennedy to Prime Minister Nehru. Finally, Stevenson gives as examples of United States efforts to solve the problem in advance, two personal appeals to Indian officials to ask them to suspend their preparation for invasion, and an American offer to mediate in negotiations between the Portuguese and Indian governments.

After the first session of the Security Council on the Goa Question, Stevenson, in consultation with the representatives of France, the United Kingdom, and Turkey, introduces the Council resolution which received a vote of seven in favor, four opposed, no abstentions, but because of the Soviet veto, failed. UN resolutions themselves have rhetorical significance, both with *epideictic* and *deliberative* components. In the preamble paragraphs of the resolution, the Council expresses praise or blame for current conditions, through participles: "Recalling Council efforts," or "Noting with alarm," and in the operational paragraphs call for specific deliberative action: "Calls upon," "Demands," "Urges." The resolutions thus inherently appear to have cause–effect logic.

STEVENSON'S APPEALS FOR ETHOS IN HIS STATEMENTS

Finding it necessary to offer stringent criticism of the Indian occupation of Goa, Damao, and Diu, Stevenson goes to great pains to praise their Government's previous contributions to the peaceful efforts of the UN, calling Gandhi and Prime Minister Nehru great peacemakers, extolling their contingent of UN forces in the Congo, and their ongoing support of UN goals and principles. He suggested: "The Indian tradition of nonviolence has inspired the whole world." Several times, Stevenson tried to create good will for the American government by linking it to the highest principles of the Charter, with international law, and as anticolonialists. Stevenson's frequent linkage with the Charter as a means of creating ethos for his country, is seen by his remark: "The Charter, in its categorical prohibition of the use of force in the settlement of international disputes, makes no exceptions, no reservations. The Charter does not say that all Members shall settle their international disputes by peaceful means except in colonial areas." Although it is common for nearly all delegations to associate themselves closely with the UN Charter, some delegates ridiculed the concepts of international law in relationship to colonial powers and territories, which they argued had been formulated by Europeans who were the masters of the colonial empires.

Ambassador Benites of Ecuador acknowledged Stevenson's high credibility in diplomatic circles by saying: "We were particularly impressed by the statement by the representative of the United States, Mr. Stevenson, whose intellectual and moral authority merit our highest tribute" (Benites, cited in Prosser, 1964, p. 185). In terms of creating goodwill with some of the other delegations, Stevenson probably made a mistake in emphasizing that the American Government was anticolonialist and that the American government was not interested in the actual dispute between Portugal and India, but only that the Charter and international law had been violated. Ambassador Jha of India praised and condemned Stevenson's remarks within the context of one paragraph.

> We have had an important statement by the representative of the United States. His statements are always important and we pay very great attention to them, but what has he told us? He says, "We are not concerned with the substance of the dispute." That is to say, the basic problem, which is the colonial problem of Goa, does not interest him. Does not that statement show some kind of disregard, some kind of indifference, towards the motivations, the feelings, of people, the great movement of our times, the yearning for freedom—the passionate yearning for freedom? (Jha, cited in Prosser, 1964, p. 185)

Ambassador Malalasekera of Ceylon (now Sri Lanka) dismissed Stevenson's appeals by saying: "The representative of the United States who spoke here today made a fervent and appealing statement about the use of force by India. We were moved by his statement, but we are not quite sure of its relevance. . . . If Portugal conquered Goa, then the people of Goa have the right of rebellion" (Malalasekera, cited in Prosser, 1964, p. 184). Ambassador Zorin attacked him more harshly: "When the matter involves assistance to them (colonial powers), then you apply one standard, the standard of the colonial Powers: whereas when it is a case of condemning the Portuguese colonial empire, then you once more assist that colonial empire and condemn those who are fighting against it" (Zorin, cited in Prosser, 1964, p. 184).

STEVENSON'S EMOTIONAL APPEALS

Ambassador Stevenson appears to have been touched very strongly by the crisis involved in the Goa Question. He spoke of "this fateful hour in the life of the United Nations," of the American government's "anxiety for the future of this Organization as a result of this incident," of the urgent duty for the Security Council to act in the interest of international peace and security, and of the potential enfeeblement of the UN peace-keeping machinery. As Stevenson concluded his first statement, he stressed that the Council had an urgent duty, "in our judgment, to bring this dispute back from the battlefield, so fraught with danger for the world, to the negotiation table."

In the second brief statement late on the evening of December 18, 1961, Stevenson reacted strongly to the request of Ambassador Barnes of Ghana to delay the vote on the American, British, French, and Turkish resolution, so that he could receive directions from his home government, by saying:

> I see no need whatever for any further delay in reaching a vote. This is an urgent and pressing matter. This is war. People are being killed [In the second statement, Stevenson made a highly emotional appeal to the assembled representatives in the Council:] I believe that I am the only representative at this table who was present at the birth of this Organization. Tonight we are witnessing the first act in a drama which could end in its death. The League of Nations, died, I remind you, when its members no longer resisted the use of aggressive force. So it is with a most heavy heart that I must add a word of epilogue to this fateful discussion, by far the most important in which I have participated since this Organization was founded sixteen years ago.

STEVENSON'S EFFORTS AT REFUTATION

Stevenson made several efforts to refute the arguments of Ambassador Jha and others who had denigrated his appeals to establish ethos for the US government and for himself. He repeated that the United States had a forthright stand on colonial questions, including the situation in Angola, in which Portugal was the colonial power. Stevenson said: "We wholeheartedly believe in progress, in self-government and in self-determination for colonial peoples. . . . We have not altered that stand." After hearing the negative remarks of some of the neutral representatives and Ambassador Jha of India, Stevenson asked: "Do I detect in this debate an implication that a country such as the United States, for example, is not really anticolonial unless it approves the abolition of colonies by international armed attack: If so, the United States delegation totally rejects this implication. We are against colonialism and we are against war; we are for the Charter." In response to their comments, Stevenson, possibly unsuccessfully, tried to prove that the Indian arguments that the Goa Question revolved around "self-determination," in reality, was a cause of international armed aggression.

SOME ESTIMATES OF STEVENSON'S LONG-TERM ETHOS AND RHETORICAL EFFECTIVENESS

Stevenson's appeals for establishing credibility, trustworthiness, and high standards for the US Government and for himself, appear to have been in question in this particular situation, the Goa Question in the December 18, 1961, UN Security Council. His remarks were disparaged or ridiculed. The United States, British, French, and Turkish resolution failed because of the Soviet veto. At his press conference on December 21st at the conclusion of the Fifteenth General Assembly, Stevenson appeared to be in despair that the UN was so ineffective in solving such a short-lived crisis as the Goa Question.

Stevenson continued to spar with Ambassador Zorin and other Soviet representatives, as a continuing part of the United States–Soviet tensions in the Cold War, especially in the Cuban missile crisis of 1962. In American society, he was one for whom his opponents often offered the enthymeme that he was "too liberal for too long," and "too much the idealist and therefore not practical enough." As Aristotle suggested, however, the summing up of one's life is less while it is in progress, and more at the end. Stevenson died in London on July 14, 1965, just before he was preparing to host a luncheon for a group of Japanese Cabinet members and 3 weeks after he and President Johnson had spoken at the 20th-anniversary celebration of the founding of the UN in San Francisco.

At the UN Memorial Ceremony for Ambassador Stevenson, in the General Assembly, July 19, 1965, Secretary General U Thant said that Stevenson had demonstrated

> with rare distinction how it was possible to combine the highest form of patriotism with loyalty to the idea of international peace and cooperation. . . . I was repeatedly impressed by his dedication to the basic concepts of peace, justice, and freedom. . . . During the four and a half years that he served at the United Nations, he stood as the embodiment of dedication to the principles of the United Nations. (U Thant, cited in Prosser, 1969, pp. 453–454)

President of the 1964 and 1965 General Assembly Sosa Rodriguez, said of Stevenson:

> America has lost one of its most enlightened sons and the United Nations one of its most faithful champions. . . . Of the many qualities that adorned the shining personality of Adlai Stevenson, perhaps the most outstanding were his moderation and his profound human feeling. Perhaps this is the reason why he never inspired hatred but only affection, and always respect. (Rodriguez, cited in Prosser, 1969, pp. 458–459)

American Poet Laureate Archibald MacLeish praised him:

> Those qualities in Aldai Stevenson which seemed, in other surroundings, to be traits of character, attributes of personality—his warmth, his charm, his considerateness, his intelligence, his humor, his devotion, his incisiveness, his eloquence—were fused here [in the United Nations], in their employment in the noblest of all causes, to compose a complete man, a man so balanced, so harmonious as a human being, that his greatness passed almost unnoticed while he lived. (MacLeish, cited in Prosser, 1969, p. 463)

US Secretary of State Dean Rusk remarked:

> He had the capacity for forceful advocacy—when advocacy was needed. But he also had the perception to see that all issues worthy of debate are complex and are seen differently—and honestly—from other points of view. . . . The words of the Charter—and his own ringing phrases which will live in literature—were more than symbols to him. They were calls to action. He used language as few men have—but used it to summon himself and others to work. (Rusk, cited in Prosser, 1969, p. 486)

APPLICATION

1. Although these two brief statements by Adlai Stevenson were given in the moment of a crisis in the UN Security Council, most of his speeches and statements at this time were drafted, at least in part, by staff of the US Mission to the UN. Comparing the two statements, given approximately an hour apart, his own personal feelings are demonstrated in the second statement very clearly when he speaks of being present at the birth of the UN. Using this commitment as a guideline, can you identify remarks in the first statement which appear to have Stevenson's own hand in preparing it?
2. These statements are clearly part of the *deliberative* genre of which Aristotle spoke as moving an audience toward belief, policy, or action. However, as in most speeches and statements, there are also elements of *epideictic* rhetoric involved in these two statements as well. Can you identify several instances in which Stevenson used the *epideictic* elements of praise and blame? Was he successful?
3. Given the nature of these statements, one can also see aspects of *judicial or forensic* rhetoric, that is attempting to prove innocence or guilt. Can you provide several instances in these statements in which Stevenson attempted to interject such innocence or guilt, beyond the *epideictic* examples of praise and blame?

4. The *stasis (status,* or *basis)* or central point of dispute in this situation seems clearly articulated on both sides—an unwarranted international invasion from the perspective of Stevenson, the Portuguese ambassador, and the representatives of the United Kingdom, France, and Turkey or "self-determination" from the perspective of Ambassadors Jha of India, and Malalasekera of Ceylon, other Third World representatives and the Soviet delegate. Are there other points of clash between the opposing sides than this one? If so, are they more or less important than the one identified above?
5. Stevenson's basic premises are repeated in the resolution which he and the representatives of the United Kingdom, France, and Turkey have proposed. We have indicated that resolutions in themselves are rhetorical, as well as the statements that are made in a crisis such as this one. We have indicated that the preamble paragraphs of a resolution tend to be *epideictic* in nature and the operative or call to action paragraphs tend to be *deliberative* in nature. Why is this likely? Can we also find *judicial* elements present either in a resolution's preamble or in its operative paragraphs? How would you describe such elements if they are present?
6. We have identified several possible syllogisms which might develop out of Stevenson's hypothetical syllogisms, as well as some enthymemes, which are called truncated syllogisms. Why is an enthymeme a truncated syllogism? Can you create several other examples of syllogisms that Stevenson developed or might have developed? Can you make new enthymemes out of these new syllogisms? Utilizing the few quoted remarks made by other representatives in the Council meeting, what syllogisms or enthymemes can you develop from their rhetoric?
7. Stevenson worked hard to create *ethos* for his government. Although criticizing the Indian statements, he also attempted to show his goodwill for that delegation. As we have noted, some representatives believed that he had not been successful. Without giving up on his point of view in the clash of ideas, or relinquishing his basic premises from which he derives his arguments, what could Stevenson have done to create greater *ethos* both for the American Government and himself in this situation? In the four eulogies after his death by the Secretary General U Thant, President of the General Assembly Rodriguez, the US poet Archibald MacLeash, and the US Secretary of State Rusk, he appears to have developed his *ethos* over time. Is it likely that his ethos in the eyes of his opponents, except for Ambassador Zorin, actually was high during the crisis related to the Goa Question, or that this situation diminished his *ethos* only in this particular crisis? Why? Why not?

8. Stevenson was very emotionally agitated when he made his second brief statement on the Goa Question on December 18, 1961. In his press conference at the end of the session of the General Assembly on December 21st, he appeared highly pessimistic about the potential future for the UN in its responsibility to maintain international peace and security. Is it likely that this emotional agitation and apparent distress was personally genuine, or was he simply representing the position that the US Government wanted him to make, whether or not be believed it personally? Should he have made his emotional appeals stronger or weaker to fit the occasion?
9. Stevenson made efforts to refute the opposing viewpoint of the Indian delegation and others of the opposite side of the conflict. Was he successful? If not, what extra efforts would he need to make to become emotionally more successful in creating adequate *pathos* in the audience as linked to his own emotional perspective? Should he, despite the odds of failure at the end of the General Assembly session, because of the increasing number of third world countries which had recently joined the UN, have used the "Uniting for Peace" resolution to move the Goa Question from the Security Council to the General Assembly? From the moral point of view as related to the Charter and international law, should he have taken the risk of having the United States lose again in the General Assembly? Or, is it possible that he could have been persuasive enough to have won? After all, the United States continued to win votes, although with a smaller and smaller majority, against the admission of the People's Republic of China until 1971. If it could win on the Chinese representation question, could the United States have won on an issue of international invasion of another territory over the opposing position of "self-determination"? Would losing still have been a moral victory?
10. The American, French, British, and Turkish resolution did win in terms of seven required votes out of the eleven cast. The resolution was lost, however, because of the Soviet veto. From a rhetorically persuasive perspective, would you argue that Stevenson did win the argument because several delegations voted in favor of his resolution, or that he lost it persuasively because he could not convince his hostile audience, the Soviet delegation, to vote in favor of his resolution, or at least to abstain, so that the will of the majority of the Council would be honored?

The excerpts from four eulogies given for Stevenson at his Memorial Service at the UN General Assembly give us clear examples of Aristotle's genre of *epideictic* rhetoric, praising Stevenson for his contributions. The example of this set of two statements by Stevenson himself on the Goa Question in the UN Security Council on December 18, 1961, shows clearly how we can begin to analyze his *deliberative* rhetoric, using the classical Greek rhetorical analysis.

ANALYSIS OF STEVENSON'S STATEMENTS UTILIZING CONTEMPORARY WESTERN CONTRIBUTIONS

1. It is now appropriate for you to return to the "Goa Question." Substituting Chaim Perelman's method of argument, and utilizing his special vocabulary, consider the following questions. Was there a "universal audience" for this Security Council debate? Are you part of this "universal audience? Why or why not? From what "places" did Ambassador Stevenson find the basis for his arguments? From what "places" did his opponents find their arguments? You remember that Stevenson and his allies in the debate called the "stasis," or "clash point" of the debate whether the question revolved around an international invasion or self-determination? In what areas could both Stevenson and his allies and Ambassador Jha of India and his allies find basic agreements on? Was one argument or the other more rational, or was one or both positions "quasi-logical"? Why or why not? How did Ambassador Stevenson use his own "experience" as a part of his argument? How did Ambassador Jha of India use "experience" to come to a different conclusion than Stevenson's? Where did each opposing side find "the starting place of argument" for their position? Did Stevenson apply Perelman's "rule of justice" in treating similar categories fairly? Did Jha apply this rule fairly? How did the Soviet veto affect the "disassociation of concepts" from the rhetoric of appearance to the rhetoric of reality or the reverse? Were either Stevenson or Jha guilty of utilizing the rhetoric of appearance versus the rhetoric of reality? Applying concepts from both Toulmin and Perelman with their practical argumentation can you reconstruct both the pro and con arguments for the Indian action in Goa, Dam, and Diu in 1961?.

2. In your mind, and the minds of people throughout the world, what does the phrase "UN," or "*l'Organization des Nations Unies,*" or "*las Naciones Unidas*" mean? Do you understand the words to be involved with international conflict resolution or failure to resolve conflicts, peacekeeping or peacemaking, a world government, "the blue berets," the world's debating society, sustainable development, or adjuration of disputes? Do you think only of the UN, or do you think only of the Security Council or the General Assembly, or the UN building in New York, or of

UNESCO that in Geneva, Switzerland, the International Court of Justice of the World Court in the Hague in the Netherlands, or of other UN organizations around the world? Do you think of your country's membership in the UN? Do you think that diplomats of the world bring their misunderstandings to the UN and cure them? Or do you believe that greater misunderstandings are created at the UN than cured? Do you see it as the setting for power politics? Do you believe that the UN should be confirmed, strengthened, or abandoned?

3. I.A. Richards would ask what is the context in the setting of addresses, statements, debates, and speeches at the United Nations? For example, there are several different contextual dynamics at work in the General Assembly, one when heads of state or government are escorted ceremoniously into the Assembly by the President of the General Assembly and the Secretary General, and provide "an address" to assembled delegates and visitors and even to a "universal audience." During the annual 3-week "General Debate" at the beginning of each General Assembly session, the context allows all heads of state and government, foreign ministers, and official ambassadors or representatives of the approximately 190 nations in the international organization to speak on issues or questions about which their country is concerned. These messages take on the nature of "omnibus speeches" as they deal with various matters, often receiving one or two paragraphs of attention each. When specific issues or committee recommendations are being debated in the General Assembly, heads of state or government, foreign ministers, ambassadors, and other official representatives make "statements" on these issues of questions. There are also special sessions of the General Assembly, for example, the Fifth Emergency Special Session in 1967 on the Middle East crisis, or special sessions on such topics as sustainable development, disarmament, international trade, and human rights. The context changes for 5-, 10-, 20-, 25-, 30-, 40-, and 50-year anniversaries, the last major anniversary that happened in 1995, where dozens of heads of state and government addressed the General Assembly. Some of the 50th-anniversary celebrations were held in June 1995, in San Francisco where the Charter was written and approved, and thus the context changes again.

4. In the Security Council, the context is very different than in the General Assembly. The latter is normally in session for 3 months each September to December, which is more given to listening to speakers, receiving and approving reports, and debating often more general issues and questions. In the Security Council, a seated body, in constant session as the need arises, the contextual responsibility is to take actions which will resolve specific international conflicts and to further international peace. With 15 members seated, and five permanent members having the

vested interest of the veto, the monthly presidency rotates alphabetically by country, and the contextual meaning changes regularly. Later, we provide for your analysis a chapter including several statements by world leaders in an "unprecedented Security Council meeting at the level of heads of state and government." Certainly, the context would have been different for that meeting—which offered a vision for the future—than in a meeting such as the Goa Question, where the definition of terms was seen as contextually different for those perceiving a violation of the Charter by an international attack on a foreign territory versus a view of the question as self determination. Even the context of Security Council resolutions, with their preambles and operative sections, as well as the possibility of a defeat by a single permanent member's veto, changes the meaning of the context considerably.

5. In the International Court of Justice, one of the major organs of the UN, how is the meaning of the context seen differently by different delegations? The United States supported the finding of the Court in its favor in an Iranian–US dispute over the hostages taken in the late 1970s, but rejected its findings in favor of Nicaragua in its complaint against the United States for violating and mining its harbors. When we compare the General Assembly, the Security Council, the International Court of Justice, the secretariat, the Trusteeship Council (now largely without work), and UNESCO (which the United States and United Kingdom governments withdrew from in the 1980s under the Reagan and Thatcher Administrations), the context and its meaning certainly are different in each situation. Richards would ask, are there various different contexts at work in the same setting? After all, there are many different organs and committees at work simultaneously, both within the headquarters in New York, and in various other countries. The UN has more than 3,000 subsidiary organizations attached officially, and more than 1,500 Nongovernment Organizations (NGOs) affiliated more indirectly.

6. Many of the addresses, speeches, and statements may be highly poetic and metaphoric. At the same time, the UN produces many annual reports of an empirical nature on many international subjects. Would Richards ask us to consider whether one can better describe the UN through metaphor and poetry or through empirical research? Or would he ask whether the UN can be considered in both ways—emotively and scientifically?

7. We could ask ourselves whether Marshall McLuhan is right in his statement that: "The new electronic interdependence recreates the world in the image of a global village"? Today there are more than 50 cities that have more than 5 million people, and more than 200 cities have more than 1 million people. Many of these cities are in developing societies. Is

this new electronic interdependence recreating the world rather in the image of a "global city"? Or, if McLuhan is correct, is the UN itself analogous to a "global village"? Members of the secretariat and diplomats and representatives functioning there, either in the Security Council, the General Assembly, or other organs of the UN, come from approximately 190 countries, and in some ways may be more like each other—either international civil servants or elite diplomats and other representatives—than like their own country's people, with whom they may be out of touch. Generally, languages spoken at the UN focus on the two working languages—English and French, and even if speaking other official languages, Arabic, Chinese, Russian, or Spanish, the speakers probably also know one of the two working languages, perhaps as their third or fourth language. Does this make the UN building itself with its secretariat members and diplomats a global village? Jurisdictionally, the UN building itself, like foreign embassies, is outside the authority of the city of New York, the state of New York, or the United States, even with its own postal system. Does that make it a global village?

8. Members of a "village" tend to know every one's business, and much of the work of the UN is done in "corridor diplomacy" even more than in the formal addresses, debates, and statements. Most diplomats and other representatives frequent diplomatic receptions several times weekly, smoking, eating, and drinking together, and engaging in the idle chit chat of the diplomatic "village." Many are personal friends, over an extended time as was illustrated in the eulogies of Secretary General U Thant and the President of the General Assembly at the memorial service in the General Assembly for Adlai Stevenson in 1965.

9. On the other hand, the diplomats and representatives have constituencies from countries with populations as small as 100,000 or as large as the People's Republic of China population in 1995 as 1,190,431,000. In this case, is the UN itself a "global city"? A global city usually has a communication overload, its members are detached from each other, each person is out for him- or herself, and there are few close bondings. New York City, the world's diplomatic capital, is busy and bustling during the day; at night many of its districts are forbidding and dangerous. Tokyo appears to be an exception to the isolation that people may feel in the typical global city, but even there the nighttime comfort level in major downtown areas is now less supportive than only a few years earlier.

10. Again, if he is correct, would McLuhan tend to say that the UN itself is the *message,* which is more important than the content of the addresses, speeches, and statements given there? In such a case, does the UN itself serve as a *massage* for the members of the secretariat, the diplomats, and other representatives working there? To put it another way, if

the UN had not existed for more than 50 years, would diplomats have had to create such an organization for the message it conveys, even if the reality is different? Toward the end of *Diplomatic Discourse,* we have an example of the statements made by heads of state and government in an unprecedented meeting of the Security Council at the level of heads of state and government expressing their vision for the future. Was the fact that thirteen heads of state and government, and two foreign ministers, gathered for one day to chart their vision for the future of the UN itself more important than what each one of them said? McLuhan would say yes. Secondly, by their presence together, were the heads of government of the five permanent members of the Security Council, and the heads of state or government, or foreign ministers of ten elected country members in the Security Council more important as a message and massage for each other, and perhaps for a wider audience, than for what they had to say in each of their brief statements?

11. Li Peng, the Premier of the People's Republic of China, was vigorously protested, primarily by Chinese students, outside of the UN headquarters, because of his role in the Tiananmen Square massacres in 1989. Was Prime Minister John Major of the United Kingdom, who served as the host of the one-day summit, more impressed with the message of having all, or nearly all of the Council members represented by a head of state or government, than with the message which Li Peng's presence caused to the outside protesters? President Boris Yeltsin made his first appearance at the UN after the collapse shortly before of the Soviet Union and the newly emerged Russian Federation and Council of Independent States. Was his presence a message which was more important than what he had to say at the Council meeting? The draft document was prepared, probably by the British Government, before the actual one day event actually occurred. In this case, did the medium itself become the message and the massage?

12. Conor Cruise O'Brien and Felix Topolski, in *The United Nations: Sacred Drama,* make the metaphor about the UN as a holy temple, the universal shrine of survival, with the Secretary General as the high priest, the speaking rostrum as the high altar, and those who come to speak in the General Assembly as the high priest's acolytes. They emphasize: "Rhetoric has its own dynamics, and the dynamics of a rhetoric which involves arguments of international law—when such arguments are used by those who have means to impose their concepts of international law—are powerful and dangerous. The 'power' of the United Nations,' and in particular of the General Assembly, is the power to evoke such a rhetoric and squeeze it towards action" (O'Brien & Topolski, 1968, p. 52). What metaphors could you create positively about the

UN? Negatively? About the Secretary General? About those heads of state and government who travel from their home countries to speak in the General Assembly? About the ability to squeeze rhetoric towards action in the UN?

13. Aristotle separated three genre, epideictic, deliberative, and judicial rhetoric, while at the same time indicating that there is overlap among the three. Based on what Richard Weaver says about language being sermonic, does it seem possible that there could be three distinct genre of addresses, speeches, or statements in the UN, or is there only one—deliberative—which seeks to move delegates and nations toward supporting the status quo, new policy or action? Can Queen Elizabeth's address be considered ceremonially neutral, or must her ideas have consequences? When we consider the two versions: in English—the UN—or translated from French, "Nations Uniting," according to Weaver, which would be a stronger noun phrase? When you consider the god and devil terms identified as related to the UN, with which ones would you agree that they are god or devil terms? If you were applying these terms to the United States and the former Soviet Union as a member of either nation, how would you react? If you were a Chinese student today studying in the United States, how would you react to being identified as a "Red Chinese"? If you were a member of the People's Republic of China delegation when protest signs appeared calling the Chinese Premier "Butcher of Tiananmen Square," how would you handle this situation for your delegation? With UN officials? With members of the international media accredited to the UN? With television reporting to the citizens of the PRC of your visit to the UN?

14. In an earlier discussed statement by the foreign minister of the Democratic Republic of Korea, would you assume that this designation means South or North Korea without noting the word "North"? Why? If the foreign minister of the Democratic Republic of Korea calls his country's head "the great leader Kim II Sung," how would you react, if you were friendly toward that government, or antagonistic?

15. In resolutions before the Security Council and other organs of the UN, the preamble paragraphs are based on present states of being in the language framework of a participle or gerund: The Security Council: *noting, understanding, recalling, angered at, dismayed at,* and so forth. The operative paragraphs, however, became very forcefully active: *calls upon, demands, insists, urges, recommends, requests,* and so forth. Following is an imaginary resolution:

Sponsor: The United States; Cosponsors: the United Kingdom, France, and Turkey.

The Security Council: *Highly Distressed* at the unauthorized and unprecedented Iraqi troops movements near the borders of Turkey.

Recalling Security Council resolutions SC. 1,000 and 1,001 deploring the Iraqi troop movements in that region.

Therefore, *Calls upon* the Iraqi Government to respect seriously and completely international borders and Security Council resolutions 1,000 and 1,001.

Urges the complete withdrawal immediately of their troops from the Turkish border regions, *and Instructs* the Secretary General to keep the Council apprised of developments of a military nature in that region.

Considering Weaver's emphasis on the sentence (which begins with "*The Security Council,*" and ends with "border regions"), and the forceful versus secondary parts of speech, in the sentence, what would you consider the most persuasive or forceful elements of the sentence, and which the most subsidiary? Why? As a rhetorical stratagem, how do you see the Security Council resolution addressing a realistic situation to a specific audience rooted historically for members of the Security Council, for residents and citizens inside the immediate borders of Turkey, and for members of the government and military units of Iraq? What is the difference in force between the preamble paragraphs and the operative paragraphs of the resolution? What is the difference in the forcefulness of the term *preamble* versus *operative*? Who is taking the action: the United States, the United Kingdom, France, and Turkey, or the UN Security Council? Why?

16. Utilizing Stephen Toulmin's method of argument, can you make arguments related to addresses, speeches, or statements in the UN to show how this practical method will actually work? In the preceding chapter, we synthesized Toulmin's practical reasoning and applied it to an article on the UN from *The US News and World Report*. Taking that same situation of arguments, for and against Stevenson's points, can you reconstruct from Toulmin's perspectives, how Stevenson would have moved to his major conclusions?

JUDICIAL OR FORENSIC RHETORIC AT THE INTERNATIONAL COURTOF JUSTICE CONCERNING THE COMPLAINT OF NICARAGUA AGAINSTTHE UNITED STATES BOMBING ITS HARBORS AND OTHER HOSTILE ACTS

Here, instead of analyzing the messages themselves of the Nicaraguan and US advocates in the International Court of Justice, we are providing guidelines about understanding the *judicial* rhetoric involved from the perspective of the elite media's views of the issue before the International

Court of Justice (ICJ). An easy starting point for the crisis itself is *The World Almanac and Book of Facts: 1995,* which tells us, among other information: "Relations with the US were strained as a result of Nicaragua's aid to leftist guerrillas in El Salvador and US backing of anti-Sandinista contra guerrilla groups. In 1983, the Contras launched their first major offensive; the Sandinistas imposed rule by decree. In 1985, the US House rejected President Reagan's request for military aid to the Contras. The subsequent diversion of funds to the Contras from the proceeds of a secret arms sale to Iran caused a major scandal in the US" (1994, p. 806). Interestingly enough, however, though one media writer called the Nicaraguan complaint in the ICJ the most politically sensitive the World Court has ever adjudicated, as well as representing its first involvement in an international conflict still under way, *The World Almanac* fails to mention this aspect of the situation.

Today, through computer search in almost any technologically advanced college or university library, one can find extensive information on Nicaraguan–US relations in the 1980s, the Contra–Sandinista conflict, the Reagan–Bush policies toward Nicaragua, and the Nicaraguan complaint in the ICJ against the United States for mining the Nicaraguan harbors. Utilizing only the decade of the 1980s, and considering only a small segment of the elite press and media resources available in English, various specific articles were found in the *New York Times,* Reuters North European Service, *The Christian Science Monitor, Newsweek,* Information Access Company—ASAP, *The United Nationals Chronicle,* Reuters Ltd., *The Financial Times Ltd., The Chicago Tribune, The Reuter Library Report,* and *The Boston Globe.* Many articles in other elite newspapers such as *The Times* (of London) and *The Sunday Times* simply repeated Associated Press or Reuters files, without much independent news gathering of their own.

Before turning to the actual Nicaraguan complaint itself, the American response, the decisions of the ICJ, and illustrative elite media reactions in English, let us return to and briefly expand the classical views of *judicial* rhetoric.

Classical views of judicial rhetoric reviewed

First, it is important to remember that unlike *epideictic* and *deliberative* genre of rhetoric, the ancient Greeks and Romans did have differing views of *judicial* rhetoric. Both Plato, through the Socratic dialogues, and Aristotle in *Rhetorica,* advocated a major consideration for any speaker (writer) to be *justice* and *injustice.* Roman rhetoricians such as Cicero, a foremost legal mind in his period, and Quintilian, the first state paid teacher of rhetoric, expanded on the Greek contributions. Because there were no attorneys for the defense in the Greek city-states, the defendant was required to plead his own case in front of very large spectator juries. However, wealthy defendants did hire logographers or ghost writers, who often wrote the same defense for several different clients, with some minor modifications for a particular situation or client. Thus, just as in the Aristotelian discussions of "commonplaces" or "topics," there were also legal "commonplaces" which the defendant could call upon as he needed. As we have noted earlier, only freeborn citizens, excluding women, foreigners, and slaves, would be involved seriously in jury trials, either as defendants or members of the large and often unwieldy jury for whom it was a sort of spectator sport. If a slave or foreigner were called in front of a jury trial, it could be assumed that he had been tortured to extract the called-for response. Women appeared only with children, often in a bedraggled state, for a defendant to provide a certain element of *pathos* in front of his male peers. Beyond weeping and wailing, women and children did not speak for the jury to hear them present arguments.

In Plato's *Phaedrus,* Socrates pushes Phaedrus to identify the purpose of rhetoric as: "the art of speaking and writing is exercised chiefly in lawsuits, and that of speaking also in public assemblies." Socrates continues: "Tell me, what do the parties in a lawsuit do in court? Do they not contend in speech, or what shall we say they do? . . . (Do they speak) about the just and unjust? . . . Then he whose speaking is an art will make the same thing appear to the same persons at one time just and at another, if he wishes, unjust?" "Certainly," Phaedrus responds (Plato, cited in Benson & Prosser, 1969b, p. 25). Later, Socrates establishes a principle in legal rhetoric that still is in force today, but which he considers a negative, when he says disparagingly to Phaedrus: "In the courts, they say, nobody cares for truth about these matters, but for that which is convincing; and that is probability. For sometimes one must not even tell what was actually done, if it was not likely to be done, but what was probable, whether in accusation or defense; and in brief, a speaker must always aim at probability, paying no attention to truth" (Plato, cited in Benson & Prosser, 1969, p. 73).

In *Rhetorica ad Alexandrum,* pseudo-Aristotle defines forensic or judicial rhetoric: "the oratory of accusation is the recital of errors and offenses, and that of defense and refutation of errors and offenses of which a man is accused or suspected" (Benson & Prosser, 1969, p. 73). Aristotle considers deliberative rhetoric "less knavish than Forensic, and embraces larger interests. . . . In forensic speaking . . . it is important to win over the hearer. . . . Truth and the likeness of truth come under the observation of the same faculty. (It may be added that men are adequately gifted for the quest of truth and generally succeeded in finding it.) Hence the same sort of man who can guess about truth, must be able to guess about probabilities" (Aristotle, cited in Benson & Prosser, 1969, p. 55).

The Nicaraguan complaint against the United States in the International Court of Justice

Virtually as soon as Ronald Reagan became the US President in 1981, his administration suspended aid to the Sandinistas in power in Nicaragua, accusing them of arming Marxist rebels in El Salvador. In 1982, the United States supported a group of mercenaries, called the Contras. They launched raids against the Sandinistas into Nicaragua from Honduras, starting a war that claimed 30,000 lives in 8 years. In 1983, the Contras blew up two key bridges in Nicaragua, with US support, and in 1984, the CIA role in the mining of the Nicaraguan harbors created an international uproar. In November 1984, Daniel Ortega was elected president with two thirds of the vote when the opposition pulled out. In this particular review of the decade of the 1980s, an article is headlined: "Decade of Conflict: A Look at Sandinista Rule; 1979; Defeat of the Sandinistas." The article included as graphics a photo of General Augusto Sandino, for whom the Sandinistas are named, a UPI File Photo of Anastasio Somoza, who was ousted by the Sandinistas, a photo of Sandinista rebels riding a small tank through the streets of Managua after their victory over Somoza in 1979, and a UPI File Photo of Commander Melchol Castellon Moreno training Contras in the province of Selaya Sur (*The Boston Globe,* February 27, 1990).

On October 9, 1982, Frank J. Prial wrote an article for the *New York Times* and its syndicate, headlined "Honduras and Nicaragua Give Opposing Views at the UN," datelined at the UN the previous day. During the then General Debate of the General Assembly, the Foreign Minister of Honduras spoke to assembled diplomats saying that his country had been working to solve some of the Central American conflicts, but was not threatened by those conflicts and regional terrorism. He said that his country was working with Costa Rica to establish a forum for peace, with hopes that Nicaragua would join them. Earlier, however, the Nicaraguan Foreign Minister in a news conference at the UN said that an imminent US-inspired invasion from Honduras was expected. Foreign Minister Rev. Miguel d'Escoto Brockman of Nicaragua indicated that there had been many incursions into Nicaragua from Honduras. He praised the proposed Mexican–Venezuelan proposal for direct talks between Nicaragua and Honduras, and criticized US Secretary of State George Schultz for not meeting with him during the Secretary's General Assembly visit the week before. Speaking to the General Assembly, the Cuban Foreign Minister, Isidoro Malmierca Peoli, blamed the United States for the Central

American unrest, saying "Blinded by stupidity and lack of realism, Mr. Reagan's Administration has rejected dialogue and a negotiated political solution in this explosive area and is preparing the conditions for an armed intervention that would prevent a revolutionary triumph in El Salvador and drown the Nicaraguan revolution in blood." Prial said that intended military intervention in Nicaragua and El Salvador would create a new Vietnam in Central America (Prial, 1982 [Online]).

On June 8, 1983, the Reuters North European Service ran a nearly 1,000 word article, bylined by Walker Simon, with the headline: "Nicaraguans Outraged over Consulate Closures." Daniel Ortega charged that the closure of six of its seven consulates in the United States "fortifies its warlike line to spread Bloodletting in Central America." Three American diplomats were accused of trying to kill the Nicaraguan Foreign Minister, a Catholic priest, with a drink "laced with poison." Simon indicated that this assassination attempt had become the subject of a humor program on the official Radio Sandino. Pro-government newspaper *Nuevo Diario* was quoted several times in Simon's article, calling the alleged US move against the Foreign Minister "disproportionate and haughty," stating that the closure of the consulates amounted to an economic blockade and caused serious hardships for the 40,000 Nicaraguans living in the United States. *Nuevo Diario,* calling the consulates' closure a barbaric move, was identified as hoping that the US decision would "rebound like a boomerang against the haughty men who made it." Ortega was paraphrased as saying that the move went hand in hand with US Reagan Administration "criminal military backing of more than 7,000 rightist rebels based in Honduras, with Honduran artillery providing cover for their incursions into Nicaragua." Simon said that Washington had acknowledged giving undercover support to "freedom fighters" opposed to the Marxist Sandinistas, but denied that its intention was to overthrow the government. In turn, the United States was noted as accusing the Managua regime of funneling Soviet-Bloc arms to leftist guerrillas trying to topple the US-backed government in El Salvador. The US diplomat Richard Stone, who was to arrive in Managua in 2 days, was described by Foreign Minister D'Escoto as a "tremendous reactionary—with a total lack of moral values" (Simon, 1983 [Online]).

Daniel Southerland (1983), writing with the headline "Many Voices on Reagan's Central America Policy," for *The Christian Science Monitor,* emphasized that considerable confusion existed about the Reagan Administration Central American policy, both outside and within the government. Henry A. Kissinger's, Richard Stone's, and Langhorne A. Motley's official involvement in the Central American situation was aided by the active participation of CIA Director William J. Casey, plus William P. Clark, President Reagan's National Security Adviser, and that of UN Ambassador

Jean J. Kirkpatrick. Southerland points out that it was increasingly difficult to tell who was calling the shots in the Central American affairs, and that the US administration pronouncements seemed to lack any clear sense of coordination, with State Department officials dismayed by Defense Department officials who spoke openly about trying to "intimidate" Nicaragua. Southerland indicates that leaks to the press make it seem that Reagan was a warmonger bent on crushing the Sandinista regime at all costs. Whether the overthrow of the Sandinista regime in Nicaragua was the immediate aim or a long-range one, Southerland stresses that the President's policy at the moment was designed to put the pressure on the Sandinistas, with a strategy either to push them to negotiations, or to prevent the overthrow by Marxist guerrillas of another government (El Salvador) in Central America. President Reagan was quoted as saying that it would be difficult to settle the issues in Central America with the Sandinistas remaining in power, because "they're being subverted, or they're being directed by outside forces." However, some US officials felt that a naval blockade, or quarantine "is a remote possibility indeed." An unidentified State Department official was quoted as saying: "Some of the macho types really want to rattle the cage, and see what birds fall out." Southerland's conclusion was that while it might appear that the administration knew exactly where it was going, it was more likely to be working things out on a day-to-day basis (Southerland, 1983 [Online]).

In the August 1, 1983 US edition of *Newsweek*, a 3,203-word article by Mark Whitaker, with others in Washington, and Beth Nissen in Managua, was headlined "Reagan's Gunboat Diplomacy." The article's highlight was "The President sends the US fleet south and puts Nicaragua on warning." It describes the surprise of an expected 7-month cruise of Pearl Harbor, Singapore, and the Philippines, the USS Ranger, suddenly setting a new course for Central America, where it rendezvoused with seven other ships, and headed for international waters off of Nicaragua. In a press conference in Washington, President Reagan denied that he was trying to impress Nicaragua with "gunboat diplomacy" and said that he did not intend to blockade Nicaragua as an open act of war, an eventuality which he said he hoped would not arise. The article indicates that Reagan's address to longshoremen in Florida charged that Soviet and Cuban meddling in Central America was the first real communist aggression on the American mainland. At a ceremony marking "Captive Nations" week, Reagan accused the Soviet government of "cranking up a war machine in Nicaragua." Part of Reagan's effort, the article speculates, was to get more attention from Congress, and thereby more committed funds, including $110 million in US emergency military aid for El Salvador. He also wished to block a US House of Representatives proposal to cut off all covert US aid to insurgents battling the Nicaragua junta, and to convert $80 million in open aid earmarked solely for interdicting arms shipments to leftist guerrillas in El Salvador.

The *Newsweek* article continues to assess Reagan's intentions in Central America and the potential effectiveness of his "Teddy Roosevelt big stick" approach, and indicates that it appears that the American efforts were poorly planned and coordinated. National Security Adviser William Clark ordered the new maneuvers without first consulting either the State or Defense Department, or the government in Honduras, where most of the military activities were to take place. The article indicates that a "US quarantine or blockade would have a devastating effect. Although the administration cut off all direct aid to the Sandinistas in 1981, the United States remains the country's most important trading partner." Offering its own assessment of US diplomatic and military prospects in El Salvador and Nicaragua, the article suggests that:

> The administration's effort at diplomacy looked very tentative. . . . But the administration's line did seem tougher than ever. Hard liners . . . are convinced that the only way to squeeze the leftist insurgency in El Salvador is to cut off its supplies at the source—in Nicaragua. At the same time, they believe that if the Soviets and Cubans are given much more time to build a "warehouse" for revolution in Nicaragua, the only way to stop them will be a full-scale invasion, something no one wants. (Whitaker, et al., 1983 [Online])

In what appears to be the sort of ending of an article that both *Time* and *Newsweek* use with some regularity, the article speculates: "Hotter heads in Washington now talk giddily about 'beating the communists' for the first time since the Berlin airlift. . . .If the White House continues on its course and the Sandinistas retreat into Fortress Nicaragua, the more plausible outcome is a long and perhaps even more destructive face-off." The article includes ten photos to support various parts of the assessment and analysis by Mark Whitaker and his *Newsweek* colleagues (Whitaker, et al., 1983).

Twelve days later on August 12, 1983, Reuters Ltd. carried a brief 188 word article about the USS Ranger joining the fleet of six ships which was to locate in the international waters off of Nicaragua, and the planned joint ground troop exercises of 5,600 US troops in Honduras (Reuters, Ltd., 1983). In November, 1983, *The United Nations Chronicle* had a 961 word article headlined: "Nicaragua Complains of United States Support for Counter-revolutionaries." Nicaragua had taken its complaint to the UN Security Council on September 13, that "new acts of aggression had been committed against it by Somozist and mercenary counter-revolutionary forces trained and financed by the present Administration of the

United States of America" The Nicaragua representative was the only speaker at the Council meeting. The Nicaragua representative emphasized that the US government was speaking of dialogue on one hand, while sending a war fleet to the coast of Nicaragua for joint maneuvers with Honduras. The Nicaragua representative reiterated Nicaragua's "constant readiness and understanding with the United States and with even greater reason with our Central American brothers." The Security Council took no action about the complaint, and the Council President said that the matter would remain on the Security Council agenda (*United Nations Chronicle,* 1983).

However, on April 11, 1984, *The Christian Science Monitor,* provides an editorial of 603 words entitled "Mines and Law," and an article of 779 words in its National Section entitled "US Troubles Mount over Nicaragua." On the same day, Reuters North European Service has a 405-word article with the headline: "Senate Passes Bill to Cut Off Nicaragua Mine Laying Funds." The April 16 United States edition of *Newsweek* has an 801 word article headlined "The CIA's Harbor Warfare," written by Steven Strasser, and others in Washington. Reuters Northern European Service provides a 389-word dispatch by Robert Trautman, headlined "Harbor Mining Seen Damaging Reagan Central American Policy." The British *Financial Times* offers a brief article by Reginald Dale (1984) entitled "CIA Chief 'Apologizes' after Outcry on Mining."

In fact, according to the chronology supplied by Reuters North European Service (1986a), the Reagan Administration, on April 6, 1984, said it would not accept World Court rulings on Central America for 2 years. On April 9th, Nicaragua filed suit, alleging that the United States broke the UN Charter, the Organization of American States Charter, a bilateral treaty between Nicaragua and the United States and various fundamental international laws by creating, training, arming, and directing a rebel army with the purpose of toppling the Managua government. It further charged that the United States directed the minings of the Nicaragua harbors, and asked for war reparations, to be determined at a later date. Between April 25 through 30, 1984, the chronicle of events continues, the US counsel argued that the Court had no jurisdiction in a political case, that Nicaragua had never formally recognized the Court, and that the Managua regime was using it as a forum for propaganda.

On May 10, 1984, the ICJ made a provisional judgment, ordering a halt to the mining, calling for respect for Nicaragua's frontiers, and telling both sides to refrain from action which might aggravate the dispute. On August 15, 1984, El Salvador applied to intervene in the case on behalf of the United States with the argument that Nicaragua, through armed subversion in El Salvador, was guilty of the same offense of which it accused Washington. The ICJ rejected the El Salvadorian request. From October 8 through 18, 1984, the United States took part in the jurisdiction hearings, challenging the Court's right to deal with the case. On November 26, 1984, the Court rejected the US pleas and ruled, in a series of majority decisions, that it had jurisdiction to hear the full case and judge on its merits. On January 18, 1985, the United States called the jurisdiction decision "clearly erroneous" and declared that it would take no further part in proceedings on the case. From September 12 through 21, 1985, Nicaragua provided a group of witnesses, and demanded $375 million in reparations. On October 7, 1985, the United States gave notice of its withdrawal from compulsory jurisdiction of the ICJ, saying it would not obey, leaving only the United Kingdom among the five permanent members of the UN Security Council accepting compulsory jurisdiction of the World Court (Reuters North European Service, 1986a).

For further information about this phase of the issue see: BBC (1985); Engelberg (1986); Kirk (1985); Latin American Newsletters, Ltd. (1986); Lewis (1986); Manuel (1985); Reuters North European Service (1986a); and Reuters, Ltd (1986).

After a Norwegian cargo ship was extensively damaged when it hit a US-placed mine in the Nicaraguan harbor, Reuters North European Service (1986b), provides a short dispatch headlined "Judge Dismisses Suit Against US in Nicaraguan Ship Incident," which emphasizes that the suit which the US Federal Judge dismissed claimed that the US CIA under instructions of the US President had carried out actions in mining the harbor "in a negligent, malicious or wanton manner." The judge noted that the White House, the CIA and the State Department all denied responsibility for mining the Nicaraguan harbors in the early months of 1984, with a Reagan Administration argument that the suit raised political questions outside of the court's jurisdiction. However, the Knight-Ridder Newspapers (1987) ran the headline "Documents Link North to Mining of Nicaragua." Finally, on October 6, 1988, *The Reuter Library Report* (1988) is headlined "New Proposal Made on Use of World Court, US Says," while at the same time, the US State Department spokesperson said that the proposal did not alter the Reagan Administration position that issues involving the use of force and national security should be exempt from the World Court's jurisdiction. This dispatch ends: "The United States rejected the court's jurisdiction after a dispute with Nicaragua over US involvement in the mining of Nicaraguan harbors."

Let us now consider more directly the complaint of Nicaragua in the International Court of Justice against the United States that it mined the Nicaraguan harbors and engaged in other hostile actions, and the US rejection of the Court's jurisdiction on this matter more precisely from the perspective of the media noted above from April 11, 1984, to the October 6, 1988, report cited above. Daniel Southerland's *The Christian Science Monitor* article of April 11, 1984 reports that both the US Congress and US's European allies were very upset about the US mining of the Nicaraguan harbors, with the latter expressing their concerns (a) that the mining of Nicaraguan ports disrupts the universally recognized principle of the freedom of navigation, (b) that European seamen may be killed or injured in Nicaraguan ports, and (c) that Soviet or East European ships could be damaged, thus leading a regional conflict further in the direction of superpower conflict. The French government was reported as stating that the mining of the harbors had prevented humanitarian supplies from unloading, and indicated that it would help Nicaragua sweep its harbors of the mines. The British government had indicated its disapproval of the US actions, especially after a ship carrying British seamen under the Liberian flag had struck a mine in a Nicaraguan port. Ships from six nations, including a Soviet ship, were reported damaged by the mines in the past 6 weeks alone. The US government was reported to indicate that the mining of the harbors was "fair play," because Salvadorean guerrillas, with Nicaraguan backing, had attacked economic targets such as bridges, coffee mills, and transportation facilities. Four foreign ministers in the Contadora group, trying to facilitate a regional peace settlement, including Mexico, Venezuela, Colombia, and Panama were quoted by Southerland that the mining of the harbors had "contributed to a 'grave deterioration' in Central America."

Southerland continued: "But what concerns some senators and congressmen more than anything else at the moment is the Reagan administration's decision last week to refuse to accept for the next two years the jurisdiction of the International Court of Justice for any cases arising from US actions in Central America" despite the request of Nicaragua to the ICJ to order a stop to the US-sponsored mining of its ports and attacks on its territory. The article ends with a statement by the Speaker of the US House of Representatives, Thomas P. O'Neill Jr., that the administration policy was not only "immoral" but also "illegal" (Southerland, 1984 [Online]).

The editorial in the same issue of *The Christian Science Monitor* argues:

> Whatever the World Court's "jurisdiction" over Reagan Central American actions, one would expect the administration to welcome making its case. But again, as in its attitude toward the United Nations and the other world bodies, the White House seems not to want to suffer review of its policies by international organizations. It is strengthening its unilateralist image. . . . Taken together, the four issues—the mining, contingency troop plans, World Court boycott, and charges against Congress—are working in reverse. (*The Christian Science Monitor,* 1984 [Online])

The Reuters North European Service (1984) dispatch of the same day stresses: "An angry US Senate tonight overwhelmingly approved a resolution advocating a cut-off of all funds to be used for laying mines in Nicaraguan harbors. . . . The Motion . . . is not binding on the President but expresses 'the Sense of the Congress.' " Senator Edward Kennedy had proposed this amendment to a tax billing, with the willing support of the Republican Senate leadership by agreeing to defer a second proposal calling on the Administration to reverse its decision to deny the jurisdiction of the World Court to hear Nicaragua's complaint about the mining of its ports. Reuters reported an unnamed senior Senate Republican aide saying that the Administration agreed to allow a vote on the mining itself, but was adamant about preventing a vote on the second Kennedy measure. The aide said the issue had been mishandled and "The White House wanted to get rid of it." Later, the dispatch notes that "Conservative Senator Barry Goldwater, Chairman of the Senate Intelligence Committee and normally a Reagan Administration supporter, condemned the mining of Nicaraguan waters as 'an act of war' " (Reuters North European Service, 1984 [Online]).

The US edition of *Newsweek* on April 16, 1984, reports that the Reagan Administration had routinely credited the disruptions with six ships being damaged from the mined harbors as the work of Nicaragua counterrevolutionaries. However, Steven Strasser notes:

> Last week there was increasing evidence of direct CIA involvement in the harbor war against Nicaragua. According to intelligence sources, American agents supplied Italian-made mines and a vessel of Panamanian registry to serve as a covert mother ship. CIA speedboats delivered the devices—and CIA contract agents helped sow the explosive charges. (Strasser et al., 1984, [Online])

Newsweek expanded on various elements of the mining operation already identified a week earlier by *The Christian Science Monitor* and Reuters, noting that a CIA spokesman had said "there are no Americans involved in Nicaragua or its waters," but that CIA Director William Casey had briefed the House Intelligence Committee on the mining program. Strasser et al. cited specific countries whose ships had been damaged by the mines, plus negative statements in the US Senate and House of Representatives and overseas (Strasser et al. 1984). A Reuters North European Service dispatch's major emphasis was that the mining of the harbors had hurt Reagan's Central American policy more than it had damaged the Nicaraguans, in fact, causing physical damage to seven non-Nicaraguan commercial vessels and injuring fifteen crewmen (Trautman, 1984).

Ronald Van De Krol (1984) details specifically the Nicaraguan complaint being lodged against the United States in the ICJ. Van De Krol (1984) points out that Nicaragua asked the Court to restrain the United States from covert action against Nicaragua while deciding if it had jurisdiction. On April 6th, however, the Reagan Administration had said it would not recognize the Court's jurisdiction in cases involving Central America for 2 years. The Court President said the United States had filed a letter with the Court saying it had information that Nicaraguan had not accepted the compulsory jurisdiction of the Court, which the Nicaraguan ambassador to the Hague indicated was untrue. Part of the evidence supplied by Nicaragua, including Senator Barry Goldwater's letter to CIA Director Casey expressing his dismay that the Senate had not been told about the CIA's mining of the harbors, referred to Reagan giving the CIA written permission to help mine the Nicaraguan harbors (Van De Krol, 1984). Dale (1984) for the *Financial Times* of London indicates that CIA Director Casey had "apologized" or had "come as close to an apology as could be expected," not for the CIA involvement in mining, but for having failed to brief the Senate Intelligence Committee as fully as needed about the event. This is the extent of most of the elite media coverage in English about the Nicaraguan complaint before the ICJ for nearly a full year.

An Inter Press Service dispatch, written by Alejandro Kirk (1985), indicates that the UN Secretary General Javier Perez de Cuellar backed dialogue in the Nicaraguan situation, but not intervention, and reports that Washington had sent approximately $100 million to the "Contras" through the CIA since December, 1981. Kirk notes that the US-Congress had cut off funding in May, 1984, following revelations that the CIA had directed the mining of Nicaragua's principal harbors (Kirk, 1985).

In the BBC (1985) Summary of World Broadcasts, Moscow in English for North America, Russian media commentary is introduced related to the Nicaraguan complaint against the United States in the ICJ. Here, we have an example of Soviet commentary while the United States and Soviet Union were still in a cold war mentality toward each other. The first two paragraphs represent a reasonably parallel list of facts in the development of the Nicaragua complaint to the ICJ and the US rejection of ICJ jurisdiction. Then editorializing, the commentary continues:

> Nothing can justify Washington's involvement in the atrocious crimes committed by the Contras. That is why Washington could submit no evidence to the court in The Hague because conflicts in Central America could be resolved only by political and diplomatic means and not because it has nothing to say for itself. . . . What are the objectives of the Reagan administration in dealing with Nicaragua? It clearly follows from its moves that its goal is to topple the Sandinista government. The most recent pronounce-

> ment by the administration indicates that the USA does not rule out the possibility of an armed intervention in Nicaragua. (BBC, 1985 [Online])

Manuel (1985), emphasizing that the UN had announced that it would limit its recognition of the authority of the World Court only to deem it as "appropriate," provided a good balance of testimony from specific Reagan administration spokespersons, Charles Redman of the State Department, and its top legal expert, Judge Abraham Sofaer with a counterbalance of opposing views by John Lawrence Hargrove, a Professor of International Law at the School for Advanced Strategic and International Affairs at Georgetown University, Democratic Senator Christopher Dodd of Connecticut, and New York Democrat Representative Ted Weiss. On the one hand, Judge Sofaer was quoted as saying that Nicaragua's case "is part of a general effort by communist regimes to take over democracies, to undermine democracies"; on the other hand, Weiss stated that the administration "has brazenly made lawlessness a guiding principle of its foreign policy."

Without any judgmental statement by the Inter Press Service, Manuel writes that the US decision related to the ICJ marked the third time that the Reagan Administration had limited its role in a UN agency, following its 1984 withdrawal from UNESCO, and the week before the US administration's announcement that it was indefinitely suspending its funding of the UN Fund for Population Activities to protest the UNFPA support for China's objectionable family planning program (Manuel, 1985). Inter Press Service (1985) highlighted Nicaraguan President Daniel Ortega's address to the United Nations General Assembly, October 21, 1985, an address 3 days before President Reagan's scheduled address. The Inter Press Service dispatch noted that President Ortega, in an impassioned address, called upon the United States to bring its Central American policies in line with the UN Charter and international law, as the United States had placed itself "outside the law" by rejecting the ICJ jurisdiction over the Nicaraguan complaint against the United States' relation to the mining of its harbors. After summarizing Ortega's address, and noting that his US speaking tour had been suspended because the United States refused to provide him a visa until 24 hours before his scheduled UN address, Inter Press Service noted that 400 persons had demonstrated outside the UN in support of Nicaragua (Inter Press Service, 1985).

A Reuters Ltd. dispatch (1986), headlined "Nicaragua To Take its Case to UN in New York," indicates that with the World Court declaration that President Reagan's support for the Contras was illegal, despite an unenforceable order that the funding should be halted, Nicaraguan Foreign

Minister Manuel D'Escoto called it "a victory for peace." The Reuters Ltd. dispatch cites that on most issues by a vote of 12 to 3, the ICJ judges produced a whole battery of decisions (15) against the United States, which indicated that it would ignore these decisions:

> The verdict declared that the United States broke a 1956 treaty of friendship between the two countries and a range of customary international laws banning intervention in the internal affairs of another state, the use of force against another state, violation of the sovereignty of another state and interruption of peaceful commerce.
>
> It threw out a US argument that Nicaragua was the regional aggressor and condemned aid to the Contras as illegal.
>
> It also found the United States responsible for a series of air and sabotage attacks on Nicaraguan ports and installations and for the mining of Nicaraguan harbors.
>
> It declared illegal a US embargo on trade with Nicaragua and reminded Washington it had a duty to obey international law. (Reuters Ltd., 1986 [Online])

The New York Times expanded on this information in an article by Lewis (1986) by citing the 15 specific instances in which the court supported Nicaraguan claims against the United States. Lewis notes that throughout the case the argument that the United States was giving military aid to the Contras was never in doubt, but that before the United States withdrew from the case, it had argued that the US actions were "collective self-defense" against Nicaragua support of leftist guerrillas in El Salvador and elsewhere. Lewis further speculates that: "The Nicaraguan case is widely seen by legal scholars as the most politically sensitive the World Court has ever adjudicated as well as representing its first involvement in an international conflict that is still under way" (Lewis, 1986 [Online]). Both Latin American Newsletters, Ltd. (1986) and Lewis (1986) indicate that the ICJ rejected the Nicaraguan claim that the United States created the contra force, for lack of substantial proof, and found no clear evidence that the United States exercised such a degree of control as to justify treating the Contras as acting on its behalf. Thus, the Court also found that the Contras remained responsible for their own acts, especially violations of a human rights nature (Latin American Newsletters, Ltd., 1986; Lewis, 1986). Although reported elsewhere as well, *The Chicago Tribune* highlights Lt. Oliver North's extensive involvement in aiding the Contras, and in the CIA mining of the Nicaraguan harbors, and in proposing the US sinking of an oil tanker (Knight-Ridder Newspapers, 1987). Later North was convicted of illegally aiding the Contras, lying to Congress, and being part of the Iran-Contra cover up. The decision was overturned and North ran for the Senate seat of Senator Charles Robb during 1994 in Virginia, being defeated by the incumbent.

APPLICATION

1. Here, we have an example not of the judicial rhetoric itself relating to the Nicaragua complaint to the International Court of Justice against the United States for mining its harbors and other actions. We have, instead, selected reports in the elite media assessing Nicaragua–US tensions and media reports about the complaint of Nicaragua itself in the International Court of Justice, with the subsequent American withdrawal from the jurisdiction of the Court. The actual statements by Nicaraguan and American lawyers in the ICJ are not available here, but would resemble standard legal briefs. Recalling the classical definition of *forensic* or *judicial* rhetoric as accusation and defense, and based on our media information, can you isolate three major clash points between the Nicaraguan and United States basic premises in their cases before the ICJ? What are the major accusatory arguments presented by the Nicaraguan government against the US government? What are the major defense arguments presented by the US government? What accusatory arguments did the United States make in the ICJ against Nicaragua? What evidence did each party to the conflict present?
2. Utilizing the Platonic and Aristotelian range between absolute truth and probability, why does the US position seem to change from "There are no Americans in Nicaragua or its waters," to "The mining of the harbors appears to be the work of the Contras," to CIA Director Casey's apology to the Senate Intelligence Committee, not for the mining itself, but for failing to brief the Committee fully on the issue? In this case, what was the difference between truth and probability? Was the Nicaraguan government honest in its complaint and related details against the United States in the ICJ? Was the US government honest in its initial response to the ICJ complaint by Nicaragua?
3. What was the impact of the elite media's reporting noted above in determining whether the US CIA *actually* caused the harbor mining or whether it *probably* caused the mining? What was the effect of the public information about the mining on the US Senate and House of Representatives? On the European allies? Why did the potential damage to Soviet or Eastern European ships in the Nicaraguan harbors from the mining provide a possible or probable global threat?

Were the media from which we have seen excerpts themselves involved persuasively in trying to sway opinion in one direction or the other in terms of Nicaragua–US tensions and in relation to the mining of the harbors? Can you give examples where the media appeared to be moving away from simple reporting toward proposed probabilities of accusation or defense of one side or the other? Noting the excerpts from various elite media above, which seemed more balanced in its reporting, the American or the European media (e.g. Reuters)? Why? How do you react to the BBC World Wide Commentary from the Moscow media in relation to this complaint?

4. After nearly 40 years where the United States had accepted the compulsory jurisdiction of the ICJ, why did it indicate first that it would not be bound by any ICJ decisions related to US activities in Central America for two years, later withdrew from the case entirely, and finally refused to accept any compulsory jurisdiction of the Court in the future, except when it chose? Would this appear to strengthen the probability of just or unjust behavior on the part of the United States against Nicaragua? Why? Why not? Would it strengthen or weaken the US ethos in terms of its sense of justice in relations to the small countries in its region?
5. Because each of the classical Greek genre of rhetoric, *epideictic, deliberative,* and *forensic* or *judicial,* tend to overlap to some extent, as we reflect back to the two statements in the Security Council by Ambassador Adlai Stevenson on the GOA Question, are there identifiable elements of *forensic* rhetoric in the information coming out of the Security Council debate on the GOA Question? If so, can you provide specific examples? In this ICJ case as reported by the elite media, are there elements of *epideictic* and/or *deliberative rhetoric*? If so can you provide examples? What comparisons or contrasts can be found in the US rhetoric in the UN Security Council by Ambassador Stevenson in 1961 that the UN Charter makes no exceptions in terms of the acceptability of international attacks on other countries or territories and the US rhetoric in the mid 1980's about its actions relating to Nicaragua and El Salvador?
6. We may develop the following syllogism. Major Premise: "Countries which attack other countries violate the United Nations Charter and international law." Minor Premise: "The United States has mined the Nicaraguan harbors." Conclusion: "The United States has violated the UN Charter and international law." Out of this, an enthymeme could develop as follows: "The United States is a war monger in Central America." A different syllogism, however, is possible. Major Premise: "Communistic ideology is evil." Minor Premise: "The

Nicaraguan Government accepts Communism." Conclusion: "The Nicaragua Government is evil." An enthymeme develops, for example: "Stamp out communism in the Americas." If you were to build syllogisms from aspects of the Nicaraguan complaint in the ICJ against the United States, what would be some of your examples? If you were then to develop truncated syllogisms or enthymemes from these syllogisms, what would be some of your examples? If you were to build syllogisms from the US arguments in the ICJ case accusing the United States of mining Nicaraguan harbors, what would be some examples? If you were then to develop enthymemes from these syllogisms, what would be some examples?

7. From the moment of his inauguration, President Ronald Reagan appeared obsessed with the situations in El Salvador and Nicaragua. In the media excerpts cited above, we see President Reagan calling the Contras "freedom fighters." In a statement, he called them "the moral equivalent of our founding fathers." As cited in the media excerpts above, the US government indicated that its efforts against Nicaragua were the first time that the United States had challenged communism directly on the mainland. Why were the United States and the Reagan administration so taken up with this challenge to communism in the Americas during this period? How did their public rhetoric reflect this obsession in relation to Nicaragua?
8. During the Reagan–Bush presidencies, the United States directly or indirectly attacked through military means the Sandinista Government in Nicaragua, the rebels in El Salvador, Libya, Granada, Panama, and Iraq. In general, the *ethos* of the American leaders through such efforts was high. Why does this seem a reasonable assumption? In relation, however, to the mining of the Nicaraguan harbors, the Reagan Administration *ethos* with members of the US Senate and House of Representatives, as well as with European allies, seemed strained, with some Republican and Democratic Senate and House leaders calling the decision "brazenly lawless," "an act of war," and "criminal activity." Why did the two American presidents, Reagan and Bush, appear to have high *ethos* among many Americans with the direct or indirect attacks of several of the countries noted earlier, but much less so with the mining of the harbors?
9. The International Court of Justice, by a vote of 12 to 3 on most counts of the Nicaraguan complaint against the United States, declared that the United States had acted in violation of international law and against Nicaraguan sovereignty on 15 different counts of the complaint. A majority of the judges rejected the American claim that it was acting in the "collective self-defense" of El Salvador, Costa

Rica, and Honduras because Nicaragua was supporting rebel movements in these countries. Did the Court treat the United States justly or unjustly in its decisions on this complaint? The Court held in favor of the United States on the count that it could not be held responsible for specific acts by the Contras because the United States did not directly control their actions. Did the Court treat the United States on this count justly or unjustly? Why? Did the Court treat Nicaragua on this count justly or unjustly? Why?

10. Because the ICJs decision in this complaint was unenforceable, because the United States refused to accept its jurisdiction, Nicaragua could have taken the Question to the UN Security Council, where the United States could veto any decision by the majority. The Nicaraguan Foreign Minister said that if the United States failed to respect the Court's judgment, the United States' "reputation as a member of the international community will be tarnished, perhaps irreparably." Based on your understanding of this complaint, was he correct or incorrect? Why? Should Nicaragua have proceeded to take the Question to the Security Council, despite the fact that the United States would veto any favorable resolution in favor of Nicaragua? Recalling the situation earlier with Ambassador Stevenson on the GOA Question in the Security Council being thwarted by the Soviet veto, and his decision not to take it to the General Assembly under the "Uniting for Peace" resolution, which is rhetorically and symbolically more important, to proceed with the alternative, despite a sure or probable failure, or to accept whatever symbolic victory has already been achieved, and be done with the matter?

CONCLUSION

In this chapter, we have offered examples of three different genre of rhetoric, the General Assembly *epideictic* address of Queen Elizabeth II in 1957, the Security Council *deliberative* statements of Ambassador Adlai Stevenson on the Goa Question in 1961, and 1980's elite media reports of *forensic* or *judicial* rhetoric of Nicaragua and the United States in the International Court of Justice on the Nicaraguan complaint against the United States in relation to the mining of its harbors, and other hostile actions.

Among the classical Greek concepts for rhetorical analysis, we have noted key elements of each genre, and their possible applications, questions and guidelines relating to the clash points of conflicts, the basic premises which can be developed in the different rhetorical genre, the use of rhetorical proofs which can be utilized, such as *ethos, logos,* and *pathos,* arguments based on syllogisms and enthymemes and examples, and refutation.

Understanding that Greek (and Roman) classical rhetoric is the basis for contemporary rhetorical theories, which often simply expand on the classical theories of practice and criticism, we have illustrated some samples of how contemporary rhetorical applications can be made, particularly in relation to the Stevenson statements.

We now turn to the other conflict situations and their resolutions, as reflected in addresses to the UN by Nobel Peace Laureates Yassar Arafat, Nelson Mandela, and Mikhail Gorbachev, as well as Ronald Reagan, Francois Mitterand, Boris Yeltsin, and Pope John Paul II, and a speech by Hillary Rodham Clinton to the United Nations Beijing Forum on Women.

PART III

APPLICATIONS

9

MIDDLE EASTERN CONFLICT: ISRAEL AND THE PLO

In 1919, the Balfour Declaration affirmed that two countries should emerge in the Middle East: Israel and Palestine. After the founding of the UN, when Israel was created in 1948, its troops immediately moved to take control over the areas in which Palestinians were living, and forced many Palestinians to become permanent refugees. During the 1948 Arab–Israel War, the West Bank and East Jerusalem were added to the Kingdom of Jordan. In the 1956 Suez crisis, the United States and the Soviet Union were surprisingly on the same side with Egypt against Israel, the United Kingdom, and France. In 1964, the Palestinian Liberation Organization (PLO) was founded with Yassar Arafat as its Chairman. Its initial purpose was to gain a Palestinian homeland and to destroy the state of Israel. In the 1967 Middle East Six Day War between Israel and the United Arab Republic, the Kingdom of Jordan, and the Syrian Arab Republic, the Soviet union called an emergency session of the General Assembly under the 1950 "Uniting for Peace" resolution that allowed two thirds of the General Assembly membership to agree to become involved in a crisis which the Security Council had been unable to solve. In this conflict, Israel took control over the West Bank, the Gaza Strip and the Golan Heights, all of which became known under international law as "the occupied territories of Israel." In 1968, PLO-related terrorists killed members of the Israeli athletic teams at the Munich Olympics. In the 1973 Yom Kippur War against Israel, the Israeli forces were again victorious. In 1974, the Arab Summit designated the PLO as the official representation on the West Bank. The PLO obtained Observer Status at the UN, and Arafat was received at the UN and in many world capitals as the equivalent of a head of government.

For a number of years, the PLO was headquartered in Beirut, Lebanon, but after the intensive Israeli raids and massacres of residents in the refugee camps by Israeli and Lebanese Christian militia in 1982, the PLO moved its headquarters to Tunis, Tunisia. In 1988, Jordan cut its administrative ties with the West Bank, thus forcing Israel to assume the entire financial burden for the area. Arafat sought in 1988 to speak to the UN General Assembly, but the Reagan administration blocked his visa access, in contravention of its agreement with the UN, and in a period of otherwise improved relations between the United States and the Soviet Union. The entire General Assembly met in Geneva, instead of New York, to hear Arafat speak at the cost for the UN of nearly a half million dollars.

In response to the killing of Palestinians in 1990, first by a deranged Israeli gunman, and then by Israel troops, Arafat and 22 members of the Arab League called for an urgent Security Council meeting. Because the United States had previously denied Arafat the visa in 1988, the Bush administration was caught in a quandary in 1990. The United States had to consider its stated immigration policy, its past support of Israel, the ongoing *Intifadah* uprising against Israeli military forces in the occupied territories, and the recent Israeli attacks against unarmed Palestinian citizens. The United States agreed to hold the Security Council meeting in Geneva if Arafat would not push his visa request. By this arrangement, the PLO was accorded a small victory. Media reports of the day expected that Arafat would "demand that the UN immediately send a peacekeeping force to the occupied territories." His action was further expected to embarrass Israel and possibly undermine the Israeli–American relations. Israel, on its part, argued that the UN was showing bias by selectively choosing to react to the violence in Israel and not at others, and that UN aid to the area would go beyond refugees and end up helping the PLO.

QUESTIONS FOR ANALYSIS

1. Would Arafat perform as expected, and if so, how early and forcefully would he speak about a UN peacekeeping force?
2. Would his address be conciliatory in any way toward Israel or would he mainly be condemning Israeli oppressive efforts in the occupied territories?
3. What stand would Arafat be likely to take toward the United States, if any?
4. Would he give special acknowledgment to the Arab states which helped make his address possible in Geneva?

CHAIRMAN YASSAR ARAFAT, CHAIRMAN OF THE PALESTINIAN LIBERATION ORGANIZATION UNITED NATIONS SECURITY COUNCIL, MAY 25, 1990

(Interpretation from the Arabic)

I greet my brother the representative of the Republic of Yemen, the unified Arab State whose birth was announced a few days ago.

It is a source of great pride for me to be present today for the second time in a year and a half in this hospitable country, where I have already had the honor to address the United Nations, in order to speak with the voice of Palestine, and deliver the word of the Palestine Liberation Organization (PLO).

I should like, Mr. President, to thank you for having given me this special opportunity to undertake this mission on behalf of Palestine and the Palestine people. While we consider this as a token of your deep understanding of the dangerous situation in our area, we also view it as an expression of sympathy for, and solidarity with, the Palestinian people, who are now being subjected to the ugliest oppression and terrorism while struggling for their freedom and for the implementation of the goals, principles and values consecrated by this international Organization.

When the Palestine Liberation Organization (PLO), with the support of the Arab Group, requested the convening of this urgent meeting of the Security Council, its request stemmed from the realization that the situation has reached an extremely dangerous and explosive point. No longer can hesitation be acceptable or verbal condemnation sufficient. The situation now requires urgent action to enforce reverence for international legitimacy.

Last Sunday—"Black Sunday"—a heinous massacre was perpetrated against Palestinian workers who early that morning were in search of bread for their children. They had already been uprooted from their land by policies of the Israeli occupation and were forced to seek labor under the worst possible conditions of exploitation and repression.

Further, the massacre is being continued by the Israeli forces in the West Bank, the Gaza Strip and Jerusalem, accompanied by an outburst of Israeli racism against the Palestinian masses in the Galilee, the Triangle and the Negev. As a result of those policies, more than 25 Palestinian martyrs have fallen and more than 2,000 have been injured during the last five days. All this constitutes but one link in the chain of the Israeli iron-fist policy and Israeli racist practices against the Palestinian people, policies and practices which the international community, Governments and peoples have unanimously denounced.

It was not the insanity or derangement of an individual that was responsible for the Black Sunday massacre, as Israeli officials have claimed. The primary responsibility falls on the insanity and derangement of the whole system, a system which is haunted by mythical ghosts, by defunct illusions of racial superiority and by an obsession with expansion and invasion, stemming from the stupid arrogance of military superiority, in order to create a "Greater Israel."

I am addressing the Council while the wounds of my people are still bleeding and the graves of their martyrs are still exposed. Every moment, Palestinian children, faced with the organized Israeli machine of oppression and terrorism against our Palestinian people, who are struggling for a free and dignified life. During the 30 months of the brave *intifadah* of the Palestinian masses against occupation forces saturated with hatred and aggression, the occupiers have been arrogantly waging a brutal war of extermination.

Over the past 30 months, 1,200 Palestinian martyrs have fallen under the bullets of the occupiers. More than 80,000 citizens have been injured as a result of various kinds of repression ranging from severe beatings, the breaking of bones and the use of rubber bullets and live ammunition to the use of internationally prohibited poison gases, which have caused more than 6,000 miscarriages and permanent handicaps to thousands of children, women, and men, in addition to other kinds of terrorism and repression. Over those 30 months, the Israeli occupation forces have been waging a war of extermination on all fronts. Our people have been the victims of crimes prohibited by international law, divine law and moral and human values: from the war of starvation waged by laying siege to population centers, the destruction of the infrastructure of our national economy through continuing expropriation of land and water resources thereby devastating farms, and the imposition of huge taxes and attempts to collect them through terrorism and theft as happened in Beit Sahour and elsewhere, to the war of imposed ignorance which has led to the closing for three years of all education centers in our country from kindergartens to universities.

The universities and most schools are still closed, as verified by reports and other documents available at the United Nations. This has been accompanied by the closing of many philanthropic, cultural and vocational institutions and by the opening, on the other hand, of mass detention camps and prisons for more than 85,000 detainees, scores of whom have been physically eliminated—in addition to deportations and house arrests. At the same time there has been an escalation of the policy of demolishing the houses of Palestinian citizens, by which the occupation forces have demolished, destroyed and shut down more than 2,000 houses during the years of the *intifadah*, a policy which has left 10,000 persons, including 5,000 Palestinian children, homeless. All of this is in addition to burning and devastating 80,000 *dunums* of land and 188,000 trees, the application of collective punishment and the imposition of huge fines by the courts of the Israeli occupation. All this is being carried out with premeditation and racism on the part of the Israeli Government and the fanatic armed settlers against unarmed citizens in the Palestinian and Arab occupied territories.

The recently published report of the Swedish Save the Children organization states that 159 Palestinian children 16 years of age or younger were killed during the first two years of the *intifadah* by prohibited terrorist methods, including internationally prohibited gas bombs, as reports by two United States and Belgian medical teams have proved. That figure now stands at 256. The same Swedish report states that during the same period between 50,000 and 63,000 Palestinian children were injured and required medical treatment. Twenty-five thousand children, some six years of age or younger, were beaten and their bones broken. Further, 675,000 Palestinian children in the West Bank and the Gaza Strip were subject to curfews, with their attendant psychological and educational implications for everyday life.

Betselem, an Israeli human-rights organization, has reported that, out of 102 cases examined by them in which Palestinian children were killed, only one Israeli soldier was imprisoned—for a mere two months. That confirms the conclusions of the Swedish report, which shows the contempt of Israeli soldiers for the lives of our Palestinian children.

The Palestinian people expect the Security Council to shoulder its responsibilities to put an end to the Israeli occupation and to begin forthwith to adopt the necessity measures to protect the lives of the children, women and men of our Palestinian people and their property under occupation, especially in the light of the Israeli Government's refusal to abide by United Nations resolutions, such as Security Council resolutions 465 (1980) and 605 (1987), which condemn and deplore Israeli practices and crimes against the Palestinian people and call upon Israel scrupulously to abide forthwith by the fourth Geneva Convention of 1949 relative to the Protection of Civilian Persons in Time of War.

The Israeli Government, not content with these crimes and this official organized terrorism against our people, has followed them up by bringing in new waves of Jewish immigrants from all parts of the world and by starting to settle them in the occupied Palestinian territories, including Holy Jerusalem, and other Arab territories in place of the Palestinian and Arab owners of those occupied lands, against whom Israel practices organized official terrorism and brutal oppression in order to drive them from their homeland and the homeland of their ancestors.

In addition, Israel has displaced Palestinian families. Within this very short period of the *intifadah*, more than 256 families have thus far been expelled from their homeland. Placing new immigrants in the quarters belonging to the Greek Orthodox Church and the assaulting the Patriarch of Jerusalem and other priests are part and parcel of the policies practiced by the Israeli Government, policies that were preceded and followed by aggression against Islamic and Christian Holy Places in Jerusalem and the rest of the Holy Land, places viewed as symbols of sanctity, love, peace and tolerance by Muslims and Christians throughout the world.

I have photographic and other evidence of the aggression against the Patriarch of Jerusalem; of the children, many of them nine years of age or younger, killed by Israel; of miscarriages caused by the use of poison gas, which is prohibited internationally. I shall leave these documents for the use of members of the Security Council.

In all it perpetrates and in its repressive, bloody actions and practices against the Palestinian people in the occupied territories, Israel considers itself to be outside the bounds of international responsibility which apply to all States of the world. Indeed, Israel—which was established by a decision of the United Nations—is the only State which ignores and challenges United Nations resolutions and which does not commit itself to implement them.

Israel even refuses to deal with the international Organization when it requests it to carry out its decisions and resolutions. It has now become necessary for the international community to take a stand on this subject and for the Security Council, and especially its permanent member States, to shoulder their responsibility to maintain international peace and security, to implement international resolutions, to end the occupation and to protect the lives of the Palestinian children, women and men under Israeli occupation, in order to arrive at a just and permanent peaceful political solution to the conflict in the Middle East through convening the International Peace Conference on the Middle East, under the auspices of the United Nations.

At a time when the international community is determined to build a world based on cooperation, fruitful dialogue and democracy, when the atmosphere of international detent is being enhanced and when the peoples of the world are preparing to welcome the coming century by underscoring the values of freedom, democracy and human rights, Israel and its leaders insist on clinging to their defunct racist and terrorist policies. Our peaceful initiatives, together with our approach and our *intifadah*, represent a model that has been emulated and that has inspired many peoples struggling for freedom and democracy, peoples which have affirmed the harmony and congruence between the realities of our era and the direction of that model's principal course.

Members of the Council undoubtedly know that, on 13 December 1988 in this hospitable country, in the name of the Palestinian people, I presented to the General Assembly the Palestinian peace initiative adopted by the Palestine National Council in Algiers on 15 November 1988, which was based on international legitimacy and resolution and which was adopted by the Arab summit conference in Casablanca in May 1989.

That initiative also received the support of the summit of the Movement of Non-Aligned Countries, the African summit and the conference of foreign ministers of Islamic countries, in addition to that of many States in Western and Eastern Europe, the Soviet Union, China, Japan and the Scandinavian and other countries. The Palestinian peace initiative found support inside Israeli society and daily increasing support among Israeli democratic and peace-loving forces. It also had a positive influence among Jewish groups in Europe and the United States of America.

Basing itself on Palestinian priorities and rights which are in harmony with international legitimacy, the PLO has shown itself to be totally responsive and responsible. We remain flexible; we continue to approach flexibly and sincerely all international peace initiatives adopted by the United Nations, as well as other proposals, including the five points of the United States Secretary of State Baker. We have also reacted positively to the 10 Egyptian points and to the United States proposals conveyed to us by Mr. Sven Andersen, the Swedish Foreign Minister, on 16 September 1989. The PLO is still committed to its declared peace initiative and is ready to participate in arriving at a political solution through which the Palestinian people will be enabled to realize its legitimate national rights, including the right to return, to self-determination and to the establishment of an independent State of its own on its Palestinian national soil, on the basis of international legality and United Nations resolutions.

Regrettably, those peace initiatives have met with rejection and stubbornness on the part of the Israeli Government, which has escalated its iron-fist policy in order to move further from the peace process in the Middle East, thereby defying all international resolutions relating to the conflict in the Middle East, primarily General Assembly resolution 176/43 of 15 December 1988 relative to the convening of the International Peace Conference on the Middle East. In addition, Israel has ignored and refused to implement Security Council resolutions 242 (1967) and 338 (1973).

As for the city of Jerusalem and the Israel decision to annex it and change its status, proclaiming it the capital of the State of Israel—which was unfortunately followed by a decision on Jerusalem by the United States Congress, encouraging Israel and its occupation, terrorism and crimes—Israel still refuses to carry out any international resolutions on the Holy City, including Security Council resolution 252 (1968) of 21 May 1968, General Assembly resolution 2253 (ES-V) of 4 July 1967, which affirmed the inadmissibility of changing the status of the city of Jerusalem, Security Council resolution of 476 (1980) of 30 June 1980, which declared null and void the measures taken by Israel to change the status of the city of Jerusalem, and Security Council resolution 478 (1980) of 20 August 1980 on the non-recognition of Israel's "basic law" on Jerusalem.

Israel continues to carry out the policy of settlement by expropriating the lands of the Palestinians building Jewish settlements on those lands and changing the demographic nature of the occupied Palestinian territories, in defiance of Security Council resolution 452 (1979) of 20 July 1979, which stipulated that the Israel occupation authorities should cease settlement operations in the occupied Arab territories, resolution 446 (1979) of 22 March 1979, which considered the Israeli practice of establishing settlements a serious obstruction to achieving peace, and resolution 465 (1980) of 1 March 1980, which called upon Israel to dismantle existing settlements and cease the construction and planning of settlements.

Recently Israel has exploited the conditions that have permitted opening the doors of immigration to Soviet Jews and Jews from Eastern European and other States, thereby transforming the right to emigrate into a political and colonial aim, as represented in forced immigration to Israel only, which deprives emigrants and those forced to emigrate of their right to choose their own destination. This constitutes a violation of the rights of those Jews. We would recall that the rights of any individual or people cease where the rights of other individuals or peoples—including the Palestinian people—begin.

Israel has endeavored by all means to close all doors but one to Soviet Jewish emigration, keeping only Palestinian land open for them. Israel has been helped in that endeavor by decisions made and obstacles raised by some States, especially the United States and Australia, within the framework of a special understanding and a fundamental and dangerous distortion of the concept of the right of emigration as stipulated in the Helsinki accords, transforming it to achieve the aggressive political aim of preventing the Palestinian people from living in their homeland and depriving Palestinian refugees of the right to return in order to settle new immigrants in the homeland to which the original owners have a right.

It is necessary for me to point out most responsibly that the issue of Soviet Jewish emigration to Palestinian lands represents a danger to the whole region, not only to the occupied Palestinian lands themselves. The threat extends to neighboring Arab States. Indeed, it has begun to threaten the Golan Heights and southern Lebanon, where bitter experience in the Middle East proves that Israel's greed and expansionist appetites know no limits.

I see it as my duty to point out that, most regrettably, the United States of America has given Israel unlimited support at all levels; this has encouraged Israel to continue its occupation and escalate its terrorist and barbaric practices against the Palestinian people, challenging the decisions of the international community and impeding all peace initiatives in the Middle East region, including the United States proposals themselves, quite apart from all other peace initiates.

The United States, which raises the slogan of human rights, has totally neglected the Palestinians and their human rights and has ignored the comprehensive human and moral dimensions of the concept of human rights. This has encouraged Israel to persist in its barbaric acts; Lebanese villages and Palestinian refugee camps are exposed to Israeli air raids, destructive bombardment and, in the South, occupation.

In view of the dangers in the surrounding Middle East region that arise from the continued Israel occupation of Arab and Palestinian lands and Israel's escalation of State-organized terrorism and the war of annihilation against our people, with aggressive and expansionist threats against many Arab States, especially Iraq, Lebanon and Jordan, through Israel's continuous preparations for aggression and war, it is high time for the Council to shoulder its responsibility to implement United Nations resolutions relating to the Arab–Israeli conflict before it is too late. Through its practices, threats and war preparations, Israel is leading the entire region to a catastrophe whose danger is unprecedented in the light of the fact that the Middle East is among the regions where conventional, nuclear, chemical and biological weapons are stockpiled, which raises the prospect of a catastrophe which will go beyond the borders of the Middle East region to threaten international peace and security.

The dimensions of the danger threatening the prospect of peace in the Middle East are now visible every day. They are beginning to manifest themselves in mass killings, in increased escalation, in the tense situation which is leading the area to the brink of war, and in Israel's insistence on continuing its occupation of Palestinian lands, which only a few days ago Shamir officially declared to be "liberated and inherited lands."

The Palestine Liberation Organization, which affirms its strategic commitment to peace, submits to the Security Council the following practical steps which will realize the international community's consensus, transforming its resolutions into practice and inspiring confidence and hope with respect to the Council's role and effectiveness in achieving world peace, security and justice.

Before outlining those steps, I should like to bring to the attention of the Council a document concerning "Greater Israel" as depicted on the 10-agora coin. The document was published in the *Jewish Journal* in the United States on 19 February 1989. That document speaks of "Greater Israel," which is depicted on Israeli currency, and the map comprises all of Israel, all of Lebanon, all of Jordan, half of Syria, two thirds of Iraq, one third of Saudi Arabia up to the holy city of Al-Mandinah and half of Sinai. The document contains a detailed map, with "Greater Israel" marked in blue.

The first step would be the designation by the Secretary General of a permanent special envoy to work full-time on the peace process and engage in the contacts necessary to secure a peaceful, just and lasting solution to the Arab–Israel conflict. Alternatively, the Secretary General might himself undertake the duties of that mission.

The second step would be adoption by the Council of a resolution providing international protection to the Palestinian people to safeguard their lives, property and holy places in the occupied territories, under the flag of the United Nations and by means of international emergency forces, to supplement the United Nations observer force now stationed in Jerusalem, with the purpose of ending completely the Israeli occupation of our Palestinian land.

The third step is the adoption by the Council of a clear resolution—and the Council's assurance of its supervision and implementation—to stop settler immigration to the occupied Palestinian territories, a decision that will prevent completely the construction and expansion of Israeli settlements, military or civilian, in the occupied Palestinian lands, particularly in Arab Jerusalem, in implementation of the relevant international resolutions.

The fourth step would be for the Council to call the representatives of its permanent members to an immediate meeting to discuss the peace settlement and the peace process and to prepare for the convening of the International Peace Conference on the Middle East, in implementation of international resolutions.

The fifth step is to start to adopt the necessary arrangements and preparations for the imposition of sanctions on Israel in accordance with Chapter VII of the Charter of the United Nations as a response to the crimes committed by Israel against the Palestinian people in the occupied territories and as a consequence of its breach and violation of the Fourth Geneva Convention of 1949 relative to the treatment of civilians in time of war, as well as for its refusal to implement the relevant international resolutions, for its deliberate defiance and its impeding of the peace process in the Middle East, and in particular, for its refusal to implement the Council's own decisions and resolutions.

The experience of the United Nations in imposing sanctions against South Africa has borne fruit in Namibia, where the heroic Namibian people have gained their independence through the New York Agreement, implemented under the auspices of the United Nations. It has also started to bear fruit for the people of South Africa, with the release of the militant hero Nelson Mandela and with the start of building peace and fulfilling the rights of the people of South Africa, far from racial discrimination and *apartheid.* In this context, I should like to express our deep appreciation of the active and extremely important role of the Secretary General, Mr. Perez de Cuellar.

Obligation and commitment to the human heritage and to the concepts of justice and righteousness to which that heritage has been dedicated require that the Council should decide to form an international investigation committee composed of members of the Council to investigate all the crimes against humanity that have been perpetrated by the Israeli Government against the Palestinian people.

While reaffirming that our choice of the path of peace is a genuine strategic alternative, we also affirm our right to continue our resistance and our self-defense until an end is put to the Israeli occupation. That is a sacred right guaranteed to us by the law of human rights, the Charter of the United Nations, international decisions and the will of the Palestinian people. The heroic people's *intifadah* against the Israeli occupation of our country will continue until we wrest our right to freedom and national independence on our national soil.

Our people are committed to the issue of peace and to the initiative that I announced in the name of the Palestinian people a year and a half ago before the General Assembly. Our people are determined to attain their political, national and human rights like all other peoples in the world. We are determined to do so because we are an indivisible part of the community of nations and of human society, with which we have participated in carrying the torch of culture, for it was in our land that the three heavenly religions were formed, flourished and lived side by side in harmony.

It is high time that people enjoyed security, peace and independence. We are not asking for the moon. We are not asking for the impossible. It is high time for our children to live as peacefully as other children of the peoples of the world, far from fear, destruction and death. It is high time to stop the spilling of the blood of our people and for our flag to be raised over their liberated soil. It is high time for us to realize our freedom and for the curtain to fall once and for all, for the last time and forever, on the last racist, settler military occupation of Palestine, that holy [city] and of our planet Earth. (Arafat, 1990)

ELITE MEDIA REACTION TO THE ARAFAT STATEMENT TO THE SECURITY COUNCIL IN GENEVA

In the immediate period after Arafat's Security Council statement, there were reports, among many others, over the next week from the Xinhua General Overseas News Service of the PRC May 25th and 28th, Reuters on May 26th, 27th, 30th, and through its Melbourne, Australia service on May 30th. Among the American newspapers providing the poststatement coverage were *The Chicago Tribune* and *The New York Times* on May 26th with essentially an identical story in its main components, though the *New York Times* story was longer, *The Los Angeles Times*, May 26th, *The New York Times* with a long article on May 27th, and *The Chicago Tribune* on the same day; in the United Kingdom: *The Times* of London, *The Daily Telegraph,* and *The Financial Times,* May 26th, and *The Independent,* May 17th, and *The Jerusalem Post* on May 29th.

The Xinhua files of May 25th, indicated the praise of Palestinians for Arafat's statement: "Wild applause erupted among some 200 Palestinian listeners in East Jerusalem who chanted 'long live Abu Ammar' (Arafat)," but the files noted that the Israelis had sharply rejected the statement, as Prime Minister Shamir's aide called it "a vicious attack on Israel," which was "full of lies and distortions." Xinhua reported that Shamir told Israeli radio: "Our position is clear. We think that it is unnecessary and damaging to send observers of any kind" (Xinhua General Overseas News Service, 1990 [Online]). The Xinhua file of May 28th, indicated that Arafat had followed up his Security Council statement with a call at the Arab Summit meeting for provisional UN supervision over the occupied territories to protect the native Palestinians from Israeli suppression, and demanded an International Middle East Peace Conference. He warned the Arab leaders that Israel was seeking to establish a "greater Israel . . . from the Nile to the Euphrates." Arafat was reported to have said that "encouraged by the United States, Israel has launched a new aggression that aims to empty Arab territories of their original inhabitants and settle Jewish emigrants in their place. . . . We are duty-bound to use all weapons, including sanctions—economic boycotts and political psychological pressures—against countries, states, establishments and companies that participate in aggression against Arab territories," adding that the Palestinian uprising in the occupied territories will continue until victory is won. "We are not war-mongers, but seekers of rights and freedom" (Xinhua General Overseas News Service, 1990 [Online]).

The US media had generally similar reports after the statement in the Security Council. The May 26th *New York Times* article emphasized the American decision to allow the UN to conduct a small fact-finding operation in the occupied territories, but said that the United States would use its veto against an observer force. This appeared to be a shift from Secretary of State Baker's statement a few days earlier in which he said the United States was now willing "to discuss the question of a UN observer team" if the Arabs asked for one at the May 26th session of the Security Council. It repeated the same information about the Israeli report of Israeli claims of Arafat's statement having been "full of lies and distortions" (Times Wire Services, 1990 [Online]). *The Los Angeles Times* May 26th article on page 24, essentially repeated earlier information in the other American papers.

On May 27th, *The New York Times* had a long opinion article by Alan Cowell, reporting from Cairo, headlined "Arab Anger at Israel: Has Mubarak Caught It Too?" He started his article saying that President Hosni Mubarak of Egypt had warned of a slide to war caused by Soviet Jewish immigration to Israel, and that some considered this evidence that a new wave of Arab anger toward Israel had swept him up too. Cowell continued, however, by noting Mubarak's moderate stance toward Israel and his cooperation with Arafat to assure a Palestinian–Israeli settlement in the Arab world would not become unsettled by the changed relationship between the superpowers and the collapse of totalitarian rule in Eastern Europe. Cowell cited various recent reverses in the peace process with Israel. One Arab diplomat was quoted as saying "What Mubarak is trying to do is to avoid being outmaneuvered by Saddam Hussein" (Cowell, 1990 [Online]).

On the same day, *The Chicago Tribune* offered a long opinion article "Arab Summit May Offer Support for Iraq," with a byline by Stephen Franklin reporting from Tunis, leading with the statement that not only Presidents Bush and Gorbachev were holding summits this week, but that the Arab Summit in Baghdad, Iraq, would be a crucial test of the Arab's world unity, its support for the PLO, and its independence from the superpowers, called by President Saddam Hussein of Iraq. Hussein is reported as "riding a wave of support from the PLO and a number of Arab countries because of his recent tough talk and warning to Israel that an attack on Iraq will spur a retaliation that will 'burn' half of Israel." Basically, Franklin indicated that it was a struggle between moderates led by Egypt and radicals led by Iraq. Franklin concluded by saying: "A veteran Egyptian diplomat, who expected no major achievements from the summit, would be happy if the Arabs just 'decide to cooperate' " (Franklin, 1990 [Online]).

Reuters dispatches and the British newspapers included headlines "Palestinians Applaud Arafat; Israel Says He Exploited Tragedy" (Siegel, 1990); "Israel Hits Back after Arafat Plea for UN Protection" (*The Times,*

1990); "Arafat Presses UN to Take Action; Security Council in Geneva Hears Demand for West Bank Emergency Force" (Dullforce, 1990); "Arafat Tells UN of War Threat to Middle East" (Bishop, 1990); "Israel–US Relations Headed for Crisis: (Israel) Ambassador Says" (Weizman, 1990); and "Israelis Anxious about Arab Summit, Palestinians Skeptical" (Siegel, 1990). Reuters and the elite British newspapers, while adding some new information to that provided by the elite American newspapers had more or less the same tone in their reporting on the Security Council meeting and Arafat's statement.

The Jerusalem Post, May 29, 1990, included a 1,666 word opinion article, with a byline by Douglas M. Bloomfield, and headlined "Going Over the Edge at the Summit," referring to the Bush–Gorbachev summit in Washington, indicated that friends of Israel were worried that Bush would push the Soviet president to take a more active role in the Middle Eastern conflicts. Bloomfield remarked that Bush was looking more and more like Carter in relation to the Middle East:

> [In his] enthusiasm for Gorbachev and his dislike of Yitzhak Shamir, Bush could well be tempted to abandon the Shamir Peace Plan and opt for an International Conference . . . one of the major recommendations arising out of the Arab League's summit in Baghdad this week. Yasser Arafat renewed the call in his lengthy speech to the UN Security Council in Geneva last Friday, and the chief Soviet delegate endorsed it. . . . Bush, in his frustration with Israel, now nearing its third month of political paralysis, could well endorse the international conference urged upon him by Gorbachev, King Hussein, Hosni Mubarak, Hafez Assad and Saddam Hussein. Arafat's American acceptance has been achieved in stages. . . . Each time he asked (for a visa to enter the US) he was turned down, but not sent away empty handed. . . . Arafat . . . got the last word by giving the grizzled terrorist a consolation prize. In December, 1988, the UN General Assembly held a special session in Geneva for Arafat. . . . This time, Arafat got his own, personal Security Council session in Geneva, and a pronouncement by the American Secretary of State that the US would look favorably on sending a UN observer team to Israel. . . . THE SPECTACLE of Arafat in Geneva bemoaning the fate of Palestinian children was one of the most transparent pieces of theater in recent memory. . . . Yet the Bush Administration went to Capitol Hill last week to defend this murderer and declare him an honorable man." (Bloomfield, 1990 [Online]).

In the 1990 *Facts on File,* June 1st, we learn that the plan for an observer team collapsed May 26th, when the United States in an apparent shift of policy that dismayed moderate Arab diplomats, said it could not accept the proposal. Arab League UN envoy Clovis Maksoud is quoted as saying: "This is a sad day for Arab moderates. Israel has shown it still has a stranglehold on American policy." In the UN Security Council on May 31st, the United States formally vetoed a Security Council resolution, supported by all 14 other Council members that would have dispatched an observer mission to the occupied territories (*Facts on File*, 1990 [Online]).

QUESTIONS FOR ANALYSIS

You have now read Arafat's statement, and illustrative media reporting and opinion articles on the event and those immediately surrounding the Security Council statement by Arafat.

1. Would you judge that your responses to the prestatement questions were reasonable? If so, why? If not, why not?
2. Did Yassar Arafat meet the expectations that the media had anticipated before he gave his statement, or did he emphasize other points more or less than expected? In what ways?
3. Noting the samples of media reports, we have given separate emphasis to the Xinhua General Overseas News Service of the People's Republic of China, a more or less combined emphasis to the American and British newspapers and Reuters, and a separate emphasis to the article in *The Jerusalem Post* by Michael Bloomfield. Based on the information that you have available, what major similarities and differences in emphasis can you identify between the three major sources, Xinhua; the American and British press and Reuters, and *The Jerusalem Post?* What similarities or differences of emphasis can you identify in the opinion articles noted in the American press and the *Jerusalem Post?* Which is more emotionally charged? Why?
4. What similarities or differences in emphasis do you identify in quoted material by Israeli and Arab leaders in the Middle East on the conflict?
5. What principles from discourse analysis and rhetorical analysis can you utilize, singly or jointly, to provide your own analysis of the Arafat statement?
6. With the media citations, what follow up can you make in these articles to support your own analysis of the Arafat statement and the surrounding events related to this Israeli–Palestinian, Israeli–Arab, Israeli–United States situation?

EVENTS BETWEEN ISRAEL AND ARAB STATES AND BETWEEN ISRAEL AND THE PLO SINCE 1990

Jordan and Israel signed in 1993 a framework accord, intended to lead to a peace treaty, and officially agreed in 1994 to end their state of war. Israel and the PLO met several times in 1993 in Norway, France, and Egypt over Palestinian self-rule. On December 29, 1993, Israel offered the PLO joint control over border areas and increased Palestinian autonomy around Jericho, which Chairman Arafat rejected, requesting a larger area of self-rule. In February 1994, Israel and the PLO initialed an agreement which resolved some of the contentious issues, but that month an American-born Israeli gunman killed 29 worshipers in a Moslem Mosque, calling a halt to the talks. Arafat asked the UN to send emergency forces to the occupied territories on February 25, 1994. In March 1994 talks were resumed. The final agreement for self rule was reached in April, and the Self-Rule Accord was signed on May 4, 1994, in Cairo between Chairman Arafat and Prime Minister Rabin of Israel. Palestinian self-rule began in the occupied territories on July 1, 1994 with Arafat officially crossing into Gaza from Egypt, for the first time in 27 years, where he addressed 100,000 people in Jericho. On July 5th, he took the oath as head of the new Palestinian National Authority (*The World Almanac*, 1994). Both Prime Minister Yitzak Rabin of Israel and Yassar Arafat jointly won the Nobel Peace Prize, and spoke at the 50th anniversary commemoration of the United Nations in New York. On November 4, 1995, Rabin was assassinated by a right-wing Israeli. President Mubarak of Egypt and King Hussein of Jordan attended the funeral in Jerusalem. Arafat did not attend because of the danger of renewed tensions, but was shown by the media watching the funeral on television, and sent a delegation. On May 30, 1996, Prime Minister Shimon Peres lost a tight national election, to LIKUD leader Benjamin Netenyahu. Since that time, there have been serious clashes between the Israeli soldiers and the Palestinians on the West Bank.

CONCLUSION

Because the Israeli–PLO conflict was long term, and part of a broader Arab–Israeli conflict, this statement of Yassar Arafat to the Security Council meeting was considered highly significant. Subsequently, the Council took several decisions condemning acts of violence against the Palestinians by the Israeli security forces, and calling for Israel to abide scrupulously by its legal obligations and responsibilities under the Geneva Convention relative to the Protection of Civilian Persons in Time of War of August 12, 1949. Resolutions 672 on October 12, 1990, 673 of October 24, 1990, and 681 of December 20, 1990, which all were made to help resolve the conflict were all adopted unanimously by the Council, as well as several others that were adopted without veto by the required number of nine Council votes.

The developments in resolving the Israeli–PLO conflict since 1990 have been heartening, but the assassination of Prime Minister Rabin in 1995 plus later actions in 1996 by both the Israeli government and the Palestinian authority indicates how fragile this peace has been.

10

AN AFRICAN CONFLICT RESOLVED

In 1994, Nelson Mandela became the first South African head of government ever to address the UN General Assembly. South Africa's last major speech at the UN had been by the Foreign Minister in 1972. Mandela's election as President in April 1994 "officially" ended "apartheid," a policy of racial and ethnic segregation instituted by the White minority government increasingly since 1948. A lawyer and leader of the African National Congress, Mandela became an early activist against apartheid and was put into prison for treason, a charge unproven. Nevertheless, he was again arrested, tried, and imprisoned for 27 years until his release by a presidential decree of State President F.W. DeKlerk in 1990. Four years later, he was elected President in the country's first multiracial election. Despite South Africa's First World development in many ways, its Black citizens remain plagued by poverty, a lack of education, and unemployment, although the "colored" (mixed race population) and Asian population are somewhat better off. The General Assembly had barred South Africa from all UN activities because of its apartheid policies in 1974. South Africa was fully readmitted to the UN in July 1994. As a 76-year-old President, Mandela came to the United States and the UN in 1994, blending a good will celebration of South African democracy and seeking an investment to solve these problems and to help his country become a model as "the new nonracial and nonsexist South Africa."

QUESTIONS FOR ANALYSIS

1. What role, if any, is Mandela likely to recognize the UN as having had in abolishing apartheid?

2. What proportion of content in his address is Mandela likely to devote to celebrating South Africa's new age and to facing the country's problems?
3. In what way is he likely to evince or not evince a conciliatory attitude toward the White minority of his country?
4. Is Mandela likely to stress the past evils of apartheid or the future that lies ahead for South Africa?
5. What is the meaning of the phrase "the new nonracial and nonsexist South Africa"?

NELSON RORIHLAHLA MANDELA
PRESIDENT OF THE REPUBLIC OF SOUTH AFRICA
UNITED NATIONS GENERAL ASSEMBLY, OCTOBER 3, 1994

It surely must be one of the great ironies of our age that this Assembly is being addressed, for the first time in its 49-year history, by a South African Head of State drawn from among the African majority of what is an African country.

Future generations will find it strange in the extreme that it was only so late in the 20th Century that it was possible for our delegation to take its seat in the Assembly, recognized both by our people and by the nations of the world as the legitimate representative of the people of our country.

It is indeed most welcome that the Organization will mark its 50th anniversary next year with the apartheid system vanquished and consigned to the past. That historic change has come about not least because of the great efforts in which the United Nations engaged to ensure the suppression of the apartheid crime against humanity. Even as it was still in the process of establishing its institutions, the United Nations was confronted by the challenge of the accession to power of the party of apartheid domination in our country. Everything that that system stood for represented the very opposite of all the noble purposes for which the Organization was established. Because apartheid reduced and undermined the credibility of the United Nations as an effective international instrument to end racism and secure the fundamental human rights of all peoples, the establishment and consolidation of apartheid constituted a brazen challenge to the very existence of the Organization.

The United Nations was born out of the titanic struggle against nazism and fascism, with their pernicious doctrines and practices of racial superiority and genocide. It therefore could not stand by while, in South Africa, a similar system was being established by a government which also had the temerity to claim representation within the United Nations.

We believe that it was indeed of great importance to the universal efficacy of, and respect for, the Universal Declaration of Human Rights and the United Nations Charter that the United Nations should have spurned the pleas of the apartheid regime that the gross violation of human rights in South Africa was a domestic matter of no legal or legitimate concern to the world body.

We stand here today to salute the United Nations and its Member States, both singly and collectively, for joining forces with the masses of our people in a common struggle that has brought about our emancipation and pushed back the frontiers of racism.

The millions of our people say "Thank you" and "Thank you again, because the respect for your own dignity as human beings inspired you to act to ensure the restoration of our dignity as well."

We have together traversed a course which we are convinced has strengthened human solidarity in general and reinforced the bonds of friendship between our peoples and the nations of the world. This dates back to the early days when India put the question of racism in South Africa on the Assembly's agenda, to the moment when the world community, as represented here, could adopt consensus revolutions against apartheid with none dissenting.

It was therefore with great joy that at our inauguration as President of our Republic we received, among others, such high and distinguished officials of the Organization as the Secretary General, the President of the General Assembly and the Chairman of the Special Committee against Apartheid. Their presence reaffirmed the incontrovertible truth that the victory over apartheid, the success of the cause of democracy, non-racialism and non-sexism in our country belongs as much to our people as it does the United Nations.

And so we have embarked on the road to the remaking of our country, basing ourselves both on the democratic Constitution, which came into force on 27 April this year, and on the Reconstruction and Development Program, which has become the property of all our people.

Clearly, these documents would have no life unless the people gave them life. The words printed in them must inspire common ownership by all our people and their common allegiance to the process and the results which these documents intend. For this to happen, as we propagate the vision these documents contain we must at the same time engage in a historic effort of redefinition of ourselves as a new nation.

Our watchwords must be justice, peace, reconciliation and nation-building in the pursuit of a democratic, non-racial and non-sexist country. In all that we do we have to ensure the healing of the wounds inflicted on all our people across the great dividing line imposed on our society by centuries of colonialism and apartheid.

We must ensure that color, race and gender become only a God-given gift to each one of us, and not an indelible mark or attribute that accords a special status to any.

We must work for the day when we as South Africans see one another and interact with one another as equal human beings and as part of our nation united, rather than torn asunder, by its diversity.

The road we shall have to travel to reach this destination will by no means be easy. All of us know how stubbornly racism can cling to the mind and how deeply it can infect the human soul. Where it is sustained by the racial ordering of the material world, as is the case in our country, that stubbornness can multiply a hundredfold.

And yet, however hard this battle may be, we will not surrender. Whatever the time it may take, we will not tire. The very fact that racism degrades both the perpetrator and the victim commands that, if we are true to our commitment to protect human dignity, we fight on until victory is achieved.

We firmly believe that we who have particular experience of the destructive and anti-human force of racism owe it to ourselves to center our transformation on the creation of a truly non-racial society. Because we know racism so intimately, we must stand a good chance of developing and nurturing its opposite.

It will perhaps come to be that we who have harbored in our country the worst example of racism since the defeat of nazism will make a contribution to human civilization by ordering our affairs in such a manner that we strike an effective and lasting blow against racism everywhere.

Some of the steps that we have already taken—including the establishment of a Government of National Unity, the orderly transformation of the institutions of State and the cultivation of a national consensus on the major issues of the day—have started us off on a correct footing with regard to continuing the processes leading to the creation of the just society we have been speaking of.

Our political emancipation has also brought into sharp focus the urgent need to engage in the struggle to secure our people's freedom from want, from hunger and from ignorance. We have written this on our banners: that the society we seek must be a people-centered society; all its institutions and its resources must be dedicated to the pursuit of a better life for all our citizens. That better life must mean an end to poverty, joblessness, hopelessness and the despair that comes on deprivation. This is an end in itself because the happiness of the human being must, in any society, be an end in itself.

At the same time, we are intensely conscious of the fact that the stability of the democratic settlement itself and the possibility actually to create a non-racial and non-sexist society depend on our ability to change the material conditions of life of our people so that they not only have the vote but have bread and work as well.

We therefore return to the United Nations to make the commitment that, as we undertook never to rest until the system of apartheid was defeated, so do we now undertake that we cannot rest while millions of our people suffer the pain and indignity of poverty in all its forms.

At the same time, we turn once more to this world body to say, "We are going to need your continued support to achieve the goal of the betterment of the conditions of life of our people." We are pleased and inspired that both the Secretary General and the specialized agencies of the United Nations have taken up the development challenge in South Africa with the enthusiasm that they have shown.

We believe that it is in the common interest that we sustain the common victory that we have scored in South Africa, and take it further by achieving success not only in politics but also in the socio-economic sphere.

It is perhaps common cause among us that everywhere on our globe there is an unmistakable process leading to the entrenchment of democratic systems of government. The empowerment of the ordinary people of our world freely to determine their destiny, unhindered by tyrants and dictators, is at the very heart of the reason for the existence of this Organization.

But it is equally true that hundreds of millions of these politically empowered masses are caught in the deathly trap of poverty, unable to live life in its fullness.

Out of all this are born social conflicts that produce insecurity and instability, civil and other wars that claim many lives, millions of desperate refugees and the destruction of the little wealth that poor countries are able to accumulate. Out of this cauldron are also born tyrants, dictators and demagogues who not only take away or restrict the rights of the people but also make it impossible to do the things that must be done to bring lasting prosperity to the people.

At the same time, the reality can no longer be ignored that we live in an interdependent world which is bound together to a common destiny. The very response of the international community to the challenge of apartheid confirmed this very point that we all understood—that so long as apartheid existed in South Africa, so long would the whole of humanity feel demeaned and degraded.

The United Nations understood very well that racism in our country could not but feed racism in other parts of the world as well. The universal struggle against apartheid was therefore not an act of charity arising out of pity for our people, but an affirmation of our common humanity. We believe that that act of affirmation requires that this Organization should once more turn its focused and sustained attention to the basics of everything that makes for a better world for all humanity.

The elaboration of a new world order must, of necessity, center on this world body. In it we should find the appropriate forum in which we can all participate to help determine the shape of the new world.

The four elements that will need to be knit together in fashioning that new universal reality are the issues of democracy, peace, prosperity and interdependence.

The great challenge of our age to the United Nations is to answer the question, "Given the interdependence of the nations of the world, what is it that we can and must do to ensure that democracy, peace and prosperity prevail everywhere?"

We are aware of the fact that the United Nations is addressing these questions in many ways; yet there can be no gainsaying the fact that such progress as we have made has been made more by stealth than in the bold and determined fashion that the world crisis demands today.

Perhaps a new and forceful initiative is required. Such an initiative should inspire all of humanity because of the seriousness of its intent. It should also have a chance to succeed because it will have been underwritten by the commitment of the masses of the people in each member country to join hands with other nations, to address together the related issues of democracy, peace and prosperity in an interdependent world.

We are aware of the fact that the dictates of *realpolitik* militate against the speedy realization of such an initiative. But we do believe that the reality of life and the realism of policy will, at some point, bring to the fore the fact that the delay we impose on ourselves today will serve only to increase the pressure on all of us to incorporate, within what we consider possible, a sustainable vision of a common world that will rise or fall together.

Undoubtedly, to inspire greater confidence in itself among all the member nations and to reflect better the impulse towards the democratization of international relations, the United Nations will have to continue looking at itself to determine what restructuring of itself it should effect. This process must naturally affect, among others, the structure and functioning of the Security Council and the peacemaking and peacekeeping issues raised by the Secretary-General in "An Agenda for Peace."

Democratic South Africa rejoins the world community of nations determined to play its role in helping to strengthen the United Nations and to contribute what it can to the furtherance of its purposes. Among other things, we have this morning acceded to the covenants and conventions adopted by this Organization, which address various matters such as economic, social and cultural rights, civil and political rights, and the elimination of all forms of racial discrimination, to say nothing of our irrevocable commitment to the realization of the objectives contained in the Universal Declaration of Human Rights.

We are determined to play our full part in all processes that address the important question of the non-proliferation and elimination of weapons of mass destruction. Our Government has also decided to become a signatory to the Convention on prohibition and restrictions on the use of certain conventional weapons.

In a similar vein, we shall not be found wanting in the quest for sustainable development that is keeping with the Rio de Janeiro Declaration on Environment and Development as well as with Agenda 21.

Equally, our own national interest dictates that we join forces with the United Nations and all its Member States in the common struggle to contain and end the traffic in narcotics.

Even in constitutional terms, we are committed to the advancement of the objective of the emancipation of women through the creation of a non-sexist society. Apart from anything else, we are therefore actively engaged in the preparations for what we are convinced will be a successful Beijing Conference.

We are part of the region of southern Africa and the continent of Africa. As members of the Southern African Development Community and the Organization of African Unity (OAU), and an equal partner with other Member States, we will play our role in the struggles of these organizations to build a continent and a region that will help to create for themselves and all humanity a common world of peace and prosperity.

Ours must become a continent free of such tragedies as those which have afflicted our own country as well as Rwanda, Somalia, Angola, Mozambique, the Sudan and Liberia. Happily, the OAU is actively addressing the issues of peace and stability on our continent.

We are greatly encouraged that the countries of our region, faced with a crisis in Lesotho, acted together speedily and, with the cooperation of the Government and the people of that country, succeeded in demonstrating that together we have the will to defend democracy, peace and national reconciliation.

Furthermore, as members of the Non-Aligned Movement and the Group of 77, we are committed especially to the promotion of South-South cooperation and to the strengthening of the voice of the poor and disadvantaged in the ordering of world affairs.

We would like to take this opportunity to express our appreciation to the members of the General Assembly for the speed and readiness with which they accepted the credentials of democratic South Africa, enabling us to participate in the work of the last General Assembly. We are pleased to note that this same spirit characterizes the approach of other international organizations toward our new democracy, including the Commonwealth and the European Union.

We would like to close by congratulating you, Mr. President, on your election to your high post, and we express our confidence that you will guide the work of the Assembly with the wisdom and sense of purpose for which we admire you.

The millions across our globe who stand expectant at the gates of hope look to this Organization to bring them peace, to bring them life, to bring them a life worth living.

We pray that the new South Africa, which the General Assembly helped bring into being and so warmly welcomed among the community of nations, will, in its own and in the wider interest, make its own contribution, however small, to the realization of those hopes.

Our common humanity and the urgency of the knock on the door of this great edifice demand that we must attempt even the impossible.

(Mandela, 1994a)

ELITE MEDIA REACTION TO THE MANDELA GENERAL ASSEMBLY ADDRESS AND RELATED EVENTS

President Nelson Mandela actually gave two UN addresses shortly after his election as President of the Republic of South Africa: the October 3, 1994, address to the General Assembly as part of his 8-day visit to the United States and a second brief speech in March 1995 at the UN World Summit for Social Development (called by some media "the Poverty Summit") in Copenhagen, Denmark, at which 120 world leaders spoke in a marathon session. During his October 1994 visit to the United States, besides the UN address, Mandela held a postaddress news conference in which he indicated his desire to lift foreign exchange controls for foreign investors, as well as doing away with subsidies for domestic industries. He participated in a very busy 8-day schedule, giving speeches and news conferences, meeting with various business leaders, and participating in cultural events in his honor.

Reuters in an October 2nd dispatch indicated that the visit was an effort to "blend a goodwill celebration of South African democracy with a bid for foreign investment" (Reuters, Ltd., 1994 [Online]). This dispatch, several other dispatches, and media articles, gave much more attention to Mandela's investment efforts than on his UN address. In the UN address,

Mandela emphasized that millions of South Africans, though politically empowered, were still "caught in the deadly trap of poverty."

The October 4th *The Times* of London noted that as he spoke to the 184 member delegation at the UN, he thanked them for standing by the South African people in their attempt to throw off the burden of apartheid, but reminded the delegates that if South Africa were to establish genuine nonracist and nonsexist democracy, the material conditions of the life of the people had to be improved dramatically (Bone, 1994). *The New York Times* article of the same day stressed that Mandela's address seemed less aimed

> at making a policy statement than at ceremonially declaring the end of apartheid before the group of nations that had made dismantling apartheid one of its main official aims. . . . Mr. Mandela's appearance in the vast chamber clearly had an emotional significance for many of the delegates, who rose and applauded as Mr. Mandela was introduced and again when he finished speaking. (Bernstein, 1994 [Online]).

Agence France Press, on the same day, in its 1,720 word dispatch, repeated many of the same statements included in the Reuters and *New York Times* articles, including his frequently quoted UN statement: "Our watchwords must be justice, peace, reconciliation and nation-building in the pursuit of a democratic, non-racial and non-sexist country."

Agence France Press expanded Mandela's post UN address press conference, by discussing his commitment to working on African problems, external to South Africa, through the United Nations and the Organization for African Unity, rather than unilaterally. Mandela was reported as having also raised the issue of reform of the UN itself, a topic which we will see addressed in a later chapter by world leaders in the Security Council. Agence France Press indicated that while Japan and Germany are considered leading contenders for permanent seats on the Security Council, South Africa, Nigeria, and Egypt all are possible contenders for a permanent African seat (Mannion, 1994).

Mandela was hosted by Governor Mario Cuomo of New York and New York City Mayor Rudolph Gulliani for meetings with business executives; he held meetings with President Clinton and received a 21-gun salute for his White House Lawn speech in front of 4,500 people. He held a joint news conference with Clinton and meetings with Vice President Albert Gore and President Jean Bertrand Aristide of Haiti, was a personal guest of David Rockefeller, and attended religious services at the Canaan Baptist church in Harlem. He was only the third foreign leader to speak twice to a joint session of the US Congress, and spoke to the National Press

Club as well as to the the New York Foreign Trade Council. He received an honorary doctorate at Howard University. Mandela was the first foreign leader to share President Clinton's weekly radio broadcast. As a private citizen in 1992, Mandela had attended Clinton's inauguration and they had become friends.

The Clinton–Mandela news conference of October 5th was carried live by CNN and provided a 3,862 word transcript. President Clinton announced that the United States has provided $35 million to assure the free elections in April of 1994 throughout South Africa, and had committed a $600 million trade and investment pattern, $220 million of which had already been delivered. Additionally, Clinton announced the formation of a joint, binational commission to assist in projects involving energy, education, and development, with Russia having the only other joint binational commission. Loans of a half billion dollars would be committed by the United States for housing, $50 million to help bring electricity to the townships, and $30 million to support basic health care, and the Overseas Private Investment Corporation was launching its second $75 million dollar fund to promote investment in South Africa. Clinton indicated that the Peace Corps would establish a presence there in 1995 to train nurses and teachers, and to create South Africa's own volunteer corps. Because the development of South Africa was integrally connected to the development of the whole southern African area, Clinton announced the establishment of a $100 million development fund for the entire region.

President Mandela's remarks in the CNN joint press conference emphasized the need for economic reconstruction in South Africa, and repeated his remarks at the UN and in his post UN press conference, thanking the American government for its positive economic stimulus both to South Africa and the southern African region, saying:

> Success will not only underpin the consolidation of democracy in South Africa, but will also enable South Africa to play its role as the powerhouse of the South African region in a mutually beneficial partnership with our South African Development Community neighbors. . . . I believe that the whole South African region and Africa in general can also benefit from these efforts. South Africa's transition to democracy has created an historic opportunity for South Africa to play its rightful role for the first time on the world stage. (Sesno, 1994 [Online])

One of Mandela's final efforts before leaving the United States, was his October 7, 1994, National Press Club Luncheon speech, whose transcript was 6,082 words. The speech was both witty and later serious as he defended the freedom of communication:

> When our voice was silenced, you lent your voices to our demand for freedom of expression and information, and gave support to South African writers, artists, and journalists who were persecuted for daring to use . . . against tyranny and in support of freedom. . . . Our experience of repression and our persecution has only strengthened the commitment to the rights of freedom of information, freedom of expression, and freedom of the press, not merely as constitutional rights, but as a daily reality. (Mandela, 1994b [Online])

Because Mandela's address to the UN was only one part of his 8-day visit to the United States, which had the primary purpose of encouraging business investments in South Africa, it is interesting to assess how the elite media felt immediately following his visit about his success. Seth Faison, writing in the *New York Times* in a long article on October 8th, indicated that while Mandela had seemed to cast a spell over 800 business executives at a dinner at the Waldorf Astoria Hotel, "yet his main goal—attracting more American investment to South Africa—may be harder than wowing the crowd. . . . 'The world is not breathless to invest anywhere,' said Anthony J.F. O'Reilly, chief executive of the H.J. Heinz Company. South Africa is going to have to fight to make its case" (Faison, 1994 [Online]). Faison offered several comments of business executives whom Mandela met during his US visit, showing divergent positive and cautious views about the viability of investment in South Africa. He speculated that Black business owners in the United States may be the most likely to invest quickly, but reminded his readers that the "Gandhi-like experience" of meeting Mandela would not move all potential investors to make their investments based on their enthusiasm for Mandela (Faison, 1994 [Online]).

QUESTIONS FOR ANALYSIS

1. Among President Mandela's various addresses, speeches, and press conference's during his 8-day visit to the UN, which of these three events would you consider most attended to by the American public: his October 3rd UN address, his October 5th live joint press conference with President Clinton carried by CNN, or his National Press Club luncheon speech on October 7th carried live by national public radio and television? Why?
2. If you could have been an invited guest to one event at which Mandela spoke, which would you choose: his United Nations address, his speech to 800 business executives at the Waldorf Astoria Hotel

in New York, his joint press conference with President Clinton, his speech before the joint houses of Congress, his speech before 15,000 at Howard University when he received his honorary doctorate, or his speech to the National Press Club? Why? What would be his major changes of emphasis from speech to speech?

3. Which American media, print or electronic, were more likely to provide the largest amount of coverage of his visit? Why?
4. In his UN address, what was the extent of his contrast between the former apartheid situation in South Africa, and the postapartheid situation in South Africa? Did he spend more time criticizing the past events surrounding apartheid in South Africa, or in seeking reconciliation for and toward his countrymen and women?
5. In his UN address, what sort of commendation did he provide to the UN itself for ending the apartheid government of South Africa?
6. In his UN address, to what extent did Mandela demonstrate the new South African commitment to the UN and its subsidiary organizations, to the southern African region, and to Africa as a whole?
7. Would you consider his UN address a success? If so, by what measures would you identify it as a success? If not, how did he fail to meet your criteria for a successful address?
8. What principles developed earlier in *Diplomatic Discourse* either from the perspective of discourse analysis or rhetorical analysis or both in an integrated analysis would you choose for your personal analysis of his UN address? Why?
9. The title we have given to this chapter is "An African Conflict Resolved." If this is a correct title, what African conflict was resolved? What African conflict was only partially resolved? What African conflict remained after his address to be resolved? If this is not a correct title, what new title would you provide? Why?

CONCLUSION

Nobel Peace Prize Laureate Nelson Mandela's *The Long Road to Freedom* was begun during his 27-year imprisonment, and demonstrates his growing involvement in the struggle against apartheid, ending with his election as the President of South Africa. In 1993, Mandela received the William J. Fulbright Award for International Understanding, and has been honored throughout the world for his efforts. Vice President Al Gore and the US First Lady, Hillary Rodham Clinton, led the US delegation to his inauguration as President in May of 1994. President Mandela welcomed Pope John Paul II to South Africa in September 1995.

Mandela was also among the 140 heads of state and government to speak briefly at the UN during its 50th anniversary in 1995. Subsequently, he led efforts by the Commonwealth nations to suspend Nigeria from their membership for its execution of nine human rights activists and dissidents against the military rule in Nigeria. His actions while in prison, his negotiations with the National Party in South Africa to end apartheid, and his contributions to peaceful solutions to conflicts, have given him the status of one of the major world leaders and moral exponents in Africa.

11

SUPER POWER CONFLICTS AND RESOLUTIONS

President Ronald Reagan gave seven addresses to the UN, including six to the General Assembly and a 1982 statement to the special session on disarmament. President Truman gave five addresses to the UN; Presidents Eisenhower and Bush, each four; President Johnson, three; Presidents Kennedy, Nixon, and Clinton, two; and President Carter, only one. President Mikhail Gorbachev of the Soviet Union gave only one address to the UN, after a 21-year absence by Soviet heads of government. Premier Aleksei Kosegin had spoken at the Fifth Special Emergency General Assembly in 1967 during the Middle East crisis. Premier Nikita Khrushchev had spoken in 1959 during his 3-week visit to the United States, and twice in 1960 for the "World Summit" in the General Assembly.

Elite media reaction before Reagan's September 20, 1988, address at the opening of the 43rd session of the General Assembly indicates an expected shift on his part toward the UN, from a nearly 7-year hostility toward it, to a more friendly and supportive position both for the UN and toward Secretary General Javier Perez de Cuellar. The United States had withheld 60% of its dues to the UN in the last several years, as pressure for UN management reforms, improved personnel policies, and better budgeting priorities, but before coming to the UN for his last address, Reagan pledged that the United States would soon pay the world body its accumulated dues of $188 million. Some media noted, however, that the actual dues owed the UN by the United States was closer to $500 million. In 1995, the figure reached $1.5 billion.

Reagan's National Security Adviser Colin Powell stated that the Reagan address would be "a major foreign policy speech, broad in scope," that would look to the future of United States to UN relations whereas also boasting of administration accomplishments, as well as offering an important new initiative on chemical weapons: "As a result of the president's involvement (in UN affairs), I think it's fair to say that our relations with the UN are excellent, better than they have been in a long time" (Powell, cited in Arieff, 1988 [Online]). Irwin Arieff argued in the Reuters dispatch, however, that Reagan's 2-day visit to the UN, including meetings with several foreign leaders, was not expected to produce any major diplomatic breakthroughs, but simply to be a series of farewell visits. Arieff speculated that although arms control was expected to be a part of his various meetings at the UN, "Washington and Moscow agree, too many obstacles remain to complete a major new United States–Soviet strategic arms accord before Reagan leaves office" (Arieff, 1988 [Online]).

The Japan Economic Newswire indicated that Reagan's final appearance before the UN would offer "a message of hope" and would urge curbs on chemical weapons, quoting Reagan's September 24th radio speech as saying: "My message this year to the delegates of the UN will be a message of hope. For eight years around our nation and around the world, I've been saying that the key to world peace and human freedom is the strength and determination of the great democracies." The newsservice indicated that Reagan had met with Soviet Foreign Minister Eduard Shevardnadze on September 23rd, and that in his September 24th weekly radio address, Reagan stressed that he would speak in the UN about the intermediate-range nuclear forces (INF) treaty with the Soviet Union and "other successes for our philosophy of peace through strength" (Japan Economic Newswire, 1988 [Online]).

Later in the 43rd session of the General Assembly, Mikhail Gorbachev, President of the Soviet Union, spoke to the UN on December 7, 1988, the 47th anniversary of the Japanese attack on Pearl Harbor. Robin Gedye of the United Kingdom's *Daily Telegraph* quoted Soviet Foreign Minister Andrei Gromyko's statement during his 1985 support of Mikhail Gorbachev for Soviet leadership: "He has a winning smile, but I warn you he has iron teeth" (Geyde, 1988 [Online]). The December 6th dispatch of the Soviet Union's TASS, headlined "New Political Thinking–Soviet Press Conference at UN" began by saying:

> All people are now interested in the visit of Mikhail Gorbachev, General Secretary of the CPSU Central Committee and President of the Presidium of the USSR Supreme Soviet, to the UN Organization, his upcoming speech at the UN, a conversation with the United States President Ronald Reagan and Vice President George Bush. [In a press conference by N. Shishlin, Deputy Head of the Soviet Press Centre, and others, Shishlin said] It is clear that the time has come to think together what we must do so that the "cold war" could recede into the past for good, so that international relations could develop calmly and harmoniously, and so that we could find

> a balance of interests of major powers and small states. And, of course, Gorbachev's meetings with Reagan and Bush will show that there is no pause in the Soviet–American dialogue. A greater predictability of Soviet–American relations is already a gain scored by the new political thinking." (TASS, 1988 [Online]).

The Rome-based newsservice specializing for the media of the third world, Inter Press Service (1988b) provided a dispatch the same day. It indicated that this was the first time since Khrushchev addressed the United Nations in 1960 that a Soviet head of government would address the United Nations General Assembly. Although this is technically correct, Premier Aleksei Kosegin addressed the UN Fifth Emergency Special Session of the General Assembly during the Middle East crisis in June of 1967. The Inter Press Service stated that Gorbachev's December 6th arrival in New York emphasized his promise that his UN address would outline the new thinking of the Soviet Union on a range of global issues, but that Gorbachev had not specified what new ideas he would actually speak about. Among the speculations offered by Inter Press Service for his address were Soviet commitments to respect human rights and to press for world-wide respect for the "rule of law" in international relations. There was widespread speculation that Gorbachev would outline proposals to reduce conventional weapons in Europe, to speed up the process for ending the conflict in Afghanistan, to convene an international conference on the Middle East, and to increase the integration of the Soviet economy in the world economy.

Following the Soviet leader's UN address, Inter Press Service noted that he was scheduled to meet with US President Reagan and Vice President and President-Elect Bush. The Inter Press Service dispatch of December 6 said that despite speculation that Gorbachev would offer new ideas to the US leaders in their meeting, both the Reagan administration and the Bush transition team had downplayed the meeting, saying that it was not a summit. Gorbachev was quoted as saying: "There is no formal agenda. Either side will be free, openly and frankly, to raise any questions that it wishes," and that the talks "will doubtless promote greater dynamism in the US–Soviet dialogue and an expansion of cooperation between our two countries in the interest of the whole world" (Inter Press Service, 1988b [Online]).

QUESTIONS FOR ANALYSIS

Note that in Chapters 9 and 10, we have provided a single address on an issue of conflict and conflict resolution for your consideration. Here, we are presenting two UN addresses, those of US President Ronald Reagan on September 26, 1988, and Soviet President Mikhail Gorbachev on December 7, 1988. It was Reagan's seventh address to the UN and Gorbachev's only address to the General Assembly. Identifying the Cold War which had begun immediately after World War II, Prime Minister Winston Churchill of the United Kingdom spoke at Fulton, Missouri, in 1946 and said that a giant "iron curtain" had descended over Eastern Europe. This metaphor refers to the "iron curtain" that descends in British theaters during the intermission to prevent fire from spreading from the stage to the seating area or vice versa. George Bush gave a campaign speech in 1988 in Fulton, and used the metaphor to refer to the possible end of the Cold War. In 1993, during the 250th anniversary of the birth of Thomas Jefferson, as Gorbachev, now out of power, gave a series of speeches in the United States in which he announced in Fulton that the iron curtain metaphor no longer applied, as the Cold War was over.

1. Based on the preliminary media information cited earlier, which leader in the autumn of 1988, about to speak at the UN, appeared more optimistic about his forthcoming address? Why?
2. Would Reagan cite the precedence of the addresses of former American presidents to the UN and his own earlier six addresses to the UN? What issues would Reagan emphasize most?
3. Would Gorbachev cite the presence of Khrushchev and Kosegin with addresses to the UN? Would he mention the long lapse of time, 21 years, since a Soviet head of government had spoken? What issues would he emphasize most?
4. Although there was a lapse of more than 2 months between the two addresses, which would appear to suggest more major contributions in his UN address to the resolution of international conflict and world peace? Why?
5. In speculating on Reagan's diplomatic initiatives expected in his UN address, several of the elite media noted his intention to provide a new American perspective on the control and elimination of chemical weapons, particularly relating to conflicts in the Middle East. Which initiatives would you expect Reagan to emphasize most in his address: the improved United States–UN relations; improved United States–Soviet Union relations; American accomplishments toward peace, or the expected American initiative on chemical weapons? Why?
6. Although Colin Powell indicated that Reagan's address would be a major foreign policy statement and the Japan Economic Newswire dispatch quoted President Reagan as calling it "a message of hope," there was also the speculation by Irwin Arieff, writing for Reuters,

that "his two-day farewell visit was not expected to produce major diplomatic breakthroughs." Before reading the address, which view would you consider more likely. Why?

7. Because President Reagan was expected to boast at the UN of US efforts as he completed his administration, would you assume that these efforts included improved United States–Soviet Union relations? Why? Why not?
8. Although President Gorbachev's Soviet Press Center's representatives indicated that his UN address would offer "new political thinking," the Inter Press Service stressed on December 6th that President Gorbachev "did not indicate the new ideas that he is widely expected to unveil in his UN speech." Why do you assume that Gorbachev declined to identify the specific issues which he would raise in his UN address? What was his strategy?
9. Typically bilateral meetings between the heads of government of the United States and the Soviet Union have been called summit meetings. Why would you speculate that both the American and Soviet leaders downplayed this meeting after Gorbachev's UN address as "not a summit"?
10. Because Gorbachev was seen as the leader of one of two superpowers, why was it speculated that he would specifically speak in his UN address about the need to incorporate the Soviet economy into the world economy? Would he be conciliatory toward the United States and Reagan specifically? If he was conciliatory, how would the Soviet media handle this situation?
11. In the last two chapters, we have presented media statements about Yassar Arafat and Nelson Mandela before and after their UN addresses. Based on the information which you have at present, which of the four world leaders speaking at the UN would you assume had the highest level of media interest? Why?

RONALD REAGAN, PRESIDENT OF THE UNITED STATES UNITED NATIONS GENERAL ASSEMBLY SEPTEMBER 26, 1988

Half a world away from this place of peace, the firing, the killing, the bloodshed in two merciless conflicts have for the first time in recent memory diminished. After terrible new names, names such as Halabja, Maidan Shahr and Spin Suldak, have been added to the roll-call of human horror, there is today hope of peace in the Persian Gulf and Afghanistan.

So, too, in the highlands and coastal cities of southern Africa, places of civil war, places of occupation by foreign troops, talk of peace is heard, peace for the tortured nation of Angola. Sixty-five hundred miles east, in the South-East Asian country of Cambodia, there is hope now of a settlement and the removal of Vietnam's occupying forces. Finally, in this hemisphere, where only 12 years ago one third of the people of Latin America lived under democratic rule, some 90 percent do so today. And especially in Central America, nations such as El Salvador, once threatened by the anarchy of the death squad and the spectre of totalitarian rule, now know the hope of self-government and the prospect of economic growth.

Another change, a change that if it endures may make future generations shake their heads in wonder, is also upon us; a change going to the source of post-war tensions and to the once seemingly impossible dream of ending the twin threats of our time—totalitarianism and thermonuclear world war.

For the first time, the differences between East and West—fundamental differences over important moral questions dealing with the worth of the individual and whether Governments shall control people or people control Governments—for the first time these differences have shown signs of easing, easing to the point where there are not just troop withdrawals from places such as Afghanistan, but also talk in the East of reform and greater freedom of the press, of assembly and of religion. Yes, fundamental differences remain, but should talk of reform become more than that, should it become reality, there is the prospect of not only a new era in Soviet-United States relations but a new age of world peace; for such reform can bring peace. History teaches, and my country has always believed that, where the rights of the individual and the people are enshrined, war is a distant prospect. For it is not people who make war; only Governments do that.

I stand at this rostrum, then, at a moment of hope; hope not just for the peoples of the United States and the Soviet Union, but for all the peoples of the world, and hope too for the dream of peace among nations, the dream that began the United Nations. Precisely because of these changes, today the United Nations has the opportunity to live and breathe and work as never before.

Already, Mr. Secretary General, you, through your persistence, patience and unyielding will, have shown in working towards peace in Afghanistan and the Persian Gulf how valuable the United Nations can be. We salute you for these accomplishments.

There are numerous negotiations under way: multilateral negotiations at the Conference on Disarmament, as well as bilateral negotiations on a range of issues between the Soviets and ourselves. These negotiations, some of them under United Nations auspices, involve a broad arms-control agenda: strategic offensive weapons, strategic defense and space, nuclear testing, and chemical warfare—whose urgency we have witnessed anew in recent days.

And the negotiators are busy. Over the last few years they have been engaged in more than an academic exercise. There is movement; the logjam is broken. Only recently, when the United States and the Soviet Union signed the intermediate-range nuclear forces (INF) agreement, an entire class of United States and Soviet nuclear missiles was eliminated for the first time in history. Progress continues on negotiations to reduce strategic weapons in massive number, with effective verification, and talks will begin soon on conventional reductions in Europe.

Much of the reason for all this goes back, I believe, to Geneva, to the small chateau beside the lake where I and the Soviet General Secretary had the first of several fireside chats—exchanges characterized by frankness, but friendliness too. I said at the first meeting in Geneva that this was a unique encounter between two people who had the power to start a third world war or to begin a new age of peace among nations. I also said that peace conferences, arms negotiations and proposals for treaties could make sense only if they were part of a wider context, a context in which we sought to explore and resolve the deeper underlying differences between us. I said to Mr. Gorbachev then, as I have said to the Assembly before, that nations do not mistrust each other because they are armed; they are armed because they mistrust each other.

In that place, by that peaceful lake in neutral Switzerland, Mr. Gorbachev and I did begin a new relationship based not just on engagement over the single issue of arms control but on a broader agenda about our deeper differences, an agenda of human rights, regional conflicts and bilateral exchanges between our peoples. Even on the arms-control issue itself we agreed to go beyond the past, to seek not just treaties that permitted building weapons to higher levels, but revolutionary agreements that actually reduced and even eliminated a whole class of nuclear weapons.

What was begun that morning in Geneva has shown results: in the INF Treaty; in my recent visit to Moscow; in my opportunity to meet there with Soviet citizens and dissidents and speak of human rights; and to speak too, in the Lenin Hills of Moscow, to the young people of the Soviet Union about the wonder and splendor of human freedom. The results of that morning in Geneva are seen in peace conferences now under way around the world on regional conflicts and in the work of the United Nations here in New York as well as in Geneva.

But history teaches caution. Indeed, that very building in Geneva, where important negotiations have taken place—those on the Geneva Accords on Afghanistan, and the Iran–Iraq negotiations, for example—we see today as stone-like testimony to a failed dream of peace in another time. The Palais des Nations was the headquarters of the League of Nations, an institution that was to symbolize an end to all war. Yet that institution and its noble purpose ended with the Second World War; ended because the chance of peace was not seized in the 1930s by the nations of the world, ended because humanity did not find the courage to isolate the aggressors, to reject schemes of government that served the State, not the people. We are here today determined that no such fate shall befall the United Nations. We are determined that the United Nations shall succeed and serve the cause of peace for humankind.

So we realize that, even in this time of hope, the chance of failure is real, but this knowledge does not discourage us: it spurs us on. For the stakes are high: Do we falter and fail now, and bring down upon ourselves the just anger of future generations? Or do we continue the work of the founders of this institution, and see to it that, at last freedom is enshrined and humanity knows war no longer, and that this place, this floor, shall be truly "the world's last battlefield"?

We are determined that it shall be so. So we turn now to the agenda of peace. Let us begin by addressing a concern that was much on my mind when I met with Mr. Gorbachev in the Kremlin as well as on the minds of Soviet citizens I met in Moscow. It is also an issue that I know is of immediate importance to the members of this Assembly who, this fall, commemorate the 40th anniversary of the Universal Declaration of Human Rights.

That Declaration says plainly what those who seek peace can forget only at the greatest peril that peace rests on one foundation: observance of the "inalienable rights of all members of the human family." In a century where human rights have been denied by totalitarian governments on a scale never before seen in history, with so many millions deliberately starved or eliminated as a matter of State policy—a history, it has been said, of blood, stupidity and barbed wire—few can wonder why peace has proved so elusive.

Well, let us understand. If we would have peace, we must acknowledge the elementary rights of our fellow human beings, in our own land and in other lands. If we would have peace, the trampling of the human spirit must cease. Human rights is not for some, some of the time. Human rights, as the Universal Declaration adopted by this Assembly in 1948 proclaims, is "for all peoples and all nations." And for all time.

This regard for human rights as the foundation of peace is at the heart of the United Nations. Those who starve in Ethiopia, those who die among the Kurds, those who face racial injustice in South Africa, those who still cannot write or speak freely in the Soviet Union, those who cannot worship in the Ukraine, those who struggle for life and freedom on boats in the South China Sea, those who cannot publish or assemble in Managua—all of these are more than just an item on your agenda. It must be a first concern, an issue above others. For when human rights concerns are not paramount at the United Nations—when the Universal Declaration of Human Rights is not honored in these halls and meeting rooms—then the very credibility of this Organization is at stake, the very purpose of its existence in question.

That is why, when progress is made in human rights, the United Nations grows stronger and the United States is glad of it. For example, following a two-year effort led by the United States, the United Nations Commission on Human Rights took a major step towards ending the double standards and cynicism that had characterized too much of its past. For years, Cuba, a blatant violator of its citizens' human rights, has escaped United Nations censure or even scrutiny. This year, Cuba has responded to pressure generated by the Commission on Human Rights by accepting an investigation into its human rights abuses. Fidel Castro has already begun to free some political prisoners, improve prison conditions, and tolerate the existence of a small, independent national human rights group.

More must be done. The United Nations must be relentless and unyielding in seeking change, in Cuba and elsewhere. And we must also see to it that the Universal Declaration itself is not debased with episodes like the resolution "Zionism is racism." Respect for human rights is the first and fundamental mission of this body, the most elementary obligation of its members. Indeed, wherever one turns in the world today, there is a new awareness, a growing passion for human rights. The people of the world become United: new groups, new coalitions form, coalitions that monitor government, that work against discrimination, that fight religious or political repression, unlawful imprisonment, torture or execution. As those I spoke to at Spaso House said to me last June: Such movements make a difference.

Turning now to regional conflicts, we feel again the uplift of hope. In the Gulf War between Iran and Iraq—one of the bloodiest conflicts since the Second World War—we have a cease-fire. The resolution and the firmness of the allied nations in keeping the Persian Gulf open to international shipping not only upheld the rule of law, it helped prevent further spread of the conflict and laid the basis for peace. So, too, the Security Council's decisive resolution in July a year ago has become the blueprint for a peaceful Gulf. Let this war—a war in which there has been no victor or vanquished, only victims—let this war end now. Let both Iran and Iraq cooperate with the Secretary General and the Security Council in implementing resolution 598 (1978). Let peace come.

Moving on to a second region, I would recall that when I first addressed the United Nations General Assembly in 1983, world attention was focused on the brutal invasion and illegal occupation of Afghanistan. After nearly nine long years of war, the courage and determination of the Afghan people and the Afghan freedom fighters have held sway—and today, an end to the occupation is in sight. On April 14, the USSR signed the Geneva Accords, which were negotiated under United Nations auspices by Pakistan and the Kabul regime. We encourage the Soviet Union to complete its troop withdrawal at the earliest possible date, so that the Afghan people can freely determine their future without further outside interference.

In southern Africa, too, years of patient diplomacy and support for those in Angola who seek self-determination are having their effect. We look forward to an accord between the Governments of Angola, Cuba, and South Africa that will bring about a complete withdrawal of all foreign troops—primarily Cuban—from Angola. We look forward as well to full implementation of United Nations Security Council resolution 435 (1978) and our longstanding goal of independence for Namibia. We continue to support a growing consensus among African leaders who also believe there can be no end to conflict in the region until there is national reconciliation within Angola.

There are new hopes for Cambodia, a nation whose freedom and independence we seek just as avidly as we sought the freedom and independence of Afghanistan. We urge the rapid removal of all Vietnamese troops and a settlement that will prevent the return of the Khmer Rouge to power, permitting instead the establishment of a genuinely representative government—a government that will, at last, respect fully the rights of the people of Cambodia and end the hideous suffering they have so bravely and needlessly borne.

In other critical areas, we applaud the Secretary General's efforts to structure a referendum on the Western Sahara. In the Mediterranean, direct talks between Greek and Turkish Cypriot communities hold much promise for accord in that divided island nation. Finally, we look to a peaceful solution to the Arab-Israeli conflict. So, too, the unnatural division of Europe remains a critical obstacle to Soviet-American relations.

In most of these areas, then, we see progress and, again, we are glad of it. Only a few years ago, all of these and other conflicts were burning dangerously out of control. Indeed, the invasion of Afghanistan and the apparent failure of will among democratic and peace-loving nations to deter such events seemed to cause a climate where aggression by nations large and small was epidemic, a climate the world had not seen since the 1930s. Only this time, larger war was avoided—avoided because the free and peaceful nations of the world recovered their strength of purpose and will. And now the United Nations is providing valuable assistance in helping this epidemic to recede.

And because we are resolved to keep it so, I would be remiss in my duty if I did not now take note here of the one exception to progress in regional conflicts. I refer here to the continuing deterioration of human rights in Nicaragua and the refusal of the tiny elite now ruling that nation to honor promises of democracy made to their own people and to the international community. This elite—in calling itself revolutionary—seeks no real revolution; the use of the term is subterfuge, deception for hiding the oldest, most corrupt vice of all: man's age-old will to power, his lust to control the lives and steal the freedom of others.

That is why, as President, I will continue to urge the Congress and the American public to stand behind those who resist this attempt to impose a totalitarian regime on the people of Nicaragua; that the United States will continue to stand with those who are threatened by this regime's aggression against its neighbors in Central America.

Today, I also call on the Soviet Union to show in Central America the same spirit of constructive realism it has shown in other regional conflicts; to assist in bringing conflict in Central America to a close by halting the flow of billions of dollars worth of arms and ammunition to the Sandinista regime, a regime whose goals of regional domination, while ultimately doomed, can continue to cause great suffering to the people of that area and risk to Soviet–American relations unless action is taken now.

With regard to the arms reduction agenda, I have already mentioned the importance of the INF Treaty and the momentum developed in the strategic arms reduction talks (START). The draft START treaty is a lengthy document filled with bracketed language designating sections of disagreement between the two sides. But through this summer in Geneva, those brackets have diminished; there is every reason to believe this process can continue. I can tell this Assembly that it is highly doubtful such a treaty can be accomplished in a few months, but I can tell you that a year from now is a possibility—more than a possibility. But we have no deadline. No agreement is better than a bad agreement. The United States remains hopeful, and we acknowledge the spirit of cooperation shown by the Soviet Union in these negotiations. We also look for that spirit to be applied to our concerns about compliance with existing agreements.

So, too, our discussions on nuclear testing and defense and space have been useful. But let me here stress to the General Assembly that much of the momentum in nuclear-arms-control negotiations is due to technological progress itself, especially in the potential for space-based defensive systems. I believe that the determination of the United States to research and develop and, when ready, deploy such defensive systems—systems targeted to destroy missiles, not people—accounts for a large share of the progress made in recent years in Geneva. With such systems, for the first time, in case of accidental launch or the act of a madman somewhere, major Powers will not be faced with the single option of massive retaliation, but will instead have the chance of a saner choice: to shield against an attack instead of avenging it. So, too, as defensive systems grow in effectiveness, they reduce the threat and the value of greater and greater offensive arsenals. Only recently, briefings I have received in the Oval Office indicate that progress toward such systems may be even more rapid and less costly than we had at first thought. Today, the United States reaffirms its commitment to its strategic defense initiative and our offer to share the benefits of strategic defenses with others.

And yet, even as diplomatic and technological progress holds out the hope of at last diminishing the awful cloud of nuclear terror we have lived under in the post-war era, even at this moment another ominous terror is loose once again in the world, a terror we thought the world had put behind, a terror that looms at us now from the long-buried past, from ghostly, scarring trenches and the haunting, wan faces of millions dead in one of the most inhumane conflicts of all time.

Poison gas; chemical warfare: the terror of it; the horror of it! We condemn it. The use of chemical weapons in the Iran-Iraq war, beyond its tragic human toll, jeopardizes the moral and legal strictures that have held those weapons in check since the First World War. Let this tragedy spark reaffirmation of the Geneva Protocol outlawing the use of chemical weapons. I call upon the signatories to that Protocol, as well as other concerned States, to convene a conference to consider actions that we can take together to reverse the serious erosion of this treaty. We urge all nations to cooperate in negotiating a verifiable, truly global ban on chemical weapons at the Conference on Disarmament in Geneva.

It is incumbent upon all civilized nations to ban, once and for all—and on a verifiable and global basis—the use of chemical and gas warfare.

Finally, we must redouble our efforts to stop further proliferation of nuclear weapons in the world. Likewise, proliferation in other high-technology weapons such as ballistic missiles, is reaching global proportions, exacerbating regional rivalries in ways that can have global implications. The number of potential suppliers is growing at an alarming rate, and more must be done to halt the spread of these weapons. This was a matter of discussion last week between Secretary Shultz and Foreign Minister Shevardnadze. Talks between American and Soviet experts begin on this today; and we hope to see a multilateral effort to avoid having areas of tension like the Middle East becoming even more deadly battlegrounds than they already are.

But in most of these areas we see not only progress but also the potential for an increasingly vital role for multilateral efforts and institutions like the United Nations. That is why now more than ever the UN must continue to increase its effectiveness through budget and program reform. The United Nations already is enacting sweeping measures affecting personnel reductions, budgeting by consensus, and the establishment of program priorities. These actions are extremely important. The progress on reforms has allowed me to release funds withheld under congressional restrictions. I expect that the reform program will continue and that further funds will be released in our new fiscal year.

Let me say here that we congratulate the United Nations on the work it has done in three areas of special concern. First, our struggle against the scourge of terrorism and state-sponsored terrorism must continue; and we must also end the scourge of hostage-taking. Second, the work of the World Health Organization in coordinating and advancing research on AIDS is vital. All international efforts in this area must be redoubled. The AIDS crisis is a grave one; we must move as one to meet it.

So, too, is the drug crisis. We are moving now toward a new anti-drug-trafficking convention. This important treaty will be completed in December. I am confident that other strong United Nations drug-control programs will also follow. The American people are profoundly concerned and deeply angered. We will not tolerate the drug traffickers. We mean to make war on them—and we believe this is one war the UN can endorse and participate in.

Yes, the United Nations is a better place than it was eight years ago—and so, too, is the world. But the real issue of reform in the United Nations is not limited to fiscal and administrative improvements; it includes also a higher sort of reform, an intellectual and philosophical reform, a reform of old views about the relationship between the individual and the State.

Few developments, for example, have been more encouraging to the United States than the special session on Africa that this body held two and a half years ago—a session at which the Members of the United Nations joined in calling as one for free-market incentives and a lessening of State controls to spur economic development.

At one of the first international assemblies of my presidency, in Cancun, Mexico, I said that history demonstrates that, time and again, in place after place, economic growth and human progress make their greatest strides in countries that encourage economic freedom; that individual farmers, laborers, owners, traders and managers are the heart and soul of development. Trust them, because where they are allowed to create and build, where they are given a personal stake in deciding economic policies and benefiting from their success, societies become more dynamic, prosperous, progressive and free. We believe in freedom; we know that it works.

This is the immutable lesson of the post-war era: that freedom works; that, even more, freedom and peace work together. Every year that passes, everywhere in the world, this lesson is taking hold—from the People's Republic of China to Cameroon, from Bolivia to Botswana, and, yes, in the citadel of Marxism-Leninism itself. No, my country did not invent this synergy of peace and freedom, but, believe me, we impose no restrictions on the free export of our more than two centuries of experience with it. Free people, blessed by economic opportunity and protected by laws that respect the dignity of the individual, are not driven towards war or the domination of others. Here, then, is the way to world peace. But we Americans champion freedom not only because it is practical and beneficial but because it is also just, morally right.

Here I would like to note that I have addressed this assemblage more often than any of my predecessors and that this is the last occasion on which I shall do so. Therefore I hope that I may be permitted some closing reflections.

The world is currently witnessing another celebration of international co-operation. At the Olympics we see nations joining together in the competition of sports, and we see young people, who know precious little of the resentments of their elders, coming together as one.

One of our young athletes, from a home of modest means, said that she drew the strength for her achievement from another source of wealth. "We were rich as a family" she said about the love she was given and the values she was taught. I dare to hope that in the sentiment of that young athlete we see a sign of the rediscovery of old and tested values: values such as family—the first and most important unit of society, where all values and learning begin, an institution to be cherished and protected; values, too, such as work, community, freedom and faith, for it is here we find the deeper rationale for the cause of human rights and world peace.

Our own experience on this continent, the American experience, though brief, has had one unmistakable encounter, an insistence on the preservation of one sacred truth: it is a truth that our first President, our founding father, passed on in the first farewell that I hope you will permit me to mention in these remarks of farewell, a truth embodied in our Declaration of Independence: that the case for inalienable rights, the idea of human dignity, the notion of conscience above compulsion, can be made only in the context of higher law, only in the context of what one of the founders of this Organization, Secretary General Dag Hammarskjold, called "devotion to something which is greater and higher than we are ourselves."

This is the endless cycle, the final truth to which humankind seems always to return—that religion and morality, faith in something higher, are prerequisites for freedom, and that justice and peace with ourselves is the first step toward justice and peace in the world and for the ages.

Yes, this is a place of great debate and grave discussion. Yet I cannot help but note here that one of our founding fathers—the most worldly of men, an internationalist, Benjamin Franklin—interrupted the proceedings of our own constitutional convention to make much the same point.

I cannot help but think this morning of other beginnings—of where and when I first read those words "and they shall beat their swords into ploughshares" and "your young men shall see visions and your old men shall dream dreams." This morning, my thoughts go to her who gave me many things in life but whose most important gift was the knowledge of the happiness and solace to be gained in prayer. It is the greatest help I have had in my presidency, and I recall here Lincoln's words when he said

"Only the most foolish of men would think he could confront the duties of the office I now hold without turning to someone stronger, a power above all others."

I think, then, of her and others like her in that small town in Illinois, gentle people who possessed something that those who hold positions of power sometimes forget to prize. No one of them could ever have imagined that the boy from the banks of the Rock River would come to this moment and have this opportunity. But, had they been told that it would happen, I think they would have been a bit disappointed if I had not spoken here for what they knew so well: that when we grow weary of the world and its troubles, when our faith in humanity falters, it is then that we must seek comfort and refreshment of spirit in a deeper source of wisdom, one greater than ourselves.

So, if future generations do say of us that in our time peace came closer, that we did bring about new seasons of truth and justice, it will be cause for pride. But it will be a cause of greater pride still if it is also said that we were wise enough to know that the deliberations of great leaders and great bodies are but an overture, that the truly majestic music, the music of freedom, justice and peace, is the music made in forgetting self and seeking in silence the will of Him who made us.

Thank you for your hospitality over the years. I bid you now farewell, and God bless you.

MIKHAIL GORBACHEV, GENERAL SECRETARY OF THE CENTRAL COMMITTEE, COMMUNIST PARTY OF THE SOVIET UNION, PRESIDENT OF THE PRESIDIUM OF THE SUPREME SOVIET OF THE UNION OF SOVIET SOCIALIST REPUBLICS, UNITED NATIONS GENERAL ASSEMBLY, DECEMBER 7, 1988
(Interpretation from Russian)

We have come here to show our respect for the United Nations, which increasingly has been manifesting its ability to act as a unique international center in the service of peace and security.

We have come here to show our respect for the dignity of this Organization, capable of accumulating the collective wisdom and will of mankind.

Recent events have been making it increasingly clear that the world needs such an organization, and that the Organization itself needs the active involvement of all its Members, their support for its initiatives and actions and their potentialities and original contributions that enrich its activity.

A little more than a year ago, in an article entitled "Realities and safeguards for a secure world" (A/42/574), I set out some ideas on problems of concern to the United Nations.

The time since then has given fresh food for thought. World developments have indeed come to a crucial point.

The role played by the Soviet Union in world affairs is well-known, and in view of the revolutionary *perestroika* under way in our country, which contains a tremendous potential for peace and international cooperation, we are now particularly interested in being properly understood.

That is why we have come here to address this most authoritative world body and to share our thoughts with it. We want it to be the first to learn of our new, important decisions.

What will mankind be like when it enters the 21st Century? People are already fascinated by this non-too-distant future. We are looking ahead to it with hopes for the best, and yet with a feeling of concern.

The world in which we live today is radically different from what it was at the beginning, or even in the middle, of this century, and it continues to change, as do all its components.

The advent of nuclear weapons was just another tragic reminder of the fundamental nature of that change. A material symbol and expression of absolute military power, nuclear weapons at the same time revealed the absolute limits of that power. The problem of mankind's survival and self-preservation came to the fore.

We are witnessing most profound social change. Whether in the East or the South, the West or the North, hundreds of millions of people, new nations and States, new public movements and ideologies have moved to the forefront of history. Broad-based and frequently turbulent popular movements have given expression, in a multidimensional and contradictory way, to a longing for independence, democracy and social justice. The idea of democratizing the entire world order has become a powerful socio-political force.

At the same time the scientific and technological revolution has turned many economic, food, energy, environmental, information and population problems, which only recently we treated as national or regional, into global problems.

Thanks to the advances in mass media and means of transportation the world seems to have become more visible and tangible. International communication has become easier than ever before. Today, the preservation of any kind of closed society is hardly possible. This calls for a radical review of approaches to the totality of the problems of international cooperation as a major element of universal security. The world economy is becoming a single organism, and no State, whatever its social system or economic status, can develop normally outside it. That places on the agenda the need to devise fundamentally new machinery for the functioning of the world economy, a new structure of the international division of labor.

At the same time, the growth of the world economy reveals the contradictions and limits inherent in traditional-type industrialization. Its further extension and intensification spell environmental catastrophe.

However, there are still many countries without sufficiently developed industries, and some have not yet moved beyond the pre-industrial stage. One of the major problems is whether the process of their economic growth will follow the old technological patterns or whether they can join in the search for environmentally clean production. And there is another problem: instead of diminishing, the gap between the developed and most of the developing countries is increasingly growing into a serious global threat. Hence the need to begin a search for a fundamentally new type of industrial progress, one that would meet the interests of all peoples and States.

In a word, the new realities are changing the entire world situation. The differences and contradictions inherited from the past are diminishing or being displaced, but new ones are emerging. Some of the past differences and disputes are losing their importance, but conflicts of a different kind are taking their place.

Life is making us abandon established stereotypes and outdated views. It is making us discard illusions. The very concept of the nature and criteria of progress is changing. It would be naive to think that the problems plaguing mankind today can be solved with the means and methods that were applied or that seemed to work in the past. Indeed, mankind has accumulated a wealth of experience in the process of political, economic and social development under highly diverse conditions. But that experience belongs to the practices and to a world that have become, or are becoming, parts of the past. That is one of the signs of the crucial nature of the current phase of history.

The greatest philosophers sought to grasp the laws of social development and find an answer to the main question: how to make man's life happy, just and safe. Two great revolutions, the French Revolution of 1789 and the Russian Revolution of 1917, exerted a powerful impact on the very nature of history and radically changed the course of world developments. Both of them, each in its own way, gave a tremendous impetus to mankind's progress. To a large extent those two revolutions shaped the way of thinking that is still prevalent in social consciousness. It is a most precious spiritual heritage.

But today we face a different world, for which we must seek a different road to the future. In seeking it, we must, of course, draw upon accumulated experience and yet be aware of the fundamental differences between the situation yesterday and what we are facing today. Yet the novelty of the tasks before us, as well as their difficulties, goes well beyond. Today, we have entered an era when progress will be shaped by universal human interests. Awareness of that dictates that world politics, too, should be guided by the primacy of universal human values.

The history of past centuries and millennia was a history of wars that raged almost everywhere, of frequent desperate battles to the point of mutual annihilation. They grew out of clashes of social and political interests, national enmity, ideological or religious incompatibility. All that did happen. And even today, many would want those vestiges of the past to be accepted as immutable law.

However, concurrently with wars, animosities and divisions among peoples and countries, another trend, with equally objective causes, was gaining momentum: the process of the emergence of a mutually interrelated and integral world. Today, further world progress is possible only through a search for universal human consensus as we move forward to a new world order.

We have come to a point where the disorderly play of elemental forces leads to an impasse. The international community must learn how it can shape and guide developments in such a way as to preserve our civilization and to make it safe for all and more conducive to normal life.

We are speaking of cooperation, which could be more accurately termed co-creation and co-development. The formula of development at the expense of others is on the way out. In the light of existing realities, no genuine progress is possible at the expense of the rights and freedoms of individuals and nations or at the expense of nature.

Efforts to solve global problems require a new scope and quality of interaction of States and socio-political currents, regardless of ideological or other differences.

Of course, radical changes and revolutionary transformations will continue to occur within individual countries and social structures. This is how it was and this is how it will be. But here, too, our time marks a change. Internal transformations can no longer advance their national goals if they develop only along parallel courses with others without making use of the achievements of the outside world and of the potential inherent in equitable cooperation.

In those circumstances, any interference in such internal developments designed to redirect them to someone's liking would have all the more destructive consequences for the establishment of a peaceful order.

In the past differences were often a factor causing mutual rejection. Now, they have a chance of becoming a factor for mutual enrichment and mutual attraction.

Behind differences in social systems, in ways of life and in preferences for certain values stand different interests. There is no escaping that fact.

But, equally there is no escaping the need to find a balance of interests within an international framework, which has become a condition for survival and progress.

Pondering all this, one comes to the conclusion that, if we are to take into account the lessons of the past and the realities of the present, if we are to reckon with the objective logic of world development, we must look together for ways to improve the international situation and build a new world, and, if so, we ought to agree on the basic, truly universal prerequisites and principles of such action.

It is obvious, for instance, that the use or threat of force can no longer, and must no longer, be an instrument of foreign policy. This applies, above all, to nuclear arms, but that is not the only thing that matters. All of us, and primarily the stronger of us, must exercise self-restraint and totally rule out any outward-oriented use of force. That is the first and the most important component of a nonviolent world, an ideal which we proclaimed, together with India, in the Delhi Declaration and which we invite you to follow.

After all, it is now quite clear that building up military power makes no country omnipotent. What is more, one-sided reliance on military power ultimately weakens other components of national security.

It is also quite clear to us that the principle of freedom of choice is mandatory. Its non-recognition is fraught with extremely grave consequences for world peace. Denying that right to peoples, under whatever pretext or rhetorical guise, jeopardizes even the fragile balance that has been attained. Freedom of choice is a universal principle that should allow of no exceptions.

It was not simply out of good intentions that we came to the conclusion that that principle was absolute. We were driven to it by an unbiased analysis of the objective trends of today. More and more characteristics of them is the increasingly multi-optional nature of social development in different countries. This applies both to the capitalist and to the socialist systems. The diversity of the socio-political structures that have grown out of national liberation movements over the past decades also attests to this.

This objective fact calls for respect for the views and positions of others, tolerance, a willingness to perceive something different as not necessarily bad or hostile, and an ability to learn to live side-by-side with others, while remaining different and not always agreeing with each other. As the world asserts its diversity, attempts to look down on others and to teach them one's own brand of democracy become totally improper—to say nothing of the fact that democratic values intended for export often lose their worth very quickly.

What we are talking about, therefore, is unity in diversity. If we assert this politically, if we reaffirm our adherence to freedom of choice, then there is no room for the view that some live on Earth by virtue of divine will, while others are here quite by chance. The time has come to discard such thinking and to shape our policies accordingly. This would open up prospects for strengthening the unity of the world.

The new phase also requires de-ideologizing relations among states. We are not abandoning our convictions, our philosophy or traditions, nor do we urge anyone to abandon theirs. However, neither do we have any intention of being hemmed in by our values, which would result in intellectual impoverishment, for it would mean rejecting a powerful source of development—the exchange of everything original that each nation has independently created.

In the course of such exchange, let everyone show the advantages of their social system, their way of life and their values, not just by words or propaganda, but by real deeds. That would be a fair rivalry of ideologies. But it should not be extended to relations among states, otherwise we should simply be unable to solve any of the world's problems, such as developing wide-ranging, mutually beneficial and equitable cooperation among nations; making efficient use of the achievements of scientific and technological revolution; restructuring the world economy and protecting the environment; and overcoming backwardness and eliminating hunger, disease, illiteracy and other global scourges. Similarly, we would not be able to eliminate the nuclear threat and militarism.

These are our reflections on the patterns of world development on the threshold of the twenty-first century.

Of course, we are far from claiming to be in possession of the ultimate truth, but on the basis of a thorough analysis of the past and newly emerging realities, we have concluded that it is on these lines that we should jointly seek the way to the supremacy of the universal human idea over the endless multitude of centrifugal forces, and to preserve the vitality of this civilization which is possibly the only one in the entire universe.

Could this view be a little too romantic? Are we not overestimating the potential and maturity of the world's social consciousness? We have heard such doubts and such questions, both in our country and from some of our Western partners.

I am convinced that we are not floating above reality. Forces have already emerged in the world that in one way or another stimulate the arrival of a period of peace. The peoples and large sectors of the public do, indeed, ardently wish for an improvement in the situation. They want to learn to cooperate. It is sometimes amazing how powerful this trend is. It is also important that it is beginning to shape policies.

Changes in philosophical approaches and in political relations form a solid prerequisite for imparting, in line with worldwide objective processes, a powerful impetus to the efforts designed to establish new relations among states. Even those politicians whose activities used to be geared to the Cold War and sometimes linked with its most critical phases are now drawing appropriate conclusions. Of all people, they find it particularly hard to abandon old stereotypes and past practices, and, if even they are changing course, it is clear that, when new generations take over, opportunities will increase in number.

In short, the understanding of the need for a period of peace is gaining ground and beginning to prevail. This has made it possible to take the first real steps toward creating a healthier international environment and towards disarmament.

What are the practical implications of that? It would be natural and sensible not to abandon everything positive that has already been accomplished and to build on the gains of the past few years, on all that we have created working together. I refer to the process of negotiations on nuclear arms, conventional weapons and chemical weapons and the search for political approaches to ending regional conflicts. Of course, I refer, above all, to political dialogue—a more intense and open dialogue aimed at the very heart of problems instead of confrontation, at an exchange of constructive ideas instead of recriminations. Without political dialogue, the process of negotiations cannot advance.

We regard prospects for the near and more distant future quite optimistically. Just look at the changes in our relations with the United States. Little by little, mutual understanding has started to develop and elements of trust have emerged, without which it is very hard to make headway in politics.

In Europe, such elements are even more numerous. The Helsinki process is a great process. I believe that it remains fully valid. Its philosophical, political, practical and other dimensions must all be preserved and enhanced, while taking into account new circumstances.

Current realities make it imperative that the dialogue that ensures normal and constructive evolution of international affairs involve, on a continuous and active basis, all countries and regions of the world, including such major Powers as India, China, Japan and Brazil, and other countries—big, medium and small.

I am in favor of a more dynamic and substantiative political dialogue, or strengthening the political prerequisites for improvement of the international climate. That would make it easier to find practical solutions to many problems. Tough though it may be, this is the road that we must travel.

Everyone should join in the movement towards greater world unity. Today this is particularly important, for we are approaching a very important point at which we shall have to face the question of how to ensure world solidarity and the stability and dynamism of international relations.

Yet, in my talks with foreign government and political leaders, with whom I have had over 200 meetings, I have sometimes sensed their dissatisfaction that at this crucial time, for one reason or another, they sometimes find themselves on the sidelines, as it were, of the main issues of world politics. It is natural and appropriate that no one is willing to resign himself to that.

If, although different, we are indeed part of the same civilization, if we are aware of the interdependence of the contemporary world, this fact must be increasingly present in politics and in practical efforts to harmonize international relations. Perhaps the term *perestroika* would not be quite appropriate in this context, but I do call for the building of new international relations.

I am convinced that our time and the realities to today's world make it necessary to internationalize dialogue and the negotiating process. This is the main, most general conclusion that we have come to in studying the global trends that have been gaining momentum in recent years and in participating in world politics.

In this specific historical situation we face the question of a new role for the United Nations. We feel that states must to some extent review their attitude to the United Nations—this unique instrument without which world politics would be inconceivable today. The recent reinvigoration of its peace-making role has again demonstrated the ability of the United Nations to assist its members in coping with the daunting challenges of our time and working to humanize their relations.

Regrettably, shortly after it was established the Organization sustained the onslaught of the Cold War. For many years it was the scene of propaganda battles and continuous political confrontation. Let historians argue who is more and who is less to blame for this. What political leaders today need to do is to draw lessons from that chapter in the history of the United Nations, which turned out to be at odds with the very meaning and objectives of our Organization. One of the most bitter and important lessons lies in the long list of missed opportunities. As a result, at a certain point the authority of the United Nations diminished, and many of its attempts to act failed.

It is highly significant that the reinvigoration of the role of the United Nations is linked to an improvement in the international climate. In a way, the United Nations blends together the interests of different States. It is the only Organization capable of merging into a single current their bilateral, regional and global efforts.

New prospects are opening up for it in all areas that fall naturally under its responsibility—the politico-military, economic, scientific, technological, environment and humanitarian areas. Let us take, for example, the problem of development, which is a truly universal problem. The conditions in which tens of millions of people live in a number of third-world regions are becoming a real threat to all mankind.

No closed entities or even regional communities of States, important though they are, are capable of untangling the main knots that tie up the principal avenues of world economic relations—North–South, East–West, South–South, South–East, and East–East. What is needed here is to combine the efforts and take into account the interests of all groups of countries—something that only this Organization, the United Nations can accomplish.

External debt is one of the gravest problems. Let us not forget that in the age of colonialism the developing world, at the cost of countless losses and sacrifices, financed the prosperity of a large portion of the world community. The time has come to make up for the losses that accompanied its historic and tragic contribution to global material progress.

We are convinced that here, too, the internationalization of our approach offers a way out. Looking at things realistically we have to admit that the accumulated debt cannot be repaid or recovered on the original terms. The Soviet Union is prepared to institute a lengthy moratorium of up to 100 years on debt-servicing by the least developed countries, and in quite a few cases to write off the debt altogether.

As regards other developing countries, we invite members to consider the following: limiting their official debt-servicing payments, depending on the economic performance of each of them, or granting them a long period of deferral of the repayment of a major portion of their debt; supporting the appeal of the United Nations Conference on Trade and Development for reduction of debts to commercial banks; guaranteeing government support for market arrangements to assist in third-world debt settlement, including the formation of a specialized international agency that would repurchase debts at a discount.

The Soviet Union favors a substantiative discussion in multilateral forums of ways of settling the debt crisis, including consultations, under the auspices of the United Nations, among Heads of Government of debtor and creditor countries.

International economic security is inconceivable unless related not only to disarmament but also to the elimination of the threat to the world's environment. In a number of regions the state of the environment is simply frightening. A conference on the environment within the framework of the United Nations is scheduled for 1992. We welcome this decision and are working to ensure that this forum produces results commensurate with the scope of the problem.

But time is running out, although much is being done in various countries. Here again I should just like to underscore most emphatically the prospects opening up in the process of disarmament—particularly, of course, nuclear disarmament—for environmental revival.

Let us also think about setting up within the framework of the United Nations a center for emergency environmental assistance. Its function would be to send international groups of experts without delay to areas with a badly deteriorating environment. The Soviet Union is also ready to co-operate in establishing an international space laboratory or manned orbital station designed exclusively for monitoring the state of the environment.

In the general area of space exploration the outlines of a future space industry are becoming increasingly clear. The position of the Soviet Union is well known: Activities in outer space must rule out the appearance of weapons there. Here again there has to be a legal base. The groundwork for it—the provisions of the 1967 Treaty and other agreements—is already in place.

However, there is already a strongly felt need to develop an all-embracing regime for peaceful work in outer space. Verification of compliance with that regime would be entrusted to a world space organization. We have put forward on more than one occasion our proposal to establish such an organization. We are prepared to incorporate within its system our Krasnoyarsk radar station. A decision has already been made to place that radar under the authority of the USSR Academy of Sciences. Soviet scientists are prepared to receive their foreign colleagues and discuss with them ways of converting it into an international center for peaceful cooperation by dismantling and refitting certain units and structures, and to provide additional equipment. The entire system could function under the auspices of the United Nations.

The whole world welcomes the efforts of this Organization, its Secretary General, Mr. Perez de Cuellar, and his representatives in untying knots of regional problems. I should like to elaborate on this. Paraphrasing the words of the English poet that Hemingway took as an epigraph for his famous novel, I will say this: The bell of every regional conflict tolls for all of us.

That is particularly true since those conflicts are already taking place in the third world, which already faces many ills and problems of such magnitude that it has to be a matter of concern to us all.

The year 1988 has brought a glimmer of hope in this area of our common concerns as well. That has been felt in almost all regional crises. On some of them, there has been movement. We welcome it, and we did what we could to contribute to it.

I will single out only Afghanistan.

The Geneva Accords, whose fundamental and practical significance has been praised throughout the world, provided a possibility for completing the process of settlement even before the end of this year. That did not happen.

That unfortunate fact reminds us once again of the political, legal and moral significance of the Roman maxim *pacta sunt servanda*—treaties must be observed.

I do not want to use this rostrum for recriminations against anyone.

But it is our view that, within the competence of the United Nations, the General Assembly resolution adopted last November could be supplemented by some specific measures.

In the words of that resolution, for the urgent achievements of a comprehensive solution by the Afghans themselves of the question of broad-based Government, the following should be undertaken.

A complete cease-fire, effective everywhere as of 1 January 1989, and the cessation of all offensive operations or shelling, with the opposing Afghan groups retaining, for the duration of negotiations, all territories under their control; linked to that, stopping as of the same date any supplies of arms to be belligerents; for the period of establishing a broad-based Government, as provided for in the General Assembly resolution, sending to Kabul and other strategic centers of the country a contingent of United Nations peace-keeping forces. We also request the Secretary General to facilitate early implementation of the idea of holding an international conference on the neutrality and demilitarization of Afghanistan.

We will continue most actively to assist in healing the wounds of the war and are prepared to cooperate in that endeavor both with the United Nations and on a bilateral basis.

We support the proposal to create under the auspices of the United Nations a voluntary international peace corps to assist in the revival of Afghanistan.

In the context of the problems of settling regional conflicts, I have to express my opinion on the serious incident that has recently affected the work of this session. The Chairman of an organization that has observer status at the United Nations was not allowed by the US authorities to come to New York to address the General Assembly. I am referring to Yassar Arafat.

What is more, that happened at a time when the Palestine Liberation Organization had made a constructive step that facilitates the search for a solution to the Middle East problem with the involvement of the United Nations Security Council. It happened at a time when a positive trend had become apparent towards a political settlement of other regional conflicts, in many cases with the assistance of the USSR and the United States. We voice our deep regret over the incident and our solidarity with the Palestine Liberation Organization.

The concept of comprehensive international security is based on the principles of the United Nations Charter and is predicated on the binding nature of international law for all States.

Being in favor of demilitarizing international relations, we want political and legal methods to prevail in solving whatever problems may arise.

Our ideal is a world community of States which are based on the rule of law and which Subordinate their foreign policy activities to law.

The achievement of that goal would be facilitated by an agreement within the United Nations on a uniform understanding of the principles and norms of international law, their codification with due regard to new conditions and the development of legal norms for new areas of cooperation.

In a nuclear age the effectiveness of international law should be based not on enforcing compliance but rather on norms reflecting a balance of State interests.

In addition to the ever-increasing awareness of the objective commonality of our destiny, that would make every State genuinely interested in exercising self-restraint within the bounds of international law.

Democratizing international relations means not only a maximum degree of internationalization in the efforts of all members of the world community to solve problems; it also means humanizing those relations.

International ties will fully reflect the genuine interests of the peoples and effectively serve the cause of their common security only when the human being and his concerns, rights and freedoms become the center of all things.

In that context, I should like to join the voice of my country in the expressions of high appreciation of the significance of the Universal Declaration of Human Rights adopted 40 years ago on 10 December 1948.

Today, that document retains its significance. It, too, reflects the universal nature of the goals and objectives of the United Nations.

The most fitting way for a State to observe the anniversary of the Declaration is to improve its domestic conditions for respecting and protecting the rights of its own citizens.

Before I inform you on what specifically we have undertaken recently in that respect, I should like to say the following.

Our country is going through a period of truly revolutionary uplifting.

The process of *perestroika* is gaining momentum. We began with formulation of the theoretical concept of *perestroika*. We had to evaluate the nature and the magnitude of problems, to understand the lessons of the past and express that in the form of political conclusions and programs. That was done.

The theoretical work, a reassessment of what is happening, the finalization, enrichment and readjustment of political positions have not been completed. They are continuing.

But it was essential to begin with an overall concept, which, as now confirmed by the experience of these past years, has generally proved to be correct and has no alternative.

For our society to participate in efforts to implement the plans of *perestroika,* it had to be democratized in practice. Under the sign of democratization, *perestroika* has now spread to politics, the economy, intellectual life and ideology.

We have initiated a radical economic reform. We have gained experience. At the start of next year, the entire national economy will be redirected to new forms and methods of operation. That also means profoundly reorganizing relations of production and releasing the tremendous potential inherent in socialist property.

Undertaking such bold revolutionary transformations, we realized that there would be mistakes, and also opposition, that new approaches would generate new problems. We also foresaw the possibility of slow-downs in some areas.

But the guarantee that the overall process of *perestroika* will steadily move forward and gain strength lies in a profound democratic reform of the entire system of power and administration.

With the recent decisions by the USSR Supreme Soviet on amendments to the Constitution and the adoption of the Law on Elections, we have completed the first stage of the process of political reform.

Without pausing, we have begun the second stage of this process with the main tasks of improving the relationship between the center and the republics, harmonizing inter-ethnic relations on the principles of Leninst internationalism that we inherited from the Great Revolution, and at the same time reorganizing the local system of Soviet power.

A great deal of work lies ahead. Major tasks will have to be dealt with concurrently.

We are full of confidence. We have a theory and a policy, and also the vanguard force of *perestroika*—the Party, which is also restructuring itself in accordance with new tasks and fundamental changes in society as a whole.

What is most important is that all our peoples and all generations of citizens of our great country support *perestroika.*

We have become deeply involved in building a socialist State based on the rule of law. Work on a series of new laws has been completed or is nearing completion.

Many of them will enter into force as early as 1989, and we expect to meet the highest standards from the standpoint of ensuring the rights of the individual.

Soviet democracy will be placed on a solid normative base. I am referring, in particular, to laws on the freedom of conscience, *glasnost,* public associations, organizations, and many others.

In places of confinement there are no persons convicted for their political or religious beliefs.

Additional guarantees are to be included in the new draft laws that rule out any form of persecution on those grounds.

Naturally this does not apply to those who have committed actual criminal offenses or State crimes, such as espionage, sabotage, terrorism and so on, whatever their political or ideological beliefs. Draft amendments to the penal code have been prepared and are awaiting their turn. Among the articles being revised are those relating to capital punishment.

The problem of exit from and entry to our country, including the question of leaving it for family reunification, is being dealt with in a humane spirit. As the Assembly will know, one of the reasons for refusal of permission to leave is a person's knowledge of secrets. Strictly warranted time limitations on the secrecy rule will now be applied. Every person seeking employment at certain agencies or enterprises will be informed of this rule. In case of disputes there is a right of appeal under the law. This removes from the agenda the problem of the so-called refuseniks.

We intend to expand the Soviet Union's participation in the human rights monitoring arrangements of the United Nations and the Conference on Security and Cooperation in Europe (CSCE). We believe that the jurisdiction of the International Court of Justice at The Hague as regards the interpretation and implementation of agreements on human rights should be binding on all States. We regard as part of the Helsinki process the cessation of jamming of all foreign radio broadcasts beamed at the Soviet Union.

Overall, this is our credo: political problems must be solved by political means only; human problems in a humane way only.

Let me now turn to the main issue without which none of the problems of the coming century can be solved: disarmament.

International development and communications have been distorted by the arms race and the militarization of thinking. As the Assembly will know, on 15 January 1986 the Soviet Union put forward a program for building a nuclear–weapon-free world. Translated into actual negotiating positions, it has already produced material results. Tomorrow marks the first anniversary of the signing of the Treaty between the United States of America and the Union of Soviet Socialist Republics on the Elimination of Their Intermediate-Range and Shorter-Range Missiles—INF Treaty. I am therefore particularly pleased to note that the implementation of the Treaty—the elimination of missiles—is proceeding normally in an atmosphere of trust and businesslike work. A large breach has thus been made in a seemingly unbreakable wall of suspicion and animosity. We are witnessing the emergence of a new, historic reality: a turning away from the principle of super-armament to the principle of reasonable defense sufficiency.

We are present at the birth of a new model of ensuring security, not through the build-up of arms, as was almost always the case in the past, but on the contrary through their reduction on the basis of compromise. The Soviet leadership has decided to demonstrate once again its readiness to reinforce this healthy process, not only by words but also by deeds.

Today I can report to the General Assembly that the Soviet Union has taken a decision to reduce its armed forces. Within the next two years their numerical strength will be reduced by 500,000 men. The numbers of conventional armaments will also be substantially reduced. This will be done unilaterally, without relation to the talks on the mandate of the Vienna meeting.

By agreement with our Warsaw Treaty allies we have decided to withdraw, by 1991, six tank divisions from the German Democratic Republic, Czechoslovakia and Hungary and to disband them. Assault landing troops and several other formations and units, including assault crossing units with their weapons and combat equipment, will also be withdrawn from the groups of Soviet forces stationed in those countries. Soviet forces stationed in those countries will be reduced by 50,000 men and their armaments by 5,000 tanks.

All Soviet divisions remaining for the time being on the territories of our allies are being reorganized. Their structure will be different from what it is now; after a major cutback in their tanks it will become clearly defensive.

At the same time time we shall reduce the numerical strength of the armed forces and the numbers of armaments stationed in the European part of the Soviet Union. In total, Soviet armed forces in this part of our country and in the territories of our European allies will be reduced by 10,000 tanks, 8,500 artillery systems and 800 combat aircraft.

Over these two years we intend to reduce significantly our armed forces in the Asian part of our country too. By agreement with the Government of the Mongolian People's Republic a major portion of Soviet troops temporarily stationed there will return home.

In taking this fundamental decision the Soviet leadership is expressing the will of the people, who have undertaken a profound renewal of their entire socialist society. We shall maintain our country's defense capabilities at a level of reasonable and reliable sufficiency so that no one can be tempted to encroach on the security of the Soviet Union and our allies.

By all our activities in favor of demilitarizing international relations we wish to draw the attention of the international community to yet another pressing problem: the problem of transition from the economy of armaments to an economy of disarmament. Is conversion of military production a realistic idea? I have already had occasion to speak about this. We think that it is indeed realistic.

For its part the Soviet Union is prepared to take the following steps: within the framework of our economic reform to draw up and make public our internal conversion plan in the course of 1989 to draw up as an experiment, conversion plans for two or three defense plants; and to make public our experience in providing employment for specialists from military industry and in using its equipment, buildings and structures in civilian production.

It is desirable that all States, and in the first place the major military Powers, should submit their national conversion plans to the United Nations. It would be useful also to set up a group of scientists to undertake a thorough analysis of the problem of conversion as a whole and as applied to individual countries and regions and report to the Secretary General of the United Nations, and subsequently for this matter to be considered at a session of the General Assembly.

Finally, since I am here on American soil, and also for other obvious reasons, I have to turn to the subject of our relations with this great country. I have a chance to appreciate the full measure of its hospitality during my memorable visit to Washington exactly a year ago. Relations between the Soviet Union and the United States of America have a history of five and a half decades. As the world has changed, so have the nature, role and place of those relations in world politics. For too long they developed along the lines of confrontation and sometimes animosity, either overt or covert. But in the last few years the entire world has been able to breathe a sign of relief, thanks to the changes for the better in the substance and the atmosphere of the relationship between Moscow and Washington.

No one intends to underestimate the seriousness of our differences and the toughness of our outstanding problems. We have, however, already graduated from the primary school of learning to understand each other and seek solutions in both our own and the common interest.

The USSR and the United States have built the largest nuclear and missile arsenals; but it is those two countries that, having become specifically aware of their responsibility, have been the first to conclude a treaty on the reduction and physical elimination of a portion of their armaments which posed a threat to both of them and to all other countries. Both countries possess the greatest and most sophisticated military secrets; but it is those two that have laid a basis for and are further developing a system of mutual verification both of the elimination of armaments and of the reduction and prohibition of their production. It is those two countries that are accumulating experience for future bilateral and multilateral agreements.

We value this. We acknowledge the contributions made by President Ronald Reagan and by the members of his Administration, particularly Mr. George Schultz.

All this is our joint investment in a venture of historic importance. We must not lose that investment, or leave it idle.

The next United States administration, headed by President-elect George Bush, will find in us a partner who is ready—without long pauses or backtracking—to continue the dialogue in a spirit of realism, openness and goodwill, with a willingness to achieve concrete results working on the agenda which covers the main issues of Soviet–United States relations and world politics.

I have in mind, above all, consistent movement towards a treaty on 50% reductions in strategic offensive arms while preserving the Treaty on the Limitation of Anti-Ballistic Missile Systems (ABM Treaty); working out a convention on the elimination of chemical weapons—here, as we see it, prerequisites exist to make 1989 a decisive year, and negotiations on the reduction of conventional arms and armed forces in Europe.

I also have in mind economic, environmental and humanistic problems in their broadest sense.

It would be quite wrong to put the positive changes in the international situation exclusively to the credit of the USSR and the United

States. The Soviet Union highly appreciates the major and original contribution of socialist countries in the process of creating a healthier international environment.

During the course of negotiations we are constantly aware of the presence of other major Powers, both nuclear and non-nuclear. Many countries, including medium-sized and small countries, and of course the Non-Aligned Movement and the intercontinental Group of Six, are playing a uniquely important constructive role.

We in Moscow are happy that an ever-increasing number of statesmen, political, party and public figures and—I should like to emphasize this—scientists, cultural figures, representatives of mass movements and various churches, and activists of the so-called people's diplomacy are ready to shoulder the burden of universal responsibility.

In this regard I believe that the idea of convening on a regular basis, under the auspices of the United Nations, an assembly of public organizations deserves attention.

We are not inclined to simplify the situation in the world.

Yes, the trend towards disarmament has been given a powerful impetus, and the process is gaining a momentum of its own. But it has not yet become irreversible.

Yes, the willingness to give up confrontation in favor of dialogue and co-operation is being felt strongly. But it is still far from becoming a permanent feature in the practice of international relations.

Yes, movement towards a nuclear-weapon-free and non-violent world is capable of radically transforming the political and intellectual identity of our planet. But only the first steps have been taken, an event they have been met with mistrust in certain influential quarters and face resistance.

The legacy and the inertia of the past continue to be felt. Profound contradictions and the roots of many conflicts have not disappeared. And there remains another fundamental fact, which is that a peaceful period will be taking shape in the context of the existence and rivalry of different socio-economic and political systems.

However, the thrust of our international efforts and one of the key elements of the new thinking is that this rivalry should be given a quality of reasonable competition with due regard for freedom of choice and a balance of interests. Then it will become even more useful and productive from the standpoint of global development.

Otherwise, if as in the past the arms race remains its basic component, this rivalry will be deadly. More and more people throughout the world—leaders as well as ordinary people—are beginning to understand that.

I conclude my first address to the United Nations with the same feeling that I had when I began it—a feeling of responsibility to my own people and to the world community.

We are meeting at the end of a year that has meant so much for the United Nations and on the eve of a year from which we all expect so much.

I should like to believe that our hopes will be matched by our joint efforts to put an end to an era of wars, confrontation and regional conflicts, to aggressions against nature, to the terror of hunger and poverty as well as to political terrorism.

That is our common goal and we can only reach it together.

(Gorbachev, 1988)

THE ELITE MEDIA REACTION TO REAGAN'S ADDRESS

After President Reagan's address to the UN, the Soviet news agency TASS on September 26th gave about half of a 1-page dispatch to quote Reagan favorably

> There is the prospect of not only a new era in Soviet–American relations, but a new age of world peace. . . . There is movement. The logjam is broken. . . . We [Reagan and Gorbachev meeting in Switzerland] agreed to go beyond the past. To seek not just treaties that permit building weapons to a higher level, but revolutionary agreements that actually reduced, and even eliminated, a whole class of nuclear weapons. (Reagan, cited in TASS, 1988 [Online])

The second half of the dispatch became more critical of Reagan's statements

> However the program he set out, was distinguished for its unbalanced character and, in many cases, for clearly biased and confrontational assessment of several problems. Putting to the fore human rights, the president "forgot" about the need for ensuring them in his own country, concentrating on his attacks against some other countries, including the Soviet Union. His references were especially crude with respect to Cuba, and Nicaragua. . . . Touching on the situation in Afghanistan, the US president preferred to bypass completely the burning problem complicating the implementation of the Geneva accords: their truce violation by Pakistan which supports extremists. (TASS, 1988 [Online])

Irvin Arieff, in two additional Reuters dispatches, one on September 26th and one on September 27th related to Reagan's UN address, noted his emphasis on a worldwide conference on chemical weapons, the possibility of a superpower agreement on strategic arms reductions being possible in 1989, and his reconfirmation of the US commitment to his so-called "Star Wars" space-based missile defense system, opposed by the Soviet Union. As he had predicted before the address, Arieff indicated that it contained no new major foreign policy initiatives, but it was warm in its praise of the UN, "a world body the president has not always held in high esteem." Arieff indicated that Reagan's proposal for the world-wide ban on chemical weapons was greeted enthusiastically by Eduard Shevardnadze, who told the president that it was "a very good idea," and speaking on Visnews (a world-wide television news service, a majority of which is owned by Reuters): "Today's statement was different from those of the past. There were more positive moments, elements," and that the Soviet government had been "supportive of this for a long, long time" (Arieff, 1988b [Online]). In his later article, Arieff emphasized that Reagan had shunned substance in his farewell talks with Allied ministers, failing to mention his proposed chemical weapons ban at all in his bilateral discussions, or the conventional arms talks in Vienna, or a proposed US–Soviet treaty to halve long-range nuclear weapons, or the strategic arms proposal all of which had been mentioned in his UN address (Arieff, 1988c).

Robinson's (1988a) Inter Press Service dispatch of September 26 said that one Western European diplomat suggested that "It sounded like an acceptance speech for the Nobel Peace Prize" which was to be announced in Oslo, Norway, on September 29. Robinson identified several areas in which the Reagan administration had shown its hostility earlier to the UN, and complemented its improvements. Robinson wrote however that Reagan had not pointed out that the UN reforms had not been matched by adequate external financial resources, including the failure of the United States and other creditor countries to live up to the session's expectations on resource flows. Robinson continued: "While noting the UN's successes, Reagan did not outline a vision of the future for the organization as had been suggested in some quarters including an editorial in the *New York Times* newspaper today" (Robinson, 1988a [Online]). Helen Thomas, dean of the White House Press Corps, filed an article for the United Press International, in which she suggested that several of Reagan's statements were expanded or clarified by State Department officials and White House aides (Thomas, 1988).

The Inter Press Service (1988a) dispatch of September 26 focused its headline on "Central America: Reagan Calls for 'Constructive' Soviet Policy," and devoted its entire dispatch to the tensions between the United States and Nicaragua, which Reagan had mentioned as one of the US disappointments in the UN address, and which several other media reported. The Inter Press Service (1988a) offered several rebuttal statements by the deputy foreign minister of Nicaragua: "After eight years, the [US] policy [against Nicaragua] has brought only death and suffering." Deputy Foreign Minister Tinoco said that Reagan's military backing for the "contras," opposition to the regional peace plans, and the direct involvement of the US Central Intelligence Agency in mining Nicaraguan harbors and other acts of hostility were responsible for the continuation of the conflict. The Inter Press Service dispatch ended with the words: "For his part, Tinoco said he hoped that Reagan's tacit admission that his Central America policy had failed would be a signal for the next administration (President Bush) to chart a new course in the region" (Inter Press Service, 1988a [Online]).

E.A. Wayne, writing for *The Christian Science Monitor,* headlined "US–UN Chill Starts to Thaw," indicated that Reagan's address symbolized a new attitude toward the world body, quoting Reagan as saying "Today, the UN has the opportunity to live and breathe as never before. Already you, Mr. Secretary General, through your persistence, patience, unyielding will, have shown . . . how valuable the UN can be" (Reagan, cited in Wayne, 1988 [Online]). Most of Wayne's nearly 900 word article explained that Reagan's UN address linked the new cooperation between the United States and USSR and the US support for the UN itself. Wayne noted: The new love affair with the UN doesn't mean that the US thinks it will work for everything, officials stress. It can still be painfully difficult to build consensus for action. . . . But to the degree that the big powers are reining in their rivalries and can find consensus on resolving international conflicts, US officials say, the UN may well be a growth industry (Wayne, 1988 [Online]).

THE ELITE MEDIA REACTION TO GORBACHEV'S ADDRESS

Following Gorbachev's UN address, a variety of news media reported on and evaluated his efforts in lengthy articles and dispatches, including, among others, the Inter Press Service: "UN: Gorbachev's Troop-Cutting Proposals Hailed," "Soviet Union: Official Welcomes Continuity with Bush," "UN: A Year of Political Advances, Economic Struggles," *Newsday:* "For Reagan, Gorbachev a Cordial Last Meeting," and "It Was Going Well," *The Los Angeles Times:* "A Day That Will Live on, Famously," *The Chicago Tribune:* "Addresses Close Cold War Curtain," the US edition of *Newsweek:* "Special Report: Hope and Tragedy: Brave New World," *Financial Times:* "A Time of Hope, A Hint of Peace: 1988: The Watershed Year," and *Maclean's* (of Canada): "The Year of the Peacemakers." *The Los Angeles Times'* headline: "A Day That Will Live on, Famously," was a pun on President Franklyn D. Roosevelt's reaction to the Japanese bombing of Pearl Harbor on December 7, 1941, when he called it "A day that will live in infamy."

Just as Nikita Khruschev's 1959 General Assembly address, "Let Us Disarm Now" was among the important addresses given during the first 15 years of the UN, President Gorbachev's December 7, 1988 UN address could properly be called a disarmament speech of considerable magnitude. He announced a major unilateral reduction in Soviet troop strength in Europe and Asia by 500,000 men over the next 2 years, the dismantling of military hardware, steps to ease Third World debt, to hasten the resolution of regional conflicts, and to improve relations with the United States. Claude Robinson's nearly 1,000-word Inter Press Service dispatch of December 7, 1988, noted positive responses from Zimbabwe's ambassador and chairman of the 101 nation Non-Aligned Movement, US Secretary of State George Schultz, and senior UN officials. Robinson wrote that

> The speech came against a background of the 'new thinking' emanating from Moscow since Gorbachev became party leader and initiated a policy of more openness or 'glassnost' in Soviet society, modernization of the domestic economy, reduction of East–West tension and reduction of regional conflicts. The policy has been widely credited as being the main force behind the Soviet–US agreement last year to eliminate a whole class of nuclear weapons. (Robinson, 1988b [Online]).

Robinson reported that although Gorbachev announced Soviet debt relief to third world nations, African delegations were disappointed that not a single reference was made to Africa. Khrushchev had strongly emphasized Soviet sympathies with the new African delegations in 1960, and had called for a resolution totally abolishing colonialism. Robinson praised Gorbachev's increasing enthusiasm for the UN, reversing "earlier suspicion of the organization which, in its early stages, was regarded by Moscow as sympathetic to US foreign policy interests," and Gorbachev's statement that "de-ideologizing" of international relations was a prerequisite for solving the world's major problems (Robinson, 1988b [Online]).

Curiously, Robinson indicated in his December 7 article that it was the first Soviet Chairman's address to the UN since Nikita Khrushchev came in 1960. The media error is clear, since Premier Alexi Koseigin had addressed the Fifth Emergency Special Session of the General Assembly during the 1967 Middle East crisis. Saul Friedman, writing for Newsday December 8, repeated the same error. Both errors indicate a lack of knowledge or forgetfulness on the part of the media writers of the 1967 Middle East crisis and the important role that Koseigin played in bringing the issue to the UN.

Charles M. Madigan's 1,300-word *Chicago Tribune* opinion article of December 8th began:

> A mere eight years before Mikhail Gorbachev, general secretary of the Soviet Communist Party, came to visit the UN, Ronald Reagan decided to spend almost every penny the United States government had—and borrow some beyond that—to wage the Cold War. . . . There was a declaration of US victory in the Cold War on Wednesday. That it came from Gorbachev only added irony to the moment. . . . British Prime Minister Margaret Thatcher recognized it four years ago when she said the Cold War was over and that she could do business with Gorbachev. (Madigan, 1988 [Online]).

Madigan listed many of the Cold War actions taken by both sides, but especially by the Soviet Union, and concluded:

> What Gorbachev offered was nothing less than a new definition of the relationship between the most powerful nations in the world, a challenge to abandon the horror of a contest kept in check by the threat of oblivion. If the military buildup was the defining element in Soviet–American relations during the Reagan years, President-elect Bush will have the advantage of dealing with a Kremlin leader who is clearly willing to rethink his nation's place, and America's place, in the world. (Madigan, 1988 [Online])

In a 2,542-word article in the US edition of *Newsweek,* Russell Watson and others, highlighted the article with the words: "Playing a weak hand brilliantly, Gorbachev loosens Moscow's ideological straitjacket and announces a unilateral cut in his country's armed forces." Called back to the Soviet Union and unable to visit Cuba as scheduled because of the devastating Armenian earthquake, Gorbachev spent only 46 hours in New York, *Newsweek* reported, but his UN address "drew applause from Ronald Reagan and George Bush," "snatched the initiative from both Reagan and Bush," caused George Bush to be 'sobered' by Gorbachev's gambit, and was called a "brilliant tour de force," by a Bush adviser: "It has elevated his standing at home, engendered enormous good will for him outside the Soviet Union and passed a serious challenge to the cohesion of the (NATO) alliance—all in one dramatic proposal." *Newsweek,* noting continued weaknesses for the Soviet economy, nonetheless assessed his UN address as "a virtuoso performance" with his major theme being "continuity between the USSR and the United States."

Robert E. Hunter started his *Los Angeles Times* article of December 8th

> On the 47th anniversary of Pearl Harbor, America has again been assaulted by a principal rival for power. This time it is a peace offensive, launched on American television by the Soviet president, Mikhail S. Gorbachev. Like Pearl Harbor, Gorbachev's actions are likely to transform how we look at the world and our place in it. . . . Before his UN speech, Gorbachev was already topping opinion polls in Western Europe as more a man of peace

> than Ronald Reagan. Now Reagan's successor will start out even further behind, and will have to labor even harder to prove a match—in Europe and elsewhere—for the wily Soviet leader. (Hunter, 1988 [Online]).

The Gorbachev-Reagan-Bush lunch, *Newsweek* indicated was not a business meeting "because neither side was interested in conducting business," but Gorbachev left Reagan amused, and Bush backed off from campaign rhetoric critical of the Soviet position on Strategic Arms Reduction Talks. Reagan administration officials, including President Reagan and Secretary of State George Schultz, however, stated that the discussion covered the full range of United States–Soviet relations, including arms control, regional conflicts, and human rights (Friedman, 1988). Immediately after the luncheon, *Newsweek* reported:

> Gorbachev took Manhattan by storm." Crowds chanted "Gorby, Gorby". . . . Bathed in the red glow of a Coca-Cola sign, Mikhail and Raisa Gorbachev emerged from their massive ZiL limousine into the kaleidoscopic sights and sounds of Broadway. They smiled and waved while their bodyguards hyperventilated. . . . On the way up Third Avenue, Gorbachev got out of his car again near Bloomingdales. "There are two men I wouldn't mind having as a client," said Republican consultant Ed Rollins. "The pope is one, and Gorbachev is the other." (Watson, et al., 1988 [Online]).

In a 1,731-word editorial, Edward Mortimer, writing for *The Financial Times* of London, on December 19, 1988, picked up Reagan's UN message with his headline: "A Time of Hope, a Hint of Peace; 1988 The Watershed Year." He gave his highly optimistic view of the year: "On the world political stage 1988 has been one of the most hopeful years since 1945." Listing the resolution of several international and regional conflicts troubling international relations and the UN for years, Mortimer wrote:

> Two weeks ago it was the turn of President Mikhail Gorbachev himself to use the UN General Assembly as a platform for further proposals on virtually the whole range of problems currently facing the world, though this time it was his announcement of unilateral cuts in Soviet conventional forces that caught the headlines. (Mortimer, 1988 [Online])

President-Elect Bush

> has clearly stated his desire to develop the new US–Soviet relationship. If the "new detente" does indeed continue, it will probably result in a further strengthening and broadening of the UN's role in a wide variety of issues. A few years ago, the UN was widely seen as increasingly irrelevant to the world's

> real problems. Whenever the two superpowers have been able to agree on a course of action affecting third parties—for instance an intervention to secure a cease fire in successive Arab-Israeli wars—they have found it convenient to work through the Security Council. . . . That discovery of common ground is primarily the result of Mr. Gorbachev's "new thinking."

Gorbachev and his advisers have been inspired

> to embarrass the UN system with all the wide-eyed enthusiasm of the born-again convert. . . . Clearly the international community is finding it difficult to digest such a rich diet of ideas all in one meal, and there are serious doubts about the ability of the UN machinery to handle it. But at the same time there is widespread recognition that many of the problems Mr. Gorbachev is raising are real ones, and that the improved international atmosphere does provide better opportunities for dealing with them. (Mortimer, 1988 [Online]).

Maclean's of Canada, in its "Images of 1988," in its December 19, 1988 issue, headlined its 900-word article "The Year of the Peacemakers." Noting that the UN military forces had won the Nobel Peace Prize in Oslo, *Maclean's* said that some people had expected that the prize might go jointly to Ronald Reagan and Mikhail Gorbachev,

> the leaders of the superpower nations that have been known for 40 years for building up overkill in nuclear weaponry and for military interventions within and beyond their claimed spheres of influence. . . . Gorbachev, who pressed his peace initiatives abroad and reforms at home in a series of diplomatic and political initiatives, was the year's major news-maker." [*Maclean's* assessment of the year noted that George Bush in an October campaign speech at Fulton, Missouri, admitted that] "Gorbachev's initiative "shows promise" [and called for] a kinder, gentler America [and that the "Iron Lady," Margaret Thatcher in her tenth year as Prime Minister of the United Kingdom, appealed to her party to accept the importance of] caring and compassion. [Concluding the article by citing Stephen Hawking's best selling book *A Brief History of Time, Maclean's* said that Hawkings had taken a longer view:] The most immediate threat is from nuclear weapons. We will need luck to get through the next 200 years. But if we do, it must be because we are conducting our affairs in a more sensible way. (*Maclean's,* 1988 [Online]).

Claude Robinson's nearly 1,300-word dispatch for the Inter Press Service of December 28, 1988, "UN: A Year of Political Advances: Economic Struggles," called Reagan's address one of the 43rd General Assembly's more remarkable events because of his praise for the progress of the UN:

His remarks came in sharp contrast to the UN-bashing that had characterized the Reagan Administration in the past. . . . The positive mood prevailed throughout most of the session, and came to a dramatic peak as the Assembly wound down in December, when Soviet leader Gorbachev addressed the body in New York, and Palestine Liberation Organization Chairman Yassar Arafat made an appearance in Geneva. . . . His [Gorbachev's] call for the "de-ideologizing" of international relations and for a new role for the UN in preventing conflicts from escalating into bloody wars was also welcomed as signaling the beginning of an end to East–West ideological competition. . . . In Perez de Cuellar's view, the Gorbachev speech "shows the importance of the mission of the UN as a forum for peace." (Robinson, 1988c [Online])

QUESTIONS FOR ANALYSIS

1. Having read both UN addresses and an illustrative sample of the elite media surrounding both, which address, that of President Reagan or President Gorbachev, would you consider having the most broad impact? Why?
2. If you could have been an invited guest to one, but not both of these addresses, which would you have chosen? Why? What would you have advised this speaker to emphasize, from your point of view as someone interested in world affairs?
3. Whose initiatives, identified in their addresses, would you consider to have had a greater appeal to the diplomatic audience attending the addresses? Why?
4. Considering one of the thrusts of *Diplomatic Discourse* to be international conflict and its resolution or potential resolution, what proposals did both President Reagan and President Gorbachev make in their addresses to resolve these conflicts? Which one appeared more successful in presenting his proposals? Why?
5. What sort of credit did each speaker give to the other leader, Reagan and Gorbachev, in the context of his UN address, for helping to move toward the resolution of international conflict and toward world peace?
6. Which leader, Reagan or Gorbachev, appeared to take more personal credit for helping to resolve international and regional conflicts, and moving toward world peace? Why? Which leader appeared more confident of his own position and that of his country in his UN address? Why?

7. Both leaders gave strong support to the UN as a growing major factor in resolving international and regional conflicts. Several authors, articles, and dispatches indicated that this support had seemed "newfound" for both Reagan and Gorbachev. What caused each leader to provide such positive acclaim to the UN after years of suspicion and belligerence toward the UN?
8. Several authors indicated that because relations between the United States and Soviet Union had improved, this allowed the UN to work more efficiently in resolving international and regional conflicts. Do you agree? Why? If not, why not?
9. TASS in its December 6, 1988, dispatch about the Gorbachev address on December 7th, was headlined "New Political Thinking." Several of the other media utilized the same term. Is it likely that Gorbachev or TASS planted this phrase for other media reports, articles and dispatches, or that TASS picked it up from other media that may have first coined the term?
10. One dispatch suggested that Reagan's address to the UN seemed as if he were receiving the Nobel Peace Prize to be awarded a few days later in Oslo. By the time that Gorbachev spoke to the UN in December, the UN Forces had already been announced as the year's award winner. Gorbachev, however, had seemed to make great strides with his "peristroika" and "glassnost," in opening up the Soviet Union to new opportunities and ideas. Perhaps earlier in the year, he may have thought it possible for him to win the Nobel Peace Prize. In *Diplomatic Discourse,* three of our world leaders speaking at the UN whose addresses are included did receive the Nobel Peace Prize: Gorbachev in 1990, Mandela in 1993, and Arafat in 1994. Which one of these addresses by our three Nobel Peace Prize awards would you consider the most constructive as a statement for world peace? Why?
11. Various leaders and media announced that the Cold War was now over, and if so, this would mean the beginning of a whole new era in the resolution of international conflict and in Soviet–American relations. Based on events that have occurred since these addresses in 1988, would you agree with the assessment that the Cold War is over? Why? If not, why not? What world events have happened more recently that support or reject this optimistic assessment of 1988? Some critics suggest it is now a "Hot Peace." Why?
12. Utilizing principles and concepts from discourse analysis and rhetorical analysis, both singly and jointly, how would you establish your framework to analyze these addresses?

CONCLUSION

President Ronald Reagan was widely regarded as unfavorable to the UN. Through his administration's decision, he decided to end the US involvement in UNESCO and other UN agencies, and refused the competency of the United Nations' judicial organ, the International Court of Justice in relation to the Nicaraguan–United States dispute. During the Reagan Administration, the United States refused to pay its required UN dues, a condition that continued both through the Bush and Clinton Administrations. Nonetheless, Reagan gave more addresses to the UN (seven) than any other American president. It was also Reagan who frequently had referred to the Soviet Union as the "evil empire." Yet, both Reagan and President Gorbachev indicated publicly their esteem for each other toward the end of the Reagan Administration, allowing both Presidents Bush and Clinton to build on developments which Reagan's administration had initiated. Assuming that Reagan believed that both he and Gorbachev may jointly receive the Nobel Peace Prize, as DeKlerk and Mandela in South Africa did become joint Laureates, and as Rabin of Israel and Arafat of the PLO also became joint Laureates, he was obviously disappointed, whereas Gorbachev who did receive the Nobel Peace Prize was delighted.

While identifying the major role of disarmament in the resolution of any world conflicts in the 20th Century and beyond, Gorbachev unleashed forces through *glastnost* and *perestroika* that eventually led to an unsuccessful coup attempt against him, foiled in part by his successor, Boris Yeltsin. The new independence of countries and territories controlled by the Soviet Union led to extraordinary regional and global changes, many of which are still developing. It is possible to say clearly that the Soviet revolution of 1917, which Gorbachev called one of the two great modern revolutions, was matched or surpassed by the Russian Revolution of the late 1980s and early 1990s in its historical importance. In 1992, when he was no longer President even of the new Russian Federation, Gorbachev gave the 250th anniversary address of the birth of Thomas Jefferson at the University of Virginia, which Jefferson founded as his last major act, and acknowledged the importance of Jefferson in the American revolution—as one of the great events of history, a linkage which he failed to make in his 1988 address to the UN. On September 10, 1996, the United Nations passed a Nuclear Test Ban Treaty with a vote of 153 in favor, 3 against, and 8 abstaining.

12

TOWARD A FUTURE WORLD ORDER

The UN Security Council, on January 31, 1992, held an unprecedented summit meeting of heads of state or government. A Russian television station heralded it as "probably the most important international event since the United Nations Organization was set up in 1945" (BBC, 1992 [Online]). *The New York Times* expressed it well:

> Three decades after Nikita S. Khrushchev banged his shoe on a desk at the United Nations, creating one of the most enduring images of the Cold War, the leaders of 15 nations—the permanent and temporary members of the Council—are coming together in a new spirit of cooperation with an avowed purpose of shaping a more humane and peaceful world order. (McFadden, 1992 [Online])

For the Russians, it had the added significance that they were to assume the former seat of the Soviet Union, now dissolved. Thus, a new world order had to be forged. Work toward that end was begun by the permanent members, China, France, Russia, United Kingdom, and the United States, as well as the temporary ones, Austria, Belgium, Cape Verde, Ecuador, Hungary, India, Japan, Morocco, Venezuela, and Zimbabwe.

In terms of speechmaking, the nature of the event encouraged broad topics about the world, rather than narrow. In this regard, these addresses parallel those usually found in the General Assembly. British Prime Minister John Major, the then President of the Security Council, called the summit meeting at the suggestion of President Mitterrand of France. "UN officials [said that] the purpose [was] for the leaders to sort out new directions for the UN and offer a more solid commitment to it in a period of upheaval" (Mouat, 1992a [Online]). The world was entering a transition period created by the break up of the Soviet Union and collapse of the old world order. In a word, the leaders were engaging in "preventive" diplomacy as opposed to that for a crisis. Hopes were high also that cooperation could long last mark their meetings rather than the confrontation symbolic of the Cold War. Nevertheless, conflict always exists, at least potentially, for that is the *reason d'etre* of the UN.

The special nature of this meeting and its zeal to chart a new course for international affairs signal an important transition. Because of space limitations, only two of these addresses could be included. In the end, it was decided to include an address from President Mitterrand of France, for it was his idea for the conference. President Yeltsin of Russia also deserved special consideration because this was such an important juncture for both Russia and the world. Yeltsin's address is provided unabridged; Mitterrand's, with judicious deletions.

FRANCE

> While neither the US President, Mr. Bush, nor the British Prime Minister, Mr. Major, suggested anything of substance during their speeches, several other countries, including France, Russia [and some others], put forward proposals for change or in some cases made veiled criticisms of the US for having financially crippled the world body for not paying its full membership dues in recent years. (Peers, 1992 [Online])

Little was found in media reports of the day about President Mitterrand's address. Nevertheless, the circumstances of the end of the Cold War are well enough known to proceed. Read Mitterrand's address and respond to the pre- and post-questions.

QUESTIONS FOR ANALYSIS

1. If you were to remind a superpower (the US) that it owed back membership dues to the UN, how would you say it in your speech and when?
2. What vision does Mitterrand cast for a future world order?

FRANCOIS MITTERRAND
PRESIDENT OF FRANCE
UNITED NATIONS SECURITY COUNCIL, JANUARY 31, 1992
(Interpretation from French; Abridged)

First, Mr. President [Major], I should like to thank you for your initiative which has brought us together here as members of the Security Council. It is a very important event, as the Secretary General has just emphasized. I should like to tell him how pleased we are to see him today heading our great international society. I wish him every success in his work, in which we shall be unsparing in our support.

In addition to those words of encouragement, I should like to express our gratitude to Mr. Perez de Cuellar, gratitude which has already been so well expressed by you, Mr. President.

I myself had hoped for a meeting such as this 10 months ago, when we were at the end of a war waged to deal with aggression and to restore law and order, under the aegis of the United Nations. That was a new, but essential step, though the war of course inevitably brought suffering in its wake.

There have been many upheavals since then, with people thrown onto the road, civil wars and the disruption of vast political entities of long standing.

Where are we heading? We are looking for signposts, but we do not always find them. It is the role of the Security Council and the General Assembly to point the way.

Disorder and unpredictability have become the rule. It will be said that perhaps there are too many things happening at the same time and that the only constant today is change. But are we now to mourn the old order and prefer, with Goethe, the great German writer, injustice to disorder? Surely not! Liberty has grown in the world; we must continue to help it.

Are there any clear responses? It is true that a time of crisis, such as we are living through now, is also a time of choice. On the one hand there is war, exodus, the break-up of States and terrorism. Are they unavoidable? We can prevent them. That is my first assertion. Preventing them is precisely the primary task of the Security Council of the United Nations, in accordance with the Charter.

A meeting like today's has been needed since March of last year. Prime Minister Major was absolutely right: the time was ripe for inviting us here. By no means does everything depend on us—but a great deal does.

Let me join my colleagues in tracing the route we should follow. First of all, a world in crisis requires instruments for comprehensive, universal action; secondly, we must guarantee collective security; and finally, we must create new forms of solidarity.

Needless to say, my statement will not be exhaustive, for we have only a limited amount of time to say what we want to say—and that may be a good thing. I shall merely put forward a few ideas, a few plans.

It is a fact that since 1945 all the world's major problems have required a universal approach. We must now create the instruments for that universal action: instruments on security, on how to expand the means available to the Security Council for intervention. Take, for example, resolution 687 (1991), which put an end to the Kuwait war. Its strict implementation is necessary to restore peace in the Middle East, but it is not enough. The situation clearly calls for the creation of a zone free of weapons of mass destruction, which means the participation of all the States of the region—and of other regions. It also calls for universal adherence to the Treaty on the Non-Proliferation of Nuclear Weapons. For its part, France is in the process of ratifying that Treaty. France will also become a party to Additional Protocol I of the Treaty for the Prohibition of Nuclear Weapons in Latin America—the Treaty of Tlatelolco—whose twenty-fifth anniversary will be marked in two weeks.

But the establishment of such a zone requires also the adoption of a convention banning chemical weapons. That is possible, which is why I call upon all States to come to Paris to sign such a convention before the end of the year.

We should also try to monitor and limit arms transfers and, as so aptly proposed by President Bush and President Yeltsin, to accelerate genuine reductions in nuclear weapons. We should establish a closer link between the concepts of nonproliferation and disarmament, and so forth.

We are no longer engaged in a race towards over-armament; on the contrary. That is excellent news.

Everyone must now participate in nuclear disarmament, provided first and foremost that all States in question are able to see that their security is assured. There should not be vast differences among the nuclear potentials of various parties.

Economic interdependence [deserves attention also]. We have a great deal of ground to cover in order to reap the practical benefits of such interdependence. We are now in a position to decrease military budgets for the benefit of development. . . . We must continue the work already begun, for example, on the question of debt by considering the position of intermediate-income countries among the less wealthy. I would mention the case of Venezuela and France: without any great fanfare, we have been working since July to achieve an agreement between a consumer and a producer of oil.

We must revise many of our methods, our concepts and our approaches.

I shall not dwell on the question of the environment. Soon a conference on the subject will be held in Rio de Janeiro, where we shall have to take a broad view in order to save the planet while still enabling peoples to make progress. Peoples are often compelled to alter the natural balance, because they lack the means to live in any other way.

Human rights have triumphed—and I hope it is no temporary triumph—in the ideological struggle of the Cold War.

I am not proposing a new system. I merely remind the Council that democracy begins in the schools. We must consider and renew the role of the United Nations Educational, Scientific and Cultural Organization (UNESCO), to make it exemplary; we must consolidate it. It is time for the States that have left UNESCO to return and contribute to its great task.

Collective security will be jeopardized very quickly if we do not create up-to-date conditions for it. Past experience has shown that nothing can be done without the determination of States, particularly the major Powers, to reject the law of the jungle and the principle that might is right. That determination is reflected in the Charter of the United Nations. For a long time, the Charter was hobbled, but today all its provisions are usable, and we must implement them immediately.

I am certain that other colleagues will also be making proposals to ensure the greater effectiveness of peace-keeping operations. I state that for its part France is ready to make available to the Secretary General a 1,000-man contingent for peace-keeping operations, at a time, on 48-hours notice. That figure could be doubled within a week. Such deployments would involve activity by the Military Staff Committee, as provided for in the Charter.

Secondly, it is indispensable that we develop preventative diplomacy. Members of the Council should undertake systematically to provide the Secretary General with information on international security and to give him the mandate to maintain regular contacts with his counterparts, the leaders of regional organizations. Chapter VIII of the Charter, on regional arrangements, should no longer be disregarded, We must be able to turn as necessary to new bodies to meet specific needs.

On the relationship between disarmament and development, suggestions have recently been made, for example by Germany. Those are good suggestions, which is why France recommends the establishment of regional funds for the conversion of military research and development to civilian production [to benefit new] States: republics, with urgent needs, which once formed part of the former Soviet Union. I am certain that other countries too will be able to benefit, including States of the Middle East.

Similarly, on the model of Europe, why should we not establish in each region appropriate arbitrating bodies? The European Community already has such a body.

Those are a few of the possible instruments.

We must, moreover, ensure that the United Nations has regular, increasing financing. To that end, arrears must be paid. I am not making any specific allusions, but I would remind the Council that this would make it possible to demonstrate that a spirit of cooperation will be present in our work.

My third and last point concerns the conditions for a new solidarity. Security cannot be conceived solely in military terms. Obviously, it has an economic aspect which is in fact supreme over the other as time passes and so long as economic insecurity does not generate new military conflicts.

Many proposals can be made. North-South confrontation should not be allowed to replace the East-West confrontation. I am sure all will agree to that. Politics, like economics, disarmament, social development and the environment, takes us back to the same law—that of solidarity. For a long time now the general term "developing countries" has not been in keeping with reality. Twenty years ago, we could believe in general and uniform progress. Today, there is in truth two basic categories of countries: some have succeeded in making progress, but many others—particularly in Africa but elsewhere as well, such as in the Indochinese peninsula—are bogged down in a situation from which they cannot emerge without our assistance.

If there are many kinds of developing countries—to use the traditional term that I am challenging—we need adapted forms of aid. Those developing countries which really are developing need private and public investment, cheap credit, and growth in international trade. Hence the importance of international negotiations currently under way.

As for other countries which have not yet succeeded in bringing about true development, let us not mince words: how can they be reinjected into the world economy? We should really examine this, giving particular thought to the necessary control of primary commodities. Otherwise, intolerable situations will arise and countries of goodwill, which work and require a great deal of their citizens, often find themselves in terrible crises. Their two-, three- or five-year plans for recovery are demolished simply because in a single week international speculation has come into play.

Those are a few of the issues I would like the Council to consider. I very much hope—and my country is requesting it—that there will be a world summit on social development that will enable us to rejuvenate our thinking on development itself and to highlight the human dimension of things.

That is what I wished to say today. We are experiencing in Europe—in Western Europe particularly—an exceptional experiment: that of a community which has known atrocious wars. These wars monopolized the entire history of this century, piled destruction upon disaster, and long destroyed any chance our continent had. Well, we decided more than 40 years ago to settle our differences by negotiation, to bring about the necessary reconciliations and to learn to share our sovereignties and resources equally in the interests of security and the common good.

I do not wish to set that up as an example. Many others elsewhere have much to teach us by way of example. All are rich in tradition, culture and contributions to world civilization. I simply ask Your Excellencies to be good enough, on behalf of the Security Council of the United Nations, to exploit them.

Council President Major: I thank President Mitterrand for his remarks. The initiative for a meeting of this sort did originally spring from President Mitterrand some months ago, and I am delighted to have been able to bring it about today. (Mitterrand, 1992, pp. 13–22)

Questions for Analysis (Continued)

3. How are devices or apparent strategies used to organize this address?
4. How well are the topics ordered?
5. When and how are elements of dialogue used in the address?

6. How much does this address appear from someone who first suggested this Summit meeting?

THE RUSSIAN FEDERATION

"Boris Yeltsin, a giant at home but an uncertain quantity abroad, steps onto a world stage that is so far immune to [his] charms" and so began Lyons's (1992 [Online]) report on the Russian president before the Summit. The "uncertain quantity" about him arose from his reputation for drink and his skipping out on scheduled appointments with foreign dignitaries. Thus, "UN leaders basically [had] a dark image of Yeltsin" (*The Daily Yomiuri*, 1992 [Online]). "On what [was] widely regarded as the most important diplomatic trip of his career" (McFadden, 1992 [Online]), the future of Yeltsin's government rested on his gaining western support for his domestic reforms. Western financiers had concerns about the Russian financial condition, the breakup of the former Soviet military, and control of their nuclear weapons (Burke, 1992 [Online]). Yeltsin, therefore, had to "convince his western counterparts that his government [had] a coherent plan to ensure future economic, political, and military stability in the Commonwealth [of Independent States (CIS)]" (Burke, 1992 [Online]). In short, "if Yeltsin [could] demonstrate that he [was] a dependable pro-democracy leader and that he ha[d] a firm control over the CIS' nuclear weapons, his debut [as a world leader would] be a success" (*The Daily Yomiuri*, 1992 [Online]). One speech hardly could be expected to do it all, but it was Yeltsin who "stole the limelight" that day at the UN (Leopold, 1992 [Online]). His speech, then, merits attention all the more. Read President Yeltsin's address and respond to the pre- and post-questions.

QUESTIONS FOR ANALYSIS

1. Does Yeltsin project a "dark image" that others had of him before the Summit?
2. What vision does Yeltsin cast for a future world order?

BORIS YELTSIN
PRESIDENT OF THE RUSSIAN FEDERATION
UNITED NATIONS SECURITY COUNCIL, JANUARY 31, 1992
(Interpretation from Russian)

This summit meeting of the Security Council, the first of its kind on the political Olympus of the contemporary world, is a historic and unprecedented event. The end of the twentieth century is a time of great promise and new anxieties. The age-old search for truth and the attempt to discern what the future has in store for humanity seem to be getting a kind of a second wind. Perhaps for the first time ever there is now a real chance to put an end to despotism and to dismantle the totalitarian order, whatever shape it may take. I trust that after all the unthinkable tragedies and tremendous losses it has suffered, [human]kind will reject this legacy; it will not allow the twenty-first century to bring new suffering and privation to our children and grandchildren.

The process of profound change is already under way in various spheres of life, and above all in the economic sphere. It is a problem that concerns not just individual nations or states, but the whole of [human]kind. After all, it is an economy mutilated by ideological diktat and built in defiance of all common sense that forms the principal material base of totalitarianism. A profound awareness of this causal relationship has led the Russian leadership to embark upon a most difficult course of economic reform. We have taken that risk in a country where an all-out war was waged against economic interests for many decades.

I am grateful to the world community for its support of our efforts and for understanding that the future not only of the people of Russia but of the entire planet largely depends on whether or not these reforms are successful. I am also grateful to the people of Russia for their courage and steadfastness. They should take a great deal of credit for the fact that the world community is moving ever farther away from the totalitarian past.

Democracy is one of the major achievements of human civilization. All times and all countries have known people who have risen up selflessly in its defense. The people of Russia defended democracy at the walls of our Moscow White House. Now we must accomplish the most difficult task—that is, the creation of legal, political and socio-economic guarantees to make democratic changes irreversible.

All of us [are] weighed down by a tremendous burden of mutual mistrust. It is no secret that a most profound abyss has separated the two States that until recently were referred to as the super-Powers. This abyss must be bridged. That is the wish of our nations and the commitment of the Presidents of the United States of America and the Russian Federation.

The new political situation in the world makes it possible not only to advance new, original ideas but also to make even the most ambitious of them practicable. Our proposals have been outlined in our messages to the Secretary General of the United Nations, Mr. Boutros Boutros-Ghali, and the President of the United States, Mr. George Bush. Russia believes that the time has come to reduce considerably the presence of means of destruction on our planet. I am convinced that together we are capable of making the principle of minimum defence sufficiency a fundamental law of the existence of contemporary States. Today there are real opportunities for implementing deep cuts in strategic offensive arms and tactical nuclear weapons; resolutely moving towards significant limitations on nuclear testing and even towards its complete cessation; making antiballistic-missile defenses less complicated and costly and eliminating antisatellite systems; considerably reducing conventional armaments and armed forces; ensuring practical implementation of international agreements on the prohibition of chemical and bacteriological weapons; and enhancing the reliability of barriers to the proliferation of weapons of mass destruction.

The problem of experts engaged in the development and production of such weapons, including nuclear physicists, has lately become a top priority. No country has the right to use its talents for political gains, at the expense of international security. Russia is fully aware of its own responsibility and is taking steps to make provision for the social security of such experts. At the same time, we support the idea of establishing international centers which could coordinate appropriate research and support the most promising areas of work.

I think the time has come to consider creating a global defense system for the world community. It could be based on a reorientation of the United States Strategic Defense Initiative, to make use of high technologies developed in Russia's defense complex.

We are ready to participate actively in building and putting in place a pan-European collective security system—in particular during the Vienna talks and the upcoming post-Helsinki-II talks on security and cooperation in Europe.

Russia regards the United States and the West not as mere partners but rather as allies. This is a basic prerequisite for, I would say, a revolution in peaceful cooperation between progressive nations. We reject any subordination of foreign policy to pure ideology or ideological doctrines. Our principles are clear and simple: primacy of democracy, human rights and freedoms, legal and moral standards. I hope that this is something that our partners in the Commonwealth of Independent States also hold dear. We support their early admission to the United Nations and believe that this will have a beneficial impact on the evolution of the Commonwealth itself. The Commonwealth has been formed by the participating States on the basis of full equality and of their own free will. It rests on natural human ties among tens of millions of people. Russia is fully aware of its responsibility for making the Commonwealth of Independent States an important factor of stability in the world. This applies above all to nuclear forces. The participating states of the Commonwealth share the view that nuclear weapons are an integral part of the strategic forces of the Commonwealth under a single command and unified control.

Today talks are under way about the future of the armed forces of the former Union. The main task is to carry out the transformation of them in a civilized manner and on a clearly defined legal basis.

Our top priority is to guarantee all human rights and freedoms in their entirety, including political and civil rights and decent socio-economic and environmental living standards.

I believe that these questions are not an internal matter of States, but rather their obligations under the United Nations Charter, international covenants and conventions. We want to see this approach become a universal norm. The Security Council is called upon to underscore the civilized world's collective responsibility for the protection of human rights and freedoms.

In the near future Russia intends to adopt legislation that will reflect the highest international standards in the field of the protection of human freedom, honor and dignity. This applies above all to ensuring personal security, to the Criminal Code and the Correction Labor Code, to protection of Russian citizens abroad, to alternative military service and to other issues.

We are prepared to accede to the international instruments on migration and to join in the efforts of the United Nations High Commissioner for Refugees. I believe that the experience of the world community in these areas will be useful for Russia and other States of the Commonwealth.

A few days ago the 10 remaining political prisoners were pardoned by a decree of the President of the Russian Federation. There are no longer any prisoners of conscience in free Russia.

A special role in establishing a new international climate in the world belongs to the United Nations. This Organization has stood the test of time and managed, even in the ice age of confrontation, to preserve the nascent norms of civilized international cohabitation contained in its Charter.

We welcome the United Nations increased efforts to strengthen global and regional stability and to build a new democratic world order based on the equality of all States, big or small.

Russia is prepared to continue partnership between the permanent members of the Security Council. The current climate in the activities of this body is conducive to cooperative and constructive work.

For us, the peace-making experience of the United Nations is particularly valuable.

The new Russian diplomacy will contribute in every possible way to the final settlement of conflicts in various regions of the world that have been unblocked with the assistance of the United Nations. We are ready to become more fully engaged in these efforts.

We will make use of the effective role of the United Nations and the Security Council and take part in the search for lasting solutions to the Yugoslav and Afghan problems and for a normalization of the situation in the Near and Middle East, in Cambodia and in other regions.

I believe that we need a special rapid-response mechanism, as mentioned by President Mitterrand of France, to ensure peace and stability.

Upon decision of the Security Council it could be expeditiously activated in areas of crisis.

We are prepared to play a practical role in United Nations peace-keeping operations and contribute to their logistical support.

My country firmly supports steps to consolidate the rule of law throughout the world. It is necessary to enhance the prestige of the International Court of Justice as an effective instrument for the peaceful settlement of international disputes.

On the whole, I think it is high time we considered serious reform of the United Nations. The world has changed and certain areas of United Nations activities have lost their relevance. We should do away with those structures which yield no practical benefits to Member States. We are ready to present our proposals for reform of the United Nations.

It is a historical irony that the Russian Federation, a State with centuries-long experience in foreign policy and diplomacy, has only just appeared on the political map of the world. I am confident that the world community will find in Russia, as an equal participant in international relations and as a permanent member of the Security Council, a firm and steadfast champion of freedom, democracy and humanism.

Last year's events have confirmed that the nations of the world have now come of age and are capable of adopting responsible and meaningful decisions.This was vividly demonstrated by the developments in the Gulf, when our joint efforts resulted in the just punishment of the aggressor, and by the defeat of the coup in Moscow last August.

Difficult work lies ahead for us all to consolidate the positive trends in the evolution of today's world and to make them irreversible. It is only on this basis that we can ensure a decent and prosperous life for our nations and every individual. Russia is prepared to do all it can to achieve this goal.

In conclusion, permit me to wish Mr. Boutros-Ghali every success in his important post of Secretary General of the United Nations.
(Yeltsin, 1992, pp. 42–48)

Questions for Analysis (Continued)

3. What stance does Yeltsin take toward the United States and what are his related discourse strategies?
4. What telltale element of UN speechmaking is untypically used in Yeltsin's address?
5. In what ways did he break the mold of past Russian speechmaking at the UN?
6. How does he try to develop ethos for himself and his country?
7. How important is the role of topical order in this address?

CONSOLIDATION EXERCISE

1. Compare and contrast the addresses by Mitterrand and Yeltsin in regard to their apparent strategies of discourse. How did the purposes and situation of each speaker differ? How may have that influenced their organization and content?
2. Which speaker contributes more toward developing a vision for a future world order and why?

FOR FURTHER STUDY

Space does not permit including the other addresses made at the Summit. However, for those interested in further study, we would suggest obtaining them through interlibrary loan (unless your local library is a depository for UN collections) by requesting the UN records for the Security Council, S/PV.3046, pages 1 through 147. Selections include:

- Austria: Franz Vranitzky (pp. 61–67)
- Belgium: Wilfried Martens (pp. 67–75)
- Cape Verde: Carlos Carvalho Veiga (pp. 76–85)
- China: Li Peng (pp. 86–94)
- Ecuador: Rodrigo Borja-Cerallos (pp. 23–31)
- India: P. V. Narashimha Rao (pp. 95–102)
- Japan: Kiichi Miyazawa (pp. 102–112)
- Morocco: King Hassan II (pp. 32–42)
- Venezuela: Carlos Andres Perez (pp. 54–61)
- United Kingdom: John Major (pp. 135–147)
- United States: George Bush (pp. 49–55)

Addresses from Hungary and Zimbabwe are not listed because they were not from heads of state or government but from foreign ministers.

Suggested Starter Questions

1. A media report cited in this chapter found that the addresses from Bush and Major were unremarkable. Read their addresses to determine whether that report was justified.
2. Consider Major's address in terms of conflicting motivations of his for calling the Summit, as reported by *The Daily Yomiuri* (1992): One opinion was that Major, "fully aware of the global concern over the

collapse of the Soviet Union, realize[d] a renewed international call for a stronger UN [was] needed." The other had it that "Major's efforts [were] an attempt to divert people's attention from the knotty domestic issues" of the day.

3. Compare Major's with Mitterrand's in terms of the need for a renewal of the UN or for projecting a vision for a new world order. Which address appears more effective and why?
4. Compare the addresses collectively from the permanent members with those of the nonpermanent ones for commonalties and contrasts.
5. Consider more comprehensively why Yeltsin captured the limelight. Was this more a result of the Soviet Union's breakup or a matter of his speech address? What other address (or addresses) from the Summit rival his in effectiveness?
6. (If able to have a nearly complete set of addresses): Compare Major's language used as the moderator for the addresses. Does he use a formula? If so, what is that formula? Or does he make individual comments for each address and speaker? If so, how does he differ his comments?

13

FREEDOM, HUMAN RIGHTS, AND WOMEN'S RIGHTS

In this chapter, two final addresses are presented, without guidelines, media reports, or application, so that you may undertake your own investigation, and also because both addresses stress major ethical, cultural, and moral perspectives as presented to UN audiences, and both which have a much broader appeal than the immediate audience.

In September 1995, the UN World Forum on Women was held in Beijing, People's Republic of China. An American delegation leader, the former Congresswoman Bella Abzug, said that it was not the world forum on woman, but the women's forum on the world. This was the sixth of the major UN conferences leading up to and away from the 50th anniversary: the UN Conference on Children in 1990, the UN Summit on the Environment in 1992, the UN Conference on Human Rights in 1993, the UN Conference on Social Development in 1994, the UN Conference on Population in 1995, the UN World Forum on Women in 1995, and the UN Habitat II on Cities in 1996. More than 30,000, mostly women, attended the Beijing Nongovernmental Preparatory meetings before the actual conference. There were 5,000 delegates at the Forum itself. Hillary Rodham Clinton attended the conference for 2 days and gave a speech to the World Health Organization Forum on Women and Health Security, September 5, 1995, emphasizing the health rights of women as human rights.

In 1995, during the 50th anniversary of the UN, Pope John Paul II made his second visit to the UN. His first visit was in 1979. His leadership of the Roman Catholic Church represented at the UN by the Holy See and as Head of State of the tiny Vatican State provided him a far greater moral voice than is typical for the heads of state or government for many world leaders. His high charisma was evident in most of the more than

70 countries that he visited during his papacy. His celebration of Mass and his homily at the 1994 World Youth Conference in the Philippines is estimated to have attracted the most people at any single event in the world—more than 5 million. In his address to the UN, October 5, 1995, he spoke in Arabic, Chinese, English, French, Russian, and Spanish—the six working languages of the UN. His theme of human freedom was widely praised in the media.

HILLARY RODHAM CLINTON
FIRST LADY OF THE UNITED STATES OF AMERICA
WORLD HEALTH ORGANIZATION FORUM
ON WOMEN AND HEALTH SECURITY
BEIJING, CHINA, SEPTEMBER 5, 1995

Thank you, Dr. Nakajima.

Dr. Nakajima, Dr. Sadik, Gertrude Mongella, delegates to the Fourth UN Conference on Women, and guests from all over the world, I am honored to be here this morning among women and girls everywhere.

I commend the World Health Organization for making women's health a top priority and for establishing the Global Commission on Women's Health.

I am proud that in the Preparatory meetings for this Fourth World Conference on Women, the United States took the lead in highlighting importance of a comprehensive approach to women's health. That approach builds on actions taken at previous women's conferences and the recent conferences at Cairo and Copenhagen, whose goals to promote the health and well-being of all people were endorsed by 180 nations.

Cairo was particularly significant as governmental and non-governmental participants worked together to craft a Program for Action which, among other things, calls for universal access to good quality reproductive health care services, including safe, effective, voluntary family planning; greater access to education and health care; more responsibility on the part of men in sexual and reproductive health and childbearing; and reeducation of wasteful resource consumption.

Here at this conference, improving girls and women's health is a priority of the draft Platform for Action. It includes such goals as: Access to universal primary health are for all people—a goal not yet achieved in many countries, including my own. The promotion of breast feeding. The provision of safe drinking water and sanitation. Research in and attention to women's health issues, including: environment hazards, prevention of HIV/AIDS and other sexually transmitted disease, encouragement for adolescents to postpone sexual activity and childbearing, and discouragement of cultural traditions and customs that deny food and health care to girls and women.

Goals such as these illustrate a new commitment to the well-being of girls and women and a belief in their rights to live up to there own God-given potentials.

At long last, people and their government everywhere are beginning to understand that investing in the health of women and girls is as important to the prosperity of nations as investing in the development of open markets and trade. The health of women and girls cannot be divorced from progress on other economic and social issues.

Scientists, doctors, nurses, community leaders and women themselves are working to improve and safeguard the health of women and families all over the world. If we join together as a global community, we can lift up the health and dignity of all women and their families in the remaining years of the 20th century and on into the next millennium.

Yet, for all the promise the future holds, we also know that many barriers lie in our way. For too long, women have been denied access to health care, education, economic opportunities, legal protection and human rights—all of which are used as building blocks for a healthy and productive life.

In too many places today, the health of women and families is compromised by inadequate, inaccessible and unaffordable medical care, lack of sanitation, unsafe drinking water, poor nutrition, insufficient research and education about women's health issues, and coercive and abusive sexual practices.

In too many places, the status of women's health is a picture of human suffering and pain. The faces in that picture are of girls and women who, but for the grace of God or the accident of birth, could be us or one of our sisters, mothers or daughters.

Today, at least fifteen percent of pregnant women suffer life threatening complications and more than one-half million women around the world die from childbirth. Most of these deaths could be prevented with basic primary, reproductive and emergency obstetric health care. In some places, there are 175,000 motherless children for every one million families. Many of those children don't survive. And of those who do, many are recruited into a life of exploitation on the streets of our world's cities, subjected daily to abuse, indignity, disease, and the specter of early death.

There must be a renewed commitment to improving maternal health. The WHO launched in 1987 Safe Motherhood initiative to halve maternal mortality by the year 2000. To reach that goal, more attention must be paid to emergency medical care as well as primary prenatal care. Providing emergency obstetric care is a relatively cheep way of saving lives—

and along with family planning service is among the most cost-effective interventions in even the poorest of countries.

The commitment of the WHO and its Global Commission on Women's Health to make childbearing and childbirth a safe and healthy period of every woman's life deserves action on the part of every nation represented here.

One hundred million women cannot obtain or are not using family planning services because they are poor, uneducated or lack access to care. Twenty million of these women will seek unsafe abortion—some will die, some will be disabled for life. A growing number of unwanted pregnancies are occurring among young women, barely behind childhood themselves. As we know, when children have children, the chance of schooling, jobs, and good health is reduced for both parent and child. And our progress as a human family takes another step back.

The Cairo document recognizes "the basic rights of all couples and individuals to decide freely and responsibly the number, spacing and timing of their children and to have the information and means to do so." Women should have the right to health care that will enable them to go safely through pregnancy and childbirth and provide them with the best chance of having a healthy infant.

Women and men must also have the right to make those most intimate of all decisions free of discrimination, coercion and violence, particularly any coercive practices that force women into abortions or sterilizations.

On these issues, the US supports the provisions in the Beijing Platform for Action that reaffirm consensus language that was agreed to at the Cairo Conference about a year ago. It declared that "in no case should abortion be promoted as a method of family planning." The Platform asks governments "to strengthen their commitment to women's health, to deal with the health impact of unsafe abortion as a major public health concern and to reduce the recourse to abortion through expanded and improved family planning services."

Violence against women remains a leading cause of death among girls and women between the ages of 14 and 44—violence from ethnic and religious conflicts, crime on the streets and brutality in the home. For women who survive the violence, what often awaits them is a life of unrelenting physical and emotional pain that destroys their capacity for mothering, homemaking or working and can lead to substance abuse, and even suicide.

Violence against girls and women goes beyond the beatings, rape, killings and forced prostitution that arise from poverty, wars and domestic conflicts. Every day, more than 5,000 young girls are forced to endure the brutal practice of genital mutilation. The procedure is painful and life-threatening. It is degrading. And it is a violation of the physical integrity of a women's body, leaving a lifetime of physical and emotional scars.

HIV, AIDS, and sexually transmitted disease threaten more and more women—and experts predict that by the end of this decade more than half of the people in the world with HIV will be women. AIDS, which threatens whole families and regions, demands the strongest possible response. Government and the international community must address head-on the growing number of women who are being infected.

More then 700,000 women worldwide face breast cancer each year—over 300,000 die of it. It's the leading cause of death for women in their prime in the developed world. In the time I speak to you today, 25 women around the world will die of breast cancer. In my own country it is hard to find a family, an office, or a neighborhood that has not been touched by this disease. My mother-in-law struggled against breast cancer for four years before losing her battle.

Tobacco use is the number one preventable cause of death. Ninety percent of women who smoke began to smoke as adolescents—leading to high rates of heart disease, cancer, and chronic lung disease later in life.

As the WHO points out, we also need to recognize and effectively address the fact that women are far more likely to be exposed to work related and environment health hazards. Policies to alleviate and eliminate such health hazards associated within the home and in the workplace demand action.

Research also indicates that certain communicable diseases affect women in greater numbers. Tuberculosis, for example, is responsible for the deaths of one million women each year and those in their early reproductive years are most vulnerable.

When health care systems around the world don't work for women; when our mothers, daughters, sisters, friends, and co-workers are denied access to quality care because they are poor, do not have health insurance, or simply because they are women, it is just not their health that is put at risk. It is the health of their families and communities as well.

Like many nations, the United States brings to this conference a serious commitment to improving women's health. We bring with us a series of initiatives which represent the first steps to carrying out this conference's Platform for Action.

We are continuing to work for health care reform to ensure that every citizen has access to affordable, quality care.

We are proposing a comprehensive and coordinated plan to reduce smoking by children and adolescents by 50 percent.

We are working to address the many factors that contribute to teenage pregnancy, our most serious social problem, by encouraging abstinence and personal responsibility on the part of young men and women; improving access to health care and family planning services; and supporting health education in our schools.

We are pursuing a public policy agenda on HIV/AIDS that is specific to women, adolescent and children.

We are continuing to fund and conduct contraceptive research and development.

We are addressing the health needs of women through initiatives such as these:

- The National Action Plan on Breast Cancer—a public, private partnership working with all agencies of government, the media, scientific organizations, advocacy groups and industry to advance breast health and eradicate breast cancer as a threat to the lives of American women.
- An Expansion of the National Breast and Cervical Cancer Early Detection Program—which will ensure that women who need regular screening and detection services have access to them, and that those services meet quality standards.
- The inclusion of women in clinical trials for research and testing or drugs or other interventions that probe specific differences between men and women in patterns of disease and reactions to therapy.
- The special health care needs of older-women will be addressed through educational campaigns about osteoporosis, cancer and other disease.
- And the US is conducting the largest clinical research study ever undertaken to examine the major causes of death, disability and frailty in post-menopausal women.

Women's health must be a priority of all people and governments working together. Without good health, a woman's God-given potential can never be realized. And without healthy women, the world's potential can never be realized.

So let us join together to ensure that every little boy and girl that comes into our world is healthy and wanted; that every young woman has the education and economic opportunity to live a healthy life; and that every woman has access to the health care she needs throughout her life to fulfill her potential in her family, her work, and her community.

If we care about the futures of our daughters, our sons, and the generations that will follow them, we can do nothing less.

Thank you for the work you do everyday to bring better health to the women, children, and families of this world. Thank you for helping governments and citizens around the world understand that we cannot talk about equality and social development without also talking about health care.

Most of all, thank you for being part of this historic and vital discussion, which holds so much promise for our future.

(Text as prepared for delivery, First Lady Hillary Rodham Clinton, Remarks for the World Health Organization Forum on Women and Health Security, Beijing, China [Online: CRTNET].)

POPE JOHN PAUL II
THE HOLY SEE
UNITED NATIONS GENERAL ASSEMBLY, OCTOBER 5, 1995

Mr. President, ladies and gentlemen,

It is an honor to have the opportunity to address this international assembly and to join the men and women of every country, race, language and culture in celebrating the 50th anniversary of the founding of the United Nations Organization.

In coming before this distinguished assembly, I wish to express my heartfelt gratitude in the first place to the secretary general, Dr. Boutros Boutros-Ghali, for having warmly encouraged this visit. And I thank you Mr. President, for your cordial welcome. I greet all of you, the members of this General Assembly: I am grateful for your presence and your kind attention.

Ladies and gentlemen! On the Threshold of a new millennium, we are witnessing an extraordinary global acceleration of that quest for freedom which is one of the great dynamics of human history. This phenomenon is not limited to any one part of the world; nor is it the expression of any single culture. Men and women throughout the world, even when threatened by violence, have taken the risk of freedom, asking to be given a place in social, political, and economic life which is commensurate with their dignity as free human beings. This universal longing for freedom is truly one of the distinguishing marks of our time.

It is important for us to grasp what might be called inner structure of this worldwide movement. It is precisely its global character which offers us its first and fundamental "key" and confirms that there are indeed universal human rights, rooted in the nature of the person, rights which reflect the objective and inviolable demands of a universal moral law.

These are not abstract points; rather, these rights tell us something important about the actual life of every individual and of every social group. They also remind us that we don't live in an irrational or meaningless world. On the contrary, there is a moral logic which is built into human life and which makes possible dialogue between individuals and peoples. If we want a century of violent coercion to be succeeded by a century of persuasion, we must find a way to discuss the human future intelligibly. The universal moral law written on the human heart is precisely that king of "grammar" which is needed if the world is to engage this discussion of its future.

The moral dynamics of this universal quest for freedom clearly appeared in Central and Eastern Europe during the nonviolent revolutions of 1989. Unfolding specific times and places, those historical events nonetheless taught a lesson which goes far beyond a specific geographical location. For the nonviolent revolution of 1989 demonstrated that the quest for freedom cannot be suppressed. It arises from a recognition of the inestimable dignity and value of the human person, and it cannot fail to be accompanied by a commitment on behalf of the human person. Modern totalitarianism has been, first and foremost, an assault on the dignity of the person, an assault which has gone even to the point of denying the inalienable value of the individual's life.

The revolutions of 1989 were made possible by the commitment of the brave men and women inspired by a different, and ultimately more profound and powerful, vision: the vision of men as creatures of intelligence and free will, immersed in a mystery which transcends his own being and endowed with the ability to reflect and the ability to choose—and thus capable of wisdom and virtue. A decisive factor in the success of those nonviolent revolutions was the experience of social solidarity: In the face of regimes backed by the power of propaganda and terror, that reminder that it is possible for men's historical journey to follow a path which is true to the finest aspirations of the human spirit.

The quest for freedom in the second half of the 20th century as engaged not only individuals but nations as well. Fifty years after the end of the Second World War, it is important to stress the rights of nations.

Unfortunately, even after the end of the Second World War, the rights of the nations continued to be violated. To take but one set of examples, the Baltic states and extensive territories in Ukraine and Berlarus were absorbed into the Soviet Union, as had already happened to Armania, Azerbaijan, and Georgia in the Caucasus. At the same time, the so-called "People's Democracies" of Central and Eastern Europe effectively lost their sovereignty and were required to submit to the will dominating the entire bloc. The result of this artificial division of Europe was the "Cold War," a situation of international tension in which the threat of a nuclear holocaust hung over humanity. It was only when freedom was restored to the nations of Central and Eastern Europe that the promise of the peace which should have come with the end of the war began to be realized for many of the victims of that conflict.

A study of these rights is certainly not easy, if we consider the difficulty of defining the very concept of "nation," which cannot be identified a priori and necessarily with the state. Such a study must nonetheless be made, if we wish to avoid the errors of the past and ensure a just world order.

A proposition of a nation's right is certainly its right to exist: Therefore no one—neither a State nor another nation, not an international organization—is ever justified in asserting that an individual nation is not worthy of existence. This fundamental right to existence does not necessarily call for sovereignty as a state, since various forms of juridical aggregation between different nations are possible, as for example occurs in federal states, in confederations or in states characterized by broad regional autonomies. There can be historical circumstances in which aggregations different from single state sovereignty can even prove advisable, but only on condition that this takes place in climates of true freedom, guaranteed by the exercise of the self-determination of the people concerned. Its right to exist, naturally implies that every nation also enjoys the right to its own language and culture, through which a people expresses and promotes that which I would call its character.

History shows that in extreme circumstances (such as those which occurred in the land where I was born) it is precisely its culture that enables a nation to survive the loss of political and economic independence. Every nation therefore has the right to shape its life according to its own traditions, excluding, of course every abuse of basic human rights and in particular the education for the younger generations.

During my pastoral pilgrimages to the communities of the Catholic Church over the past 17 years, I have been able to enter into dialogue with the rich diversity of nations and cultures in every part of the world. Unhappily, the world has yet to learn how to live with diversity, as recent events in Balkans and central Africa have painfully reminded us. The fact of "differences" and the reality of "the other" can sometimes be felt as a threat. Amplified by historic grievances and exacerbated by the manipulations of the unscrupulous, the fear of "difference" can lead to a denial of the very humanity of "the other": with the result that people fall into a cycle of violence in which no one is spared, not even the children. We are all very familiar today with such situations; at this very moment my heart and my prayers turn in a special way to the sufferings of the sorely tried people of Bosnia-Herzegovina.

From bitter experience, then, we know that the fear of "difference," especially when it expresses itself in a narrow and exclusive nationalism which denies any rights to "the other," can lead to a true nightmare of violence and terror. And yet if we make the effort to look at matters objectively, we can see that, transcending all the differences which distinguish individuals and peoples, there is a fundamental commonality. For different cultures are but different ways of facing the question of the meaning of personal existence. And it is precisely here that we found one source of the respect which is due to every culture and every nation: Every culture is an effort to ponder the mystery of the world and in particular of the human person. It is a way of giving expression to the transcendent dimension of the human life. The heart of every culture is its approach to the greatest of all mysteries: the mystery of God. Our respect for the culture of others is therefore rooted in our respect for each community's attempt to answer the question of human life. And here we can see how important it is to safeguard the fundamental fight for freedom of religion and freedom of conscience, as the cornerstones of the structure of human rights and the foundation of every truly free society. No one is permitted to suppress those rights by using coercive power to impose an answer to the mystery of man.

We need to clarify the essential difference between unhealthy forms of nationalism, which teaches contempt for other nations or cultures, and patriotism, which is a proper love of one's country. True patriotism never seeks to advance the well-being of one's own nation at the expense of others. For in the end, this would harm one's own nation as well: doing wrong damages both aggressor and victim. Nationalism, it's most radical forms, is thus the antithesis of true patriotism, and today we must ensure that extreme nationalism does not continue to give rise to new forms of the aberrations of totalitarianism.

Ladies and gentlemen! Freedom is the measure of man's dignity and greatness. Living the freedom sought by individuals and peoples is a great challenge to man's spiritual growth and to the moral vitality of nations. The basic question which we must all face today is the responsible use of freedom, in both its personal and social dimensions. Our reflection must turn then to the question of moral structure of freedom, which is the inner architecture of the culture of freedom.

Freedom is not simply the absence of tyranny or oppression. Nor is freedom a license to do whatever we like. Freedom has an inner "logic" which distinguishes it and ennobles it: Freedom is ordered to the truth, and is fulfilled in a man's quest for truth and in man's living in truth. Detached from the truth of the human person, freedom deteriorates into license in the lives of individuals, and, in the political life, it becomes the caprice of the most powerful and the arrogance of power. Far from being a limitation upon freedom or a threat to it, reference to the truth about the human person—a truth universally knowable through the moral law written on the hearts of all—is, in fact, the guarantor of freedom's future. In the light of what we said we understand how utilitarianism, the doctrine which defines morality not in terms of what is good but what is advantageous, threatens the freedom of individuals and nations and obstructs the building of a true culture of freedom. Utilitarianism often has devastating political consequences, because it inspires an aggressive nationalism (where a) smaller or weaker claimed to be a good thing solely because it corresponds to the nation's interest. No less grave are the results of economic utilitarianism that drive more powerful countries to manipulate and exploit weaker ones.

Nationalistic and economic utilitarianism are sometimes combined, a phenomenon which has too often characterized relations between the "North" and the "South," for the emerging countries, the achievement of political independence has too frequently been accompanied by a situation of de facto economic dependence on other countries. Such situations offend the conscience of humanity and pose a formidable moral challenge to the human family.

Yes, distinguished ladies and gentlemen! The international economic scene needs an ethic of solidarity, if participation, economic growth, and a just distribution of goods are to characterize the future of humanity. The international cooperation called for by the Charter of the United Nations for "solving international problems of an economic, social, culture, or humanitarian character" cannot be conceived exclusively in terms of help and assistance, or even by considering the eventual returns on the rescue provided. When millions of people are suffering from a poverty which means hunger, malnutrition, sickness, illiteracy, and degradation, we must not only remind ourselves that no one has a right to exploit another for his own advantage, but also above all we must recommit ourselves to that solidarity which enables others to live out, in the actual circumstances of their economic and political lives, the creativity which is a distinguishing mark of the human person and the true source of wealth of nations in today's world.

As we face these enormous challenges, how can we fail to acknowledge the role of the United Nations Organization? The United Nations Organization needs to raise more and more above the cold status of an administrative institution and to become a moral center where all the nations of the world feel at home and develop a shared awareness of being, as it were, a "family of nations." The idea of "family" immediately evokes something more than simple functional relations or a mere convergence of interests. The family is (worthy of lasting) and sincere respect. In an authentic family the strong do not dominate; instead, the weaker members, because of their very weakness, are all the more welcomed and served.

Raised to the level of the "family of nations," these sentiments ought to be, even before the law itself, the very fabric of relations between peoples. The United Nations has the historic, even momentous, task of promoting this qualitative leap in international life, not only by serving as a center of effective mediation for the resolution of conflict but also by fostering values, attitudes and concrete initiatives of solidarity which prove capable of raising the level or relations between nations from the "organizational" to a more "organic" level, from simple "existence with" others to "existence for" others, in a fruitful exchange of gifts, primarily for the good of the weaker nations but even so, a clear harbinger of greater good for everyone.

None of this should appear an unattainable utopia. Now is the time for new hope, which calls us to expel the paralyzing burden of cynicism from the future of politics and of human life. The anniversary which we are celebrating invites us to this by reminding us the idea of "united nations," an idea which bespeaks mutual trust, security and solidarity. Inspired by the example of all those who have taken the risk of freedom, can we not recommit ourselves also to taking the risk of solidarity—and thus the risk of peace?

It is one of the great paradoxes of our time that man, who began the period we call "modernity" with a self-confident assertion of "coming of age" and "autonomy," approaches the end of the 20th Century fearful of himself, fearful of what he might be capable of, fearful for the future. Indeed the second half of the 20th Century has seen the unprecedented phenomenon of a humanity uncertain about the very likelihood of a future, given the threat of nuclear war. The danger, mercifully, appears to have receded—and everything that might make it return needs to be rejected firmly and universally; all the same, fear for the future and of the future remains.

In order to ensure that the millennium now approaching will witness a new flourishing of the human spirit, mediated through an authentic culture of freedom, men and women must learn to conquer fear. We must learn not to be afraid; we must rediscover a spirit of trust. Hope is not empty optimism springing from a naive confidence that the future will necessarily be better than the past. Hope and trust are the premise of responsible activity and are the assurance that man is "alone with God" and he thus perceives that he is not alone amid the enigmas of existence, for he is surrounded by the love of the Creator.

Hope and trust: These may seem beyond the purview of the United Nations. But they are not. The politics of nations with which your organization is principally concerned, can never ignore the transcendent, spiritual dimension of the human experience, and could never ignore it without harming the cause of man and cause of human freedom. Whatever diminishes man harms the cause of freedom. In order to recover our hope and trust at the end of this century of sorrows, we must regain a sign of that transcendent horizon of possibility to which the soul of man aspires. As a Christian, my hope and trust are centered on Jesus Christ, the 2,000th anniversary of whose birth will be celebrated at the coming of the new millennium. We Christians believe that in his death and resurrection were fully revealed God's love and his care for all creations.

Jesus Christ is for us, God-made man, and made a part of the history of humanity. Precisely for this reason, Christian hope for the world and its future extends to every human person. Because of the radiant humanity of Christ, nothing genuinely human fails to touch the hearts of Christians.

Therefore, as we approach the 2,000th anniversary of the birth of Christ, the church asks only to propose respectfully this message of salvation, and to be able to promote, in charity and service, the solidarity of the entire human family.

We must overcome our fear of the future. But we will not be able to overcome it completely unless we do so together. The "answer" to that fear is neither coercion nor repression, nor the imposition of one social "model" on the entire world. The answer to the fear which darkens human existence at the end of the 20th century is the common effort to build the civilization of love, founded on the universal values of peace, solidarity, justice, and liberty. And the "soul" of the civilization of love is culture of freedom: the freedom of nations, lived in self-giving solidarity and responsibility.

We must not be afraid of the future. We must not be afraid. Every human person has been created in the "image and likeness" of the One who is the origin of all that is. We have within us the capacities for wisdom and virtue. With these gifts, and with the help of God's grace, we can build in the next century and the next millennium a civilization worthy of the human person a true culture of freedom. We can and must do so! And in doing so, we shall see that the tears of this century have prepared the ground for a new springtime of human spirit.

I should say a small greeting in the Arabic language and in Chinese: The United Nations says peace and the prosperity of the human family. I wish to the whole world and all peoples, freedom and peace in living together. The entire world can live in freedom and dignity and a truly achieved peace.

(Pope John Paul II, United Nations General Assembly, October 5 1995. He spoke in the six working languages of the UN: Arabic, Chinese, English, French, Russian, and Spanish [Online: CRTNET].)

APPENDIX

For further study of the UN, the selections that follow may prove useful. The most important document, of course, is *The Charter of the United Nations and Status of the International Court of Justice* (United Nations, n.d.). Also considered "must reading" are two annual handbook series. One is produced by the New Zealand Ministry of Foreign Affairs and Trade and is titled *United Nations Handbook* (Aorere, 1996). Another annual series is authored by Tessitore and Woolfson (e.g. 1995; 1996): *A Global Agenda: Issues before the 50th General Assembly of the United Nations* and *Issues before the 51st General Assembly.* These latter ones detail issues before the General Assembly, the Security Council, and other UN agencies.

UN publications with similar goals are *Future Role of the United Nations in an Interdependent World* (1989); *Handbook of Foreign Policy Analysis* (1989); *Global Outlook 2000* (1990); and *Basic Facts about the United Nations* (1995). *Our Global Neighborhood* is a product of the Commission on Global Governance, created by the UN General Assembly (Commission on Global Governance, 1995). *A Global Affair: An Inside Look at the United Nations,* with extensive photographs, effectively covers the first fifty years of the United Nations (Janello & Jones, 1995).

Secretary General Javiar Perez de Cuellar's *Anarchy or Order: Annual Reports 1982–1991* include all his annual reports to the UN during his 10-year term (Perez de Cuellar, 1991), and Secretary General Boutros Boutros-Ghali has authored both *An Agenda for Peace* (1995) and *An Agenda for Development* (1995).

During the late 1980s and the 1990s, the UN itself began to publish the "Blue Book Series," which basically includes UN documents on a particular issue. Of general interest among these "Blue Books" and others published by the UN are: *Future, Role of the United Nations in an Interdependent World* (1989); *Handbook of Foreign Policy Analysis* (1989); *Global Outlook: 2000* (1990); *The United Nations in the 1990's: A Second Change?* (1993); *World Court: What it is and How it Works* (1994); *World Social Situation in the 1990's* (1994); and *World Media Handbook: Selected Country Profiles* (1995).

"Blue Books" and other books relating to disarmament and peaceful resolution of disputes published by the UN include: *The Blue Helmets: A Review of United Nations Peacekeeping Forces* (1990); *Peaceful Settlement of Disputes Between States: A Selected Bibliography* (1991); *The United Nations: Disarmament and Security, Evolution* (1991); *Verification and the United Nations: The Role of the Organization in Multilateral Arms Limitations and Disarmament Agreements* (1991); *Handbook on Peaceful Settlement of Disputes Between States* (1992); *The United Nations and Nuclear Non-Proliferation* (1995); *The Unfinished Disarmament Agenda* (1995); and *United Nations Peacekeeping Information Notes* (1995).

A general human rights "Blue Book" published by the UN is *The United Nations and Human Rights 1948–1995* (1995). Related to our interest in the Middle East are the following UN publications: *Prospects for Peace in the Middle East: An Israeli-Palestinian Dialogue (Helsinki Encounter)* (1992); *Promoting a Culture for Peace in the Middle East: An Israeli-Palestinian Dialogue* (1994); and *Prerequisites for Peace in the Middle East* (1995). Based on our chapter on southern Africa, the following UN publications are helpful: *Regional and Confidence-Building Processes: The Case of Southern Africa* (1993); and *The United Nations and Apartheid 1948–1995* (1995).

Two UN sources related to women's rights and the Beijing Conference on Women are: *The United Nations and the Advancement of Women, 1945–1995* (1995); and *From Nairobi to Beijing: Second Review and Appraisal of the Implementation of the Nairobi Forward-Looking Strategies for the Advancement of Women* (1995).

REFERENCES

ABC News. (1995a, October 20). *World News Tonight* [TV broadcast].

ABC News. (1995b, October 23). *World News Tonight* [TV broadcast].

ABC News. (1996, March 26). *World News Now* [TV broadcast].

Adams, J. Q. (1969). Lectures on rhetoric and oratory. In T. W. Benson & M. H. Prosser (Eds.), *Readings in classical rhetoric.* Boston: Allyn and Bacon.

Adler, R. & Towne, N. (1978). *Looking out/looking in* (2nd ed.). New York: Holt, Rinehart & Winston.

Ahidjo, A. (1963, October 17). In Prosser (1970), pp. 981–997.

Alemán, M. (1947, May 3). In Prosser (1970), pp. 45–47.

Alford, D. K. H. (1978). The demise of the Whorf hypothesis. *Proceedings of the fourth annual meeting of the Berkeley Linguistics Society.* Berkeley, CA: Berkeley Linguistics Society.

Allerton, D. J. (1979). *Essentials of grammatical theory.* London: Routledge & Kegan Paul.

Andrews, J. R. (Ed.). (1990). *The practice of rhetorical criticism.* New York: Longman.

Anton, K. H. (1991, December 7). Japan faces the ugly truth of racial discrimination. *The Japan Times,* p. 23.

Anttila, R. (1977). Dynamic fields and linguistic structure: A proposal for a gestalt linguistics. *Die Sprache,* 23, 1.

Aorere, M. (1996). *United Nations handbook, 1996.* Wellington, N. Z.: New Zealand Ministry of Foreign Affairs and Trade.

Arafat, Y. (1990, May 25). In United Nations Security Council record S/PV/2923, pp. 3–35.

Arieff, I. (1988a, September 25). Flurry of meetings set for Reagan's final UN visit. Reuters [Online: Lexus Nexus].

Arieff, I. (1988b, September 26). Reagan in UN speech steps up bid for chemical weapons ban. Reuters, pp. 1–3.

Arieff, I. (1988c, September 27). Reagan shuns substance in farewell talks with Allied ministers. Reuter Library Report [Online: Lexus Nexus].

Aristotle. (1969). Rhetoric. In T. W. Benson & M. H. Prosser. (Eds.) *Readings in classical rhetoric.* Boston: Allyn and Bacon.

Arnold, C. C., Ehninger, D., & Gerber, J. C. (1966). *The speaker's resource book.* Glenview, IL: Scott, Foresmann & Company.

Augustine, St. (1969). On Christian doctrine. In T. W. Benson & M. H. Prosser (Eds.), *Readings in classical rhetoric.* Boston: Allyn and Bacon.

Bailey, S. D. (1964). *The General Assembly of the United Nations* (Rev. ed.). Westport, CT: Greenwood Press.

Baldwin, C. S. (1969). Medieval rhetoric and poetic. In T. W. Benson & M. H. Prosser (Eds.), *Readings in classical rhetoric.* Boston: Allyn and Bacon.

Bateson, G. (1979). *Mind and nature.* New York: E. P. Dutton.

BBC. (1985, June 11). Nicaragua's case against USA at International Court of Justice [Online: Lexus Nexus].

BBC. (1992, February 3). Yeltsin addresses Security Council. BBC Summary of World Broadcasts [Online: Lexus Nexus].

Beale, W. H. (1987). *A pragmatic theory of rhetoric.* Carbondale, Il: Southern Illinois University Press.

Beaugrande, R. de. (1984). *Text production: Toward a science of composition.* Norwood, NJ: Ablex.

Beaugrande, R. de. (1985). Text linguistics in discourse studies. In T. A. van Dijk (Ed.), *Handbook of discourse analysis: Vol. 1. Disciplines of discourse.* New York: Academic Press.

Beaugrande, R. de. & Dressler, W. (1981). *Introduction to text linguistics.* London: Longman.

Bell, D. (1978). *The cultural contradictions of capitalism.* New York: Basic Books.

Benites, Ambassador. (1964). In M. H. Prosser. A rhetorical analysis of the speechmaking of Adlai E. Stevenson on major issues in the United Nations during the fifteenth and sixteenth General Assembly. Unpublished doctoral dissertation, University of Illinois.

Benson, T. W. & Prosser, M. H. (Eds.). (1969). *Readings in classical rhetoric.* Boston: Allyn and Bacon.

Bernstein, R. (1994, October 4). Mandela thanks UN for apartheid fight. *New York Times* [Online: Lexus Nexus].

Berry, J. W., Poortinga, Y. H., Segall, M. H., & Dasen, P. R. (1992). *Cross-cultural psychology.* New York: Cambridge University Press.

Bhatia, V. K. (1993). *Analyzing genre.* London & New York: Longman.

Bishop, P. (1990, May 26). Arafat tells UN of war threat to Middle East. *The Daily Telegraph* [Online: Lexus Nexus].

Blair, H. (1968). Lectures on rhetoric and belle lettres. In J. L. Golden & E. P. J. Corbett, Jr. (Eds.), *The rhetoric of Blair, Campbell, and Whatley.* New York: Holt, Rinehart and Winston.

Bloomfield, D. M. (1990, May 26). Going over the edge at the summit. *The Jerusalem Post.* Op-Ed. [Online: Lexus Nexus].

Bone, J. (1994, October 4). UN helps sought in nation's rebirth. *The Times.* Overseas News. [Online: Lexus Nexus].

Booth, W. (1967). In M. Steinmann, Jr. (Ed.), *New rhetorics.* New York: Charles Scribners Sons.

Boston Globe, The. (1990, February 27). Decade of conflict: A look at Sandinista rule; 1979; Defeat of the Sandinistas. National/Foreign. [Online: Lexus Nexus].

Boulding, K. (1967). In G. E. Stearn. *McLuhan: Hot and cool: A primer for the understanding of and a critical symposium with rebuttal by McLuhan.* New York: Signet.

Bourhis, R. Y. (1979). Language in ethnic interaction: A social psychological approach. In H. Giles & B. Saint-Jacques (Eds.), *Language and ethnic relations.* Oxford: Pergamon.

Boutrous-Ghali, B. (1994, October 24). Message. Unpublished.

Boutrous-Ghali, B. (1995a). *Agenda for peace.* New York: United Nations.

Boutrous-Ghali, B. (1995b). *Agenda for development.* New York: United Nations.

Bradley, P. (1945). A note to the reader. In A. de Tocqueville, *Democracy in America* (Vol. 1). [P. Bradley (Ed.); F. Bowen (Trans.)]. New York: Vintage Books.

Bradsher, K. (1995, April 19). U.S. gap in riches widens. *Asahi Evening News,* pp. 1–2.

Bredo, E. (1992, April). John Dewey and situated cognition, discussion of 'situated learning: John Dewey revisited?' Presented at the American Educational Studies Association meetings, San Francisco.

Breen, M. (1992, April 30). Couple kept apart by two Koreas. *Washington Times,* p. A8.

Brislin, R. (1993). *Understanding culture's influence on behavior.* Orlando: Harcourt Brace College Publishers.

Britton, J., Burgess, T., Martin, N., McLeod, A., & Rosen, H. (1975). *The development of writing abilities (11–18).* London: Macmillan.

Brown, G. & Yule, G. (1983). *Discourse analysis.* Cambridge: Cambridge University Press.

Burke, J. (1992, January 30). Yeltsin trip seen as key to reform bid at home. *The Christian Science Monitor* [Online: Lexus Nexus].

Burke, K. (1931). *Counter-statement.* New York

Burke, K. (1941). *The philosophy of literary form: Studies in symbolic action.* New York: Vintage.

Burke, K. (1959). *Attitudes toward history.* 2nd. ed. Los Altos, CA: Hermes.

Burke, K. (1962a). *A grammar of motives.* Cleveland: World.

Burke, K. (1962b). *A rhetoric of motives.* Cleveland: World.

Burke, K. (1965). *Permanence and change: An anatomy of purpose.* Indianapolis: Bobbs Merrill.

Burke, K. (1966). *Language as symbolic action: Essays on life, literature, and method.* Berkeley: University of California Press.

Burke, K. (1970). *The rhetoric of religion: Studies in logology.* Berkeley: University of California Press.

Busia, K. A. (1969, October 17). In Prossner (1970), pp. 1387–1396.

Campbell, G. (1823). *The philosophy of rhetoric.* Boston: Charles Ewer.

Casse, P. (1980). *Training for the cross-cultural mind.* Washington, DC: SIETAR.

Castro, F. (1960, September 26). In Prosser (1970), pp. 325–372.

Charniak, E. (1979). Ms. Malaprop, a language comprehension program. In D. Metzing (Ed.), *Frame conceptions and text understanding.* Berlin: de Gruyter.

Christian Science Monitor, The. (1984, April 11). Mines and law. Editorial. [Online: Lexus Nexus].

Cicero. (1969). Orator. In T. W. Benson & M. H. Prosser (Eds.), *Readings in classical rhetoric.* Boston: Allyn and Bacon.

Clark, H. H. & Clark, E. V. (1977). *Psychology and language: An introduction to psycholinguistics.* New York: Harcourt Brace Jovanovich.

Clinton, H. R. (1995, September 5). Speech to the World Health Organization Forum, Beijing, China. [Online: CRTNET].

Clyne, M. (1994). *Inter-cultural communication at work.* Cambridge: Cambridge University Press.

CNBC Asia News. (1995, November 17). [TV broadcast].

CNN News. (1994, November 28). *Headline News* [TV broadcast].

Commission on Global Governance, The. (1995). *Our global neighborhood.* New York: Oxford University Press.

Concise Columbia Encyclopedia, The. (1983). New York: Avon.

Conley, T. M. (1990). *Rhetoric in the European tradition.* New York: Longman.

Cooper, C. R. & Matsuhashi, A. (1983). A theory of the writing process. In M. Martlew (Ed.), *The psychology of written language.* New York: John Wiley.

Covert, B. (1992, April 18). *Manga,* racism and Tezuka. *The Japan Times Weekly,* pp. 1, 3, 4.

Cowell, A. (1990, May 27). Arab anger at Israel: Has Mubarak caught it too? *New York Times* [Online: Lexus Nexus].

Crosby, H. N. & Bond, G. R. (1968). *The McLuhan explosion: A casebook on Marshall McLuhan and Understanding Media.* New York: American Book.

Crystal, D. (1980). *A first dictionary of linguistics and phonetics.* London: Andre Deutsch.

Crystal, D. (1987). *The Cambridge encyclopedia of language.* Cambridge: Cambridge University Press.

Daily Yomiuri, The. (1992, January 29). UN summit to discuss new world order [Online: Lexus Nexus].

Dale, R. (1984, April 27). CIA chief "apologizes" after outcry on mining. *Financial Times* [Online: Lexus Nexus].

DeVito, J. A. (1992). *The interpersonal communication book* (6th ed.). New York: HarperCollins.

Diefenbaker, J. G. (1960, September 26). In Prosser (1970), pp. 301–311.

Dodd, C. H. (1991). *Dynamics of intercultural communication* (3rd ed.). Dubuque, IA: Wm. C Brown.

Donahue, R. T. (1990). *Japanese non-linear discourse style.* New York: Applied Linguistics Research.

Donahue, R. T. (1994). The mysterious Orient(al) schema: Images and attribution. *Intercultural Communication Studies* IV:2, 63–86.

Donahue, R. T. (1995, July). Critical discourse analysis: Racism and the ethos of equality. Presented at "Intercultural Communication: The Last Twenty-Five Years and the Next," a conference at the Rochester Institute of Technology, Rochester, New York.

Dooling, D. J. & Lachman, R. (1971). Effects of comprehension on retention of prose. *Journal of Experimental Psychology* 8:216–222.

Dullforce, W. (1990, May 26). Arafat presses UN to take action; Security Council in Geneva hears demand for West Bank emergency force. *Financial Times* [Online: Lexus Nexus].

Easton, B. (1982). Blended beginnings: Connections and the effects of editing in a case of academic 'Japanese English.' Unpublished doctoral dissertation, University of Hawaii.

Eberstadt, N. (1992). Can the two Koreas be one? *Foreign Affairs* 72:150–165.

Eberstadt, N. & Banister, J. (1992). The reunification of Korea. *The American Enterprise* 3:24–33.

Economist, The. (1992, September 26). The Koreas: Still a conundrum. Author 32–33.

Educational Testing Service. (1992). *GRE 1992–93 registration and information bulletin.* Princeton, NJ: Author.

Edwards, J. & Giles, H. (1984). Applications of the social psychology of language: Sociolinguistics and education. In P. Trudgill (Ed.), *Applied sociolinguistics.* London: Academic Press.

Eisenhower, D. D. (1960, September 22). In Prosser (1970), pp. 185–196. [The audio tape of this address is from *UN Series,* of an unknown publisher/distributor, and is on reserve in the Arts & Sciences Media Center, School of Arts and Sciences, University of Virginia.]

Elizabeth II, Queen. (1957, October 21). In Prosser (1970), pp. 117–118.

Elsner, A. (1990, May 23). US told Arafat it would reject visa request from him. *Reuters* [Online: Lexus Nexus].

Engleberg, S. (1986, July 12). C.I.A.'s paramilitary operations: the record since the 50's. *The York Times* [Online: Lexus Nexus].

Enos, R. L. (1993). *Greek rhetoric before Aristotle.* Prospect Heights, IL: Waveland.

Facts on File. (1990). Session held in Geneva. International Affairs: Arafat addresses UN. [Online: Lexus Nexus].

Faigley, L., Cherry, R. D., Jolliffe, D. A., & Skinner, A. M. (1985). *Assessing writers' knowledge and processes of composing.* Norwood, NJ: Ablex.

Faison, S. (1994, October 8). Investors wary, despite Mandela. *The New York Times* [Online: Lexus Nexus].

Fisher, G. (1989). Diplomacy. In M. K. Asante & W. B. Gudykunst (Eds.), *Handbook of international and intercultural communication.* Newbury Park, CA: Sage.

Foucault, M. (1970). *The order of things.* New York: Vintage Books.

Foucault, M. (1972). *The archaeology of knowledge.* New York: Pantheon Books.

Foucault, M. (1977). *Language, countermemory, practice.* Ithaca: Cornell University Press.

Foucault, M. (1980). *Power/knowledge.* (Colin Gordon, Ed.). New York: Pantheon Books.

Foucault, M. (1989). In J. L. Golden, G. F. Berquist, & W. E. Coleman (Eds.), *The rhetoric of western thought* (4th ed.). Dubuque: Kendall/Hunt.

Francese, P. (1995, January 17). Interview with Paul Solman. *The MacNeill/Lehrer News Hour* [TV broadcast]. PBS.

Franklin, S. (1990, May 27). Arab summit may offer support for Iraq. *Chicago Tribune* [Online: Lexus Nexus].

Fredrickson, T. L. & Wedel, P. F. (1984). *English by newspaper.* Rowley, MA: Newbury House.

Freire, P. (1992). Keynote address. SIETAR International Congress. Jamaica.

Friedman, S. (1988, December 8). For Reagan, Gorbachev a Cordial Last Meeting. *Newsday* [Online: Lexus Nexus].

Frondizi, A. (1961, September 27). In Prosser (1970), pp. 737–745.

Georgoudi, M. & Rosnow, R. L. (1985). The emergence of contextualism. *Journal of Communication* 35:76–88.

Geyde, R. (1988, October 1). Showdown in the Kremlin: Fall of "Old Stoneface." *The Daily Telegraph* [Online: Lexus Nexus].

Gheorghiu-Dej, G. (1960, September 27). In Prosser (1970), pp. 373–394.

Giles, H. (1979). Sociolinguistics and social psychology: An introductory essay. In H. Giles & R. N. St. Clair (Eds.), *Language and social psychology.* Oxford: Basil Blackwell.

Giles, H., & Powesland, P. F. (1975). *Speech style and social evaluation.* New York: Academic Press.

Gittelsohn, J. (1992, March 20). The rite of spring. *Scholastic Update* 124:14–15.

Goffman, E. (1981). *Forms of talk.* Philadelphia: University of Pennsylvania Press.

Golden, J. L., Bergquist, G. F., & Coleman, W. E. (Eds.). (1989). *The Rhetoric of western thought* (4th ed.). Dubuque, IO: Kendall/Hunt.

Goodwin, C. & Duranti, A. (1992). Rethinking context: An introduction. In A. Duranti & C. Goodwin (Eds.), *Rethinking context.* Cambridge: Cambridge University Press.

Gorbachev, M. (1988, December 7). In United Nations General Assembly record A/43/PV.72, pp. 2–35.

Grabe, W. (1987). Contrastive rhetoric and text-type research. In U. Connor & R. B. Kaplan (Eds.), *Writing across languages: Analysis of L2 text.* Reading, MA: Addison-Wesley.

Gray, M. (1990). *A dictionary of literary terms* (6th printing). Harlow, Essex: Longman York Press.

Gudykunst, W. B. (1990). Diplomacy: A special case of intergroup communication. In F. Korzenny & S. Ting-Toomey (Eds.), *Communicating for peace.* Newbury Park, CA: Sage.

Gudykunst, W. B. & Kim, Y. Y. (1992). *Communicating with strangers* (2nd ed.). New York: McGraw-Hill.

Gudykunst, W. B. & Nishida, T. (1994). *Bridging Japanese/North American differences.* Thousand Oaks, CA: Sage.

Gundersen, E. (1990, May 25). Japanese pop star eyes west. *USA Today* (International ed.), p. 9A.

Hall, E. T. (1959). *The silent language.* Garden City, NY: Doubleday.

Hall, E. T. (1966). *The hidden dimension.* Garden City, NY: Doubleday.

Hall, E. T. (1976). *Beyond culture.* Garden City, NY: Doubleday.

Hall, E. T. (1983). *The dance of life.* Garden City, NY: Doubleday.

Halliday, M. A. K. (1978). *Language as social semiotic.* Baltimore: University Park Press.

Halliday, M. A. K. (1994). *Functional grammar* (2nd ed.). London: Edward Arnold.

Hammes, S. (1992, March 20.). South Korea. *Scholastic Update* 124:4–6.

Hart, R. P. (1984). *Verbal style and the presidency.* Orlando: Academic Press.

Hart, R. P., Friedrich, G. W., & Brooks, W. D. (1975). *Public communication.* New York: Harper & Row.

Hasan, R. (1984). Coherence and cohesive harmony. In J. Flood (Ed.), *Understanding reading comprehension.* Newark, DE: International Reading Association.

Hatch, E. (1992). *Discourse and language education.* Cambridge: Cambridge University Press.

Hatch, E. & Long, M. H. (1980). Discourse analysis, what's that? In D. Larsen-Freeman (Ed.), *Discourse analysis in second language research.* Rowley, MA: Newbury House.

Hauser, G. A. (1986). *Introduction to rhetorical theory.* Prospect Heights, IL: Waveland.

Haviland, S. E. & Clark, H. H. (1974). What's new? Acquiring new information as a process in comprehension. *Journal of Verbal Learning and Verbal Behavior* 13:512–521.

Hill, C. & Larsen, E. (1983). What reading tests call for and what children do. Washington, DC: National Institute of Education. (ERIC Document Reproduction Service No. ED 238 904)

Hill, J. H. (1988). Language, culture, and worldview. In F. J. Newmeyer (Ed.), *Language: The sociocultural context. (Vol.4 Linguistics: The Cambridge survey).* Cambridge: Cambridge University Press.

Hinds, J. (1980). Japanese expository prose. *Papers in Linguistics* 13:117–158.

Hobbs, J. (1979). Metaphor, metaphor schemata, and selective inferencing. Menlo Park, CA: SRI International.

Hoey, M. (1983). *On the surface of discourse.* London: George Allen & Unwin.

Hoey, M. (1991). *Patterns of lexis in text.* Oxford: Oxford University Press.

Hofstede, G. (1980). *Culture's consequences.* Newbury Park, CA: Sage.

Holman, C. H. (1978). *A handbook to literature.* Indianapolis: Odyssey Press.

Hörmann, H. (1986). *Meaning and context.* (Edited by R. E. Innis). New York: Plenum.

Horowitz, R. (1987). Rhetorical structure in discourse processing. In R. Horowitz & S. J. Samuels (Eds.), *Comprehending oral and written language.* New York: Academic Press.

Hunter, R. E. (1988, December 8). A day that will live on famously. *Los Angeles Times* [Online: Lexus Nexus].

Inter Press Service. (1985, October 21). United Nations: Nicaragua seeks U.S. pledge to respect international law. [Online: Lexus Nexus].

Inter Press Service. (1988a, September 26). Central America: Reagan calls for "constructive" Soviet policy. [Online: Lexus Nexus].

Inter Press Service. (1988b, December 6). United Nations: Gorbachev to outline Soviet views on global issues. [Online: Lexus Nexus].

Isocrates. (1969). Antidosis. In T. W. Benson & M. H. Prosser (Eds.), *Readings in classical rhetoric.* Boston: Allyn and Bacon.

Jaeger, M. E. & Rosnow, R. L. (1988). Contextualism and its implications for psychological inquiry. *British Journal of Psychology* 79:63–75.

Jakobson, R. (1960). Closing statement: Linguistics and poetics. In T. Sebeok (Ed.), *Style in language.* Cambridge, MA: MIT Press.

Janello, A. & Jones, B. (Eds.). (1995). *A global affair: An inside look at the United Nations.* New York: Jones and Janello.

Japan Economic Newswire. (1988, September 25). Reagan to deliver "message of hope" at UN. Kyodo News Service [Online: Lexus Nexus].

Japan Economic Newswire. (1992, January 25). Summit draft hails UN role in post cold-war world. Kyodo News Service [Online: Lexus Nexus].

Japan Economic Newswire. (1995, March 12). Poverty summit to close with declaration Sunday. Kyodo News Service [Online: Lexus Nexus].

Jeremy, M. & Robinson, M. E. (1989). *Ceremony and symbolism in the Japanese home.* Manchester: Manchester University Press.

Jha, C. S. (1964). Statement in the Security Council. In M. H. Prosser. A rhetorical analysis of the speechmaking of Adlai E. Stevenson on major issues in the United Nations during the fifteenth and sixteenth sessions of the General Assembly. Unpublished doctoral dissertation, University of Illinois.

Johannesen, R. L. (1971). *Contemporary theories of rhetoric: Selected readings.* New York: Harper and Row.

John Paul II, Pope. (1995, October 5). Pope John Paul II's speech to the United Nations. [Online: CRTNET].

Johnson, L. B. (1963, December 17). In Prosser (1970), pp. 1029–1032.

Johnson, T. (1992, January 28). Miyazawa to attend UN summit. *Japan Economic Newswire,* Kyodo News Service [Online: Lexus Nexus].

Jordan, M. P. (1984). *Rhetoric of everyday English texts.* London: George Allen & Unwin.

Kamiya, A. (1992, January 31). UN summit opens to chart new world order. *Japan Economic Newswire,* Kyodo News Service [Online: Lexus Nexus].

Kang, S. J. (1988, October 18). In United Nations General Assembly record A/43/PV.34, pp. 13–32.

Kaplan, R. B. (1987). Cultural thought patterns revisited. In U. Connor & R. B. Kaplan (Eds.), *Writing across languages: Analysis of L2 text.* Reading, MA: Addison-Wesley.

Kaplan, R. B. (1988). Cultural thought patterns in intercultural education. In J. S. Wurzel, (Ed.), *Toward multiculturalism.* Yarmouth, ME: Intercultural Press. (Originally published in 1966 in *Language Learning* 16:1–20)

Karatsu, H. (1992, March 23). Never as easy as it sounds. *The Japan Times,* p. 24.

Kasavubu, J. (1960, November 8). In Prosser (1970), pp. 653–663.

Kaufmann, J. (1980). *United Nations decision making.* Alphen aan den Rijn, Netherlands: Sijthoff & Noordhoff.

Kenkyusha's New Collegiate Dictionary (Japanese-English). (1987). Tokyo: Kenkyusha.

Kennedy, J. F. (1961, September 25). In Prosser (1970), pp. 719–729.

Kennedy, J. F. (1963, September 20). In Prosser (1970), pp. 943–951.

Khan, M. A. (1962, September 26). In Prosser (1970), pp. 855–863.

Khrushchev, N. S. (1959, September 18). In Prosser (1970), pp. 143–162.

Khrushchev, N. S. (1960a, September 23). In Prosser (1970), pp. 237–277.

Khrushchev, N. S. (1960b, October 3). In Prosser (1970), pp. 537–548.

Kidder, T. (1989). *Among schoolchildren.* New York: Avon.

King, J. (1994, October 7). Mandela urges investment in South Africa. Reuters, Ltd. [Online: Lexus Nexus].

King, M. L. (1964/1986). Nobel Prize acceptance speech. In J. M. Washington (Ed.), *A testament of hope: The essential writings of Martin Luther King, Jr.* San Francisco: Harper & Row.

Kirk, A. (1985, April 17). Nicaragua: U.N. secretary general backs dialogue, not intervention. Inter Press Service [Online: Lexus Nexus].

Kitagawa, M. M. & Kitagawa, C. (1987). *Making connections with writing.* Portsmouth, NH: Heinemann.

Knight-Ridder Newspapers. (1987, July 12). Documents link north to mining of Nicaragua. *Chicago Tribune* [Online: Lexus Nexus].

Kolker, A. & Alvarez, L. (1991). *The Japanese version* [Film]. New York: Center for New American Media.

Kubota, R. (1992). Contrastive rhetoric of Japanese and English: A critical approach. Unpublished doctoral dissertation, University of Toronto.

Lakatos, I. (1970). Falsification and the methodology of scientific research programs. In I. Lakatos & A. Musgrave (Eds.), *Criticism and the growth of knowledge.* Cambridge: Cambridge University Press.

Lakoff, G. & Johnson, M. (1980). *Metaphors we live by.* Chicago: The University of Chicago Press.

Larson, R. L. (1984). Classifying discourse: Limitations and alternatives. In R. J. Connors, L. S. Ede, & A. A. Lunsford (Eds.), *Essays on classical rhetoric and modern discourse.* Carbondale: Southern Illinois University Press.

Latin American Newsletters, Ltd. (1986, July 17). World Court rules against the US [Online: Lexus Nexus].

Lavandera, B. R. (1988). The study of language in its socio-cultural context. In F. J. Newmeyer (Ed.), *Language: The socio-cultural context (Vol 4. Linguistics: The Cambridge survey).* Cambridge: Cambridge University Press.

Leopold, E. (1992, January 31). Yeltsin proposes star wars protection at UN council summit. *The Reuter Library Report* [Online: Lexus Nexus].

Lewis, P. (1986, June 28). World Court supports Nicaragua after US rejected judges' rule. *New York Times* [Online: Lexus Nexus].

Lewis, P. (1988, October 20). North Korean, at UN, sees no quick thaw. *New York Times,* p. A6.

Lewis, P. (1990, May 26). Arafat in Geneva, calls on UN to send force to occupied areas. *New York Times* [Online: Lexus Nexus].

Lewis, P. (1992, February 1). Summit at the UN. *The New York Times* [Online: Lexus Nexus].

Li Peng. (1992, January 31). In United Nations Security Council record S/PV.3046, pp. 86–94.

Lichtenberg, J. (1992). Racism in the head, racism in the world. *Philosophy and Public Policy* 12(1):3–5.

Lipsey, Courant, Purves, & Steiner. (1992). Economic growth and competition in the global economy [Poster]. Harper Collins College Publishers. [This information is as given on the poster.]

Longacre, R. E. (1983). *The grammar of discourse.* New York: Plenum Press.

Ludden, D. (1994). Ten myths about the Japanese language. *The Language Teacher* 18:12, pp. 10, 11, 32.

Lyons, J. (1992, January 29). Three days, four cities—Yeltsin's crucial test. *The Reuter Library Report* [Online: Lexus Nexus].

Macdonell, D. (1986). *Theories of discourse: An introduction.* Oxford: Basil Blackwell.

Macleans. (1988, December 19). The year of the peacemakers. Sec.: Images of 1988 [Online: Lexus Nexus].

MacLeish, A. (1969). Statement in the General Assembly. In M. H. Prosser (Ed.), *An ethnic for survival: Adlai Stevenson speaks on international affairs, 1936–1965.* New York: William Morrow.

Madigan, C. M. (1988, December 8). Address closes cold war curtain. *Chicago Tribune* [Online: Lexus Nexus].

Magnusson, D. (Ed.). (1988). *Individual development from an interactional perspective.* Hillsdale, NJ: Lawrence Erlbaum.

Major, R. C. (1992). Losing English as a first language. *The Modern Language Journal* 76:190–208.

Mandela, N. (1994a, October 3). In United Nations General Assembly record A/49/PV.14.

Mandela, N. (1994b, October 7). National Press Club luncheon address. Gil Klein, moderator. Federal News Service. In the News, 14 pp. [Online: Lexus Nexus].

Manning, S. (1992, March 20). North Korea. *Scholastic Update* 124:6–7.

Mannion, J. (1994, October 4). Mandela urges UN to fight poverty. Agence France Press. International news [Online: Lexus Nexus].

Manuel, A. (1985, October 7). United States: Limits acceptance of World Court. Inter Press Service [Online: Lexus Nexus].

Margai, M. (1961, September 27). In Prosser (1970), pp. 747–749.

Mateos, A. L. (1959, October 14). In Prosser (1970), pp. 163–167.

Mayer, J. P. (1988). From the foreword of the 1966 edition. A. de Tocqueville, *Democracy in America* [J. P. Mayer (Ed.); G. Lawrence (Trans.)]. New York: Perennial Library.

McCarthy, M. (1991). *Discourse analysis for language teachers.* Cambridge: Cambridge University Press.

McCarthy, M. & Carter, R. (1994). *Language as discourse.* London & New York: Longman.

McFadden, R. D. (1992, January 31). Leaders gather in New York to chart a world order. *The New York Times* [Online: Lexus Nexus].

McKeon, R. (1990). Rhetoric: Essays in invention and discovery. In T. M. Conley. *Rhetoric in the European tradition.* New York: Longman.

McLuhan, M. (1962). *The Gutenberg galaxy: The making of the typographic man.* New York: Signet.

McLuhan, M. (1964). *Understanding media: The extensions of man.* New York: Signet.

MeLuhan, M. (1967). In G. E. Stearn. *McLuhan: Hot and cold: A primer for the understanding of and a critical symposium with rebuttal by McLuhan.* New York: Signet.

McLuhan, M. & Fiore, Q. (1967). *The medium is the massage: An inventory of effects.* New York: Bantam.

McLuhan, M. & Stearn, G. E. (1967). In G. E. Stearn. *McLuhan: Hot and cool: A primer for the understanding of and a critical symposium with rebuttal by McLuhan.* New York: Signet.

Mead, W. R. (1995, August 24). Interview with Ray Saurez. *Talk of the nation* [Radio broadcast]. NPR News.

Miles, J. (1976). What we already know about composition and what we need to know. *College Composition and Communication* 27:136–141.

Miller, J. (1971). *Marshall McLuhan.* New York: Viking.

Miller, J. M., Prosser, M. H. & Benson, T. W. (Eds.). (1973). *Readings in medieval rhetoric.* Bloomington, IN: Indiana University Press.

Mitterrand, F. (1992, January 31). In United Nations Security Council record S/PV.3046, pp. 13–22.

Miyazawa, K. (1992, January 31). In United Nations Security Council record S/PV.3046, pp. 102–112.

Morley, G. D. (1985). *An introduction to systemic grammar.* London: Mcmillan.

Morris, E. K. (1988). Contextualism: The world view of behavior analysis. *Journal of Experimental Child Psychology* 46:289–323.

Mortimer, E. (1988, December 19). A time of hope, a hint of peace. *Financial Times,* p. 16.

Mouat, L. (1992a, January 30). UN summit to assess role, funding crisis. *The Christian Science Monitor* [Online: Lexus Nexus].

Mouat, L. (1992b, February 3). World leaders look to 'big picture' for United Nations. *The Christian Science Monitor* [Online: Lexus Nexus].

Myers, D. G. (1994). *Exploring social psychology* (International ed.). New York: McGraw-Hill.

Nakasone, Y. (1987, September 21). In United Nations General Assembly record A/42/PV.4, pp. 50–67.

Nash, W. (1960, October 4). In Prosser (1970), pp. 581–599.

Nash, W. (1980). *Designs in prose.* London: Longman.

Nasser, G. A. (1960, September 27). In Prosser (1970), pp. 395–413.

Nehru, J. (1960, October 3). In Prosser (1970), pp. 557–570.

Neustupný, J. V. (1987). Communicating with the Japanese. Tokyo: The Japan Times.

NHK News. (1995, May 6). Asia now [TV broadcast]. Japan.

Nicholas, J. K. & Nicholl, J. R. (1985). *Rhetorical models for effective writing* (3rd ed.). New York: Harper Collins.

Nichols, M. (1971). *Rhetoric and criticism.* Baton Rouge: Louisiana State University Press.

Nida, E. A. (1984). Rhetoric and styles: A taxonomy of structures and functions. *Language Sciences* 6:287–305.

Nishida, H. & Gudykunst, W. (1982). *American communication patterns.* Tokyo: Kinseido.

Nunan, D. (1993). *Introducing discourse analysis.* London: Penguin.

O'Brien, C. C. & Topolski, F. (1968). *The United Nations: Sacred drama.* New York.

Odell, L. (1981). Defining and assessing competence in writing. In C. R. Cooper (Ed.), *The nature and measurement of competency in English.* Urbana, IL: NCTE.

Ong, W. J. (1967). *The presence of the word: Some prolegomena for cultural and religious history.* New Haven, CN: Yale University Press.

Osborne, M. (1967, April). Archtypal metaphor in rhetoric: The light-dark family. *Quarterly Journal of Speech.* LIII.

O'Sullivan, T., Hartley, J., Saunders, D., Montgomery, M., & Fiske, J. (1994). *Key concepts in communication and cultural studies* (2nd. ed.). London: Routledge.

Ould Daddah, M. (1963, October 14). In Prosser (1970), pp. 973–979.

Pan, B. A. & Gleason, J. B. (1986). The study of language loss: Models and hypotheses for an emerging discipline. *Applied Psycholinguistics* 7:193–206.

Pauk, W. (1983). *Six-way paragraphs: Middle level.* Providence, RI: Jamestown.

PBS. (1995, January 26). *The MacNeill/Lehrer news hour.* [TV broadcast].

Peers, M. (1992, February 3). Japan leads pressure for new UN structure. *Australian Financial Review* [Online: Lexus Nexus].

Perelman, C. & Olbrechts-Tyteca, L. (1969). *Treatise on Argument: The new rhetoric.* Notre Dame, IN: University of Notre Dame Press.

Perelman, C. & Olbrechts-Tyteca, L. (1990). The new rhetoric. In T. M. Conleym (Ed.), *Rhetoric in the European tradition.* New York: Longman.

Perez, C. A. (1992, January 31). In United Nations Security Council record S/PV.3046, pp. 54–61.

Perez de Cuellar, J. (1991). *Anarchy or order: Annual reports 1982–1991.* New York: United Nations.

Phillips, M. (1985). *Aspects of text structure.* Amsterdam: North-Holland.

Plato. (1969a). Gorgias. In T. W. Benson & M. H. Prosser (Eds.), *Readings in classical rhetoric.* Boston: Allyn & Bacon.

Plato. (1969b). Phaedrus. In T. W. Benson & M. H. Prosser (Eds.), *Readings in classical rhetoric.* Boston: Allyn and Bacon.

Popper, K. (1972). *Objective knowledge.* Oxford: Clarendon.

Potter, J. & Wetherell, M. (1987). *Discourse and social psychology.* London: Sage.

Prado, M. (1961, September 25). In Prosser (1970), pp. 731–736.

Pratt, M. L. (1988). Natural narrative. In R. Scholes, N. R. Comley, & G. L. Ulmer (Eds.), *Textbook.* New York, NY: St. Martin's Press.

Prentice, D. J. (1990). Malay (Indonesian and Malaysian). In B. Comrie (Ed.), *The major languages of East and South-East Asia.* London: Routledge.

Prentice, E. A. (1995, March 13). Third world goes unheard at costly UN social summit. *The Times.* Overseas News [Online: Lexus Nexus].

Prial, F. J. (1982, October 9). Honduras and Nicaragua give opposing views at the U.N. *New York Times* [Online: Lexus Nexus].

Prosser, M. H. (1964). A rhetorical analysis of the speechmaking of Adlai E. Stevenson on major issues in the United Nations during the fifteenth and sixteenth sessions of the General Assembly. Unpublished doctoral dissertation, University of Illinois.

Prosser, M. H. (Ed.). (1969). *An ethic for survival: Adlai Stevenson speaks on international affairs 1936–1965.* New York: William Morrow.

Prosser, M. H. (Ed.). (1970). *Sow the wind, reap the whirlwind: Heads of state address the United Nations,* 2 Vols. New York: William Morrow.

Prosser, M. H. (Ed.). (1978). *USIA intercultural communication course: 1977 proceedings.* Washington, D.C.: International Communication Agency.

Prosser, M. H. (1989). *The cultural dialogue: An introduction to intercultural communication.* Washington, DC: SIETAR.

Prosser, M. H. (Ed.). (in press). *United Nations addresses: toward the millennium.* Greenwich, CT: Ablex.

Prosser, M. H. & Sitaram, K. S. (Eds.). (in press). *Intercultural, International, and Global Media.* Greenwich, CT: Ablex.

Quintilian. (1969). Institutes of oratory. In T. W. Benson & M. H. Prosser (Eds.), *Readings in classical rhetoric.* Boston: Allyn and Bacon.

Quirk, R., Greenbaum, S., Leech, G., & Svartvik, J. (1985). *A comprehensive grammar of the English language.* London and New York: Longman.

Ramus, P. (1989). Dialectique. In J. L. Golden, G. F. Berquist, & W. E. Coleman (Eds.), *The rhetoric of western thought.* (4th ed.) Dubuque, IO: Kendall/Hunt.

Random House Webster's College Dictionary [RHWCD]. (1991). New York: Random House.

Rao, P. V. N. (1992, January 31). In United Nations Security Council record S/PV.3046, pp. 95–102.

Reagan, R. (1988, September 20). In United Nations General Assembly record A/43/PV.4, pp. 21–40.

Reischauer, E. O. (1988). *The Japanese today.* Cambridge, MA: Harvard University Press.

Reuter Library Report, The. (1988, October 6). New proposal made on use of World Court, US says. [Online: Lexus Nexus].

Reuter Library Report, The. (1992, January 16). Chinese premier to attend UN summit. [Online: Lexus Nexus].

Reuters, Ltd. (1983, August 12). International News [Online: Lexus Nexus].

Reuters, Ltd. (1986, June 28). Nicaragua to take its case to UN in New York. International news. [Online: Lexus Nexus].

Reuters, Ltd. (1994, October 2). *New York, South Africa business office to open* [Online: Lexus Nexus].

Reuters North European Service. (1984, April 11). Senate passes bill to cut off Nicaragua mine-laying funds [Online: Lexus Nexus].

Reuters North European Service. (1986a, June 27). Chronology of Nicaraguan case against US at World Court [Online: Lexus Nexus].

Reuters North European Service. (1986b, December 11). Judge dismisses suit against US in Nicaragua ship incident [Online: Lexus Nexus].

Rice, C. (1995, March 12). Interview with D. Brinkley. *This Week* [TV broadcast]. ABC News.

Richards, I. A. (1925). *Principles of literary criticism.* New York: Harcourt, Brace.

Richards, I. A. (1936). *The Philosophy of rhetoric.* New York: Oxford University Press.

Richards, I. A. (1990). In T. M. Conley. *Rhetoric in the European tradition.* New York: Longman.

Richards, I. A. & Ogden, C. K. (1936). *The Meaning of meaning: A study of the influence of language upon thought and of the science of symbolism.* (4th ed.). New York: Harcourt, Brace.

Robinson, C. (1988a, September 26). United Nations: Reagan, in switch, praises world body. Inter Press Service [Online: Lexus Nexus].

Robinson, C. (1988b, December 7). United Nations: Gorbachev's Troop-Cutting Proposals Hailed. Inter Press Service. [Online: Lexus Nexus].

Robinson, C. (1988c, December 28). United Nations: A Year of political advances, economic struggles. Inter Press Service [Online: Lexus Nexus].

Rodriguez, S. (1969). Statement in the General Assembly. In M. H. Prosser (Ed.), *An ethnic for survival: Adlai Stevenson speaks on international affairs, 1936–1965.* New York: William Morrow.

Roh, T. W. (1988, October 18). In United Nations General Assembly record A/43/PV.33, pp. 24–40.

Rosnow, R. L. & Georgoudi, M. (Eds.). (1986). *Contextualism and understanding in behavioral science: Implications for research and theory.* New York: Praeger.

Rusk, D. (1969). Statement in the General Assembly. In M. H. Prosser (Ed.), *An ethic for survival: Adlai Stevenson speaks on international affairs, 1936–1965.* New York: William Morrow.

Sakamoto, N. & Naotsuka, R. (1982). *Polite fictions.* Tokyo: Kinseido.

Salaam, S. (1960, October 4). In Prosser (1970), pp. 571–579.

Sanford, A. J. & Garrod, S. C. (1981). *Understanding written language.* New York: John Wiley & Sons.

Saxton, B. (1972). Introduction. In *UN Series 1* [Audio tape].

Scharfstein, B. (1989). *The dilemma of context.* New York: New York University Press.

Schiffrin, D. (1987). *Discourse markers.* Cambridge: Cambridge University Press.

Schiffrin, D. (1994). *Approaches to discourse.* Oxford, UK & Cambridge, USA: Blackwell.

Schleifer, J. T. (1980). *The making of Tocqueville's Democracy in America.* Chapel Hill, NC: The University of North Carolina Press.

Schlesinger, A. (1968). In H. N. Crosby & G. R. Bond (Eds.), *The McLuhan explosion: A casebook on Marshall McLuhan and Understanding Media.* New York: American Book.

Scott, R. L. & Brock, B. L. (1972). *Methods of rhetorical criticism: A twentieth century perspective.* New York: Harper and Row.

Sebastian, R. J. & Ryan, E. B. (1985). Speech cues and social evaluation: Markers of ethnicity, social class, and age. In H. Giles & R. N. St. Clair (Eds.), *Recent advances in language, communication, and social psychology.* London: Lawrence Erlbaum.

Selassie I, H. (1963, October 4). In Prosser (1970), pp. 959–966.

Selden, R. (1985). *A reader's guide to contemporary literary theory.* Sussex, UK: Harvester.

Sesno, F. (1994, October 5). Text of Clinton-Mandela news conference. CNN. Show: News 3:43 PMEt. Transcript #527–3 [Online: Lexus Nexus].

Shannon, D. (1988, October 19). Roh urges 6-nation peace conference with N. Korea. *Los Angeles Times,* p. 11.

Siegel, C. (1990a, May 26). Palestinians applaud Arafat, Israel says he exploited tragedy. Reuters [Online: Lexus Nexus].

Siegel, C. (1990b, May 30). Israelis anxious about Arab summit, Palestinians sceptical. Reuters, Ltd. [Online: Lexus Nexus].

Simon, W. (1983, June 8). Nicaraguans outraged over consulate closures. Reuters, Ltd. [Online: Lexus Nexus].

Sinclair, J. M. (1993). Written discourse structure. In J. M. Sinclair, M. Hoey, & G. Fox (Eds.), *Techniques of description: Spoken and written discourse.* London & New York: Routledge.

Sirevåg, T. (1991). *American patterns* (Edited by A. Iwasaki). Tokyo: Seibido.

Sitaram, K. S. & Prosser, M. H. (Eds.). (Forthcoming). *Multiculturalism, cultural diversity and global communication.* Greenwich, CT: Ablex.

Smith, F. L. (1993). The pulpit and woman's place: Gender and the framing of the 'exegetical self' in sermon performances. In D. Tannen (Ed.), *Framing in discourse.* New York: Oxford University Press.

Southerland, D. (1983, July 26). Many voices on Reagan's Central American Policy. *The Christian Science Monitor* [Online: Lexus Nexus].

Southerland, D. (1984, April 11). US troubles mount over Nicaragua. *The Christian Science Monitor* [Online: Lexus Nexus].

Stearn, G. E. (1967). *McLuhan: Hot and cool: A primer for the understanding of and a critical symposium with rebuttal by McLuhan.* New York: Signet.

Steinberg, D. D. (1982). *Psycholinguistics: Language, mind and world.* London & New York: Longman.

Steinmann, M. Jr. (Ed.). (1967). *New rhetorics.* New York: Charles Scribner's Sons.

Steinmann, M. Jr. (1982). Speech-act theory and writing. In M. Nystrand (Ed.), *What writers know.* New York: Academic Press.

Stevenson, A. (1961, December 18). The failure of the Security Council is a failure of the United Nations. In Prosser (1969), pp. 334–340.

Stevenson, A. E. (1969). A privilege abused: 100 Soviet vetoes. In M. H. Prosser (Ed.), *An ethic for survival: Adlai Stevenson speaks on international affairs, 1936–1965.* New York: William Morrow.

Strasser, S., Horrock, N. M., Salcott, J. & Lindsay, J. J. (1984, April 16). The CIA's Harbor Warfare. *Newsweek.* (International) [Online: Lexus Nexus].

Stubbs, M. (1983). *Discourse analysis.* Oxford: Blackwell.

Sukarno, A. (1960, September 30). In Prosser (1970), pp. 505–535.

Swales, J. M. (1990). *Genre analysis.* Cambridge: Cambridge University Press.

Tannen, D. (1993). What's in a frame? Surface evidence for underlying expectations. In D. Tannen (Ed.), *Framing in discourse.* New York: Oxford University Press.

TASS. (1988a, September 26). Reagan's Speech at United Nations [Online: Lexus Nexus].

TASS. (1988b, December 6). "New political thinking"-Soviet press conference at UN [Online: Lexus Nexus].

Tatematsu, K., Tateoka, Y., Matsumoto, T., & Sato, T. (Eds.). (1992). *Writing letters in Japanese.* Tokyo: The Japan Times.

Tessitore, J. & Woolfson, S. (1995). *A global agenda: Issues before the 50th General Assembly of the United Nations.* Lanham, MD: University Press of America.

Tessitore, J. & Woolfson, S. (1996). *A global agenda: Issues before the 51st General Assembly of the United Nations.* Lanham, MD: University Press of America.

Thomas, H. (1988, September 27) Proprietary to the United Press International 1988. Domestic News. [Online: Lexus Nexus].

Time Wire Services. (1990, May 26). Arafat seeks UN force to aid Arabs in W. Bank, Gaza. *Los Angeles Times* [Online: Lexus Nexus].

Times, The. (1990, May 26). Israelis hit back after Arafat plea for UN protection. Overseas News. [Online: Lexus Nexus].

Tito, J. B. (1960, September 22). In Prosser (1970), pp. 197–216.

Tocqueville, A. (1963). *Democracy in America* (Vols. 1–2). [P. Bradley (Ed.); F. Bowen (Trans.)]. New York: Alfred A. Knopf.

Tocqueville, A. (1966). *Democracy in America* (Vols. 1–2). [J. P. Mayer (Ed.); G. Lawrence (Trans.)]. New York: Harper and Row.

Tocqueville, A. (1981). *De la démocratie en Amérique.* Paris: Garnier-Flammarion.

Tocqueville, A. (1988). *Democracy in America* [Vols. combined; J. P. Mayer (Ed.); G. Lawrence (Trans.)]. New York: Perennial Library.

Toner, R. (1992, July 16). Choice is affirmed: Differences in ideology smoothed as party embraces nominee. *New York Times,* p. A1.

Toulmin, S. (1950). *Reason in ethics.* Cambridge: Cambridge University Press.

Toulmin, S. (1958). *The uses of argument.* Cambridge: Cambridge University Press.

Trautman, R. (1984, April 19). Harbor mining seen damaging Reagan Central American policy. Reuters North European Service. [Online: Lexus Nexus].

Triandis, H. C. (1990). Theoretical concepts that are applicable to the analysis of ethnocentrism. In R. Brislin (Ed.), *Applied cross-cultural psychology.* Newbury Park, CA: Sage.

Triandis, H. C. (1994). Culture and social behavior. In W. J. Lonner & R. Malpass (Eds.), *Psychology and culture.* Needham Heights, MA: Allyn & Bacon.

Triandis, H. C., Brislin, R., & Hui, C. H. (1988). Cross-cultural training across the individualism-collectivism divide. *International Journal of Intercultural Relations* 12, 269–289.

Trudgill, P. (1983). *Sociolinguistics* (Rev. ed.). London: Penguin.

Tubman, W. V. S. (1961, October 23). In Prosser (1970), pp. 777–785.

U Thant. (1969). Statement in the General Assembly. In M. H. Prosser (Ed.), *An ethic for survival: Adlai Stevenson speaks on international affairs, 1936–1965.* New York: William Morrow.

United Nations. (n.d.). *Charter of the United Nations and statute of the International Court of Justice.*

United Nations. (1989). *Future role of the United Nations in an interdependent world.* New York.

United Nations. (1989). *Handbook of foreign policy analysis.* New York.

United Nations. (1990). *The blue helmets: A review of United Nations peacekeeping forces.* New York.

United Nations. (1990). *Global outlook 2000.* New York.

United Nations. (1991). *Peaceful settlement of disputes between states: A selective bibliography.* New York.

United Nations. (1991). *The United Nations, disarmament and security, evolution and prospects.* New York.

United Nations. (1991). *Verification and the United Nations: The role of the organization in multilateral arms limitations and disarmament agreements.* New York.

United Nations. (1992). *Handbook on peaceful settlement of disputes between states.* New York.

United Nations. (1992). *Prospects for peace in the Middle East: An Israeli-Palestinian dialogue (Helsinki encounter).* New York.

United Nations. (1993). *Regional security and confidence-building processes: The case of southern Africa.* New York.

United Nations. (1993). *The United Nations in the 1990's, a second chance?* New York.

United Nations. (1994). *Promoting a culture for peace in the middle East: An Israeli-Palestinian dialogue.* New York.

United Nations. (1994). *World Court: What it is and how it works.* New York.

United Nations. (1994). *World Social Situation in the 1990's.* New York.

United Nations. (1995). *From Nairobi to Beijing: Second review and appraisal of the implementation of the Nairobi forward-looking strategies for the advancement of women.* New York.

United Nations. (1995). *A guide to information at the United Nations.* New York.

United Nations. (1995). *Prerequisites for peace in the Middle East.* New York.

United Nations. (1995). *The unfinished disarmament agenda.* New York.

United Nations. (1995). *The United Nations and apartheid 1948–1994.* New York.

United Nations. (1995). *The United Nations and the advancement of women, 1945–1995.* New York.

United Nations. (1995). *The United Nations and human rights, 1948–1995.* New York.

United Nations. (1995). *The United Nations and nuclear non-proliferation.* New York.

United Nations. (1995). *United Nations peacekeeping-information notes.* New York.

United Nations. (1995). *World media handbook: Selected country profiles.* New York.

United Nations Chronicle. (1983, November). Nicaragua complains of United States support for counter-revolutionaries. 20; 31.

US News and World Report. (1995, June 5). Pro and con: Is the U.N. beyond rescue? [Online: Lexus Nexus].

Uzawa, K. & Cumming, A. (1989). Writing strategies in Japanese as a foreign language: Lowering or keeping up the standards. *The Canadian Modern Language Review* 46:178–194.

Van de Krol, R. (1984, April 25). The Hague. Reuters Ltd. International News. [Online: Lexus Nexus].

van Dijk, T. A. (1985). Introduction: Discourse analysis as a new cross-discipline. In T. A. van Dijk (Ed.), *Handbook of discourse analysis* (Vol. 1). London & Orlando: Academic Press.

Walker, W. T. (1991). *Gospel in the land of the rising sun.* Morristown, NJ: Aaron Press.

Warriner, J. E. & Griffith, F. (1977). English Grammar and Composition (Heritage Edition). New York: Harcourt Brace Jovanovich.

Watson, R. et al. (1988, December 19). Special report: Hope and tragedy; Brave new world. *Newsweek.* United States Edition [Online: Lexus Nexus].

Wayne, E. A. (1988, September 27). US-UN chill starts to thaw. *The Christian Science Monitor.* National [Online: Lexus Nexus].

Weaver, R. M. (1948). *Ideas have consequences.* Chicago: University of Chicago Press.

Weaver, R. M. (1970a). *The ethics of rhetoric.* Chicago: Henry Regnery.

Weaver, R. M. (1970b). Language is sermonic. In R. L. Johannensen (Ed.), *Contemporary theories of rhetoric.* New York: Harper and Row.

Weaver, R. M. (1972). The ethics of rhetoric. In R. L. Scott & B. L. Brock. *Methods of rhetorical criticism: A twentieth century perspective.* New York: Harper and Row.

Weaver, R. M. (1990). The ethics of rhetoric. In T. M. Conley. *Rhetoric in the European tradition.* New York: Longman.

Weiss, P. A. (1971). Life, order, and understanding. *The Graduate Journal* (Supplement to Vol. 8). Austin: University of Texas Press.

Weizman, S. (1990, May 27). Israel-US relations headed for crisis, ambassador says. Reuters Ltd. [Online: Lexus Nexus].

Whately, R. (1968). Elements of rhetoric. In J. L. Golden & E. P. J. Corbett, Jr. (Eds.), *The rhetoric of Blair, Campbell, and Whately.* New York: Holt, Rinehart and Winston.

Whitaker, M., Horrock, N., Lord, M., Lindsay, J. J., Whitmore, J., & Nissen, B. (1983, August 1). Reagan's gunboat Diplomacy. *Newsweek* [Online: Lexus Nexus].

Widdowson, H. G. (1983). *Learning purpose and language use.* Oxford: Oxford University Press.

Wilson, H. (1965, December 16). In Prosser (1970), pp. 1075–1089.

Winter, E. O. (1976). Fundamentals of information structure: Pilot manual for further development according to student need. Mimeo. Hatfield Polytechnic.

World Almanac. (1994). *The world almanac and book of facts: 1995.* Mahway, NJ: World Almanac.

Xinhua General Overseas News Service (1990a, May 25). PLO chief's UN speech welcomed in occupied lands. [Online: Lexus Nexus].

Xinhua General Overseas News Service (1990b, May 26). Israel preparing for next war, Arafat says. [Online: Lexus Nexus].

Xinhua General Overseas News Service (1990c, May 28). Arafat on Palestine issue. [Online: Lexus Nexus].

Yeltsin, B. N. (1992, January 31). In United Nations Security Council record S/PV.3046, pp. 42–48.

Yoshida, Y. (1978). Sources and causes of Japanese emigration. In D. M. Ogawa (Ed.), *Kodomo no tame ni for the sake of the children.* Honolulu: The University Press of Hawaii. (Originally published in 1909 in *The Annals of American Academy of Political and Social Science* 34:157–167).

Youlou, F. (1960, November 18). In Prosser (1970), pp. 657–663.

Zorin, Ambassador. (1964). Statement in the Security Council, interpreted from the Russian. In M. H. Prosser. A rhetorical analysis of the speechmaking of Adlai E. Stevenson on major issues in the United Nations during the fifteenth and sixteenth sessions of the General Assembly. Unpublished doctoral dissertation, University of Illinois.

AUTHOR INDEX

SUBJECT INDEX

D

ABOUT THE AUTHORS

Ray T. Donahue (PhD, University of Virginia) is currently Associate Professor of Intercultural Communication, with joint appointments in the Departments of Foreign Studies and Japanese Studies at Nagoya Gakuin University in Japan. With credentials also in applied linguistics and in counseling, he brings a rich background in racial relations and cross-cultural counseling to the field of communication studies. He has taught at universities in Japan, the United States, and China. His publications include *Japanese Non-Linear Discourse Style*, and articles on discourse analysis, cross-cultural images, perception, and intercultural training.

Michael H. Prosser (PhD, University of Illinois), a founder of the academic field of intercultural communication, is Kern Professor in Communications at the Rochester Institute of Technology. Awarded Fulbright professorships to Swaziland and Bulgaria, he is the editor or author of several books, including *Sow the Wind, Reap the Whirlwind; Heads of State Address the United Nations*; *Intercommunication Among Nations and Peoples*; and *The Cultural Dialogue* (also translated into Japanese). His co-edited *Multiculturalism, Cultural Diversity, and Global Communication* is in progress. He is President of the United Nations Association of Rochester.

www.ingramcontent.com/pod-product-compliance
Lightning Source LLC
Chambersburg PA
CBHW071142100726
47908CB00002B/224

* 9 7 8 1 5 6 7 5 0 2 9 1 6 *